Truth Matters

Life's Five Most Important Questions

Tom Gender

Truth Matters
Life's Five Most Important Questions

Copyright © 2011 by Tom Gender

Cover produced by Jim Gibson

ISBN 13: 978-1460955031
ISBN 10: 146095503X

To Jason and Lindsey

You have brought great joy to my life.

Contents

Acknowledgements

Many fine thinkers have profoundly influenced me in understanding the answers to life's most important questions and the reasons behind them. I would especially like to thank William Lane Craig, Greg Koukl, Lee Strobel, J. P. Moreland, Norm Geisler, Gary Habermas, and Peter Kreeft for their many excellent books, articles, and lectures. They have caused me to reflect deeply about what I believe and I have become more sure of my beliefs as a result.

I am extremely grateful for the assistance of several people who enthusiastically and skillfully reviewed early manuscripts of this book and offered many corrections and helpful suggestions. For this I thank my friends Arnie Gentile, Brad Cook, Elaine Bates, Fred Brost, Jim Gibson, and Nate Uitenbroek.

Finally, I would like to thank my wife, Vicki, for her great patience and encouragement to me while I spent hours upon hours in my office researching and writing this book. Without her loving support, I would not have been able to start or complete this project.

Preface

The unexamined life is not worth living.

Socrates (c. 469-399 BC)
Ancient Greek philosopher
Plato's Apology 38a

One of the fundamental problems with modern man is that he is lost in the maze of life. He has no idea why he is here, how he came to be here, where he is going, or even how he would get there if he knew where it was.

Brian H. Edwards (1941-)
Pastor, author, lecturer
Nothing But The Truth

Trying to get to the answer before one has understood all the right questions is a prime source of error in human affairs.

Phillip E. Johnson (1940-)
Professor of Law, author
The Right Questions

I assume that you are willing to take a journey with me—a journey to discover answers to the most important questions in life. My guess is that you would like to take this journey for one of three reasons. Perhaps you have never thought about such things before and now it is time. Or maybe you have tried this earlier, but gave up because it seemed too difficult to figure out. Or it is possible that you already have answers to these questions, but would like to make sure they are consistent and worthy of a life commitment. No matter your reason, the journey is the same and the process is the same—to reflect systematically, thoughtfully, and critically about the most important questions in life.

The title of this book is a play on words because I mean Truth Matters in two senses. The first is that truth is important—it *matters*. We cannot survive without it and so it is worth pursuing passionately. The second is that there are a number of important truths that demand our attention— there are *various* matters of truth. In this book, we are concerned with both senses. We want to zero in on the really important questions in life—the ones that affect *everything else*. Then we want to carefully reason about their answers to discover what view of life best explains them all.

Many people think that finding answers to life's important questions is quite difficult, but it is sometimes harder to ask the right questions. Legal scholar Phillip E. Johnson explains, "Whenever the jolts of life force us to ask the right questions instead of the wrong ones, the experience is likely to be beneficial, even when it is painful."[1] Philosopher Peter Kreeft adds, "Once we pursue a question with our whole being...we will find answers. Answers are not as hard to come by as we think; and questions, real questioning, is a lot more rare and precious than we think."[2]

Kreeft goes on to say that finding is not the problem; seeking is. We need to seek the truth if we want to find it, know it, and live by it. Indifference and diversion are the two most common obstacles to genuine truth seeking today. Most people do not care and others are simply too busy and too distracted to take the time. A real and serious search for truth requires determined effort, however. We are accustomed to receiving information in superficial sound bites today, rather than taking the time to carefully reason about it to discern truth from error. If we take the time, the reward can be life changing.

There are *so many possible* questions that it is easy to get lost in them all. My aim is to distill the handful of really significant questions that should form the foundation of everything else we believe. When we discover the true answers to *these* questions, then they will lead us to the answers to many other questions. The 17th century philosopher Blaise Pascal described this tendency we have to focus on the wrong thing when he wrote, "Man's sensitivity to little things and insensitivity to the greatest things are marks of a strange disorder."[3] Because ideas have consequences, we need to build our lives on a few big and important ideas, rather than a hundred little ones. The aim of this book is to concentrate our attention on a few big important ideas—the ones worth believing.

---

[1] Phillip E. Johnson, *The Right Questions: Truth, Meaning, & Public Debate* (Downers Grove, IL: InterVarsity Press, 2002), 30.

[2] Peter Kreeft, *Christianity for Modern Pagans: Pascal's Pensées Edited, Outlined & Explained* (San Francisco, Ignatius Press, 1993), 216-217.

[3] Blaise Pascal, *Pensées no. 632,* as quoted in Kreeft, *Christianity for Modern Pagans*, 203.

What in the world is a worldview?

A worldview is a person's basic set of assumptions, values, and beliefs concerning the more important issues of life. Our beliefs are what we think is real or true and our values are what we think is good or best.

Beliefs and values motivate our behavior. Our worldview therefore determines how we explain and interpret the world around us and provides the basis for the decisions we make about how to live. Everyone lives their life with *some* set of beliefs and values, so we all have a worldview— whether or not we realize it, call it a worldview, or formed it intentionally. Every person will always think and eventually act from his worldview.

There are two reasons that we should be concerned with answering life's most important questions. The first is personal. Each of us has the choice to make our worldview explicit or let it develop accidentally and ambiguously. We can determine our worldview by a rational, deliberate process that seeks consistency and integration with other known truths or we can determine it by a subconscious or illogical process that consists of contradictory ideas, unjustified conclusions, false generalizations, and wishful thinking.

Many people fall into the latter category, not always by intentional decision, but more often because of social conditioning or apathy. They allow their worldview to be formed using the "salad bar" approach— casually and sporadically picking up various concepts, ideas, and principles that suit them. Unfortunately, this lackadaisical approach to forming beliefs has virtually no chance of being consistent with the way the world really is.

The second reason we should answer these questions is relational. Discussion and dialogue are still the most common and effective means of intellectual exploration. If we ever desire to persuade someone of the merit of what we believe, like our family, friends, and coworkers for instance, we need to have consistent and plausible answers to these questions.

The great questions

Our aim in this book is to be intentional about forming our worldview based on finding accurate and consistent answers to these most important questions in life:

1. *Where did everything come from?*
2. *What is wrong with the world?*
3. *What happens after we die?*
4. *Can we be sure?*
5. *How should we live?*

These questions deal with origins, evil, suffering, purpose, meaning, morality, destiny, knowledge, and faith. Solid answers to these questions will satisfy the honest truth seeker who wants to know how to explain his world and live in it wisely. Even though there are many other questions we could ask and answer, I suggest that these five are at the top of the list. If we get it right with these then all the others should fall into place.

The first three questions address what the world is really like—in the past, in the present, and in the future—and why we should believe it. Knowing *that* the world is a certain way, however, is not the same thing as knowing *why* it is that way. There is a difference in explaining the existence of something and explaining the ultimate purpose or meaning of it. That is why we must ask the last two questions. The fourth question addresses how we can make sense of our answers to the first three questions, and also to what degree we can be sure of our understanding. This will directly affect the confidence we have in our answers and consequently how committed we will be to orient our life around them. This question is so crucial that I devote almost half the book to it. The fifth question addresses the logical implications of the first four. If the world really is a certain way, then how should that affect the way we live?

These questions and their answers are not independent of one another. Rather, they are designed to lead us through a logical progression of thought that build to a conclusion—one that should profoundly affect what we believe and how we behave. Of course, we could ask these same questions in a variety of other ways. For example, "Does God exist?" seems like a vital question to ask. Indeed, we will end up asking and answering this question during the course of our investigation, but I wanted to begin with the most neutral questions possible. Hopefully this approach will engage people from all faiths, and also of no particular faith.

A conclusion is called for

My impartial starting point does not mean I will withhold assessment of the evidence, as if remaining neutral and dispassionate, and avoiding conclusions were some sort of noble virtue. These questions are designed to lead us to truth, which ultimately should affect how we live. I have been persuaded by the evidence, so I will present conclusions based on where I see it pointing and will explain why I believe certain worldviews fail to explain the evidence in a satisfactory way. I invite you to come to your own conclusions. My challenge to you is to simply follow the evidence wherever it leads in an honest pursuit of truth. Often people are not fully aware of the logical conclusions of their beliefs, so be prepared to press your own beliefs to their logical ends.

This would be a good time to consider what our standard of proof should be—that is, what it will take to convince us to change our current beliefs. Seldom is any one argument or piece of evidence so compelling that we  would change a central belief based on that thing alone. The most reasonable approach is one that fairly considers the totality of evidence and decides which of the possible worldviews best explains *all* the data.[4]

The way to discriminate between competing worldviews is to evaluate the explanatory scope and power of each—that is, assess their ability to explain and integrate all the data in the most plausible and 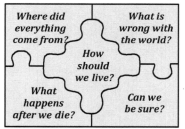 compelling way. Accordingly, think of this book as presenting a cumulative case that builds towards a conclusion which provides the best overall answer to our five questions, like puzzle pieces that fit together to form a single picture of how life works. Ultimately, you will have to decide for yourself what constitutes sufficient reason to believe something new, but I suggest that you *do* need to decide. Avoiding deliberation and withholding belief is, in fact, a decision to continue believing and behaving as you do today.

An invitation

If you are a doubter, agnostic, skeptic, nominal believer, or someone who has thus far in your life avoided answering these questions in a consistent way, I hope you will consider afresh the possibility of finding true and helpful answers to them. On the other hand, if you are a devoted believer of any faith, it is my hope that you will honestly evaluate what you believe and see if you really do have good answers to these questions. If you do, then you will affirm your faith as reasonable. If not, you might consider changing what you believe.

---

[4] This is a commonsense approach that we normally use in life all the time and is often called *inference to the best explanation*.

Introduction

Man prefers to believe what he prefers to be true.

Francis Bacon (1561-1626)
Philosopher, scientist, lawyer, author

Facts are stubborn things; and whatever may be our wishes, our inclinations, or the dictates of our passions, they cannot alter the state of facts and evidence.

John Adams (1735-1826)
Second President of the United States
Closing argument in the "The Boston Massacre" trial

Those who do not love truth excuse themselves on the grounds that it is disputed and that very many people deny it.

Blaise Pascal (1623-1662)
Mathematician, physicist, inventor, philosopher
Pensées, no. 176

The starting point of any worldview should be the ideas that are indispensable for functioning in the real world.

Nancy Pearcey (1952-)
Worldview scholar, author
Saving Leonardo

How important is truth? The question of truth is often a life and death matter. People die every day because of the truth of heart disease, the truth of a car crash, and the truth of gravity, to name only a few. People also live because of the truth of medicine, the truth of a not guilty verdict, and fleeing the truth of an impending hurricane. We all intuitively know what truth is. Truth is when a thought, statement, idea, or view actually fits the way the world really is. There is a correspondence between the claim and some objective fact in the world.

Some people deny the existence of truth, but they are terribly confused and obviously mistaken. Besides so many undeniable examples of truth in the world, those who are skeptical about truth refute themselves. They make a truth claim when they claim that truth does not exist—"It is true that there is no truth." This is contradictory and clearly false. Philosopher Roger Scruton was surely correct when he said the person who tells you truth does not exist is asking you not to believe him, so don't.[1]

The nature of truth

There are five essential characteristics of truth. First, truth about reality is *knowable*. If we couldn't know truths about the world, then we would not try to learn anything. We wouldn't investigate chemistry, biology, or physics. We wouldn't explore outer space. We wouldn't practice medicine. We wouldn't study history. We wouldn't watch news reports. We wouldn't listen to witnesses in court. The fact is, we do these things because we have learned from experience that we can know truth about our world.

Second, truth is *discovered*, not invented. We can believe a thing is true, but we cannot make it true. Truth exists regardless of who knows it. Gravity existed prior to Sir Isaac Newton discovering it.[2] A murderer is guilty of murder even if nobody knows he did it. Something could be true even if nobody believes it, and something could be false even if everybody believes it. If everybody in the world believed the Earth was flat, that wouldn't make it true. We can believe things are true, but our beliefs cannot *make* them true. Truth exists independent of anyone's trust or lack of trust in it. Jumping off a cliff and believing you will not fall does not change the fact that gravity will pull you to the ground. Truth is not dependent on our feelings about it either. We may not like that we will all eventually die, but that does not change the inevitable truth of death.

Third, truth is *universal*. It applies for everybody, everywhere, at all times, in the same circumstances. This might seem controversial to some, but consider the following: Does two plus two equal four for all people? Do computers work the same way around the world? Do human beings all die throughout history? Is gravity the same for every person on Earth? Truth is consistent and applicable for everyone.

---

[1] Roger Scruton, *Modern Philosophy: An Introduction and Survey* (New York: Penguin Books, 1994), 6.

[2] Norman L. Geisler and Frank Turek, *I Don't Have Enough Faith to Be an Atheist* (Wheaton, IL: Crossway Books, 2004), 37-38.

Fourth, truth is *exclusive*. All truths exclude their opposites by definition. If something is true, then its opposite must be false. Earth is either the third planet from the Sun or it is not—both cannot be true. Contrary beliefs are possible, but contrary truths are not possible. People might believe things that are false, but that just makes them wrong. This does not mean that truth is intolerant or offensive. Truth merely is what it is. Somebody who holds to a genuinely true belief cannot be called arrogant or intolerant simply because the challenger does not like the fact that the belief is true.

Fifth, truth is *consequential*. Truth is not avoidable. We are constrained by it and must live with it. If a doctor is right about a cancer diagnosis, then his patient ought to seek the proper treatment or the chances of dying are greater. If a skydiver does a poor job of packing his parachute, then he will suffer because of the truth of gravity. If we discover how life should be lived, then we will be better off living that way.

Kinds of truth claims

The kind of truth I have been describing is commonly referred to as *objective* truth because that which is considered to be true is the *object* of our perception or thought. This means the "truthfulness" belongs to the object of thought rather than to the thinking subject, which is you and me. When we claim that something is true about an external reality in the world, we are making an objective truth claim, like Paris is the capital of France. If such a claim is true, it will exhibit the five essential characteristics of truth listed above.

We can also make an objective truth claim about ourselves, such as where and when we were born, how tall we are, what we had for lunch today, and so on. Even though these facts may be true only for ourselves, they are objectively true because it is also the case that *they are true about us for everyone else*. For example, if someone was born in London, then someone else cannot truthfully say "It is true for me that you were born in Bangkok." That is an objectively false assertion.

However, if we claim that something is true about our internal *self*—something about our own awareness, feelings, emotions, preferences, opinions, or beliefs—then it is a *subjective* truth claim because the claim is about the subject doing the thinking. Subjective claims of truth such as "Chocolate tastes good" or "Hawaii is a great vacation destination" are not subject to dispute. No proof is necessary or can be given to show them to be true or false. They are merely statements about the internal mental states of the person making the claim. They are true for the speaker and, indeed, may not be true for someone else. However, objective claims of truth such as it is raining outside or God exists *are* subject to confirmation or refutation. An objective *claim* may or may not be true, but the important thing is that we are able to investigate it to discover the truth of the matter.

People today commonly confuse objective and subjective truth claims. Have you ever heard someone say, "That may be true for you, but it is not true for me"? For example, someone might respond that way to a friend who says, "Abortion is wrong." The friend might be stating her opinion—a subjective claim—but she might rather intend to state a universal fact, which would be an objective claim. Does she mean "My personal preference is not to have an abortion" or "Nobody should have an abortion because it is wrong for everyone"? It is therefore critically important to understand the *type of claim* that is being asserted. The first one is not open to debate, but the second one is. It should be obvious that subjective truths are rather uninteresting for our purposes because they do not describe anything about the way the world really is. They are not the kind of truths that exhibit the five characteristics listed earlier. We are focusing our attention on objective truths in this book.

Before moving on, we must make a careful but important distinction. Someone cannot challenge *that you believe something* because only you can say what you believe. However, someone can challenge *whether or not your belief is true*. This is possible (and essential) because truth is not dependent on our belief, trust, or feelings about it. Because some of our beliefs may be wrong, to know truth we must replace our false beliefs with true ones.

The realm of objective truth

Most people accept the definition of truth just described, even if they sometimes confuse objective and subjective truth claims. People do not really doubt that we can know truths in science, medicine, math, history, geography, or law courts, for example. When we begin talking about morality and religion, however, people often want to revert to the subjective realm. They think that belief in God, the meaning of life, morality, life after death, and so on are mere personal preferences, subject only to our own opinions and beliefs about them.

Why do many people tend to treat religious truth as subjective—a matter of personal opinion? We act as if morality and religion are like ice cream. "You must believe in God" sounds to many people like "You must like chocolate ice cream"—or—"You will go to Hell if you do not like my flavor."[3] When people take an objective claim of truth in this way, it sounds absurd to them. Why do people tend to think of religious truth

---

[3] Greg Koukl, "Truth Is Not Ice Cream", Ambassador Basic Curriculum, Stand To Reason, 2002.

claims this way? There are at least five reasons, each corresponding to a denial of its applicability to one of the five essential characteristics of objective truth.

First, there is a tendency to think these kinds of truths are unknowable. They have an esoteric, mysterious feel about them. If God really exists, he seems to be hidden or obscured—not plainly obvious some would say—and so people equate this with the inability to know the truth about it.

Second, people think there are no adequate tools or methods to discover the truth about God or morality. So, if this truth cannot be discovered, the only remaining option is to make it up.

Third, since there are so many different religious beliefs and they originate in so many different parts of the world, people think that religious truth cannot be universal. Therefore, the truth must be relative to different people or communities.

Fourth, it sounds arrogant to some people to claim that a belief about God and morality is true. How dare a person make such a claim, inferring that it applies to someone else?

Fifth, although the consequences are quite serious—in particular, what happens after we die—most people live apathetically with a vague feeling that "everything will work out in the end." Therefore, they rarely face the real implications about what they believe.

All of these objections are mistaken. Religion attempts to answer the very questions addressed in this book: *Where did everything come from? What is wrong with the world? What happens after we die? Can we be sure? How should we live?* In what sense can answers to these questions be personal preferences? Assume for a moment that God truly exists. If God exists, he must be the greatest being in existence. How can *that* not be true for all people? This is also the case if God is not real. If he does not exist, then he does not exist for *anyone*. If God does not exist, then there is some other explanation for origins, meaning, morality, and so on. How can *that* not be true for all people? Religions make life and death claims. Are life and death really subjective truths?

The truth about God—whether he exists or not—must be objective because the world around us is real. It has a specific nature independent of our thoughts or feelings about it. Our experience tells us it is the same for everyone. Whoever or whatever caused the world we experience must be just as real and particular as the world itself.

It seems obvious that religious truth claims are more like gravity and medicine than they are like ice cream. Statements about God and spiritual matters either correspond to reality or they do not; thus they are subject to inquiry like other topics. They can be investigated as can science and history. This is not to say that all religious truth claims are *actually* true.

Rather, all religious claims to truth try to describe the way the world really is—they make claims about universal reality, not personal preferences.

Any religious claims to truth that are actually true will exhibit the five characteristics of objective truth. First, religious truth is knowable, which means that there will be evidence to support it. Second, religious truth is discovered, not made-up, so we need to seek it to find it. Third, religious truth is true for everyone in all places at all times. Whatever answers we discover for our five questions will be true for every person who has ever lived. Fourth, religious truth excludes religious claims that contradict it. Either God exists or God does not exist—both cannot be true. Fifth, religious truth has consequences. The answers to our five questions *really* matter. In fact, since religious truth deals with the most important questions in life, its consequences are the most significant of all. They have implications that will reverberate through our lives on Earth and potentially through eternity.

The predominant worldviews

We previously defined worldview as a person's basic set of assumptions, values, and beliefs about the most important things in life. By now it should be apparent that worldview and religion are closely related since they address the same big questions of life. Religions can be generally thought of as worldviews that have been written down and studied and practiced in common by large groups of people. In addition to their beliefs, religions are known for their various practices and ritual observances. Some people may wish to distinguish religion and worldview by the association of rituals with religion, but fundamental to worldview is that behavior follows beliefs. A person's worldview describes not only what they believe, but also how they will act.

At one level there are as many worldviews as there are people in the world, since everybody has one and it is rare that two people have identical beliefs in every respect. At the heart of every worldview, though, is a commitment to a foundational belief. This is why we can group the vast majority of the world's population into one of three general worldviews: theism, pantheism, and atheism.

Theism is the belief in a personal God who created and presently sustains the universe, but is not part of the universe.[4] The major theistic religions are Judaism, Christianity, and Islam.

Pantheism is the belief in an impersonal God that literally *is* the universe, both of which are eternal. Pantheists believe that God is

---

[4] Theism is also sometimes called *monotheism*, from *mono* meaning one and *theos* meaning god.

everything that exists—the sky, the mountains, the oceans, animals, you, me, and all other things. The major pantheistic religions are Hinduism, some forms of Buddhism, Taoism, Jainism, Christian Science, Scientology, and many forms of New Age religion.

Atheism is the belief there is no God at all. Secular humanism and some forms of Buddhism would fall into this category. Sometimes practical atheism goes by other names such as naturalism, materialism, and physicalism. *Naturalism* is the view that nature is all that exists and the universe and everything in it can be accounted for entirely in terms of natural causes and laws. This is essentially the same as *materialism*, which holds that the only thing that exists is matter, and also *physicalism*, which holds that there are no kinds of things other than physical things. People often think that atheism is not a religion, but since it proposes answers to our five questions, atheism takes its place among other religions and worldviews as offering a way to explain and understand our world.

There are other worldviews believed by a smaller percentage of the world's population, such as deism, polytheism, and animism, but even these have much in common with the three main worldviews.

Deism is the belief in one deity who created the universe, but does not intervene in it. The Creator abandoned the world and set the cosmos to run on its own by natural law. He is no longer engaged or involved in the world and therefore miracles cannot happen. Deism is actually a form of theism since it holds there is only one God. It is not taught by any world religion, but is a belief held by many individuals.[5]

Polytheism is the belief in many finite gods. These gods either come from nature or were once men who became gods. Polytheistic religions include Hinduism, Taoism, Shintoism, and Mormonism.

Animism is the belief that nature is filled with spirits that influence the lives of human beings. These spirits inhabit animals, plants, and inanimate objects. Most animists believe in one supreme spirit who is distant from humans. They live in constant fear of offending the spirits and practice divination to appease them.[6] Animism is similar to pantheism in that both worship nature, however animism emphasizes the uniqueness of each individual soul whereas pantheism views everything in existence as being united in the same spiritual essence. Many primitive tribal groups around the world are animistic.

There are various combinations of these worldviews that have been adopted by different religions, but this grouping covers the primary views.

---

[5] There are softer forms of deism that allow for God's providence, answered prayer, and God-centered morality. These deists would simply say God's intervention in human affairs is more limited than what theists allow, including the rejection of miracles and written revelation.

[6] Divination is the practice of discerning the hidden significance of events and foretelling the future by occult or supernatural means.

Sometimes people claim to be *agnostic*, which means *without knowledge*. Agnosticism is a doubtful or skeptical view of finding answers to life's important questions. Agnostics usually hold one of two views towards these questions—either the answers are unknown at this time or the answers are simply unknowable. They often think this is a neutral stance, but there really is no neutral ground for these questions.[7] Agnostics essentially answer the big questions by living as if atheism were true, so theirs is in fact, a worldview choice by default.

Can they all be true?

There is a common viewpoint today that says all worldviews and religions are basically the same. They all point to the same truth and it does not really matter what you believe as long as you are sincere. This is called *religious pluralism*.[8] Hopefully by now you have seen through this deception. If all these worldviews purport to answer life's most important questions, then they are each making objective truth claims. This means that at most only one of them can be correct because they all contradict each another at key points. People who hold to religious pluralism are confusing subjective and objective truth claims. Let me illustrate with a well-known fable:

An elephant is being examined by six blind men. Each man feels a different part of the elephant and thus reaches a different conclusion about the object in front of him. One grabs the tusk and says, "This is a spear!" Another holds the trunk and says, "This is a snake!" The one hugging the leg claims, "This is a tree!" The blind man holding the tail thinks, "This is a rope!" The one feeling the ear believes, "This is a fan!" And the one leaning on the elephant's side is sure that "This is a wall!"

---

[7] This is the problem with *secularism*, as well, which is the view that public human activities and decisions, especially political ones, should not be influenced by religious beliefs.

[8] There are two other ways in which this term may be used, neither of which presents a rational problem. The first is the observation that there are many different religions in the world, thus we have a plurality of religions. The second is that we should allow freedom of conscience regarding which religion each person can believe and practice. There is no reason to object to either of these two understandings of religious pluralism. I am using this term only in the third sense where people believe that all religions are equally true or valid.

Each blind man touched the elephant, but gave a different description of the animal. Which answer was right? The pluralist concludes that all of them were at least partially correct. Religion is like the elephant, and we are all like the blind men—no one person has the complete truth. We each see only a small part of it, so all religions are true. What is wrong with this interpretation?

The pluralist has completely missed the point! Each blind man is dead wrong, which is clear from the story. How do we know the blind men are wrong? The storyteller has *told us* it was an elephant. It was not a spear, snake, tree, rope, fan, or wall. The storyteller is the only one with an objective viewpoint and he is the only one who is exactly right! It is because this objective viewpoint exists that we can know that each blind man is mistaken. We can therefore pronounce the blind men to be wrong because we know the truth. This fable is helpful, but not as the pluralist had hoped. It shows us that an objective viewpoint is possible and that we can use that viewpoint to declare something right or wrong. Only if we buy into agnosticism—that we cannot know what the world is really like—can we believe in this kind of pluralism. We have no good reason to believe this, though. We concluded earlier that our five questions fall into the realm of objective truth, so answers to them can be known.

Not all worldviews are true or even mostly true. Most are just plain wrong in important respects. Even if a worldview contains *some* truth, that does not make it worthy of our belief and trust. All worldviews are not essentially the same merely because they contain some similarities. It is the differences that set them apart. Aspirin and arsenic both come in tablet form, but their differences are crucially important.[9] Every single worldview has competing claims which contradict other worldviews.[10] Therefore, at most one of these worldviews is true. The rest are false. It is possible that all of them are false, but that would leave us with no viable explanation of the world at all, which is a dubious conclusion.[11]

We are not only seeking which *general* worldview is correct—theism, pantheism, or atheism—but since each has alternate perspectives, we want to also know which *specific* worldview is correct. For example, if theism is true, then which account of theism is true? If pantheism is true, then which version of pantheism is true? If atheism is true, then which form of atheism is true? In other words, which specific beliefs about the world are true?

---

[9] Greg Koukl, "Any Old God Won't Do", Ambassador Basic Curriculum, Stand To Reason, 2000.

[10] Interestingly, it is only the pluralist who thinks all the worldviews can be equally true or valid. Contra the pluralists, the adherents of these worldviews, for the most part, claim exclusivity of their own view. This is not surprising, given that they are making *objective* truth claims. Ironically, the pluralist is making an exclusive truth claim, too!

[11] Nevertheless, we can maintain an open mind about it at this point.

Postmodernism is a label often used today in discussions of worldviews. The fundamental idea of postmodernism is the rejection of knowable objective truth.[12] In particular, postmodernists claim that all apparent realities are only social constructions, products of human culture and language which are subject to change by people, time, and place. Postmodernists do not necessarily deny that an objective world exists. They deny that we can really know anything about it except from our own biased, culturally-based perspective, which we cannot escape. Therefore, each cultural group "discovers its own truth." This is why postmodern "truth" is not presented in propositional statements, but in stories.[13]

Postmodernism is not so much a standalone worldview as it is a perspective on truth and knowledge that people can hold in addition to other beliefs that constitute their worldview. There are postmodern atheists, postmodern pantheists, and postmodern theists, for example. I will not deal with postmodernism further except to say that when we give up on objective truth—either its existence or merely the possibility of knowing it—then we lose our grasp on reality. When that happens, we cannot know anything, and so truth becomes what we want it to be. Not surprisingly then, we see postmodernists embracing moral relativism,[14] religious pluralism, and an unhealthy over-reliance on human language, emotion, and experience. This is not a fruitful approach for discovering how the world really is.

Discovering the true worldview

Our approach to discovering the true worldview involves two simple steps. In step one, we will identify which of the general worldviews best answers our first three questions about what the world is really like. Using the principle of the  exclusivity of truth, we can eliminate from further consideration the worldviews that do not pass this step because they contradict reason and evidence.

In step two, with the general worldview that remains, we will identify which of its specific versions offers the greatest reasons for belief. We will examine the ways it provides for us to think that it is true. We will accomplish this as we answer our fourth question.

---

[12] This makes postmodernism a kind of agnosticism, although postmoderns nonetheless like to make *some* truth claims—both objective and subjective ones.

[13] A propositional statement is a declarative sentence that is either true or false. Propositional statements are the building blocks of philosophies, theories, values, and beliefs.

[14] Moral relativism will be discussed in chapter 2.

Once we complete these two steps, we will be in a position to answer our fifth, and perhaps most important, question—how we should live. A worldview not only provides beliefs and reasons to believe, but also purpose and guidance for living. This is why we are undertaking this journey, not only to believe the truth, but to live by it.

We will need to apply some truth tests to discover the answers to our five questions. These will be our truth detectors. We draw conclusions about the truth of the world in four primary ways: by reason, by observation, by experience, and by authority.

First, for something to be true, it must be rational. It must conform to the rules of logic, which are the principles and methods used to distinguish correct from incorrect reasoning.[15] An idea fails this truth test when we conclude, *"It does not make logical sense."* There are many rules of logic. One of the most important is the law of non-contradiction, which states that something cannot be both true and not true at the same time and in the same sense. A square circle is contradictory and therefore logically impossible. Another important logical principle is the law of the excluded middle, which requires that every statement be either true or false—there is no "middle ground." For example, either God exists or he does not exist; there is no third alternative.

There are also rules of logical deduction, which is a common way to argue for a particular claim by giving reasons and evidence to support it. We often refer to this as "if/then" reasoning. The general structure of a deductive argument is to make two or more logically related statements called premises that purport to justify the stated conclusion. For example, we might state that if A and B are true, then C must also be true. As long as C logically follows from A and B, then this is said to be a *valid* argument. If the premises A and B are actually true, then the argument is said to also be *sound*, and we can therefore believe that C is true. An example of this form of reasoning is as follows: All men are mortal. Socrates is a man. Therefore, Socrates is mortal. This argument is both valid and sound.

Here is an example of an invalid argument: Julie is happy when she visits her mother. Julie is happy. Therefore, Julie has visited her mother. Of course, Julie could be happy for some other reason, so the conclusion does not follow from the premises and the argument is not valid.

Here is an example of an unsound argument: All planets in our solar system other than our own are made of peanut butter. Mars is a planet in our solar system. Therefore, Mars is made of peanut butter. This argument

---

[15] Irving M. Copi and Carl Cohen, *Introduction to Logic* (Upper Saddle River, NJ: Pearson Prentice Hall, 2005, 12th edition), 4.

is valid since the conclusion follows from the premises; however the first premise is clearly false, so the argument is not sound.

Our reasoning must therefore be logically inferred from the premises we accept as true and also be free from contradictions. During our investigation we will make various assertions about the world, assuming certain premises are true, and then examine the premises to see if they are really true. Sometimes we cannot know with certainty that a given statement is true. Although there are not degrees of truth, there are degrees of plausibility and justification, so our aim will be to find the most plausible and justified premises based on the evidence.

Second, for something to be true, it should correspond with what we already observe and know about the world. An idea fails this truth test when we conclude, *"It does not fit the world as we discover it to be."* We will often test our premises using this truth test. Science is well suited to help us with this because its purpose is to discover truths about the natural world through observation and experiment.[16] For example, in chapter 1 we will test the assertion that the universe began to exist, that it is not eternal. To determine if this premise is true, we will make various mathematical and scientific observations.

Third, for something to be true, it should be affirmed by experience. An idea fails this truth test when we conclude, *"It does not fit the world as we experience it."* This truth test is closely related to the observation test, however there is a subtle difference. Science cannot answer all questions, such as what I ate for breakfast or what am I feeling right now. Our own experiences of ourselves and the world can lead us to certain kinds of truth.

Fourth, for something to be true, it should be affirmed by reliable authority. An idea fails this truth test when we conclude, *"It is not trustworthy because it lacks an advocate with adequate credentials."* Almost everything we know and every decision we make is made by trusting some authority. We trust the cook that made the food we eat to have prepared it safely. We trust that doctors have been trained and evaluate our test results correctly. We trust that news reporters accurately report events. Most of what we know of science, medicine, history, world events, and a vast amount of other information is based on authority. Even the time, place, and circumstances of our own birth we only know by the authority of our parents and the records produced by the hospital staff.

Author and speaker Greg Koukl suggests the following simple illustration to appreciate the value of authority: Suppose that I ask a

---

[16] Some people think that science can answer *all* the big questions in life, but by its very nature it cannot. This is because science deals with how things begin and how they work, not *why* things are the way they are. Science also has no ability to make us wise, happy, or good.

stranger to describe my mother. Then I describe my mother. Who will you believe? This shows two things: First, sometimes people are just wrong in what they claim. Second, some people are in a better position than others to give an accurate answer. They have access to privileged or esoteric information and thus speak with greater authority.[17] An authority's credentials can originate in many ways: through education, research, study, experience, eyewitness opportunity, or being the maker of something, such as an author, inventor, designer, or manufacturer.

Of the four truth tests, the first one—adherence to the principles of logic—acts as a truth filter that we must apply at *all* times. Whatever is true *must* satisfy these principles and, in fact, is guaranteed to do so. The last three truth tests—observation, experience, and authority—involve the collection and evaluation of evidence. The quantity and quality of the evidence will determine what we should believe and not believe.

There are dangers that lurk as we seek truth, however, so we need to carefully and thoughtfully apply these truth tests. We need to be aware of their limitations, such as faulty perceptions, flawed thinking, bad presuppositions, incomplete or misleading data, misunderstandings, biases, hidden agendas, misplaced trust, and unwillingness to believe truth that contradicts our desires. Since our truth tests have their limitations, they need to be used in combination. In this way they are mutually corrective. In other words, we can have more confidence in the truth we ascertain when reason, observation, experience, and authority all converge to point to the same conclusion. Our beliefs are less justified when they do not.

Armed with our understanding of truth and also our truth detectors, let's now begin our journey to discover the answers to life's most important questions.

---

[17] Greg Koukl, "Any Old God Won't Do".

QUESTION ONE

Where did everything come from?

If you want to maintain that something is real, then you have to say what it is and where it came from.

Francis Schaeffer (1912-1984)
Theologian, philosopher

The most fundamental question anyone must answer is one of origins. It makes little sense to try to answer any of the other important questions of life if we have not dealt with how everything we observe came into being. This is essential because the explanation of origins will profoundly influence how other aspects of life will be explained. For example, if God does not exist, then he cannot explain the existence of everything, what is wrong with the world, what happens after we die, or how we should live. If God does exist, however, it makes sense that he would be a vital part of the explanation of our other important life questions.

What kinds of things do we mean when we speak about origins? We do not mean buildings and computers and spaceships, or even you or me, for that matter. The origin of these things is obvious—human beings create things, including other human beings. We are interested in how everything got started in the first place—how the whole universe came into being and how life arose within it, including human life.

The origin of life leads us into other areas as well, such as how the wide diversity of life we observe today developed, what caused the complex life systems we see, where the information comes from in the basic unit of life—the cell, what caused consciousness, why we should trust our ability to reason, and how free will, language, significance, and morality originated. All these things are clearly evident through our observation and experience, and each requires an explanation.

CHAPTER 1

Something rather than nothing

The cosmos is all there is, or ever was, or ever will be.
Carl Sagan (1934-1996)
Atheist, astronomer, author
Cosmos

If we are to be honest then we have to accept that science will be able to claim complete success only if it achieves what many might think impossible: accounting for the emergence of everything from absolutely nothing.

Peter W. Atkins (1940-)
Chemist and Professor of Chemistry at Oxford University
The Limitless Power of Science

Everything that becomes or changes must do so owing to some cause; for nothing can come to be without a cause.
Plato (c. 428-347 BC)
Ancient Greek philosopher, mathematician, author
Timaeus

This most beautiful system of the sun, planets, and comets could only proceed from the counsel and dominion of an intelligent and powerful Being.

Isaac Newton (1643-1727)
Physicist, mathematician, astronomer, philosopher
Principia Mathematica

Have you ever thought about why there is something rather than nothing? This is a profound question—really the most foundational question we can ask. Every other important question in life is answered in light of the answer to this one. We need to begin with the most obvious fact of reality—the existence of the universe.

The immensity of the universe

The universe is stunningly vast. When we look up into the night sky, we can see a multitude of stars. There are about 2,500 stars visible to the naked eye at any one point on our planet, and six to eight thousand total  stars visible from Earth without a telescope. This is a very tiny fraction of the number of stars in the entire universe, though. In 1999, the Hubble Space Telescope project estimated there were about 125 billion galaxies in the universe. Some cosmologists now estimate there are as many as 200 billion galaxies in the universe. We are not able to see them all because our telescopes are not powerful enough. In fact, there may be many more than this since the most common kind of galaxy—the faint dwarf—is difficult to see even when close to us, and so would be undetectable at great cosmological distances.

Our own galaxy, the Milky Way, contains an estimated 200 billion stars. The nearby Andromeda galaxy is much more massive than the Milky Way and contains one trillion stars—five times as many stars as our own galaxy. The largest galaxy ever discovered is inside the Abell 2029 galaxy cluster, which contains 100 trillion stars. There is something like 10 trillion trillion stars in the entire universe.

There is another way to contemplate the size of the universe besides the incredible number of stars it contains. We can also consider its vast expanse. Because the universe is so enormous, cosmologists use the *light year* unit to measure cosmic distances. A light year is the distance that light travels in one year. Light travels fast—about 186,000 miles a second—which is 5.9 trillion miles a year. This speed is nearly impossible to fathom. Light can travel around the Earth's equator in about 13 hundredths of a second. You would need to go around our planet seven and a half times to travel 186,000 miles and more than two hundred thirty-five million times to travel one light year.

When we consider the size of the universe in terms of distance, we are quickly overwhelmed with its magnitude. The closest star to our solar system—Proxima Centauri—is 4.3 light-years away (25 trillion miles). The center of our own galaxy is about 25,000 light years away. Large galaxies like our own are about 100,000 light years across. The nearest large galaxy is Andromeda—about 2 million light years away. The nearest large cluster of galaxies—Virgo Cluster—is about 50 million light years away. The estimated width of the universe is somewhere between 80 and 150 billion light years. If you could travel at the speed of light, it would take you 100 billion years or so to cross the universe. The size of the universe is staggering!

An explanation is necessary

The fact that there is *something*—the universe and everything in it—requires a reason to explain it. Philosopher William Lane Craig tells the following story to illustrate the point:

> Imagine that you're hiking through the woods and came upon a translucent ball lying on the forest floor. You would find the claim quite bizarre that the ball just exists inexplicably; and increasing the size of the ball, even until it becomes co-extensive with the cosmos, would do nothing to eliminate the need for an explanation of its existence.[1]

Things that exist have explanations for why they are here and, with some investigation, we can discover what these explanations are.

There are only two fundamental explanations: A thing can exist either by the necessity of its own nature or by an external cause.[2] We refer to the latter as being *contingent*—that is, the thing is not necessary, but is dependent on something else for its existence. Something that exists necessarily simply *must* be. It has always existed and can never cease to exist. Since it is impossible that it does not exist, it must therefore exist in every possible world.[3] Most things are not this way because they do not have *necessary* existence. Things like stars, planets, oceans, and human beings do not *have* to exist, so they must have been *caused* by something external to themselves—something that brought them into being. If anything exists contingently, then at least one thing must exist necessarily, because not everything can be contingent. Something had to start the process.

---

[1] William Lane Craig, "Five Reasons God Exists", lecture delivered in Hyderabad, India on February 13, 2010.

[2] When we speak about a cause in this context, we are talking about the *efficient* and *final* cause of something, not its *material* and *formal* causes. A material cause explains what something is made of and a formal cause explains how it came to be arranged or formed in a particular manner. An efficient cause is what produces an effect. A final cause explains the reason for which an effect is produced—its aim or purpose. It is clear that science is well-suited to discover material and formal causes and also some efficient causes as long as they are present in the natural world, but not final causes.

[3] Philosophers often use the term *possible worlds* as a way to think about each distinct way the world *could have been*. The *actual* world is the one we, in fact, live in.

One of the most fundamental principles of philosophy is that *out of nothing, nothing comes.*[4] When we say nothing, we mean literally no thing. It is non-being. It is not merely empty space, but the absence of anything whatsoever.[5] *Nothing* has no reality, no existence, no nature, no properties, and no causal powers. Therefore, it cannot cause the existence of anything else.

If there literally ever was nothing, then there would *always* be nothing. This means that *something* must have always existed necessarily *and* eternally. Now, this could be our present universe or it could be something beyond the universe, but something has to have always been in existence, otherwise there would have always been nothing and there would always be nothing. Since nothing comes from nothing, however, and we have something, then something is eternal and we need to discover what that is in order to answer our question. We can therefore say that everything that begins to exist—that is, everything that comes into being—must have a cause external to itself.

We now need to ask if our universe had a beginning or if it has always existed. Since everything that comes into being requires a cause, if the universe began to exist, then it had a cause.[6] In fact, there is strong mathematical and scientific evidence that the universe began to exist at some time in the past. We will look at this evidence in the next two sections.

Mathematical evidence for the beginning of the universe

Infinity is a concept that refers to a quantity without bound or end. An infinite number is a number greater than any conceivable real number. If

the universe is eternal, that would be the same thing as saying it has an infinite past. If this is true, an infinite number of moments would have elapsed to get to the present moment, but *this is physically impossible.* An actually infinite number of things—like people, trees, or moments—cannot really exist. This is not to say that a *potentially* infinite number of things cannot exist, for the idea of infinity is useful as

---

[4] Perhaps the first public expression of this idea came from Parmenides in the 5th century BC.

[5] William Lane Craig, *On Guard: Defending Your Faith with Reason and Precision* (Colorado Springs: David C. Cook, 2010), 76.

[6] This is referred to as the *Kalam Cosmological Argument*, which was first developed by Muhammad Al-Ghazali in the eleventh century AD and further developed by William Lane Craig in the twentieth century. "*Kalam*" is the Arabic word for speech, and was used by Muslim thinkers to signify a theological statement or an argument supporting such a statement.

an ideal limit that can never be reached. The sequence of numbers 1, 2, 3... is an example of a potential infinity. A potential infinite can increase forever and never become an actual infinite. Adding one more thing to a finite set will always result in a larger finite set, no matter how many times it is done. An actual infinity is not merely a collection of things growing towards infinity as a limit, but is *already* complete.[7] Another way to say this is that the number of items in a collection is greater than any finite number, which is obviously impossible because we could always add one more item. This can be easily demonstrated by noting the self-contradictions that would occur if an actual infinite number of things existed. Craig invites us to contemplate the following thought experiment:[8]

> If you had an infinite number of coins numbered 1,2,3,... to infinity, and I took away all the odd-numbered coins, how many coins would you have left? Well, you'd still have all the even-numbered coins, or an infinity of coins. So infinity minus infinity is infinity. But suppose instead I took away all the coins greater than three. Now how many coins would you have left? Three! So infinity minus infinity is three! And yet in each case I took away an identical number of coins from an identical number of coins and came up with contradictory results. In fact, you can subtract infinity from infinity and get any answer from zero to infinity! This shows that infinity is just an idea in your mind, not something that exists in reality.[9]

The presence of these absurd self-contradictions when doing arithmetic on an actually infinite number of things means that an actual infinite number of things cannot exist in reality.[10] Therefore, the number of past moments in the universe must be finite. Since the series of past moments cannot go back forever, the universe must have begun to exist.

We can press this point even further, though. It is impossible to pass through an infinite number of items one at a time because we will never get to the end. Imagine trying to count to infinity. We would never get there because we can always add one more number. In fact, at any point in the process, we will always have an infinite quantity of numbers left to count! Now, if we cannot count up *to* infinity, then neither can we count down *from* infinity. This means that we could never get to the  present moment in an eternal universe that already experienced an infinity

---

[7] Craig, *On Guard*, 79.

[8] A thought experiment is a mental exercise to explore the potential consequences of some principle that is difficult or impossible to actually observe.

[9] William Lane Craig, "Five Reasons God Exists".

[10] If you doubt this, try to think of some set of a real number of things that is not finite.

of moments. Consider if each moment was a domino that knocked over the next moment's domino from an infinite past. An infinite number of dominos would have to fall before getting to today's domino, which could never happen.[11]

Mathematically, we see that it is impossible for the universe to be eternal. This evidence *alone* is sufficient to conclusively demonstrate that the universe had to have a beginning. We would expect the scientific evidence to therefore confirm this conclusion, and, in fact, this is exactly what we find.

Scientific evidence for the beginning of the universe

There are two primary lines of scientific evidence for a beginning of the universe, which we will now examine.

The Big Bang

The first scientific reason for a beginning of the universe is a series of amazing twentieth century discoveries made in the fields of cosmology, astronomy, and physics. These discoveries have shown beyond a reasonable doubt that our universe had an absolute starting point.

It began with Albert Einstein's theory of general relativity, published in 1915, which provided a unified description of gravity as a geometric property of space and time. A key implication of Einstein's theory is that

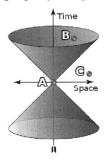

there must have been a distinct and fixed beginning point for time, space, matter, and energy, and they depend on one another—they all exist together or not at all. This beginning event of the universe is referred to as "the Big Bang."[12] This did not occur within any sort of pre-existing, empty space, but rather happened out of literally nothing at all. Prior to the Big Bang, there was no physical thing—no time, space, matter, or energy—and after that moment there was something—our physical universe.

General relativity predicted an expanding universe, which was confirmed by Edwin Hubble in 1929. Hubble found that the light coming from distant galaxies appears redder than expected. This "red shift" is due to the fact that the galaxies are moving away from us. The universe is not expanding into empty space, but rather is *creating* space as it expands.[13]

---

[11] Craig, *On Guard*, 83-84.

[12] This phrase was coined by the English astrophysicist Fred Hoyle in 1950. Hoyle, who favored a rival cosmological theory, intended "the Big Bang" to be a term of contempt, but the name became so popular that it remains today.

[13] Geisler and Turek, *I Don't Have Enough Faith to Be an Atheist*, 79.

The discovery that the universe is expanding implies that it must have had an initial starting point. This becomes clear by imagining the expansion of the universe played out as a movie. If we played this movie backwards, we would see the universe contracting as we went back in time. The size of the universe would gradually shrink from its gigantic dimensions today to literally zero dimensions at some point in the finite past.[14]

If the universe was initially very hot as the Big Bang suggests, scientists theorized that there should be some remnant today of this heat. In 1965, astronomers Arno Penzias and Robert Wilson discovered what they called cosmic background radiation pervading the observable universe.[15] This light and heat is the predicted afterglow from the event that spawned the universe.

The Big Bang theory also predicted small variations in the temperature of the cosmic background radiation that fills the universe. These temperature variations enabled matter to form galaxies. In 1989, a NASA satellite called Cosmic Background Explorer (COBE) did indeed detect these temperature variations. The radioactive glow is highly uniform in all directions, but shows a very specific pattern of irregularities, which vary with the size of the region examined. These patterns have been measured in detail and match what would be expected if a very tiny dense mass had expanded to the size of the observable universe we see today.[16]

The Second Law of Thermodynamics

The second scientific reason for a beginning of the universe is the Second Law of Thermodynamics, which is an expression of the universal principle of decay observable in nature.[17] This basically means that the universe is running out of usable energy and will eventually have none left. Once the universe reaches this point, no further change will take place. It will be in a state of equilibrium, in which the temperature and pressure will be the same everywhere and there will be no motion or life. This is what scientists refer to as the "heat death" of the universe.

The problem is that, given an infinite amount of time, the universe should have *already* reached this disastrous state. Just as a running car will run out of gas, so too will the universe ultimately "run out of gas." Your car would not still be running if you had started it up an infinitely long time ago because it would have run out of gas by now. Likewise, the

---

[14] I borrowed this movie analogy from Geisler and Turek. Ibid.

[15] Penzias and Wilson shared the 1978 Nobel Prize in Physics for this discovery.

[16] Two of COBE's principal investigators, George Smoot and John Mather, received the 2006 Nobel Prize in Physics for this discovery.

[17] The First Law of Thermodynamics states that the amount of matter and energy in the universe is constant; it is neither created nor destroyed.

universe would be out of energy by now if it had been running from eternity past.[18]

The scientific evidence for the beginning of the universe coincides perfectly with the mathematical evidence. The universe is not eternal, but came into existence at some point in the past. Because everything that begins to exist requires a cause, we can conclude the universe must have a cause for its existence.

Possible explanations for the cause of the universe

Various explanations have been proposed for the existence of the universe. The first possible explanation is that the universe is not real—it is an illusion. However, the universe is obviously real because we are experiencing it, so this explanation is irrational and can be rejected.

The second possible explanation is that the universe caused itself, but this is logically incoherent since a cause must precede its effect. The universe would have to *already* exist to be able to cause itself to exist, which is absurd, so this explanation must also be rejected.

The third possible explanation is that the universe simply popped into existence with no cause at all, but as we have seen, nothing comes from nothing. We never experience things coming into and out of existence for no reason whatsoever.[19] Have you ever seen a mountain or a building suddenly and inexplicably appear before your eyes? If our consistent experience is that this principle applies to everything *within* the universe, then why should we think the universe itself can have no cause? This explanation is nothing more than superstition, so we must reject it as well.

The fourth possible explanation is that the universe has always existed. This had been the predominant view of atheism until modern scientific discoveries proved conclusively that the universe has not always existed. This continues to be the view of pantheism, however. The

---

[18] Geisler and Turek, *I Don't Have Enough Faith to Be an Atheist*, 76.

[19] A common objection at this point is that quantum physics has discovered that subatomic particles supposedly materialize from nothing and then vanish. If this can happen at the subatomic level, then why can't the whole universe materialize out of nothing? There are several reasons to think otherwise, though. First, these particles are theoretical entities and may not really exist according to William Lane Craig, as quoted in Lee Strobel, *The Case for a Creator: A Journalist Investigates Scientific Evidence That Points Towards God* (Grand Rapids: Zondervan, 2004), 101. Second, quantum physics, by definition, operates only at the sub-atomic level. We do not observe these effects at larger scales where we can readily see the objects. Third, it would be more accurate to say, not that the particles are causeless, but that science has hit a limit where it is unable to predict their effects. Finally, these particles do not pop into existence out of literally nothing. They come into existence from a sea of fluctuating energy called a quantum vacuum that has a fixed structure, describable by physical laws. It is not nothing, but something that itself had to have a cause for its existence. The particles are thought to originate by fluctuations of the energy within the vacuum, so the analogy of something coming from nothing does not hold.

pantheist view is that an eternal god exists that is the same thing as the universe; that is, god is the universe and the universe is god. Since we have discovered good evidence that the universe began to exist at some point in the past, this option must also be eliminated.

The fifth possible explanation is really a class of explanations that seeks to avoid the conclusion of a Big Bang beginning of the universe because many scientists are troubled by the theological implications of a universe with a finite age. One of these theories is the so-called oscillating universe. This theory supposedly eliminates the need for an absolute beginning of the universe by proposing that the universe expands, then contracts, then expands again, and so on, indefinitely.[20] However, there are two main problems with this theory. First, it violates the known laws of physics.[21] Second, an oscillating universe itself would require a beginning, so this view does not really solve the problem.[22]

Another hypothesis, called "String theory," suggests a five-dimensional, eternal super-universe that contains three-dimensional membranes (universes) that collide with one another, causing them to expand as we observe our universe doing. Aside from several internal inconsistencies, this theory is really a five dimensional equivalent of a three dimensional oscillating universe, so it suffers the same problems as the previous theory.[23]

A further problem with *any* of these kinds of theories that suggest a scientific explanation for an eternal universe is that they cannot overcome the insurmountable barrier of the impossibility of an actual infinity of moments, which we discussed earlier.[24] An eternal universe is mathematically impossible.

The sixth possible explanation—and the only real remaining option—for the existence of the universe is that it was supernaturally caused. The Cause must be *super*natural because "natural" refers to everything in time

---

[20] Craig, as quoted in Strobel, *The Case for a Creator*, 113.

[21] In particular, it contradicts general relativity, which requires a beginning for the universe. Also, there are no known physics which could reverse a collapsing universe, nor does the universe have sufficient density to contract. In fact, the evidence shows that the expansion of the universe is accelerating, not decelerating. Ibid., 114.

[22] According to Craig, scientific studies have shown that entropy would be conserved from one cycle to the next, which would cause each successive expansion to be larger. If we traced that backwards, each cycle would get smaller and smaller until you come to the beginning of the universe. Ibid., 115.

[23] Ibid., 115-116.

[24] Some people might object to the existence of an eternal God on these same grounds. They would say, "Since an eternal God would have to exist through an infinite number of moments, and an actual infinity of moments is impossible, then God also cannot be eternal." However, this is not the normal understanding of a theistic God, who existed outside of time prior to creating the universe (remember that time itself came into existence at the Big Bang). Therefore, if God does exist, he did not experience an infinity of moments because he transcends time, that is, he is beyond and outside it. He only entered time when he created the universe according to this view.

and space, and the Cause created time and space, so it transcends natural causes. Natural explanations have been exhausted and none of them are convincing. The evidence seems to point to a supernatural explanation as the most probable cause for the existence of the universe.[25]

Inferences about the attributes of the Cause of the universe

We can infer several important attributes of the Cause of the universe from what we have discovered in this chapter.

One, the Cause must be necessary. There must be *something* that exists that is necessary, otherwise nothing at all would exist. Everything cannot be contingent because then there would be nothing to cause all the contingent things. Therefore the Cause *must* exist and have no cause itself. Having no prior causes or explanations, it is the First Cause of the universe. If this were not so, then we would be stuck in an endless series of causes which does not explain what caused the series.

Two, the Cause must be eternal. It has always existed. There was never a time when it did not exist. *Something* has to be eternal, otherwise there would always be nothing.

Three, the Cause is distinct from the universe. Since the Cause is eternal and the universe is not, they must be two separate entities. The Cause is not part of the universe.

Four, the Cause must exist outside of time because it created time. The consensus of modern science is that the universe, including time itself, had a beginning. Nothing that is confined to time could have created the universe, so the Cause transcends time.

Five, the Cause must be immaterial[26] because it created the material universe—all matter, space, and energy. If the Cause was not immaterial, then we could not say that all matter came into being at some finite point in the past, but that is what the scientific evidence indicates. Since the Cause transcends space, it is therefore not physical.

Six, the Cause must be unique. There is only one such Cause and nothing else is like it. The principle of *Ockham's razor* states that entities must not be multiplied beyond necessity.[27] This means that a plurality of

---

[25] If you remain unconvinced by this explanation at this point, I encourage you to remain patient, as the weight of the cumulative evidence will progressively mount.

[26] Throughout this book I use the word "immaterial" in the sense of not material or not physical. I never use it in the sense of unimportant or irrelevant.

[27] Ockham's razor is a principle attributed to the 14th century logician and Franciscan friar William of Ockham. The principle recommends selecting the competing hypothesis that makes the fewest new assumptions when the hypotheses are equal in other respects. This is sometimes stated as follows: "When you have two competing theories that make exactly the same predictions, the simpler one is preferred." The principle is referred to as a "razor" because it "shaves" away unnecessary assumptions.

causes should not be suggested if one cause is sufficient, and there is no reason to think that more than one cause is necessary for the universe.

Seven, the Cause must be a personal agent capable of deciding to cause the universe. There are two reasons to believe this: 1) The Cause cannot be mechanistic and 2) It must have a mind. The Cause cannot be some kind of mechanistic machine that necessarily causes effects because the Cause would never exist without the effect (the universe). Craig provides an example:

> The cause of water's freezing is the temperature's being below 0° Centigrade. If the temperature were below 0° from eternity past, then any water that was around would be frozen from eternity. It would be impossible for the water to *begin* to freeze just a finite time ago. So if the cause is permanently present, then the effect should be permanently present as well. The only way for the cause to be timeless and the effect to begin to exist a finite time ago is for the cause to be a personal agent who freely chooses to create an effect in time without any prior determining conditions.[28]

The only kind of immaterial thing that has causal powers is a mind. A mind is capable of thought, decision, and the will to action. The Cause had to have the power to decide and initiate a change, and this can only be done by an agent who has the power of free choice. The Cause had the complete freedom to create the universe or not create it. We can therefore say that the universe is the product of an unembodied mind.[29] When we recognize that volition is part of the explanation of the universe, then we begin to think of the Cause in terms of being a *personal Creator*.[30]

Eight, the Creator is independent. Since the Creator existed without the universe and willed that it be created, the Creator has no need for anything within the universe. The Creator is entirely self-sufficient.

Nine, the Creator is extremely powerful. The Creator's power is not only sufficient to create the universe, but also to sustain its existence every moment. This is more power than we can imagine.

Ten, the Creator is extremely intelligent. The magnificent complexity and splendor of the world requires a sophisticated mind of great intelligence.[31] The universe is far beyond anything that man could devise, so the Creator knows a great many things that we do not. The Creator must know everything about the universe down to the last detail.

Eleven, the Creator rules the universe. It is reasonable to conclude that the Creator who has the freedom, will, power, and intelligence to

---

[28] William Lane Craig, "Five Reasons God Exists".

[29] It must be unembodied because it is not physical.

[30] Since the Cause/Creator is a person, it is legitimate to refer to him using a personal pronoun.

[31] This will be further developed in chapter 3.

create the universe also rules it. We often refer to this kind of authority as *sovereignty*, which in this case includes having the authority, power, and right to govern everything in existence. The degree to and method by which the Creator actually rules the universe is an open question at this point, but at the very least this must include two things: 1) establishing the laws by which the universe operates and 2) sustaining the operation of the universe, since it continues to exist.

These eleven attributes of the Cause/Creator of the universe can be logically inferred simply by reasoning about the universe we observe. They are not proofs in a mathematical sense, but very reasonable conclusions based on the evidence. The Cause/Creator we have inferred from nature has the attributes that humanity has traditionally associated with a divine Being, whom we commonly refer to as *God*.

A thought experiment about God's attributes

God is, by definition, the greatest conceivable being.[32] If we could conceive of anything greater than God, then *that* would be God. Thus, God is the greatest being of which we can conceive—*a maximally great Being*. Maximal is a way of saying there is no way to exceed something.[33] Nothing is more powerful or knowledgeable than God. A being which did not exhibit the greatest limit of these properties would not be maximally great because we could conceive of something greater. God must therefore be *unlimited*. If he were not, he would be limited by some other thing, which would have to be in some sense greater, so *that* would be God.

Some people use this argument to prove the existence of God, but admittedly many people have trouble accepting it as *evidence* that God exists. I am using this approach in a more modest way. I believe the existence of a Creator is adequately demonstrated in other ways, one of which was presented earlier in this chapter.[34] I think there is value in this argument—or thought experiment—to show the *degree* of some of the Creator's attributes which we have already discerned from nature. For instance, a maximally great Creator is not simply very powerful, but *all*-powerful. He is not merely very intelligent—he is *all*-knowing.[35]

---

[32] What follows is referred to as the Ontological Argument for God's existence, which was first developed in AD 1011 by Anselm of Canterbury.

[33] This is what we mean when we describe God as being infinite. The term is used here in a qualitative, and not quantitative, sense, which avoids the "actual infinite" problem described earlier.

[34] Other proofs will follow in subsequent chapters.

[35] As we will see in subsequent chapters, God's other attributes of goodness, love, joy, beauty, justice, and so on, are also held by him to a superlative or maximal degree.

Preliminary conclusions about where everything came from

A supernatural explanation for the cause of the universe is consistent with both theism and deism. Theism is the belief in one deity who created the universe and remains involved with it.[36] Deism is the belief in one deity who created the universe, but does not intervene in it.[37] Both views believe in a personal God who created the universe, but who is not part of the universe. God is like a painter and his creation is like a painting. God made the painting, and his attributes are reflected in it, but God is not the painting.[38]

Pantheism can be eliminated because a god who *is* the universe cannot *cause* the universe to come into being. Both must be eternal in this view, but we know the universe is not eternal. The Creator must be distinct from the creation as a painter is distinct from his painting, but pantheists would have us believe that the painter and his painting are the same thing.

Atheism can be eliminated because natural, material, physical explanations cannot account for the cause of the universe. There simply was no "nature"—no time, space, matter, or energy—prior to its existence. Atheists claim there is no painter for the painting, which defies common sense.

Polytheism—the belief in many finite gods—can be eliminated on two grounds. First, through the principle of Ockham's razor we can conclude that a plurality of gods did not cause the universe. Second, the transcendent Cause cannot be finite in time and space because it *created* time and space. Gods who were once finite men cannot explain the origin of the universe. If the gods are not necessary, eternal, timeless, and immaterial, but rather come from nature, then they cannot be the ultimate cause. Therefore, a polytheistic theory of a plurality of finite gods cannot explain the existence of the universe.

At this point, a supernatural explanation for the cause of the universe is the most plausible, but the evidence does not end here. Now we will look into the evidence for the origin of life in the universe.

---

[36] The traditional theistic view is that God created the universe *ex nihilo*, that is, out of nothing. This does not contradict the principle that nothing can come from nothing, for there wasn't nothing; there was God. To say that God created *out of* nothing means that he used no pre-existing materials. He merely spoke the universe into being out of literally nothing.

[37] Future chapters will present evidence that argue against deism.

[38] I borrowed the painting analogy from Geisler and Turek, *I Don't Have Enough Faith to Be an Atheist*, 22-23.

CHAPTER 2

The greatest show on Earth

The inability of unguided trial and error to reach anything but the most trivial of ends in almost every field of interest obviously raises doubts as to its validity in the biological realm.

Michael Denton (1943-)
Molecular biologist, medical doctor
Evolution: A Theory in Crisis

It is not that the methods and institutions of science somehow compel us to accept a material explanation of the phenomenal world, but, on the contrary, that we are forced by our a priori adherence to material causes to create an apparatus of investigation and a set of concepts that produce material explanations, no matter how counter-intuitive, no matter how mystifying to the uninitiated. Moreover, that material-ism is an absolute, for we cannot allow a Divine Foot in the door.

Richard Lewontin (1929-)
Atheist, biologist, geneticist
The New York Review

If moral statements are about something, then the universe is not quite as science suggests it is, since physical theories, having said nothing about God, say nothing about right or wrong, good or bad. To admit this would force philosophers to confront the possibility that the physical sciences offer a grossly inadequate view of reality.

David Berlinski (1942-)
Mathematician, author
The Devil's Delusion

With apologies to the Ringling Brothers and Barnum & Bailey Circus, "the greatest show on Earth" is *life*, and human life in particular. It is nothing short of extraordinary in numerous respects. How do we explain life—both its existence and its exceptional features?

There are two main approaches to explaining what kind of world we live in. One views the world as consisting of only physical ingredients. It says that everything that exists can be completely explained in terms of chemical reactions, biological causes, and physical laws that are the result of random and unguided processes. Philosopher Victor Reppert explains this view: "The world is at bottom a mindless system of events at the level of fundamental particles, and everything else that exists must exist in virtue of what is going on at that basic level."[1] There is no immaterial or non-physical aspect of life, nor is there a supernatural explanation for it. All of life can be explained using natural processes exclusively. Everything that exists can be observed, measured, and predicted according to natural laws. Human beings are biological machines that work in deterministic ways, according to the renowned theoretical physicist and cosmologist Stephen Hawking.[2]

The second approach recognizes both physical and non-physical aspects of the world. There is no question that the physical world is real and that natural processes are working in it, which we perceive through our senses of sight, hearing, smell, taste, and touch. At the same time, we also recognize that our world is comprised of many features that are not physical. Consider that we are conscious beings that have self-awareness, that is, we sense that our *self* is distinct from our body. Why are we able to reason and why should we trust this ability if we were merely a collection of chemicals controlled by biological and physical laws? Where did human free will come from? If we are purely physical, mechanistic machines, then how could we *choose* anything? How can matter think at all? And why are there such things as value, meaning, and purpose? Why should we think that human beings have any special value just because we have a different physical arrangement than, say, a turtle? All of these things are very real—they exist in this world—so we need to account for them by giving a rational explanation for *why* they are here.

It would seem that consciousness, reason, free will, and the other features listed above are not physical in their nature. They cannot be observed, measured, and predicted like we can physical things. They are beyond matter and natural laws and so are outside the physical realm. Since immaterial features exist in the world, we must conclude that the world is not *exclusively* material. In this chapter we will examine how life

---

[1] Victor Reppert, "Confronting Naturalism: The Argument From Reason", *Contending with Christianity's Critics* (Nashville: B&H Publishing Group, 2009), Paul Copan and William Lane Craig, editors, 30.

[2] Stephen Hawking and Leonard Mlodinow, *The Grand Design* (New York: Bantam Books, 2010), 32.

arose on this planet, as well as some of the important immaterial features of life.

The origin of life

Just as the universe requires an explanation for its origin, so does the origin of life. The same stipulations apply here that applied to the origin of the universe. Life cannot arise without a cause; neither can it be self-caused; nor can it have always existed.

A naturalistic account of the origin of life

Naturalists, despite their reluctance to acknowledge a supernatural cause for life, really do not have any good theories for the origin of life. They had a glimmer of hope in 1953 when Stanley Miller, a student at the University of Chicago, performed an experiment intended to demonstrate how life could arise naturally during the primeval conditions of an early Earth.[3] Miller's doctoral advisor, Harold Urey, hypothesized that the atmosphere of the ancient Earth was probably like the atmosphere now present on Jupiter, which is comprised of methane, ammonia, and hydrogen. Miller's experiment exposed a high voltage electric spark to a mixture of these compounds and water and was able to produce a small number of simple amino acids, which are essential for the formation of living matter. The experiment was initially hailed as an astounding success, but was later discredited on multiple grounds.

First, the modern consensus is that the early Earth atmosphere was nothing like what Urey and Miller thought. Instead, the atmosphere probably consisted of carbon dioxide, nitrogen, and water vapor. If Miller's experiment is performed on this sort of atmosphere, no amino acids are produced.

Second, it is a long way to get from amino acids to a living cell. Biologists have discovered that a single cell is enormously complex. Inside each living cell is a nucleus, which contains many complicated things like chromosomes and genes. There are tens of thousands of genes in each cell. The genes are composed of a sophisticated chemical structure called DNA,[4] which is the single most important molecule in living cells because it is the genetic blueprint of life.

A single cell involves the combination of hundreds of protein molecules, which perform all the diverse functions of the cell. The building blocks of proteins are amino acids. To create a single living cell,

---

[3] The theory that life can emerge from non-living matter is referred to as *abiogenesis* and also *spontaneous generation*.

[4] DNA stands for deoxyribonucleic acid.

first the right number and kinds of amino acids must combine to create a single protein molecule, and then this must be repeated hundreds of times to create and arrange protein molecules in the right sequence. The human body has about 100 trillion cells. Referring to the possibility of all this happening by chance, molecular biologist Jonathan Wells writes, "The odds against this are astonishing. The gap between nonliving chemicals and even the most primitive living organism is absolutely tremendous."[5]

Third, life contains a distinct nonmaterial component—information—that determines what we are and what we look like. The process to get from amino acids to a living cell requires this information, which is contained in DNA. We have over 100 billion miles of DNA inside our bodies.[6] Embedded within each DNA molecule is a code that is incredibly complex—filled with the equivalent of tens of thousands of pages of information.

It is critical to recognize the difference between a message and the medium in which it is conveyed. The source of the message "I love my wife" has nothing to do with the materials I might use to express that message. I can speak it or I can write it on a piece of paper with ink or a crayon. I can paint it on the side of my house or scratch it into the concrete of my driveway. I can transmit it by letter, email, text message, or Morse code. In these examples, the message remained the same while the medium changed in each case. This illustrates that the message and the medium are two entirely different kinds of things and each requires a separate explanation. When we find information in nature, we must make this same distinction. Because the message is different than the physical thing that it resides in, we need an explanation for the origin of *each*. Miller's experiment only attempts to account for the medium, not the message.

Like a book, information written in DNA is different from the DNA material itself. In order to form a protein, a DNA molecule has to *direct* the placement of the right number and kinds of amino acids in a specific order. Philosopher and chemist J. P. Moreland says this about experiments that have tried to create life: "If life can be likened to an encyclopedia in complexity and information, then the best we have done is to synthesize a compound which carries the complexity and information of the word ME.

---

[5] Jonathan Wells, as quoted in Strobel, *Case for a Creator*, 39. Note, "chance" is a word used to describe probability, not causation. It is not a thing and it is not an explanation. It has no power to create or cause anything. Whenever "chance" is used, an explanation (e.g., mechanism, process, pathway) for *how* the thing came to be is still required, no matter its probability.

[6] We have 6 feet of DNA that is tightly coiled inside each of 100 trillion cells in our body. Lee Strobel, *Case for a Creator*, 219.

The jump from ME to an encyclopedia is so far and speculative that the relevance of progress so far is questionable."[7] Indeed, Miller had no hope of creating the enormous information content of DNA since information is not physical. Where does this information come from? All of our experience with information is that it comes from intelligence, and intelligence is the product of a mind. Who is the author and mind behind the information in living cells?

Natural accounts are wholly inadequate to explain the origin of life. We have no evidence whatsoever of life developing from non-life by means of natural processes. *Being* simply does not come from *non-being* in our observations of the world. Indeed, our uniform experience is that new life comes only from *existing* life.

Qualitative difference between life and non-life

Life has a quality about it that is radically different from things that are not alive. Life is characterized by growth, digestion, internal regulation, environmental response, adaptation, and reproduction. These are self-sustaining processes that distinguish life from non-life. On top of this, information is a fundamental component of all living cells, and information does not come from non-life. From every appearance, the boundary between life and non-life is a great chasm that cannot be bridged through purely chemical and physical processes. This fact is not lost on scientists, for many of them have come to the conclusion that the origin of life requires some sort of supernatural intervention. Here are five well-known scientists who have come to this conclusion.

Biophysicist Dean Kenyon co-wrote a very influential book called *Biochemical Predestination*, which described a theory of how life emerged naturally through biochemical processes. Kenyon later repudiated his entire theory because he could not reconcile it with the enormous molecular complexity of the cell and the information encoded within DNA. He subsequently gave up his naturalistic beliefs in favor of theism.[8]

Molecular biologist Michael Denton asks, "Is it really credible that random processes could have constructed a reality, the smallest element of which—a functional protein or gene—is complex beyond...anything produced by the intelligence of man?"[9]

Molecular biologist James Coppedge concludes, "The odds are 10^{161} to 1 that not one usable protein would have been produced by chance in all

[7] J. P. Moreland, *Scaling the Secular City: A Defense of Christianity* (Grand Rapids, MI: Baker Books, 1987), 221.

[8] Lee Strobel, *Case for a Creator*, 232.

[9] Michael Denton, *Evolution: A Theory in Crisis* (Chevy Chase, MD: Adler & Adler, 1985), 342.

the history of the earth."[10] That is one chance in the number 1 with 161 zeros after it to get a single useable protein, not even a single cell, which has hundreds of protein molecules.

Atheist astronomer, mathematician, and physicist Fred Hoyle writes, "The likelihood of the formation of life from inanimate matter is one to a number with 40,000 noughts [zeros] after it…It is big enough to bury Darwin and the whole theory of evolution…If the beginnings of life were not random, they must therefore have been the product of purposeful intelligence."[11]

Molecular biologist, co-discoverer of DNA, and religious skeptic Francis Crick admits, "An honest man, armed with all the knowledge available to us now, could only state that in some sense, the origin of life appears at the moment to be almost a miracle, so many are the conditions which would have had to have been satisfied to get it going."[12]

If life only comes from life, being only from being, and information only from a mind, then we should expect the origin of life in the universe to come from some living, personal, intelligent Being that has always existed. There must be an eternal Being who created human life and other life we observe on our planet. Building on our findings in chapter 1, where we concluded that an eternal, personal Creator created the universe out of nothing, we can reasonably conclude that life on our planet arose due to the action of this same Creator.[13]

The origin of consciousness

Consciousness is the awareness we have that we are each an individual "self"—that is, our own subjective experience of being a person, distinct from our body, with the capacities of thought, perception, memory, emotion, will, and imagination. These *mental* processes are causal factors in our behavior.

Part of this subjective experience is the notion that we have a "mind of our own" that is distinct from our brain. Our mind is not the same thing as our brain.[14] To be sure, there is a *correlation* between the mind and the brain, but they are separate entities and each requires their own explanation. While the human brain is very complex and the center of the nervous system, it can be completely described in physical terms like

---

[10] James Coppedge, *Evolution: Possible or Impossible?* (Grand Rapids: Zondervan, 1973), 109-110.

[11] Fred Hoyle, "Hoyle on Evolution", *Nature* (Vol. 294, No. 5837, Nov 12, 1981), 148.

[12] Francis Crick, *Life Itself: Its Origin and Nature* (New York, Simon and Schuster, 1981), 88.

[13] This leaves no opening for *panspermia*, the hypothesis that life exists throughout the universe and was transplanted to our planet in the distant past as the explanation for life on Earth. Even in that scenario, the origin of the *first* life must be explained.

[14] This will be further discussed in chapter 6.

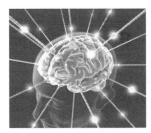 neurons, synapses, and fibers. However, the mind cannot be described using physical terms at all. There is a vast qualitative difference between the two. The brain is material and the mind is immaterial. A scientist can examine a brain, but he has no idea what thoughts are contained in it. The scientist's tools are limited to observing and measuring physical things. He can weigh and measure the container, but he has no scientific way to discover its contents. Only *we* can observe or examine *our own* mental and emotional states; no one else can do this. This is a special feature of our consciousness, which gives us the ability of introspection—the private knowledge of our own thoughts. The only way for someone to know our thoughts is if we communicate them. Therefore, our mind is different than our brain.

The special problem presented by mind and consciousness is how they could arise within a physical body through only natural processes. This is a chasm that cannot be crossed by biological functions alone. It is a conceptual gap that will always exist no matter how much we examine or describe the physical side. The gulf simply cannot be crossed using materialistic explanations because matter will never be able to think.

Physicist Erich Harth suggests, "Mind is like no other property of physical systems. It is not just that we don't know the mechanisms that give rise to it. We have difficulty in seeing how *any* mechanism can give rise to it" [emphasis added].[15] This is why materialists do not want to admit a mind/brain distinction, but this is very problematic as we have just seen. Peter Kreeft remarks, "The materialist wants us to believe that the body is a car that drives itself, or that the driver is just another one of the parts of the engine; that the *mind* is merely the *brain*. How absurd!"[16] The truth is that naturalism has no plausible way to explain the emergence of consciousness. Moreland writes, "Consciousness is among the most mystifying features of the cosmos."[17]

Mind must come from mind. Consciousness must come from consciousness. This is additional evidence that the personal Creator of the universe also created life and is a conscious Being with thoughts, perceptions, emotions, will, and imagination.

---

[15] Erich Harth, *Windows on the Mind: Reflections on the Physical Basis of Consciousness* (New York: William Morrow & Co., 1982), 15.

[16] Kreeft, *Christianity for Modern Pagans*, 59.

[17] J. P. Moreland, *Consciousness and the Existence of God: A Theistic Argument* (New York: Routledge, 2008), 1.

The origin of reason

There is a problem with the approach that atheists use when they try to persuade us of their beliefs. They propose explanations against the existence of God using logic, philosophical arguments, and their perceptions of scientific evidence, but in their view atheists have no justification to believe they can trust their own reasoning ability.

Reasoning is a mental process of human beings that provides the ability to consider and choose alternative explanations of different aspects of the world. Reppert explains, "Our processes of reasoning provide us with a systematically reliable way of understanding the world around us."[18] If reasoning does not lead us to true conclusions about the world, then all logic, math, science, and other sources  of knowledge are worthless. Therefore, to be able to reason presupposes an order and rationality to the universe.

However, according to naturalists, the universe has a fundamentally non-goal-directed explanation. It has no purpose or aim, nothing guiding or directing it to develop in a particular way or for a specific purpose. Instead, everything simply "emerged" through unguided, accidental natural processes that formed chemicals in random arrangements. But why should we suppose that a non-purposeful, non-rational universe somehow produced rational human beings? Geneticist and biologist John Haldane admits, "If my mental processes are determined wholly by the motions of atoms in my brain, I have no reason to suppose that my beliefs are true."[19] In this view, we would not come to have our beliefs because they are reasonable, but rather because we are reacting to non-rational, physical stimuli.[20]

If our ability to think is an accidental by-product of our brain chemistry, then it is difficult to see why we should place any confidence in it. This conclusion also applies to the thoughts that led us to believe that our thoughts and ways of thinking are random accidents. We get into this endless loop of being unable to trust any conclusions we draw, so this position is self-defeating. Theologian and author C. S. Lewis explains it like this: "A theory which explained everything else in the whole universe but which made it impossible to believe that our thinking was valid, would be utterly out of court. For that theory would itself have been reached by

---

[18] Reppert, *Contending with Christianity's Critics,* 32.
[19] John Haldane, *Possible Worlds* (New Brunswick, NJ: Transaction Publishers, 2009, 5th printing, orig. published 1927 by Chatto and Windus), 209.
[20] Moreland, *Scaling the Secular City*, 95.

thinking, and if thinking is not valid that theory would, of course, be itself demolished. It would have destroyed its own credentials."[21]

It seems impossible that reason should emerge from naturalistic processes. There is simply no way to connect the reliability of our cognitive faculties to random, undirected chemical processes. The most sensible way to explain the existence of rationality in the universe is by appealing to the inherent rationality of a personal Creator, who created an ordered world where reasoning about it would produce consistent and reliable results.

The origin of free will

Free will is our ability to genuinely choose between two or more alternatives without that choice being fixed, determined, or caused by some power outside our own will. It is the power we have to choose otherwise.

Determinism is the view that every event happens exactly as it does because of prior physical conditions and factors. Given all the prior conditions and factors, the event in question could not have occurred in any other way. Determinism sees every event—including the so-called choices of human beings—as the inevitable outcome of an unbreakable chain of previous events leading to that event.[22] This causal chain has a very long history which must ultimately lead back to the beginning of the universe. In this way, all events in the world are connected in some fashion. The events occur due to external forces such as physical mechanisms and processes, like some sort of complex stimulus-response machine. Determinists deny the existence of free will because, if every event has an external cause, and a free act has no outside cause, there can be no free acts. Human thoughts are merely predetermined sequences of synapse firings in the brain. There is no "choice" about them at all.

It should be apparent by now that a naturalistic view of the world is necessarily a determinist view. Everything happens as a result of chemical processes and physical laws. Human free will is not possible because that demands a conscious mind, which is separate from the brain and cannot emerge in a naturalistic world. However, as human beings, we do seem to experience genuine free will. We sense no deterministic forces at work that cause us to make the many choices we do each day. Instead, we have a clear intuitive sense that we act deliberately and consciously, we have intentions and desires, and we choose freely. Like consciousness and our

---

[21] C. S. Lewis, *Miracles* (San Francisco: HarperCollins, 2001, orig. published 1947), 21-22.

[22] J. P. Moreland and William Lane Craig, *Philosophical Foundations for a Christian Worldview* (Downers Grove, IL: InterVarsity Press, 2003), 268.

ability to reason, free will must come from a personal Creator, who also has free will, as demonstrated by his choice to create the universe.

The origin of language

Two of the most powerful things human beings can do is speak and write. Human language is an amazingly complex form of communication.

It is more than vocalization, the mere utterance of sounds. It is highly structured, consisting of a complex system of letters and sounds which are arranged in very specific ways—first into words, then sentences and paragraphs, and ultimately into entire discourses. All of this is accomplished by following a strict set of lexical, grammatical, semantic, and phonetic rules. Whenever the rules are violated, the result is nonsense and effective communication does not occur.

Human language is unique compared to communication among animals because it allows us to produce an infinite set of utterances from a finite set of letters and sounds. The known systems of communication used by animals, on the other hand, can only express a finite number of utterances that are mostly genetically transmitted.

As with consciousness, reason, and free will, the development of human language is inexplicable on naturalistic reasons alone. There is simply no way it can emerge from some arrangement of inanimate chemicals. Leading language expert and Darwinist Elizabeth Bates concludes:

> If the basic structural principles of language cannot be learned (bottom up) or derived (top down), there are only two possible explanations for their existence: either Universal Grammar was endowed to us directly by the Creator, or else our species has undergone a mutation of unprecedented magnitude, a cognitive equivalent of the Big Bang...What protoform can we possibly envision that could have given birth to constraints on the extraction of noun phrases from an embedded clause? What could it conceivably mean for an organism to possess half a symbol or three quarters of a rule?...[This is] a process that cries out for a Creationist explanation.[23]

Human language differs dramatically from animal communication in a way that does not appear to be a mere evolutionary step. On the contrary, its intricate structure and sophistication are consistent with a personal

---

[23] Elizabeth Bates, as quoted in Steven Pinker, *The Language Instinct: How the Mind Creates Language* (New York: Harper Perennial, 1994), 350, 377.

Creator who is capable of advanced communication and desires to impart it to human beings.

The origin of significance

Human beings yearn for significance. We all sense a deeper value, meaning, and purpose to life than what we normally experience, and we spend our lives seeking this significance. Value has to do with worth, so we want to know what makes us special. Meaning has to do with importance, so we ask who we are and what life is supposed to be about. Purpose has to do with a goal, so we try to discover how we are to live so that our lives really count for something.

It is important to understand that we are talking about *objective* significance, not some sort of subjective, made up to feel good kind of significance. It is not difficult for a person to manufacture significance for his own life, but ultimately there is nothing to it. This contrived significance is not *real* value, meaning, and purpose.

In 1913, explorer Ernest Shackleton placed the following announcement in a London newspaper seeking men for his forthcoming journey to the South Pole: "Men wanted for hazardous journey, small wages, bitter cold, long months of complete darkness, constant danger, safe return  doubtful, honor and recognition in case of success." Shackleton is said to have received 5,000 applications as a result of this advertisement. Why would thousands of men respond to an ad like that? What motivates a person to endure such hardships by choice? Because, deep down, we all have a longing for significance—to do something really important and special with our lives, even if it is very difficult and costs us everything. Where does that drive come from?

The atheist worldview has no resources whatsoever to account for significance, neither the reality of it nor human desire for it. If we are the result of random physical processes that did not have us in mind, then where does significance come from? Reppert explains:

> On the materialist view, purpose must reduce to Darwinian function. The purposeless motion of matter through space produced beings whose faculties perform functions that enhance their capacity to survive and pass on their genes. The physical is, on even the broadest of materialist views, a closed, non-purposive system, and any purpose that arises in such a world must be a byproduct of what, in the final

analysis, lacks purpose… In the final analysis, "purpose" exists in the world not because there is, ultimately, any intended purpose for anything, but rather because things serve Darwinian functions.[24]

If there is no transcendent Creator, then value, meaning, and purpose are ultimately human delusions. They are merely invented with no basis in anything real.[25] Indeed, if the atheist wants significance, then he has to invent it and simply live as if it were true. Pastor Mark Sayers brings the point home: "The period between birth and death is a chance to construct an identity, and to accumulate a portfolio of experiences, in order to, through a minimal force of will, create moments that *seem significant* because of the pleasure and novelty that they deliver" [emphasis added].[26]

The honest and consistent atheist would have to admit to this profoundly unhappy life of no real significance. Indeed, some have. Atheist philosopher Bertrand Russell believed that we have no choice but to build our lives upon "the firm foundation of unyielding despair."[27] The French atheist-existentialist Albert Camus regarded life as absurd and meaningless, but nevertheless invented meaning by promoting human brotherhood.[28]

Philosopher and theologian Francis Schaeffer observed that modern man lives his life on two different planes. He uses an illustration of a house that has two stories, but with no staircase connecting the upper story with the lower story. The lower story is where logic, reason, facts, and science reside. The upper story is where meaning, morality, faith, and values reside. There is no connection between the two stories. They are separated by what Schaeffer calls a "line of despair" that cannot be breached. Man's only hope to avoid despair and obtain any kind of significance is to make a blind and irrational leap onto the upper  story. But this is just a fantasy made up in our minds to make us feel better.[29] This is the only hope for the atheist—counterfeit value, meaning, and purpose.

There is reason to believe in the genuineness of significance, however. We instinctively feel that our lives need and also have real value, meaning, and purpose. In fact, this desire for significance is actually

---

[24] Victor Reppert, "The Argument From Reason", William Lane Craig and J. P. Moreland, *The Blackwell Companion to Natural Theology* (Oxford: Blackwell Publishing Ltd, 2009), 348-349.

[25] The idea that life has no objective meaning, purpose, or value is called *nihilism*.

[26] Mark Sayers, "Looking Underneath the Surface of the Millennial Generation", Christian Research Journal (Vol. 34, No. 1, 2010), 18.

[27] Bertrand Russell, *Why I Am Not a Christian* (New York: Simon & Schuster, 1957), 107.

[28] Craig, *On Guard*, 39.

[29] Francis A. Schaeffer, *Escape From Reason* (Downers Grove, IL: InterVarsity Press, 1968).

evidence that the materialistic worldview is false. C. S. Lewis explains, "Atheism turns out to be too simple. If the whole universe has no meaning, we should never have found out that it has no meaning."[30] If we had no idea of significance, then we would not feel insignificant, for we would have no way to know we were lacking it. Yet, we sense this need for significance and try to fill it. Furthermore, it seems reasonable to think that the personal Creator is the one who both implants this desire within humanity and also provides the means to attain real significance.[31]

Closely related to the idea of significance are the profound emotions of love and joy. We cannot deny their reality. We all desire them and sometimes we experience them, hopefully more often than not. From where does the desire for them come, as well as the feelings of elation that result when they are satisfied? Chemical compounds do not love and they do not experience joy. The personal Creator must be the originator for these longings as well.

The origin of morality

There is a significant and obvious contrast between humans and animals. Animals kill, rape, and oppress one another regularly and we call it normal and natural. When humans do this, however, we call it abnormal and unnatural. Indeed, we call it immoral. Why?

We all have an intuitive sense that we *ought* to behave in a certain way—that is, there are right and wrong ways to act regardless of our background, education, locality, or cultural, environmental and social influences. This intuition is universal across all people, places, and times. I am not now arguing for what the correct standard of right and wrong is, but rather that we all instinctively feel that *some* sort of standard exists. Nor am I arguing that this moral sense is fully operative in all people, for certainly we see people who behave deplorably, committing terrorism, murder, or rape, for example. We usually call these people sociopaths because they lack a sense of moral responsibility. We are able to label certain people this way because we know that they have deviated from a norm that is otherwise universally accepted. Where does such a norm come from and why does it exist?

---

[30] C. S. Lewis, *Mere Christianity* (New York: Touchstone, 1996, orig. published in 1943 by Macmillan Publishing Company), 46.

[31] At this time I am only arguing for what can legitimately ground human significance. I will explain what this significance is—in terms of value, meaning, and purpose—in chapter 12.

Moral relativism

Some people attempt to circumvent this question by denying that morality is objectively true for all people in all places at all times. Instead, they claim that moral principles are only valid relative to cultural or individual choice and can vary over time, subject to the customs and whims of the society or individual. The view that morality is defined by personal opinion or social convention is called *moral relativism.*

Many people are drawn to moral relativism because they view it as a tolerant way to live with people. According to this view, the tolerant person supposedly occupies a neutral position of complete impartiality, where he allows each person to decide moral matters for himself. Thus, he will make no judgments nor force his personal views on another.[32] This *sounds* like an appealing position to take, but in actuality, it cannot be true. In fact, moral relativism suffers from three fatal flaws.[33]

First, moral relativism is inconsistent because it assumes there is at least one universal moral principle that *every* person and *every* society must adhere to—tolerance. The relativist claims that we should all tolerate or accept the morality of others. After all, other people's views are just as valid and true as his view. Who says tolerance *must* be a virtue, though? Surely, in this view, a relativist should be free to believe that tolerance is not a virtue. If so, then he would be behaving in a perfectly moral way in being *intolerant* of another's morality. Tolerance is the one exception that relativists try to sneak in the back door, but it is inconsistent with their core premise that *all* moral views are relative. Moral relativism therefore contradicts itself because it fails to meet its own standard that there are no universal principles by requiring this one universal principle.[34]

 Second, moral relativism is unlivable. People can hold to a relativistic moral position, but they cannot consistently live that way. Let's imagine for example that Bill steals Sue's wallet and Sue is a relativist. Sue would most likely be troubled by this behavior and claim that Bill's actions were wrong, which is a moral judgment. Sue would demand punishment and

---

[32] Greg Koukl, "The Intolerance of Tolerance", Stand To Reason, http://www.str.org/site/News2?page=NewsArticle&id=5359, accessed Jan 15, 2011.

[33] These flaws are derived from Francis J. Beckwith and Gregory Koukl, *Relativism: Feet Firmly Planted In Mid-Air* (Grand Rapids, Baker Books, 2000), 61-69.

[34] The relativist is correct to regard tolerance as a virtue, but he has a distorted view of what it means. It is not tolerant to say that all views are valid. That is simply illogical, since many views contradict other views. Rather, we should tolerate other *people*, not necessarily their *views*. We are to be kind and respectful regarding persons, but be discerning and selective regarding ideas. Civility is at the heart of the classic view of tolerance. However, we must acknowledge that some ideas are better than others; otherwise we will never know the truth. Tolerance applies to how we treat people we disagree with, not how we treat ideas we think are false.

restitution. Sue has, not surprisingly, forfeited her position of being "tolerant" of Bill's morality. She cannot ultimately live out her relativism.

Third, moral relativism leads to several absurd consequences. For example, there can be no such thing as a moral reformer, since the reformer opposes some moral principle currently embraced by society. In relativism, however, this would make him intolerant. If moral relativism is true, then William Wilberforce was wrong to fight slavery and Martin Luther King Jr. was mistaken to oppose racism. Yet, our intuition tells us they were right. No moral improvement is possible in the relativist's view.

Relativists also cannot complain about the existence of evil because evil is in the eye of the beholder in their view. Admitting evil exists assumes there is a standard of goodness by which to judge something *as* evil. C. S. Lewis said that "a man does not call a line crooked unless he has some idea of a straight line."[35] Nobody could judge any behavior as being immoral, including genocide, torture, rape, theft, and so on. There can be no legitimate moral difference between Saddam Hussein's brutal murders and Mother Teresa's compassionate love in this view.

Similarly, relativists cannot place blame or accept praise or make charges of unfairness or injustice because these concepts depend on a standard outside the individual. Neither can relativists discuss morality in any significant or meaningful way since that involves comparing the merits of competing views. If all views are equally valid, how can such discussions be possible?

Moral objectivism

Moral objectivism is the view that there are universally valid moral principles that are true for all people at all times regardless of whether anybody acknowledges them or not. These moral principles are defined outside of ourselves, i.e., they transcend individuals and cultures. Like other objective truths, we *discover* these moral principles; we do not *invent* them. They are not subject to our personal thoughts or feelings about them.

We know that there is objective right and wrong for all people through our moral intuition. For example, we know by innate awareness that love, compassion, mercy, gratitude, and courage are good and right. Conversely, we know that murder, rape, racism, theft, and dishonesty are evil and wrong. We can reasonably conclude that moral objectivism is true given the large number of flaws inherent in moral relativism and our

---

[35] Lewis, *Mere Christianity*, 45.

intuitive knowledge of the existence of some universal moral principles that are true for all people in all places.

There are three important consequences of objective morality: 1) we have a sense of duty to obey it, 2) we have an internal sense of guilt when we do not, and 3) we have an intuition that we will somehow be held accountable for it. Morality is therefore like a law that we must follow—a moral law embedded within our conscience. This is one way that we are different from the animals. We have a sense of morality whereas animals do not.

Now that we have determined that there is an objective moral law, we need to identify its source. In our experience, laws are commands that come from a mind. The moral law is no different, so it must originate in a personal Moral Law Giver who transcends humanity and establishes objective moral rules for us. This is consistent with the existence of a personal Creator.[36]

Inferences about the attributes of the Creator of life

We can infer several additional attributes of the Creator who is the source of life. The main principle behind these conclusions is that a cause cannot give what it does not have. Not only do all the aspects of human life we have discussed in this chapter have their origin in the Creator, they also must be true of the Creator. In fact, the Creator must have them to greater degrees than human beings since he is the greatest conceivable Being.

One, the Creator is alive. This conclusion is rather obvious, but needs to be stated because life cannot come from non-life. Since we exist, we had to come from a living Creator.

Two, the Creator is immaterial. We also inferred this conclusion in the previous chapter, but it is worth repeating because the immaterial aspects of human life require an immaterial source.

Three, the Creator is a conscious person who experiences thought, perception, memory, emotion, will, and imagination. Because it is part of mankind's essence to be aware of his existence, to be able to think, and to experience feelings and emotions; it is also reasonable to conclude that the Being who created us must also have these characteristics.

Four, the Creator is rational and must be the source of logic. His conduct is influenced by his thoughts. He has the mental powers necessary to form conclusions and make judgments.

---

[36] This is referred to as the Moral Argument for the existence of God.

Five, the Creator has genuine free will. He chose to create the universe and the life it contains. He did not have to, but decided to create.

Six, the Creator is communicative. As the enabler of language, he obviously desires to communicate with creation in some way.

Seven, the Creator must be valuable. The value we sense in ourselves as human beings must be derived from the immense worth of the Creator himself.

Eight, the Creator has intrinsic meaning. There must be something of tremendous importance in a Creator who created a universe that seems imbued with significance.

Nine, the Creator must have a purpose for creating. There is a reason for a Creator to manufacture such an incredible place as the universe and to create human life with all the amazing qualities we have.[37]

Ten, the Creator must be loving. The Creator's love would most likely bear resemblance to the best of love displayed by his highest creation—human beings. However, where human love often fails, the maximally great Creator's love would be expressed perfectly in all its dimensions. We might expect it therefore to be universal, personal, compassionate, zealous, and perhaps even sacrificial.

Eleven, the Creator must be joyful. It would be impossible to create the soaring passion of joy and instill a desire for it in humans without having it oneself.

Twelve, the Creator is moral. We have seen that there must be such a thing as objective good, otherwise we would have no basis to judge a thing as evil. Not only this, but we find a moral intuition embedded within our human conscience. This idea and standard of morality must be rooted in the Creator.

Thirteen, the Creator must care about us because he created us and made us conscious beings with moral responsibility, the ability to reason and the freedom to choose. He also instilled within us longings for value, meaning, purpose, love, and joy, and gave us the ability to experience them.

Inferences about human beings and morality

We are able to also draw some conclusions about human beings from what we have learned in this chapter. Chemistry, biology, and physics alone cannot produce these things, so they must come from the Creator.

---

[37] The reality of value, meaning, and purpose of the Creator are reasonable conclusions from our observations of nature, but at this point, we can only speculate about what exactly is that value, meaning, and purpose. More will be said about this in chapter 12.

One, human beings are qualitatively different from animals, especially in the areas of value, meaning, purpose, and morality. The Creator must have something special in mind for humanity.

Two, objective moral truths relate to us. We instinctively realize that moral truth exists and applies to us—and only to us—not to animals.

Three, we can know what is moral. If the Creator has instilled moral intuition within our consciences, we must conclude that we can discover what those moral laws are.

Four, we have a duty to obey what is moral. If we know that moral laws exist and that they apply to us, then it follows that we have an obligation to obey them.

Five, our guilt is real. When we disobey the moral law, we often feel guilty about it. We should not suppress these feelings, but address them directly.

Six, we will be held accountable for our obedience or disobedience to the moral law. With duty comes accountability. We have a sense that we will ultimately be judged by the Moral Law Giver, and rewarded or penalized for our actions.

These are merely preliminary conclusions about human beings. We will return to them in subsequent chapters.

More conclusions about where everything came from

When we widen the circle of origins from the physical universe to include life and its various immaterial features, we begin to get a picture of a world that is deeper and richer than what we may have first contemplated. None of what we have examined so far can be explained through *purely* physical and natural processes. Only an immaterial, transcendent, personal Creator, who is distinct from the universe, can satisfactorily explain the origin of the universe, life, consciousness, reason, free will, language, significance, and morality. This view will be further corroborated when we examine design in the next chapter.

CHAPTER 3

All the world's a stage

One of the greatest challenges to the human intellect, over the centuries, has been to explain how the complex, improbable appearance of design in the universe arises. The natural temptation is to attribute the appearance of design to actual design itself.

Richard Dawkins (1941-)
Atheist, evolutionary biologist
The God Delusion

I think that the most impressive arguments for God's existence are those that are supported by recent scientific discoveries...The argument to Intelligent Design is enormously stronger than it was when I first met it.

Antony Flew (1923-2010)
Philosopher, life-long atheist turned theist
My Pilgrimage from Atheism to Theism, 2004 interview

We have never discovered why there are laws of nature, why there's not chaos. Science has been unable to tell us anything about the cause of these laws. We only know that these laws result in order, in symmetry, in harmony, in balance, in mind-boggling, complex, highly-developed living forms that we can't duplicate in the laboratory with all our efforts, let alone expect them to happen by chance.

Fred Heeren (1953-)
Science journalist
Show Me God

Have you ever contemplated the marvelous complexity and capability of the human body, the wonder of childbirth, the splendor of a night sky packed with flickering stars, or the beauty of an autumn countryside painted with yellow, orange, and red leaves? It is hard to look upon these spectacles and believe that they, and thousands of others like them, happen to exist by some random accident of nature. There is something about them that makes us intuitively recognize there is more to it than that.

If you ever found a coin while walking along the beach, you likely did not think that it was naturally created by the waves randomly washing up on shore. Similarly, while gazing upward at a towering skyscraper, you probably did not come to the conclusion that it appeared as a result of accidental and mindless acts of the weather. It is obvious to you that these objects have been *produced by someone* because of their order and sophistication. It is the same with the very world we live in. Indeed, considering the awesome beauty, complexity, precision, and elegance of the universe, it certainly *looks* designed.

To acquire a thorough appreciation of the design that is evident in the universe we will examine its features at several different levels, beginning with cosmic proportions and working down in scale to our solar system, the human body, and, finally, the individual biological cell of a living organism. We will also look at some of the more common objections to finding genuine design in nature. First, though, we will define what we mean by design.

Characteristics of design

Design is a purposeful arrangement of parts.[1] To design something means to conceive a plan in one's mind, to construct it with a definitive purpose, and then to create it in an artistic or skillful fashion to achieve that goal. Design is the mark of intelligence. As intelligence increases, designs become more sophisticated and more commonplace. Rocks and trees design nothing. Ants design anthills and beavers design dams. Human beings design paintings, computers, and cities.

We instinctively know design when we see it. The Rocky Mountains are beautiful, but we do not normally consider them to be designed. On the other hand, we instantly recognize Mt. Rushmore— another kind of scenic mountain—to be designed. What is the difference? We realize that when intelligent agents act,  they leave behind certain distinctive traces of their activity. This is what allows us to identify design in Mount Rushmore, but not the Rocky Mountains.

---

[1] Michael J. Behe, *The Edge of Evolution: The Search for the Limits of Darwinism* (New York: Free Press, 2007), 233.

Of course, all these examples of design are easily recognized as such. In the previous two chapters we saw strong evidence for a transcendent Cause of the universe. Since this Cause is also personal, it is appropriate to refer to him as the Creator who has a conscious mind. If the created universe exhibits characteristics of design, that further substantiates the case that there is an intelligent cause responsible for it.[2]

Is it more difficult to detect design in nature than in human creations, though? Until recently we had to be satisfied with intuitively discerning design in nature, but not being able to confirm it in any real scientific way. Mathematician, physicist, and computer scientist William Dembski has done pioneering work in this area. He and others have made great breakthroughs in isolating and making precise certain distinguishing trademarks of design in nature.[3]

To infer design, Dembski says that two things must be established: *complexity* and *specification*.[4] These two criteria are often combined in the phrase *specified complexity*. When they are both satisfied for some object or feature in the universe, then we can legitimately say the thing was designed by an intelligent agent. When one or both of these criteria are absent, we should think it was probably produced by natural causes, either accidentally by chance or by physical law.[5] Let's look at these two criteria more closely.

Complexity

Complexity refers to something that is characterized by a complicated arrangement of parts. With respect to design, complexity is the idea that something is not so simple that it can easily be explained by chance. If we dropped three dozen Scrabble tiles on the floor and they all wound up in a random mess, we would not

---

[2] This is referred to as the Design Argument for the existence of God.

[3] These same distinguishing trademarks indicate design by *any* personal agent, including humans.

[4] William A. Dembski, *Intelligent Design: The Bridge Between Science & Theology* (Downers Grove, IL: InterVarsity Press, 1999), 128. Dembski also adds *contingency* as a criterion, which ensures the object in question is not the result of an automatic and therefore unintelligent process that had no choice in its production. Since everything that exhibits complexity and specification is also contingent, this extra criterion can normally be assumed.

[5] We do not *have* to assume necessity or chance as the cause in these cases, though. Dembski says the absence of specified complexity is not sufficient reason to think that something was *not* designed. In other words, false negatives are possible because intelligent causes can mimic necessity and chance. Another difficulty is that detecting intelligent causes requires background knowledge on our part to recognize specification. If we do not know enough, we may miss it. Interestingly, Dembski thinks that false positives of specified complexity are not possible. Ibid., 140-146.

be surprised. However, if we observed that they all lined up in a straight line or formed a square, then we might be surprised. The difference is complexity.

Recognizing something as being complex is generally very intuitive for us—we can usually tell the complex from the simple—but in scientific terms, complexity is a matter of probability. The more complex something is, the more improbable it is to occur by chance. The improbability of opening a combination lock by chance depends on the complexity of the mechanism. As the lock mechanism increases in complexity, the greater the improbability that someone will be able to open the lock by chance. Therefore, to determine whether something is sufficiently complex to infer

design is to determine whether it has sufficiently small probability to occur accidentally.[6] Since intelligent agents normally create complex things, it is more likely that a complex thing was designed. However, a complex thing may not always indicate design. There are numerous complex phenomena in nature for instance—weather patterns, ecological systems, radioactive decay—which we wouldn't be inclined to explain by design. That is why specification is also an essential component of something that is designed.

Specification

Specification is the idea that something exhibits a pattern that is known independently of the object, thus indicating purpose. Consider these two scenarios: 1) A bottle of ink accidentally spills on a sheet of paper and 2) Someone takes a pen and writes "To be, or not to be, that is the question." on a sheet of paper. In both cases, ink is applied to paper, but in one instance we recognize chance and in the other, intelligence. The pattern is the relevant difference. A random ink blot is unspecified; it exhibits no pattern whatsoever. However, the written message is specified because it conforms to a language pattern that we know independently of the particular message. We recognize the symbols, their arrangement,

and their meaning separate from this specific instance of writing.[7]

---

[6] Ibid., 130.
[7] Ibid., 144-145.

It is important that the pattern be independent of the object or event whose design is in question. The pattern cannot be artificially imposed onto the object or event after the fact. For example, if an archer shoots an arrow at a wall and then a target is painted around the arrow, we might think he has shot a bulls-eye. However, since the pattern was imposed after the fact, it is not independent of the event, and therefore there is no specification. Conversely, if the target is set up in advance ("specified"), and then the arrow splits the center, we have an example of specification.[8]

A pattern which is independent of the object is characteristic of an intelligent cause. As with complexity, specification alone is insufficient to infer design. In our Scrabble illustration, if three of the tiles happened to spell "CAT", we would recognize that as specification, but it would not be complex. The letters could have accidentally fallen in that arrangement. We also can find examples of this in nature. A pulsar is a pair of rotating neutron stars that produce radio waves with great regularity.[9] The recognizable pattern is on-off-on-off-on-off, which is an example of specification. The problem is that the pattern has no complexity— it is too simple. Even though specification is present, without complexity, we cannot reasonably conclude that pulsars are designed.

The design filter

These two criteria—complexity and specification—work together and must both be present to indicate design. They act as a *design filter*. As we pass candidate objects and features through the design filter, the ones that meet both characteristics are the ones that we can reasonably think of as designed, and not the result of physical necessity or chance. On the other hand, we have to reserve judgment on those things that do not meet both criteria. As we examine various aspects of nature, keep in mind the following questions posed by our design filter:

- ❖ *Complexity* – Is it sufficiently improbable?
- ❖ *Specification* – Does it match an independent pattern?

The use of design principles in science

Several branches of science currently use the design filter to distinguish between chance and design. Here is a brief look at three examples.

---

[8] William A. Dembski, *The Design Revolution: Answering the Toughest Questions About Intelligent Design* (Downers Grove, IL: InterVarsity Press, 2004), 82.

[9] The regularity is so great that pulsars are considered the most precise clocks in the universe— probably more precise than atomic clocks.

Cryptography

Cryptography is the practice and study of hiding information. Code breakers apply design detection techniques to determine if a character sequence is a meaningless jumble or a message from an intelligent agent. If a complicated sequence of symbols is intercepted in a communication destined for the enemy, we have complexity. If the sequence can be deciphered into a recognizable message, then we have also established specification. We can therefore conclude that the object—the sequence of symbols—represents a coded message initiated from an intelligent source.

Forensic science

Forensics is the application of a broad spectrum of sciences to answer questions of legal interest, usually related to the circumstances surrounding a crime. Often forensic scientists try to determine if a specific event was an accident or a crime that was caused by the action of an intelligent agent who planned and carried it out.

Imagine, for the sake of illustration, that there is no obvious outward explanation for the cause of death of some unfortunate person. The investigators may begin by searching for "natural" causes of death, like a heart attack or disease. Suppose that the investigators discover the person has ingested a poisonous substance—an improbable occurrence—so complexity is established. Did the person take the poison accidentally or intentionally, or was it given to him by a murderer? If an open container of pesticide is discovered in the storage shed outside, as well as traces of it on the kitchen counter and on a glass next to the victim's body, then we have a pattern—so we have specification. At this point, we have both elements of the design filter and we can reasonably conclude that the death was caused by intelligent action, not by accidental or natural causes.[10]

Search for Extra-Terrestrial Intelligence (SETI)

 SETI is a non-profit science research center that searches for intelligence beyond the Earth. The scientists monitor radio waves from outer space and look for recognizable patterns of information using sophisticated computer programs. This is the application of complexity and specification criteria to look for intelligent agents from other planets.

---

[10] Whether the death was caused by suicide or homicide, it is still the result of an intelligent agent who willfully caused the death, either the deceased person himself or a murderer. Although this is certainly of interest to the authorities, we need not take the example any further for our purposes since intelligent action has been established.

What if SETI detected a long series of random numbers? That would be complex, but since no pattern in the series is present, it would not be specified and thus, no design inference could be made. What if they detected a sequence of numbers that correspond to the first 25 prime numbers? That would not only be complex, but would also be a recognized pattern that was independent of this particular message. From this we would conclude that specified complexity is present. Therefore, it should be characterized as an instance of intelligent causation, which is design.

Discovering design in nature

We will now examine several features of nature—both in the universe as a whole and on planet Earth—to see if they exhibit signs of intelligent design. If they do, they will have the trademark characteristics of complexity and specification. Most of the examples that follow aim to demonstrate that intelligent life could not exist in the universe unless both life itself *and* its environment were designed for this purpose.

Fine-tuning of the universe

The first evidence of design in nature we will examine is the incredible fine-tuning of the universe. The universe appears specially set up to support the existence of human life. Fine-tuning carries the idea of making very precise adjustments in the parameters of an object, such as a musical instrument, so that it would operate ideally for a particular goal. When applied to the universe, it refers to all the physical conditions being set just right in order to permit human life.

The constants of physics are a set of fundamental fixed values that, in conjunction with the laws of physics, determine the basic structure of the universe. These constant values must fall into a narrow range for intelligent life to exist. If any of them were only slightly different, no life of any kind would exist today. A brief survey of these parameters follows.

The four fundamental forces

There are four fundamental forces in nature—gravity, electro-magnetism, the weak nuclear force, and the strong nuclear force.

If gravity did not exist, masses would not clump together to form stars or planets, so there would be no solar systems in which intelligent life could live. If the gravitational force were much larger, stars would be too hot and would burn up too quickly and too unevenly. If it were smaller, stars would remain so cool that nuclear fusion would never ignite and so no heavy elements that form planets would be produced.[11] Changing this value only slightly would have a catastrophic effect on life.

The electromagnetic force causes the interaction between electrically charged particles. For life to be possible, more than forty different elements must be able to bond together to form molecules. Molecular bonding depends on the electromagnetic force, which holds electrons and protons together inside atoms. If this force did not exist, there would be no chemistry and therefore no life. If the electromagnetic force were much larger, atoms would hold onto electrons so tightly that no sharing of electrons with other atoms would be possible. If the force were much weaker, atoms would not hold on to electrons at all, and the sharing of electrons among atoms would not occur to make molecules possible. The electromagnetic force must be delicately balanced for life to exist.[12]

The weak nuclear force governs the rates of radioactive decay. If it did not exist, the life essential elements that are produced only in the core of supergiant stars would not escape, and we would not have carbon, oxygen, or nitrogen. If the force were stronger, the matter in the universe would be quickly converted into heavy elements. If it were weaker, matter would remain in the form of only the lightest elements.[13]

The strong nuclear force is what binds protons and neutrons together in an atom. If the force were too weak, protons and neutrons would not stick together and no atoms other than hydrogen would exist. If it were too strong, the affinity of protons and neutrons would be so great that they would only form the heaviest elements. In this case, there would be no hydrogen, which makes life chemistry impossible.[14] Physicist and philosopher Robin Collins explains that "just a one-percent change in the strong nuclear force would have a thirty to a thousand-fold impact on the production of oxygen and carbon in stars. Since stars provide the carbon and oxygen needed for life on planets, if you throw off that balance, conditions in the universe would be much less optimal for the existence of life."[15] Astrophysicist Hugh Ross adds that if this force were only 2% weaker or 0.3% stronger than it actually is, "life would be impossible at any time and any place within the universe."[16]

---

[11] Hugh Ross, *The Creator and the Cosmos: How the Latest Scientific Discoveries Reveal God* (Colorado Springs: NavPress, 2001), 154.

[12] Ibid., 146.

[13] Ibid., 147.

[14] Ibid., 146.

[15] Robin Collins, as quoted in Strobel, *Case for a Creator*, 131.

[16] Ross, *The Creator and the Cosmos*, 147.

The cosmological constant

The cosmological constant is part of Einstein's theory of general relativity. It is a physical property of the force that causes the universe to expand. Where gravity acts as a sort of brake on cosmic expansion by attracting large bodies, the cosmological constant works in opposition by repelling them.

If the cosmological constant had a large positive value, space would expand so rapidly that all matter would quickly disperse, and thus galaxies, stars, and planets would never form. Therefore the constant must be very close to zero for complex life to be possible. What is remarkable about this constant is that, according to the theories of particle physics, its natural range of values is between zero and 10^{53}. This upper range is one followed by fifty-three zeros, or one hundred million billion billion billion billion, which is an incomprehensibly large number. The fact that the actual value is very near zero (about 0.7)—and that is the value we need to have life—is *enormously* improbable. Collins claims that "the unexpected, counterintuitive, and stunningly precise setting of the cosmological constant is widely regarded as the single greatest problem facing physics and cosmology today...If the cosmological constant were the only example of fine-tuning, and if there were no natural explanation for it, then this would be sufficient by itself to strongly establish design."[17]

Many other finely tuned parameters

There are numerous other cosmic constants in the universe that must be in a narrow life permitting range. Ross lists *over three hundred* of them, including the ratio of proton to electron mass, the ratio of the number of protons to electrons, the mass density of the universe, the velocity of light, the average distance between galaxies, and the decay rate of protons.[18] Not only do the present physical laws and constants have to be precisely tuned to support life, but the initial conditions at the moment of the Big Bang had to be just right to even get a universe started.

Stephen Hawking writes, "The laws of science, as we know them at present, contain many fundamental numbers, like the size of the electric charge of the electron and the ratio of the masses of the proton and the electron...The remarkable fact is that the values of these numbers seem to have been very finely adjusted to make possible the development of life...It seems clear that there are relatively few ranges of values for the

---

[17] Collins, as quoted in Strobel, *Case for a Creator,* 133-134.
[18] Hugh Ross, Reasons To Believe, http://www.reasons.org/fine-tuning-life-universe and http://www.reasons.org/probability-life-earth-apr-2004, accessed Feb 9, 2011.

numbers that would allow the development of any form of intelligent life."[19]

What caused all these properties to fall exactly within the ranges that permit human life? Surely, it seems that mere chance would cause at least *some* of them—if not most of them—to fall *outside* the life permitting ranges. Ross estimates the probability at less than 1 chance in 10^{282} (one million trillion) that there exists even one planet on which life would occur anywhere in the universe without a divine miracle.[20] The probability of all of these design parameters occurring by chance is so small that it is statistically impossible. Collins suggests the following analogy to visualize the incredible odds of this happening by chance:

> One could think of the values of the initial conditions of the universe and the constants of physics as coordinates on a dart board that fills the whole galaxy, and the conditions necessary for life to exist as an extremely small target, say less than a trillionth of an inch: unless the dart hits the target, complex life would be impossible. The fact that the dials are perfectly set, or the dart has hit the target, strongly suggests that some intelligent being set the dials or aimed the dart, for it seems enormously improbable that such a coincidence could have happened by chance.[21]

Collins concludes, "Almost everything about the basic structure of the universe—for example, the fundamental laws and parameters of physics and the initial distribution of matter and energy—is balanced on a razor's edge for life to occur."[22]

These facts are so overwhelming that even the atheist astronomer Fred Hoyle writes, "A common sense interpretation of the facts suggests that a superintellect has monkeyed with the physics, as well as with chemistry and biology, and that there are no blind forces worth speaking about in nature. The numbers one calculates from the facts seem to me so overwhelming as to put this conclusion almost beyond question."[23]

---

[19] Stephen W. Hawking, *A Brief History of Time* (New York: Bantam Books, 1996), 129-130. Note, while Hawking admits fine-tuning, he rejects an intelligent designer in favor of a multiple universe theory to explain it. We will discuss this theory later in the chapter.

[20] Hugh Ross, Reasons to Believe.

[21] Robin Collins, "God, Design, and Fine-Tuning", http://home.messiah.edu/~rcollins/Fine-tuning/ FT.HTM, accessed Feb 8, 2011.

[22] Ibid.

[23] Fred Hoyle, "The Universe: Past and Present Reflections", *Annual Review of Astronomy and Astrophysics* (1982).

Can we infer from these facts that the universe was designed? There is no reason to believe that any of these parameters have the values they have out of physical necessity. They all clearly could have been different, so they are contingent. Furthermore, the total probability that the value of each parameter would be in a life-permitting range is so low that it makes it highly complex. Finally, the values combine to form a complicated, inter-related arrangement that creates a life-permitting and life-sustaining environment, so we have specification. Since this meets the criteria of the design filter, we can conclude that the universe was designed from the very first moment of its existence for the emergence of life in general and human life in particular. This intelligent design clearly points to a Creator.

Fine-tuning within our solar system

The fine-tuning we observe throughout the universe extends to our solar system as well. There are dozens of unusual conditions close to home that converge to make our planet conducive to life. We will examine a few of them.

Planetary body guards

The Earth's special placement within the solar system and the presence, location, and size of the other planets combine to make Earth the only habitable planet in our solar system. Jupiter and Saturn, the two largest planets in our solar system, act as the major protectors of Earth by shielding it from excessive meteor, comet, and asteroid bombardment. The gravitational pull of these  enormous bodies acts as a sort of cosmic vacuum cleaner for our solar system. The other planets, and even their moons, provide similar protection as well. We only have to look at all the craters on our Moon through a telescope to see what our planet was spared due to its ability to deflect collisions from us.[24] On the other hand, too many planets in a solar system would make it far less stable. It would seem we have just the right number, size, and placement of planets to make Earth habitable.

Harmony of the Sun, Moon, and Earth

The habitability of a planet varies dramatically based on the size of the planet and its host star and their amount of separation. A star similar to

---

[24] This is not to say that Earth has never been impacted by celestial debris, but rather that we have been protected from much of it.

our Sun is necessary for complex life. A bigger star has a shorter lifetime and brightens more rapidly. A smaller star radiates less energy, so a planet would have to orbit more closely to keep liquid water on its surface.[25] As for the host planet, it needs to be about Earth's size to maintain plate tectonics,[26] to keep some land above the oceans, and to retain an atmosphere.

A large moon stabilizes the rotation axis of its host planet, yielding a more stable, life-friendly climate. The Earth tilts 23 degrees on its axis. Our Moon keeps this tilt from varying over a large range, limiting it to only about 2½ degrees. To be able to do this, the Moon's mass must be a substantial fraction of Earth's mass. Small moons like those surrounding Mars will not work. If our Moon were as small as the Martian moons, Earth's tilt would vary more than 30 degrees. This would cause constant daylight and horrendously searing heat for half the year and constant night and brutal cold the other half of the year. A tilt that is too small causes other problems, such as very mild seasons with far less rain, resulting in significantly more arid land.[27]

If the Earth were closer to the Sun, then it would be too hot to support life. If it were farther away, all water would freeze. The distance of the Earth from the Sun means that water exists mainly in liquid form, which allows us to get rain. The tilt of the Earth and its precise location within the solar system provide the type of persistent climate that is stable enough to maintain widespread agriculture. These observations have led cosmologists to recognize a so-called *habitable zone*, which is a narrow region in a solar system that contains the necessary conditions for life.

This concept of a habitable zone also applies to galaxies. Large regions of typical galaxies are very hostile to life. Regions that are too close to a galaxy's center are overexposed to high doses of X-rays emanating from colliding stars and supernovas. Regions that are too far from the center of a galaxy have insufficient heavy metals to form a planet like ours. Our planet has a solid/liquid metal core, which produces a magnetic field that adequately protects the surface of the planet from space radiation.[28]

The radioactive heat from the core also fuels plate tectonics, which is necessary for maintaining planetary life. It does this in a number of ways. Plate tectonics function as Earth's global thermostat by recycling

---

[25] Guillermo Gonzalez and Jay W. Richards, *The Privileged Planet: How Our Place in the Cosmos is Designed for Discovery* (Washington DC: Regnery Publishing, 2004), 6.

[26] Plate tectonics is the movement of the planetary crust across the surface of the planet. It is found in our solar system only on Earth and is thought to be rare in the universe as a whole. Peter D. Ward and Donald Brownlee, *Rare Earth: Why Complex Life Is Uncommon in the Universe* (New York: Copernicus Books, 2004), 194.

[27] Gonzalez and Richards, *The Privileged Planet*, 4-6.

[28] Ward and Brownlee, *Rare Earth*, 28-29, 213.

chemicals essential for keeping the volume of carbon dioxide relatively uniform in our atmosphere. It also regulates the sea level to support life by spreading the sea floor through volcanic eruptions, which counters the erosion effects of the world's mountains.[29]

Earth's atmosphere

The Earth has a protective atmosphere that maintains a fairly even temperature which is ideally suited for life.[30] This is achieved through its insulating greenhouse gases such as water vapor, ozone, and carbon dioxide, which capture outgoing infrared energy from the planet's surface. Without them, Earth's temperature would be about the same as that of the Moon, which has no real atmosphere.[31]

Oxygen comprises about 21% of the Earth's atmosphere, which is the ideal amount for human life. If the cells in the body receive too little oxygen, energy production is decreased, causing cells to malfunction and die. Breathing excessive oxygen can cause injury to the lungs. Too much oxygen in the blood can also contribute to problems in the brain and eyes.

The amount of oxygen in our atmosphere is also conducive to making technology possible. Technological life needs the ability to control and shape the basic elements with fire—metals for instance. Without sufficient oxygen, fire cannot occur. If fire is exposed to pure oxygen, combustion speeds up dramatically, causing explosions.

It just so happens that we have the right amount of oxygen in our atmosphere to support both life and technology.

The essential fluid

Without water, life on Earth would be impossible. Life needs a universal solvent to provide a medium for chemical reactions.[32] The solvent needs to be able to dissolve many types of molecules; it needs to be liquid in order to be able to transport molecules; and it needs to be liquid over the same range of temperatures where the basic molecules of life remain largely intact. Water, which happens to be the most abundant chemical compound on our planet, meets these requirements perfectly.[33] Water has many other amazing properties.

---

[29] Ibid., 194-197, 205-206.

[30] The average global temperature is about 15°C (59°F), with a usual range of approximately 0-50°C (32-122°F).

[31] The Moon's average temperature is -18°C (-40°F). Ward and Brownlee, *Rare Earth,* 207.

[32] A solvent is a liquid that has the ability to dissolve, suspend, or extract other materials without causing a chemical change to the material or solvent. Solvents make it possible to process, apply, clean, or separate materials.

[33] Michael J. Denton, *Nature's Destiny: How the Laws of Biology Reveal Purpose in the Universe* (New York: The Free Press, 1998), 31-32.

Water has an ideal surface tension to support life.[34] Its surface tension is very high compared to other liquids. It must be as high as it is to draw water up through the soil to the roots of plants and to assist its rise from the roots to branches in trees. Large terrestrial plants would not be possible otherwise.[35]

Compared with other liquids, water has a very low viscosity, but again, the level is perfectly suited for life.[36] If its viscosity was much lower, it could not support delicate microscopic structures. If it was much higher, the sea would not have any life resembling fishes, since they wouldn't be able to swim. Neither would any microorganism or cell be able to move. If the viscosity of water was only a few times greater than it is, pumping blood through capillaries would require enormous pressure, rendering the circulatory system unworkable.[37]

Since living organisms are made up largely of water, the density of water largely determines their weight. If water was several times as dense, then the size of animals and humans would be much less than they are. Upright, bipedal species such as human beings would not be possible because of the excessive body weight.[38]

Water also has the unique capacity of helping larger organisms regulate their body temperatures. All activity requires the expenditure of energy which involves the generation of heat. The rise in body temperature during exertion is moderated because the heat capacity of water is greater than most other substances. Furthermore, the body is efficiently cooled by evaporation (sweat) because the latent heat of vaporization of water is the highest of any liquid in Earth's usual temperature range.[39]

Water contributes to moderating Earth's climate as well. The average surface temperature of Earth is near the triple point of water, which is a unique combination of pressure and temperature where all three states of water—liquid, solid, and gas—can coexist.[40] Water is virtually unique in being denser as a liquid than a solid. This is what makes ice float on water, insulating the water underneath from further loss of heat. Consequently, lakes and oceans do not freeze from the bottom up. If this happened, the colder ice at the bottom would never melt, and virtually all the water on Earth would completely freeze and be unavailable for life.

After careful study of water's remarkable properties, Michael Denton concludes, "Water is uniquely and ideally adapted to serve as the fluid

---

[34] Surface tension is a property of a liquid's surface that allows it to resist an external force.

[35] Denton, *Nature's Destiny*, 30.

[36] Viscosity describes a fluid's internal resistance to flow. It may be thought of as a measure of fluid friction or "thickness."

[37] Denton, *Nature's Destiny*, 33-35.

[38] Ibid., 39.

[39] Ibid., 42-43.

[40] Gonzalez and Richards, *The Privileged Planet*, 34.

medium for life on earth in not just one, or many, but in *every single one* of its known physical and chemical characteristics" [emphasis in original].[41] We find an amazing amount of fine tuning, not just in the universe as a whole, but also right here in our own solar system and on our own planet.

Earth designed for discovery

In addition to being an ideal habitation for human life, our planet has an often overlooked feature that is highly improbable. The conditions that allow for intelligent life on Earth *also* make our planet peculiarly well suited for viewing and analyzing the universe. It turns out that we are in an ideal environment to be able to observe, discover, determine, and even measure the size, age, history, laws, and other properties of the universe. We might be inclined to take this for granted, but it seems quite unlikely that the very same unusual properties that allow for our existence would *also* provide the best overall setting to make discoveries about the universe.[42] It seems more than an accident that we have an extremely rare and perfect vantage point, compared to other locations in the universe, to discover so much about the universe.

Solar eclipses

Of the more than sixty-four moons in our solar system, Earth's moon yields the best match to the Sun as viewed from a planet's surface, and this is only possible during a fairly narrow window of Earth's history, which includes the present. The Sun is about four hundred times farther from Earth than the Moon, but is also four hundred times larger. As a result, both bodies appear the same size in our sky. This makes it possible to have the kinds of solar eclipses that we observe.[43] Moreover, these are nearly *perfect* total eclipses, not only due to the visible sizes of the bodies, but also because both the Sun and the Moon are two of the roundest bodies in our solar system.

Perfect solar eclipses have played an important role in scientific discovery. In particular, they have helped reveal the nature of stars, provided a way to test Einstein's general theory of relativity, and allowed us to measure the Earth's rotation throughout history. They have also enabled historians to translate the calendar systems of ancient civilizations into our modern system, which allows us to view history on a common

---

[41] Denton, *Nature's Destiny*, 45.

[42] Gonzalez and Richards, *The Privileged Planet*, x-xv.

[43] A solar eclipse occurs when the Moon passes between the Sun and the Earth, and the Moon fully or partially covers the Sun as viewed from a location on Earth.

timeline.[44] It seems that the most habitable place in the solar system is also the very best place to view solar eclipses, at the very time when its observers can make the best use of them.

Celestial gazing

Astronomy would not be possible except for two facts about Earth that we take for granted—dark nights and an atmosphere which is transparent to visible light. Without these features, we would have little hope of learning anything about the universe in which we live. In fact, the Earth's present-day atmosphere gives us exceptional access to the wider universe at the same time it provides a sustaining environment for humans. Astronomer Guillermo Gonzalez makes these observations about the transparency of Earth's atmosphere:

> Our atmosphere participates in one of the most extraordinary coincidences known to science; an eerie harmony among the range of wavelengths of light emitted by the Sun, transmitted by Earth's atmosphere, converted by plants into chemical energy, and detected by the human eye…The near-ultraviolet, visible, and near-infrared spectra—the light most useful to life and sight—are a razor thin sliver of the universe's natural, electromagnetic emissions: about one part in 10^{25}…As it happens, our atmosphere strikes a nearly perfect balance, transmitting most of the radiation that is useful for life while blocking most of the lethal energy.[45]

The thin sliver of natural, electromagnetic emissions mentioned above amounts to one in 10 trillion trillion, which is highly improbable by chance.

The length of Earth's year is quite different from the length of its day, making it easier to separate the effects of revolution and rotation. Because of this, it is easier to discover laws of motion and gravity and to realize that they apply throughout the universe. This led to the understanding of the structure and history of the wider universe. Imagine how difficult it would be to figure out your environment while sitting on a spinning chair perched on a revolving Ferris wheel, even if they moved relatively slowly. For comparison purposes, Mercury completes three rotations every two orbits, and the orbital and rotational periods of Venus are nearly the same. This would make it confusing to understand the motion of visible planets and stars from those planet surfaces.

A very long orbital period would cause difficulty as well, providing fewer opportunities for a single individual to make multiple observations.

---

[44] Gonzalez and Richards, *The Privileged Planet,* 9-18.
[45] Ibid., 66.

For example, Saturn's period is more than 29 years, Uranus' is 84, and Neptune's is 165. Fortunately, the orbital periods of the other nearby planets are shorter (90 days to 12 years), so Earth-bound observers have ample chances to learn from them.

To study our universe, we need not only to be in a solar system with several other planets, but the orbital periods of those planets have to be substantially shorter than a human life span, and the length of our day and year have to be considerably different.[46]

Position within our galaxy

There are three basic types of galaxies in the universe: spirals, elliptical, and irregulars. Our galaxy, the Milky Way, is spiral—a sort of flattened disk. Our solar system is about halfway between the galaxy's

nucleus and visible edge. From our location, astronomers can see numerous stars, star types, star configurations (single, pairs, triplets), and stars in all life stages. We can also see matter between the stars, such as interstellar clouds and supernova remnants.[47] Astronomers could not observe such diversity from every place within our galaxy. Because of our particular location, gas and dust is quite diffused, giving us a clear view of objects in the Milky Way, as well as distant galaxies. We can see galaxies as far away as 13.2 billion light years.

It seems that any other type of galaxy or position within our galaxy would obscure much of the local and distant universe. We occupy the best overall place for observation in the galaxy to learn about stars, galactic structures, and the remote universe.

Summary

Not only is the Earth fine-tuned for *habitability*, but it is also fined-tuned for *measurability*—our ability to observe and discover many things about our universe. We appear to be more than an accidental planet in an arbitrary solar system in a random galaxy among billions of galaxies in the universe. The chances are simply too remote. The ideal ability to make a wide range of discoveries about our universe and the improbability of

---

[46] Yet, despite these favorable characteristics of our earthly platform and planetary neighbors, it still took over a thousand years—from Aristotle to Kepler and Galileo—for the human race to determine the true geometry of our solar system. Ibid., 104-106.

[47] Ibid., 144-151.

having this ability by sheer chance makes this a case of specified complexity and therefore another strong example of design.

The human body

The human body is exquisite, consisting of remarkable elegance, complexity, and function. The facts are simply mind-boggling. Here are a few of them.

The adult body is made up of 100 trillion cells, 600 muscles, 206 bones, and 22 internal organs. Every square inch of the human body has about 19 million skin cells and 20 feet of blood vessels. The average surface of the human intestine is 656 square feet. The typical human head has about 100 thousand hairs. The human brain consists of some 100 billion cells, forming trillions of interconnections. Its billions of neurons carry electrical signals to control all parts of the body. During a 24-hour period, the average human will breathe about 23 thousand times, transport blood 60 thousand miles, and replace about 24 billion cells. The average human heart will beat 3 billion times in its lifetime and pump 48 million gallons of blood.

Our ability to perceive, experience, and interact with our world is incredibly powerful due to five different sensory inputs—sight, sound, smell, taste, and touch. The light sensitive retina of the eye contains 125 million photoreceptor cells. These cells capture the light pattern formed by the lens and convert it into complex electrical signals, which are then sent to the brain where they are transformed into the sensation of vision—and all of this happens millions of times faster than the most sophisticated man-made supercomputer. It takes the interaction of 72 different muscles to produce human speech. An estimated 5 million olfactory receptors are clustered in the membrane at the upper part of our nasal passages to help us distinguish among 10 thousand different odors. There are some 9 thousand taste buds on the surface of the tongue, in the throat, and on the roof of the mouth. We have 45 miles of nerves in our skin, containing approximately 640,000 sense receptors scattered over the body's surface. Despite all of this amazing complexity and function, the human body is comprised of about 60% water and replaces most of its cells every seven to ten years.[48]

Major body systems

The human body is comprised of numerous complex, cooperating

---

[48] The cells in our bodies are constantly dividing, regenerating, and dying, but different tissues in the body replace cells at different rates. Certain parts of the brain never replace cells. Seven to ten years is often used as a rough average of cellular turnover in the body.

systems that sustain life's necessary functions. Here is a brief survey of these systems.[49]

The *skeletal system* is the framework of the human anatomy that supports the weight of the body and protects its organs. It is made up of

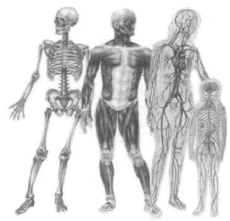

bones, ligaments, and tendons. The skeletal system works with the muscular system to permit a wide range of body movement.

The *muscular system* is made up of tissues that work with the skeletal system to control movement of the body and maintain its posture. Some muscles are voluntary, like our arms and legs. Other muscles move involuntarily, like the ones in our stomach, heart, and intestines. These muscles are controlled automatically by the nervous system and hormones, so we often do not even realize they are at work.

The *nervous system* is the body's control system, which is responsible for sending, receiving, and processing nerve impulses throughout the body. It is made up of the brain, the spinal cord, and nerves. All of the body's muscles and organs rely upon these nerve impulses to know what to do and how to respond to the environment.

The *endocrine system* is a collection of hormone-producing glands located in various parts of the body. There are many glands, including the pituitary, thyroid, adrenal, pancreas, which release hormones into the bloodstream to be transported to organs and tissues throughout the body. Hormones regulate body functions such as metabolism, growth, and sexual development.

The *circulatory system* maintains a continuous flow of blood throughout the body. The heart pumps oxygen-rich blood from the lungs through the arteries that travel all through the body. When blood enters the smallest blood vessels in body tissue, it releases nutrients and oxygen to the cells and takes in carbon dioxide, water, and waste. Veins carry the waste products away from cells and bring blood back to the heart, which pumps it to the lungs to pick up oxygen and eliminate the waste.

The *respiratory system* brings oxygen into the body and removes carbon dioxide. It includes the nose, mouth, trachea, lungs, and breathing

---

[49] Alan L. Gillen, *Body by Design* (Green Forest, AR: Master Books, 2001, 2009) and Ann Baggaley (ed.), *Human Body* (New York: Dorling Kindersley, 2001).

muscles. Every cell in the body needs oxygen to perform its metabolic processes. When we breathe in, air enters our nose or mouth and goes down a long tube called the trachea. The trachea branches into two bronchial tubes, which go to the lungs. These tubes branch off into even smaller bronchial tubes which end in air sacs. Oxygen flows through this path and passes through the walls of the air sacs and blood vessels and enters the blood stream. At the same time, carbon dioxide passes into the lungs and is exhaled out of the body.

The *digestive system* breaks down food into protein, carbohydrates, minerals, fats, and other substances, which the body needs for energy, growth, and repair. It is made up of the mouth, pharynx, esophagus, stomach, intestines, liver, pancreas, gall bladder, and rectum. After food is chewed and swallowed, it is processed by the digestive organs so that the nutrients can be absorbed and circulated around the body through the bloodstream. Any excess food that is not needed or digested is turned into waste and eliminated from the body.

The *excretory system* removes excess, unnecessary, and dangerous materials from the body, such as carbon dioxide, water, salt, urea, and uric acid. This includes filtering body fluids to remove waste products, returning other substances to body fluids as necessary, and eliminating waste from the body. It includes the skin, lungs, large intestine, kidneys, ureters, and bladder.

The *immune system* is our body's defense system against infections and diseases. It consists of bone marrow, lymph nodes and vessels, thymus, spleen, and white blood cells. There are three types of response systems in the immune system: the anatomic response which prevents substances from entering the body, the inflammatory response which removes invaders from the body, and the immune response which fights infections. Lymph nodes act as barriers to infection by filtering out and destroying toxins and germs and by reducing tissue swelling.

The *reproductive system* allows humans to produce children. Sperm from the male fertilizes the female's egg, or ovum, in the fallopian tube. The fertilized egg travels from the fallopian tube to the uterus, where the fetus develops over a period of nine months, and then leaves the mother's body through the birth canal.

The explanation

The question we must ask is whether all these complex, inter-connected systems in the human body, which are comprised of thousands of physical, chemical, and cellular interrelationships, arose inexplicably by chance or by design. Those who advocate chance rely on the ability of Evolution to explain the complexity and diversity of life, which it cannot do.[50] As with other features we have discussed in this chapter, human life exhibits the characteristic of design. Certainly, human bodies did not *have* to be the way they are, so they are clearly contingent. They are composed of incredibly complicated, interacting systems, so they are complex. They also form a pattern of intelligent life, so they are specified.

As we peer deeper into the human body—into the cell—we find evidence of even more design in the form of irreducible complexity and information.

Irreducible complexity within the cell

Modern biochemists have discovered that the living cell is operated by machines at the molecular level that are every bit as complex as today's multi-million dollar industrial factories. The machines are primarily composed of proteins, which build the structures and carry out the chemical reactions necessary for life. These biochemical machines include motors, propellers, switches, shuttles, tweezers, sensors, and logic gates. There are artificial languages, decoding systems, information memory banks, and error fail-safe and proof reading devices to control the entire construction, regulation, and operation of the cell.[51]

Scientists have discovered that these cellular structures are made up of many parts that interact in complex ways, and all the parts need to work together in a perfectly integrated manner in order to operate properly. Any single part has no useful function unless all the other parts are also present, so the larger structure is the thing that provides a useful function to the organism, not the component parts. Biochemist Michael Behe, who has done ground-breaking work in this area, refers to this as the *irreducible complexity* of molecular mechanisms. Irreducible complexity is a special form of specified complexity—with the additional attribute of irreducibility of the final arrangement—and therefore is simply another example of design.

Behe illustrates the concept using the analogy of a simple mechanical mousetrap.[52] It has five parts: a platform, hammer, spring, catch, and a holding bar. If any one piece is not present, the whole mousetrap is nonfunctional. The mousetrap has to be created with all parts intact and working together for the whole system to operate properly. This idea applies to living things as well. Many complex

---

[50] The theory of Evolution is discussed in Appendix A.

[51] Denton, *Evolution: A Theory in Crisis*, 329.

[52] Michael J. Behe, *Darwin's Black Box: The Biochemical Challenge to Evolution* (New York: Simon & Schuster, 1996), 42-43.

systems cannot be created by gradual processes because they would be nonfunctional in the intermediate stages, thereby making their survival impossible. This is why Behe calls this *irreducible* complexity—the structure is not only complex, but it also cannot function in a lesser form— that is, its individual parts do not do anything useful for life on their own.[53] Behe's point is that we have evidence of complicated things—both living and non-living—that are not the result of numerous, successive, slight modifications. Rather, they are the result of an intelligent and deliberate process and are not useful in their intermediate stages.

The bacterial flagellum

Behe cites several examples of irreducible complexity that he has studied in detail, including his most famous illustration, the bacterial flagellum.[54] This cellular structure consists of a paddle, a rotor, and a motor which allow it to swim. The motor is about 45 nanometers[55] in diameter and is assembled from about 20 different kinds of parts. Behe concludes, "As biochemists have begun to examine apparently simple structures like...flagella, they have discovered staggering complexity, with dozens or even hundreds of precisely tailored parts...As the number of required parts increases, the difficulty of gradually putting the system together skyrockets, and the likelihood of indirect scenarios plummets."[56]

Blood clotting

Behe also describes the human blood clotting mechanism as an example of irreducible complexity.[57] Blood behaves in a very unusual way. Most liquids, when they leak from a container, will eventually drain the container completely. However, when we suffer a cut, it ordinarily bleeds for only a short time before a clot stops the flow, the clot eventually hardens, and the cut heals. Obviously, this is a very good thing as it

---

[53] Not all designed systems must be *irreducibly* complex; *cumulatively* complex systems are also possible. A system is cumulatively complex if the components of the system can be arranged sequentially so that the successive removal of components never leads to a complete loss of function. A city is an example of a cumulatively complex system. We can easily envision removing people, services, and buildings until we are left with only a tiny village, all without losing the function of the community—a place to live and work and relate to others. A city is still an example of intelligent design, though. Dembski, *Intelligent Design*, 147. Today's cars, computers, and spaceships are the result of incremental advancements of earlier designs, so they are also examples of cumulative complexity in that respect. Certain aspects of cars, computers, and spaceships, however, are irreducibly complex. The loss of a wheel, a microprocessor, or a rocket motor, respectively, would render them nonfunctional.

[54] A flagellum is a tail-like projection that protrudes from the body of certain kinds of cells, which acts as a swimming device to propel the cell.

[55] A nanometer is one billionth of a meter.

[56] Behe, *Darwin's Black Box*, 73.

[57] Ibid., 78-97.

prevents us from bleeding to death. It turns out that this apparently simple process is the function of a tremendously complex system consisting of nearly two dozen interdependent protein parts. The absence of or defect in any of the components will cause the system to fail—causing the blood to not clot, clot in the wrong place, clot at the wrong time, not stop clotting, or fail to remove the clot after the wound heals.

A blood clot is formed by fibers which are produced by the protein chain called *fibrinogen*. Normally, fibrinogen floats around in the blood 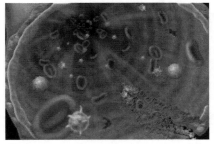 not doing anything until a cut or injury causes bleeding. Then another protein, *thrombin*, slices off small pieces from the fibrinogen to form long threads with sticky patches called *fibrin*. The fibrin threads begin sticking together in a very specific meshwork form that entraps blood cells, similar to a fisherman's net. The fiber net covers a large area with a minimum of protein, thus forming the initial clot.

We all know that when a clot initially forms it is quite fragile and can be easily disrupted, causing the bleeding to start again. So, the body has a method to strengthen the clot once it has formed by creating additional cross-links between different fibrin molecules. Once clotting begins, it must eventually stop as well, otherwise the same process would solidify all the blood in the body. A separate mechanism controls and regulates the entire process to activate and deactivate the components at exactly the right times. Additionally, the clot must be removed after the wound has sufficiently healed. A protein called *plasmin* acts as a scissors to cut up the fibrin clots at the appropriate time. Only the proteins forming the clot are severed, and not the other proteins, which would disable the system for future use.

This process is *far* more complicated than I have described here (or even for me to understand!), but you get the idea. This is an enormously complex biochemical process of many interacting parts with a precise control mechanism. If one part of it is missing or malfunctions, something dreadful happens. Behe concludes, "The formation, limitation, strengthening, and removal of a blood clot is an integrated biological system, and problems with single components can cause the system to fail. The lack of some blood clotting factors, or the production of defective factors, often results in serious health problems or death."[58]

---

[58] Ibid., 88-89.

Design indicator

Specified complexity *is* the indicator of design—improbability and conformance to an independent pattern. Irreducibility is an *additional* characteristic of some systems that makes a design inference even stronger, since the system could not have been produced by small, successive changes like naturalistic explanations require. Irreducible complexity has been shown to exist in life's smallest structures—the individual cell. Structures, which are much larger than a single cell, may also be irreducibly complex. For instance, all the body systems described earlier and even individual organs are so complicated and tightly integrated that it is difficult to envision them being produced incrementally.[59]

Information in the cell

We previously examined the incredible amount of information stored in a living cell when we looked at the origin of life in chapter 2. We will build on that in this section, especially as it relates to design.

To briefly summarize, DNA is the blueprint of life. It is stored within the nucleus of every living cell and contains the genetic information that dictates a cell's function and structure, which in turn, contributes to the determination and control of the biological characteristics of the whole living organism. We have here two distinct things that must be explained—*genetic information* (the blueprint) and the *physical structure* which holds the information (the DNA molecules). We will start with the physical structure of DNA.

Physical complexity

The complexity of a single DNA molecule is staggering. It consists of two strands that wind around each other like a twisted ladder, called a double helix. Each strand has a backbone made of sugar and phosphate. Attached to each sugar is one of four bases—adenine (A), cytosine (C), guanine (G), or thymine (T). These bases bond together in pairs on each ladder rung and are referred to as base-pairs. Each human DNA molecule has approximately 3 billion precise sequences of these base pairs, which is referred to as the *human genome*.[60] Most human cells contain two copies of the genome, for a total of 6 billion base pairs. If we unwound and tied

---

[59] Two examples of irreducible complexity in birds—the wing and lung—are presented in Appendix A.

[60] It is also referred to as the *human DNA sequence*.

together the strands of DNA in only one cell, it would stretch almost six feet, but would be a mere 80 billionth of an inch in diameter.[61]

A chromosome is a single piece of coiled DNA containing hundreds, and sometimes thousands, of genes. One chromosome can have as few as 50 million or as many as 250 million base pairs. Chromosomes package the DNA and control its functions. Genes are pieces of DNA containing hereditary information, which get passed from parent to offspring. The average gene has 10,000 to 15,000 base pairs and there are an estimated 20,000 to 25,000 genes in the human genome.[62] That is an incredible amount of complexity packed into every cell in the body, which fits our criteria of design. This only describes the *physical* structure that we refer to as DNA, not what is stored *in* the DNA.

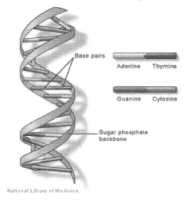

Genetic information

DNA is an *information* storage molecule. The four bases, abbreviated A-C-G-T, are chemical codes that act very much like letters in a genetic alphabet. The stairs in the DNA ladder combine the letters into complex sequences to form words, sentences and paragraphs that act as instructions to direct the development and function of the cell. The four DNA letters

are similar to the 0 and 1 binary codes that control the operation of a computer. These binary sequences must be very precise to be understood as valid instructions by the computer. A very small percentage of the possible number of sequences forms meaningful messages. In the same way, the DNA letters of the genetic language must occur in very precise sequences or they would be biologically meaningless and therefore useless.

The problem we need to consider is how all this information could arise by chance—and we are not talking about a small amount of information. If all three billion letters in the human genome were stacked one millimeter apart, they would reach a height almost 8,000 *times* that of

---

[61] The diameter of a DNA molecule is approximately 2 nanometers or 20 angstroms.

[62] Genes comprise only about 2% of the human genome. The remainder consists of non-coding regions, which means they do not generate protein sequences. The non-coding functions include protein production control and chromosomal structural integrity, among other things.

the Empire State Building.[63] It would require nearly 40,000 average size books to write the entire human genome.[64] It would take a person typing 60 words per minute, twenty-four hours a day, almost 100 years to type the whole thing.

Information meets the definition of design because it is contingent, complex, and specified. Moreover, as we have discussed, information must be the product of a mind since it transcends the physical medium in which it is contained. Therefore, we can conclude that not only is the physical structure of DNA designed, but it also contains an enormous amount of information, which is *also* designed.

Inferences about the attributes of the Designer of the universe

All the world is a stage and we are all actors in a grand drama. Just as a Shakespearean play is performed on a stage specifically designed for that purpose, this universe has been meticulously fashioned in countless ways to support intelligent life. It is far too improbable for all of it—indeed much of it—to be the result of accidental, blind, random forces of nature. All of our experience tells us that design comes from intelligence, and that intelligence is the product of a mind. A wise Creator who made the world with purpose and order *is* the Grand Designer. We can infer several important attributes of the Designer of the universe from our findings in this chapter.

One, the Designer is intelligent. We have affirmed this attribute before, but it is worth repeating. Any person who could conceive of and create an exceptionally complicated and sophisticated universe like this has an unimaginable intellect.

Two, the Designer is meticulous. Our discoveries of fine-tuning of the universe and design in the biological cell have revealed a Designer who is incredibly particular and thorough in arranging billions of fine details.

Three, the Designer is creative. This is almost too obvious to mention, as we have already made the case that the Designer is the Creator, but we are emphasizing here how original, imaginative, inventive, and resourceful the Designer is. The immense diversity and wonderful interrelationships of all the parts of the creation are astounding to consider.

Four, the Designer is beautiful. Beauty is a characteristic of something that provides a perceptual experience of pleasure or satisfaction by the mere beholding of it. There is too much excellence, elegance, harmony, and artistry on our planet—and in the whole universe—to think

---

[63] The Empire State Building is 1,250 feet (381 meters) tall.

[64] This assumes that the average size book is 400 words per page and 200 pages long.

that it does not originate with the Designer.[65] The beauty we experience and appreciate must therefore be derivative of the beauty of the Creator.

Five, the Designer is intentional. It certainly appears that he has a purpose or a goal in creation. Our human experience confirms that we design things for reasons. We have a purpose for them to fulfill. We have not yet in our investigation been able to discern the purpose of the universe and of our own lives, but suspecting there is purpose should fill us with excitement and anticipation. We will discuss this in later chapters.

Six, the Designer is involved with his creation. In the first chapter we concluded that the Creator continues to sustain the existence and operation of the universe, but his involvement appears to go much deeper than that. When we consider that the Creator is a personal being who is also the source of love, joy, beauty, goodness, value, meaning, and purpose, we cannot escape the conclusion that he profoundly cares for his creation. This is sufficient reason to reject deism—the idea that the Creator abandoned the world and set the cosmos to run on its own by natural law. Instead, he continues to intervene and remain engaged in it, and we should seek to understand how he does this.[66]

Common objections to design

Even with all these clear indications of design of the universe, some people deny it and offer various challenges that are easily disproven. We will now survey the more common ones.

Design theory is not science

Perhaps the most common charge made by opponents of design is that "It is not science." However, this is not a compelling objection for several reasons.

First, there is no generally accepted definition of what science is. Several characteristics have been suggested, such as repeatability, observability, and empirical testability, but none of them have been wholly satisfactory. There are examples of good science that do not have these characteristics and also examples of what most people would call non-science that do have them.[67] Many scientists rule out design by definition because of their materialist presuppositions. They define science to be the discovery of how the natural world operates *using only natural explanations*. But why must we limit explanations to only natural causes, especially if we have good lines of evidence that point to a supernatural

---

[65] There are also ugly things like death and evil in the world, which is the topic of Question 2.

[66] This will be the topic of Question 4.

[67] Moreland, *Scaling the Secular City*, 199.

cause? Michael Behe suggests that "science is not a word game that's decided by definitions—it's an unsentimental, no-holds-barred struggle to understand nature."[68] We should follow the evidence wherever it takes us.

Second, intelligent design is science by any reasonable definition. Dembski and others have been able to rigorously define the criteria needed to detect design in nature. We have even seen three scientific disciplines— cryptography, forensics, and the search for extra-terrestrial intelligence— that presently use design principles in their underlying theories.

Third, we must not confuse the evidence with its implications. Even if the implications of design lead to religious conclusions, *the evidence is not based on religion*. Rather, it is based on legitimate inferences—using logic, reason, and science—about the physical evidence we observe in our world. Those who pose this objection are not happy with the conclusions drawn from the design evidence. Even if some design advocates have religious motivations, that does not make design false. Truth does not depend on a seeker's motivations, but on the evidence.

Fourth, it does not matter anyway. If the truth is that the universe was designed, then asserting that we cannot know that by science is simply irrelevant. What is important is that *we do know it*. Science is not the exclusive source of knowledge about our world.[69] We should collect all the evidence we can, using all the means we have available, in order to answer life's most important questions.

It does not explain the designer

Some people claim that design inferences about the universe do not go far enough. They object that whoever designed the universe is not explained by these design theories. They say that if the universe needs an explanation, then so does its designer. If the universe designer does not need an explanation, then why think that the universe does? This challenge misunderstands how explanations work.

An explanation of something need not explain how or why it came to be. These are certainly interesting and valuable questions, but explanations come in layers. We do not need an explanation of the explanation in order to be persuaded that it is the best explanation we have. For example, if an archaeologist uncovers some objects that look like arrowheads, he is justified in asserting that the objects are man-made, designed artifacts, *even if he has no clue who designed them or why.*[70] The same is true for a

---

[68] Behe, *The Edge of Evolution*, 235.

[69] The view that science is the only way to know reality is called *scientism*, but this is a self-refuting view since this claim itself cannot be proven through science.

[70] William Lane Craig, *God is Good, God is Great: Why Believing in God Is Reasonable and Responsible* (Downers Grove, IL: InterVarsity Press, 2009), 27.

cryptologist who deciphers a coded message, or a forensics expert who finds evidence of a murder, or an astronomer who looks for messages from outer space. Each of these scientists might conclude that an intelligent agent has acted, yet have no idea *who* that agent was or *why* he acted. The identity of the designer is a different issue to be pursued separately. In the same way, we can infer the universe was designed even if we did not know *anything* about its Designer.

Of course, we can know many things about the Designer as this book aims to show using our cumulative case approach. We have already identified some two dozen attributes of the Designer. Moreover, because we believe the Designer to be eternal, he is a necessary being, and necessary things are not designed—they simply are the way they are from eternity past. Only created things can be designed.

It is only apparent design

One of the introductory quotes to this chapter was from the renowned atheist Richard Dawkins. He cautions us not to explain the improbable complexities in the universe as design, but rather to see them merely as the "appearance of design." We have to wonder, though, is a painting the evidence of an artist or does it merely "appear" that there may be an artist that painted the painting?

Dawkins would rather fight against the evidence than submit to where it leads. If we can infer design from specified complexity, then denying design requires denying an object's pattern, its improbability, or both. This is difficult to do with so many examples of highly improbable constants, laws, objects, and systems that all conspire to make the universe, and more particularly our planet, fit for life.[71]

Some scientists apply this idea of apparent design to the cosmic level. These scientists would agree that many physical constants and laws are exactly right in our universe to permit life, but they propose the existence of *many actual universes*, each of which has slightly different, random values for these properties. In this so-called *multiple universe*[72] scenario, we shouldn't think our universe so improbable since there are billions—and perhaps an infinite number—of other universes in existence. If this

---

[71] Dawkins prefers the process of natural selection as the explanation for apparent design in life forms, which is discussed in appendix A.

[72] This theory also goes by the names "Multiverse", "Many Worlds Hypothesis", and "Worlds Ensemble."

were true, we would *expect* to find at least one that was suitable for life by chance alone. There are multiple problems with this theory.

First, there is absolutely no evidence that multiple universes actually exist. By definition, a universe is any region of space-time that is disconnected from other regions in such a way that the properties of physics in that region could differ significantly from other regions.[73] Unfortunately, the same independence required to get distinct properties also means that we cannot directly observe other universes. When direct observation is not possible, scientists resort to indirect observation of causes and effects, but even this is not possible if there is no physical connection between universes. Therefore, we will never have any evidence for them.

Second, a key principle of science is the operation of Ockham's razor, which we discussed in chapter 1. This principle states that we should prefer a simpler rather than a more complex explanation if the simpler one can explain all the known relevant facts. To propose such a complicated and improbable idea as multiple universes against all the evidence, when a single universe can be explained by design, exposes the real motive with this theory—to avoid the implications of design. We would never accept this kind of reasoning in any other area of science, which normally follows the evidence wherever it leads.

Third, if multiple universes did exist, then why should we think each universe has slightly different values? What causes *that* to happen? It seems that there must exist a universe generator which controls the whole process. This universe generator itself must be a mechanism which is describable by physical constants and laws, though; so we have merely shifted the design problem up one level. From where and how did the universe generator originate?

Fourth, the number of multiple universes required to produce even one with the right values for life and sustained existence like ours is enormous, which is why some people have suggested an infinite number of them. However, we learned previously that an actual infinity is impossible, which, unfortunately for the naturalists, applies to universes as well.

Suboptimal structures cannot be designed

For the universe or any part it, such as the human body, to be intelligently designed, some people argue that we should see perfectly crafted structures that perform their individual tasks in the most elegant and efficient way possible. Thus, they argue against intelligent design based on what they view as "suboptimal design." A famous example used

---

[73] Collins, "God, Design, and Fine-Tuning".

in this challenge is the anatomy of the Giant Panda's thumb. The panda's thumb is not anatomically a finger at all, but an enlarged wrist bone, which is alleged to be "a somewhat clumsy, but quite workable, solution."[74]

The expectation for optimal designs is mistaken, however, not only for human design, but also for divine design. This is quite obvious in the case of designs produced by human beings. We frequently have to design things in ways that are suboptimal simply because of the complexity and magnitude of the task, as well as our limited resources. This does not mean that design has not occurred, however. Of course, in the case of God, we envision that he does not suffer the same limitations we do, so some people do not expect to see what they would call suboptimal divine design. Here are three reasons to think otherwise, though.[75]

First, God often uses secondary agents—like physical laws—to bring about physical structures, so we can expect to see certain patterns and processes repeated in many places and used in different ways, even though the design may not be optimal for each individual application. This concept of "reuse" is actually commonplace in human design. These repeated patterns and processes are attributes of an ordered universe that helps us understand and explain our universe. The discoverability of the structure of the universe appears to be an objective of God that we should not overlook.

Second, many of God's designs are adaptive systems, which mean they are capable of adapting to different conditions. Such systems will virtually always have components that are not being used in a given situation, so they may *appear* to be extraneous. This is not suboptimal, but rather intelligent!

Third—and this is the most important reason—divine designs may appear to be less than optimal because we are not in a position to fully understand all of the design objectives of an omniscient and omnipotent designer. It is something like a primitive cave-dweller looking at a modern-day airplane and complaining about some part he thought was unnecessary. How would he know? Similarly, what makes us think we are in a position to know with certainty why God designed something the way he did? Moreover, this objection considerably underappreciates the immense sophistication and ingenuity inherent in the structures of the cosmos and living systems. This gives us all the more reason to reserve judgment when we question some particular feature.[76]

---

[74] Stephen J. Gould, *The Panda's Thumb: More Reflections in Natural History* (New York: W.W. Norton & Company, 1980), 24.

[75] Richard Spencer, "Intelligent, Optimal, and Divine Design", *Evidence for God*, 109-110.

[76] We have since learned that the panda's "thumb" is uniquely crafted to remove bark from bamboo shoots, which is a large part of its diet.

Extinction disproves design

This argument suggests that intelligent design cannot be true because animal species have gone extinct. The idea is that an intelligent designer will have failed if a species does not survive. The same objection could probably be raised because of sickness, disease, deformities, and death in general.

The main problem with this kind of challenge is that it confuses how something came into existence with what happens to it afterwards. These are two separate questions and so they will have different answers. Take for example the chariot, steam locomotive, and buggy whip.[77] Each of these artifacts is "extinct" today because they are no longer around, but it does not follow that they were not designed. Each of these items exhibits the trademarks of intelligent causation. The fact that they have gone out of style or have been otherwise superseded by subsequent designs does not alter the fact that they, themselves, were designed. Likewise, the fact that stars or animals go extinct, or even that all organisms eventually die, says nothing about their origins. Instead, we should recognize their design and then separately investigate the causes of their extinction.

It substitutes God in the gaps

Some skeptics charge design advocates with substituting extraordinary explanations where ordinary explanations will suffice, even if they are not known at this time. This is often called *God-of-the-gaps*, since design theory is viewed as inserting God as the explanation for some gap in our understanding that science cannot presently explain. It is true that we should not be too quick to seek non-natural explanations in our investigation of the natural world, but this objection cuts both ways. We have already examined theories that substitute random chance in these same kinds of gaps—the multiple universe scenario, for example. We can just as easily accuse the challengers of using a *nature-of-the-gaps* approach—that they are too quick to appeal to nature and chance.

This illustrates the problem with the objection. The question is not really whether or not God created something, but whether or not science has the resources necessary to provide a natural explanation. To suppose that the universe *must* be explained only in natural ways exposes a bias that will restrict the investigator's field of view. There is no rule of logic, philosophy, or science that requires such a limitation. Instead, we should always follow the evidence we presently have *wherever* it leads, and sometimes we find that scientific evidence supports a conclusion that has theological significance.

---

[77] I borrowed these analogies from Greg Koukl.

It should not surprise us that we are here

If the universe were not fine-tuned for life, then human beings would not be around to observe it. We should therefore not be surprised by finding ourselves in a universe perfectly suited for us. It simply follows from the fact that we exist, or so the objection goes.

This objection has missed the whole point of the design argument, which is the enormous improbability of the universe to exist the way it does *in the first place*. The fact that "we now find ourselves here" is totally irrelevant. An explanation is still required. Philosopher John Leslie provides a helpful illustration.[78]

Imagine the scene of an execution by firing squad. The accused is blindfolded and fifty sharp-shooters aim their rifles and fire. To the astonishment of the would-be victim, he has not been hit by a single bullet. What should he conclude? The sort of objection we are dealing with here would have him think, "I should not be surprised that they missed since I am still alive." We instinctively see the problem with this explanation though—his survival is *not an explanation at all*. In fact, it has nothing to do with it since it is only the result, and not the cause, of the event. The real explanation for his continued existence is design or chance. Either the marksmen intended to miss him (design) or it was a very lucky and accidental outcome that is to be occasionally expected among thousands of attempted executions by firing squad (chance).

I will let you decide for yourself what the best explanation is in this case. However, with respect to the universe, many of its features are contingent (not necessary), complex (highly improbable), and specified (matching a pattern)—which are the sure signs of design.

---

[78] John Leslie, *Universes* (London: Routledge, 1989), 108.

CONCLUSION

Where did everything come from?

The fool says in his heart, "There is no God."

David (c. 1040–970 BC)
King of Israel

Science describes a Universe in which it is not necessary to postulate the existence of God at all.

Isaac Asimov (1920-1992)
Atheist, science fiction author
In The Beginning

For the scientist who has lived by his faith in the power of reason, the story ends like a bad dream. He has scaled the mountains of ignorance; he is about to conquer the highest peak; as he pulls himself over the final rock, he is greeted by a band of theologians who have been sitting there for centuries.

Robert Jastrow (1925-2008)
Agnostic, cosmologist
God and the Astronomers

Do you not know? Have you not heard? The LORD is the everlasting God, the Creator of the ends of the earth. He will not grow tired or weary, and his understanding no one can fathom.

Isaiah (c. 760-681 BC)
Prophet of Israel

We have surveyed the origins of the most fundamental and important aspects of our universe and planet and found that theism provides the best explanations for all of them. To this point, we have referred to the personal transcendent Cause as "the Creator" and "the Designer." We have further inferred that the Creator/Designer is necessary, eternal, distinct from the universe, timeless, immaterial, unique, personal, self-sufficient, powerful, intelligent, sovereign, conscious, rational, free to choose, valuable, meaningful, purposeful, loving, joyful, moral, caring, meticulous, creative, involved, beautiful, and communicative.

A Creator/Designer who exhibits all of these characteristics is what humanity has traditionally referred to as God for at least four millennia. We therefore have considerable rational justification to believe that God exists and that he is the Creator/Designer whom we have discovered in our examination of nature. We have not yet determined exactly who this God is or what his purposes, plans, and expectations are, but we can reasonably conclude that God is the best explanation for the following:

1. Why the universe exists instead of nothing
2. The complex order in the universe
3. The origin of life
4. The existence of consciousness
5. Our ability to reason
6. Our ability to make free choices
7. The existence of language
8. The existence of value, meaning, and purpose
9. The origin and experience of love and joy
10. The existence of objective moral values
11. The reality of irreducible complexity in biological organisms
12. The origin of information in DNA

No other worldview has anything close to the broad and persuasive explanatory scope and power that theism offers. Atheism, pantheism, polytheism, deism, animism, and agnosticism have all been shown to be implausible on multiple counts.

Atheism is perhaps the most defended worldview today other than theism, so we have spent more time addressing it.[1] We have seen that atheism simply does not have convincing answers to explain why the world is the way it is. People who believe that the universe and everything in it emerged exclusively through natural processes require a lot more faith than someone who follows the evidence leading to a supernatural Creator.

---

[1] See Appendix A for a discussion of Darwinian Evolution.

Further reading

General

> *Evidence for God: 50 Arguments for Faith from the Bible, History, Philosophy, and Science,* William Dembski and Mike Licona (editors)
> *I Don't Have Enough Faith to Be an Atheist,* Norman L. Geisler and Frank Turek
> *Reasonable Faith: Christian Truth and Apologetics,* William Lane Craig
> *The Blackwell Companion to Natural Theology,* William Lane Craig (ed.)
> *The Case for a Creator,* Lee Strobel

Intelligent design

> *Intelligent Design: The Bridge Between Science and Theology,* William Dembski
> *Intelligent Design 101,* Wayne House (editor)
> *Nature's Destiny: How the Laws of Biology Reveal Purpose in the Universe,* Michael Denton
> *The Privileged Planet,* Guillermo Gonzalez and Jay W. Richards
> *Show Me God: What the Message from Space is Telling Us About God,* Fred Heeren
> *Signature in the Cell: DNA and the Evidence for Intelligent Design,* Stephen C. Meyer
> *The Creator and the Cosmos,* Hugh Ross

What is wrong with the world?

We desire truth and find in ourselves nothing but uncertainty. We seek happiness and find only wretchedness and death.

Blaise Pascal (1623-1662)
Mathematician, physicist, inventor, philosopher
Pensées, no. 401

We do not have to look very far to notice that there is something terribly wrong with the world—cruelty, war, terrorism, crime, disease, disaster, poverty, greed, corruption, injustice—the list seems endless. Evil surrounds us. Pain and suffering are rampant, and we all experience it. Besides this, everyone experiences some degree of personal unhappiness, discontentment, disappointment, frustration, fear, and anxiety. As if all this were not enough, every one of us dies in the end. It does not seem like the world should be this way, especially in a theistic universe created and controlled by a powerful and loving God.

Many questions come to mind as we ponder these things. How did the world get to be this way? What is evil? Did God create evil? Is he responsible for it? Why does he not eliminate it or reduce it? Many people believe that evil and human suffering disprove the existence of a benevolent God. Others believe that evil shows that God has lost control of this world and therefore is not all powerful. These are important questions that we will answer as we examine what is wrong with the world.

Every worldview must give an explanation for the problem of evil and suffering. This is not only a question for theists. An answer to the question of evil and suffering should meet both the intellectual and emotional demands of the question. It must provide a rational explanation and also give us comfort and hope as we face suffering in our lives.

CHAPTER 4

Not the way it is supposed to be

Everything is broken in some way. You see it everywhere: in nature, with storms, pollution, natural disasters, vicious animals; in our physical bodies, with disease, weakness, old age; in relationships, with conflict, division, violence; in the mechanical world and its plane crashes, train wrecks, and appliance breakdowns; in human culture, with distorted values, racism, corrupt government, ethnic cleansing, and perverted justice; in work, where "weeds and thorns" and all the matters mentioned above make labor more burdensome.

Timothy S. Lane and Paul David Tripp
Pastors, speakers, authors
How People Change

There is a serious and pervasive problem in our world, and it is called evil. Billions of people suffer pain because of evil. Most of us recognize the most heinous forms of it—acts like murder, rape, child molestation, sex trafficking, and suicide bombing. What about adultery, lying, stealing, greed, and pride, though? Are they evil? When we consider a wider range of behaviors, it seems more difficult for us to draw the line at what is evil and what is not. For our present purpose let's define evil as the intention or effect of causing harm or destruction, even if we might not fully agree on what constitutes harm and destruction.

The fact that evil has a moral dimension is clear from the way we think and talk about it.[1] We call something evil because it *ought* not to happen—the world is not supposed to be that way. When human beings ought not do something, we are speaking about our moral behavior. The

---

[1] *Natural* evil, which is caused by disease and disaster, will be discussed in the next chapter.

"problem of evil" is the need we have to explain the existence and prevalence of evil we observe in the world.

Accounting for evil

One way that people choose to resolve this problem is to say that evil and suffering do not really exist. Many Eastern religions take this route.[2] They say evil is an illusion, and that we overcome pain and suffering by believing they are not real. This explanation of evil and suffering does not make sense intellectually. We see and experience the results of evil and suffering all the time. To deny it is simply irrational. This explanation also does not make sense emotionally. Imagine having to tell a victim of sexual abuse, "The evil you endured is merely a false impression; it did not really happen." This solution does not take the problem of evil seriously and is further evidence against the worldviews that advocate it.

A fundamental issue we must address is whether there is a universal, transcendent definition of evil, or whether evil is determined by our social or cultural background and customs. There are some people who say the difference between good and evil is subject to our inclinations and choices. Evil is merely what we individually or culturally decide to call evil. This view is called *moral relativism*, which we rejected in chapter 2. What counts as evil cannot be left to social custom or personal choice. Moral objectivity requires a universal standard of good and evil.

Many atheists acknowledge the objective reality of evil. At first glance it might seem that atheism has a convincing explanation for evil. What else would we expect in a godless world that is ruled by the most powerful life forms who spend their lives simply struggling to survive? It is easy to see how these organisms would disdain any sort of moral order and that evil would be prevalent. Darwin suggested as much: "That there is much suffering in the world no one disputes...The presence of much suffering agrees well with the view that all organic beings have been developed through variation and natural selection."[3]

There is a conspicuous problem ignored by the atheist when he makes this claim, however. When we say something is evil, we mean that thing *ought* to be a certain way, but it is not. There is a violation of the intended order—a deviation from some norm. Evil is a *value* judgment that must be compared against an objective moral standard in order to have any meaning. Something is evil *because* it departs from this objective standard of goodness. Otherwise, what counts as evil would be no more than

---

[2] For example, Hinduism, Taoism, some forms of Buddhism, and the Christian Science Church.
[3] Charles Darwin, *The Autobiography of Charles Darwin*, as found in Appendix A of Carroll, *On the Origin of Species*, 432.

individual or cultural preference. This would make it a mere human invention, and *not* an objective reality in the world.

An objective standard of goodness is an objective truth, which means that it is knowable, discoverable, universal, exclusive, and consequential.[4] Such a standard of right and wrong is unintelligible if there is no God. Only God can provide an *objective* standard of goodness. This is why the existence of evil is actually evidence *for* the existence of God. If there is no God, then good and evil are relative and not objective, so true evil would not exist. If there is no God, then nothing is ultimately bad, reprehensible, tragic, or worthy of blame. If there is no God then there is no standard by which we can say that Joseph Stalin or Osama bin Laden did anything wrong when they murdered so many people. Simply put, there cannot be a world in which it makes any sense to say that evil is real and at the same time say that God does not exist. So the existence of evil actually proves God exists, instead of the opposite.[5]

Evil is not a thing

Some people believe in a sort of duality between good and evil. They believe that evil cannot exist without good, nor good without evil—as if they were equal but opposite ends of some great cosmic scale that must remain in balance. The problem with this view is that it treats evil as a "thing" that exists in the universe. However, evil has no substance. Rather, it is a certain quality of particular actions and the state of bad affairs that result. Evil does not cause our actions. Instead, our actions cause evil things to happen. This is why the argument that says God created evil is not a very good one. The argument goes like this: "If God created all things, then he also created evil, which makes him evil too." The problem with this argument is that evil is not a "thing," and therefore is not created. Evil as a thing in itself, simply does not exist.

Evil seems more like the notion of coldness. Coldness is not a physical thing because it is merely the absence of heat. Heat is an energy transfer that can be measured. We refer to a condition of no heat as "cold," but there is no cold "thing" that causes the condition. The term "cold" has been created to describe what we feel when heat is not there.[6] In the same way, evil is like darkness. There is no such substance as darkness. Darkness is simply the absence of light. Light is a physical thing,

---

[4] These are the five essential characteristics of objective truth, which we discussed in the Introduction.

[5] This is not to say that atheists can't recognize moral rules or live morally; but that they cannot make sense of morality apart from God.

[6] Greg Koukl, "A Good Reason for Evil", Stand To Reason, http://www.str.org/site/News2?page=NewsArticle&id=5093, accessed Jul 31, 2011.

exhibiting properties of both waves and particles that can be measured.
Darkness is not a physical thing like that. We
wouldn't say that a shadow exists as a thing in itself;
rather it is the lack of light in a particular spot.

Evil exists the same way as dark and cold do.
Just as dark and cold exist as the absence of light and
heat, respectively, evil exists as the absence of
goodness. It is a deviation of the way things ought to
be. It is a loss of goodness in us as human beings.
You can have good without evil, but you cannot have
evil without good.

The basis of good and evil

Morality is universal because a single standard of right and wrong
applies to all people in all places at all times. Furthermore, the source of
the moral law must be God, otherwise it is simply an invention of
humanity that cannot be universal. How are we to understand the
foundation or logical basis of God's objective moral law? In other words,
what are the grounds on which God makes his moral commands?

The ancient Greek philosopher Plato posed a famous dilemma
concerning the foundation of morality when he asked, "Is the pious loved

by the gods because it is pious, or is it pious because it
is loved by the gods?"[7] More recently Bertrand Russell
restated Plato's dilemma in an attempt to show an
inconsistency in theism's concept of God. He
acknowledges that theists claim that God establishes the
moral rules of the universe and that we know these rules
by his commands.[8] Russell challenges theists to explain
the *basis* upon which God issues commands. With some
sense of triumph, he wonders if a command is good simply because God
says so or if God says a command is good because he recognizes some
moral standard beyond himself. By expressing the dilemma in these terms,
Russell has put the theist in an apparent no-win situation. The theist is
forced to choose between two dire options—one that makes God
capricious or the other which makes him subservient to some greater
reality. Let's look at Russell's two options more closely.

The first possibility that Russell suggests is what philosophers call the
"divine command theory" of ethics, which holds that moral principles
derive their validity or "rightness" simply because God commands them.

---

[7] This is commonly called the Euthyphro dilemma because, according to Plato, Socrates asked
this question of Euthyphro.

[8] We will address how we can know God's commands in Question 4.

The ultimate foundation for morality is the mere fact that God reveals his commands to humanity. For this to be true, morality would be arbitrary, subject to God's whim, which he could change whenever he wanted. Today murder is wrong, but maybe not so tomorrow. Or maybe God could have simply declared from eternity past that murder is good. In this view, God *decides* what is moral and what is not. This reduces God's goodness to his power because only he is capable of enforcing his commands.[9] Russell concludes, "For God himself there is no difference between right and wrong."[10] Theists reject this view because morality does not seem to be arbitrary—we seem to have fairly consistent moral intuitions.

Russell's challenge is that if we deny the first half of his dilemma, then we must accept the second. If God cannot simply call things right or wrong, then he must be subject to some higher law that defines right and wrong. This makes the sovereign ruler of the universe subordinate to some law outside of himself. Obviously, the theist rejects this notion as well. As the Creator, God is subordinate to nothing.

We seem to be left with the choice that God is not good or he is not supreme, unless Russell has given us a false dilemma—and indeed he has. There is another option that Russell has not considered. An objective moral standard *does* exist, which avoids the first half of the dilemma, but it is *internal* to God—not external to him—which avoids the second half of the dilemma. God's eternal and unchangeable character is perfectly good, so his commands are not arbitrary, but rooted in his righteous nature. Therefore, it is impossible for him to issue unrighteous commands.

The theist can avoid Russell's dilemma entirely. Morality is not logically prior to God as Russell suggests, but is internally fixed in God's nature. Ethics professor Scott Rae explains, "Morality is not grounded ultimately in God's commands, but in his character, which then expresses itself in his commands."[11] God's commands, in turn, constitute our moral duties and obligations. Far from being arbitrary, these commands flow necessarily from his moral nature; which is to be loving, generous, just, faithful, kind, and so forth. So whatever a good God commands will always be good.[12]

We must acknowledge that if God is wiser than we are—which seems very clear from all we have been able to infer from creation—then his judgments will likely differ from ours on many things, including what truly constitutes good and evil. What seems good to us may not be good in

---

[9] One theistic worldview, Islam, takes this position, while Judaism and Christianity deny it.

[10] Russell, *Why I Am Not a Christian*, 12.

[11] Scott Rae, *Moral Choices: An Introduction to Ethics* (Grand Rapids: Zondervan, 2000), 33.

[12] Greg Koukl, "Euthyphro's Dilemma", Stand To Reason, http://www.str.org/site/News2?page=NewsArticle&id=5236, accessed Feb 2, 2011.

his eyes, and what seems evil to us may not be so to him.[13] We approach these things from a limited and error-prone vantage point, whereas God is all-knowing and morally perfect.

We all contribute to evil in the world

We human beings have a common tendency to compare ourselves morally to one other, as individuals and also as cultures. Invariably, we judge ourselves to be more upright than our neighbors. The popular thing to do is to decry all the evil that is "out there" in the world somewhere. We hear of all the horrific and brutal acts of violence and abuse committed by one person against another, and we are outraged by it. It is right to be outraged by it, but are *we* really any better?

Perhaps the antidote to thinking we are more kind or good than the next person is to consider whether God ought to be content with the cruelty of others if they also excelled in courage or modesty.[14] We would likely think not. The point is we all do better or worse in different areas, but it is dangerous to think that we have not crossed the line of evil in *some* areas of our lives. We each have blind spots about where the line of evil should be drawn because we tend to overlook our faults in favor of our virtues. We often excuse the evil we commit ourselves, and recognize it only when we are its victim or see it in other victims. If evil is any thought, word, or action that deviates from God's perfect standard of goodness, though, then we are *all* guilty of evil—many times over throughout our lives.

C. S. Lewis claims that we all stand condemned by *our own understanding* of what is right and wrong: "The moralities accepted among men may differ—though not, at bottom, so widely as is often claimed—but they all agree in prescribing a behaviour which their adherents fail to practise. All men alike stand condemned, not by alien codes of ethics, but by their own, and all men therefore are conscious of guilt."[15] Lewis is not affirming moral relativism, but rather the reality of the human conscience that convicts each of us that we often do wrong.

We need to face the problem of evil and suffering squarely by acknowledging our own contributions to them. The answer to why the world is so messed up has something to do with our own penchant to act badly. We will look at this more closely in the next chapter.

---

[13] C. S. Lewis, *The Problem of Pain* (San Francisco: HarperCollins, 1996, 1st published 1940), 28.

[14] Ibid., 58.

[15] Ibid., 11.

CHAPTER 5

Transcendent purposes

Almost everything that is manufactured comes with a set of instructions...Of course, we may choose to ignore the maker's instructions, but if we do, then we cannot blame the manufacturer when things go wrong.

Brian H. Edwards (1941-)
Pastor, author, lecturer
Nothing But The Truth

The possibility of pain is inherent in the very existence of a world where souls can meet. When souls become wicked they will certainly use this possibility to hurt one another.

C. S. Lewis (1898-1963)
Theologian, author
The Problem of Pain

We have examined the theistic understanding of evil and concluded that evil actually proves the existence of God; otherwise we would have no universal standard against which to call something evil. However, the atheist poses two challenges that we must deal with. First, evil could not possibly exist at the same time as an all-loving, all-powerful, all-knowing God. This is called the *logical* problem of evil. Second, the extent and depth of evil make it very unlikely that an all-loving, all-powerful, all-knowing God exists. This is called the *evidential* problem of evil.[1] In addition to addressing these two problems, we will suggest some possible reasons that God allows evil to exist.

---

[1] It is also sometimes called the *probabilistic* problem of evil.

The logical problem of evil

According to this version of the problem, it is logically impossible for God and evil to coexist—since evil exists, God cannot exist. Epicurus (341-270 BC), an ancient Greek philosopher, was one of the earliest philosophers to articulate the argument against God using the logical problem of evil.[2] Basically, his argument can be summarized as follows:

1. If God was all-loving, he would have the *desire* to prevent evil.
2. If God was all-powerful, he would have the *power* to prevent evil.
3. If God was all-knowing, he would have the *knowledge* to prevent evil.
4. Since we know evil exists, it is logically impossible for an all-loving, all-powerful, and all-knowing God to exist.

It is a bold assertion to claim it is not logically possible for God to exist, especially since there is no obvious logical contradiction between the existence of God and evil. All we must do is provide one possible reason for an all-knowing, all-powerful, all-loving God to allow evil and we defeat this objection.

How should we think about this problem in light of God's attributes? Given that God is all-knowing, he certainly knew evil would result when he created humans. Since God is all-powerful, he could have created the world in other ways. Since God is all-loving, he must have had good reasons for making the world in this way. If God does have a morally sufficient reason for permitting evil, then it follows that God and evil are logically consistent. Human free will is just such a possible reason.

Evil was not created by God, but was made *possible* by God. God created human beings as free moral agents. This means we are able to choose evil as well as good. Human beings, because we have chosen to do evil things, made evil a *reality* in the world. Real love—our love of God and our love of each other—must involve a choice, but with that choice comes the possibility that people will choose instead to hate and hurt others. God might think human freedom to be worth this risk because of the great value of creatures engaging in freely chosen responses of love to him and to one another.[3] C. S. Lewis explains:

---

[2] Epicurus, as quoted by the early Christian writer Lucius Lactantius, as quoted by Clifford A. Pickover, *The Loom of God: Tapestries of Mathematics and Mysticism* (New York: Sterling Publishing Co., 2009, first published 1997), 199.

[3] Timothy O'Connor, "The Problem of Evil", *Philosophy of Religion: A Reader and Guide*, William Lane Craig, general editor (New Brunswick, NJ: Rutgers University Press, 2002), 307.

God created things which had free will. That means creatures which can go either wrong or right. Some people think they can imagine a creature which was free but had no possibility of going wrong; I cannot. If a thing is free to be good it is also free to be bad. And free will is what has made evil possible. Why then, did God give them free will? Because free will, though it makes evil possible, is the only thing that makes possible any love or goodness or joy worth having. A world of automata—of creatures that worked like machines—would hardly be worth creating.[4]

God's immense power only extends to what is logically possible. Even God cannot create a world containing logical contradictions. It is not feasible for God to create a world with no possibility of evil *and* also have creatures with free will. His omnipotence cannot prevent evil *if* he determines to allow genuine free will, which he has done. To say otherwise would mean that God would use his power to coerce non-evil choices from human beings, but then they would not have free will. This conflicts with God's desire that people should freely love him.

God made evil possible, but it is human beings who made evil a reality in the world by our choices. Since there is a possible explanation as to how God and evil can both exist, the logical argument of evil fails.[5]

The evidential problem of evil

A more compelling form of this argument against theism, at least at first glance, is the evidential problem of evil. According to this version, the existence of God and evil is logically *possible,* but it is highly *improbable.* Even if some amount of evil is expected in the way God has created the world, we endure much more than is necessary. The total amount, distribution, and intensity of evil in the world is so great that it is doubtful that God could have morally sufficient reasons for permitting all of it. God simply allows *too much* evil, so that should count against him. Therefore, it is unlikely that God exists.

The proponents of this view refer to the so-called "extra" evil as *gratuitous* evil, meaning it is pointless and unnecessary. They say there is no apparent reason or justification for it. Therefore, God probably does not exist because of the existence and amount of gratuitous evil in the world, or at least he cannot be all-loving, all-powerful, and all-knowing.

But how do we know that God *has not* limited evil? Even though we can imagine the world being better than we experience it today, we can also picture it being far worse. It is entirely possible that God *has* limited

---

[4] Lewis, *Mere Christianity*, 52-53.

[5] This refutation of the logical problem of evil was developed by philosopher Alvin Plantinga, *God, Freedom, and Evil* (Grand Rapids: William B. Eerdmans Publishing Company, 1977).

evil in the world. For instance, in the infamous terrorist attack on the U.S. on September 11, 2001, the fourth hijacked airplane crashed in a field and not into the Capitol building, saving many lives. Mercifully, there was not a fifth, sixth, or even a hundredth airplane. Could it not be possible that God did, in fact, limit the evil on that horrific day? The fact is that we cannot really know.

We have to wonder how much reduction in evil would satisfy the skeptic. Would a suicide bombing that killed only ten people instead of a hundred be acceptable? Would we be content with a world full of "only" cheating and lying, rather than murder and war? Surely we would find these lesser scenarios of evil unbearable as well. It seems that with this protest the skeptic is ultimately questioning the existence of *any* evil in the world, but we have already dealt with this objection in the logical problem of evil. In the end, none of us will accept evil simply because its quantity or severity diminishes. We want it to be eradicated completely.

This challenge assumes that we can draw a line between too much and a tolerable amount of evil. No human being, though, can know that any particular evil is "unnecessary" or that there is "too much evil" in the world. We cannot draw such a line because *it is not our line to draw.* This would require omniscience on our part. The only kind of being that could know this is God. The problem with this challenge, therefore, is its implied presumption of knowing more than God. We simply cannot know how much evil God may already be restraining in the world or how much is needed for some greater good, so this objection falls short of disproving God's existence or that he is not all-loving, all-powerful, and all-knowing.

Natural evil

At this point we should consider *natural* evil in addition to moral evil. Natural evil is what causes suffering due to events of nature, such as disaster and disease. Who has not been personally touched by, or seen, or heard about some form of natural evil? Natural disasters like earthquakes, hurricanes, tsunamis, tornadoes, floods, and drought kill hundreds of thousands each year. Disease kills millions of people every year as well. The World Health Organization lists the following diseases among the top causes of death world-wide: lower respiratory infection, coronary heart disease, diarrheal disease, HIV/AIDS, stroke, pulmonary disease, tuberculosis, neonatal infection, malaria, and cancer.[6]

Even though both moral and natural evil can cause a great amount of suffering, it is helpful to make a distinction between these two main sources of evil. Where moral evil results from the actions of free moral

---

[6] http://www.who.int/mediacentre/factsheets/fs310/en/index.html, accessed Feb 5, 2011.

agents (other human beings), there is no choice involved in natural evil. We therefore need to explain why we have both kinds of evil in the world.

Why God might allow evil

We have seen that there are no logical problems with theism regarding the presence of evil in the world. We certainly do not have to accept evil, but its presence in no way disproves the existence of God or challenges his attributes of maximal power, intelligence, or goodness. Nevertheless, we still often wonder why God allows so much evil and suffering in the world. Does he have reasons to do so?

We should admit that simply because we cannot see the good that results in a situation does not mean there is none. As human beings, we are finite, and we cannot completely understand the ways of an infinite God. Since he is powerful and intelligent and loving, yet permits evil, then we must conclude that he has reasons for evil that we cannot fully comprehend. We simply are in no position to assert that there are no valid reasons for suffering. Peter Kreeft suggests, "It's at least possible that God is wise enough to foresee that we need some pain for reasons which we may not understand, but which he foresees as being necessary to some eventual good. Therefore, he's not being evil by allowing that pain to exist."[7] God probably has many different reasons for allowing evil and the suffering that results from it. Let's explore some possible reasons, given the inferences we have already made about the attributes of God.[8]

God may allow pain and suffering to alert us to the problem that something is wrong with the world. In particular, natural and moral evil can help man see his need for God. Many people seem to ignore God, yet his loving and caring nature—exhibited by everything in creation that we have previously studied—suggests that he does not want to be ignored. Perhaps he wants to get our attention. Therefore, the reason for the magnitude, duration, and distribution of evil we observe might be to make us dissatisfied with our state of separation from God.

Pain alerts us to all sorts of serious physical problems in our everyday experience. For instance, chest pain can alert us to blocked arteries, stomach pain can alert us to an ulcer, and arm pain can alert us to a broken bone. As much as we hate pain, we have to admit that it often serves a good purpose. Pain is a siren that sounds to warn us when something goes wrong.[9] The *cause* of the distress, rather than the pain itself, is the real

---

[7] Peter Kreeft, as quoted in Lee Strobel, *The Case For Faith* (Grand Rapids, MI: Zondervan, 2000), 41.

[8] An attempt to present a positive case of why God allows evil is called a *theodicy*.

[9] Kurt De Haan, "Why Would a Good God Allow Suffering?" (Grand Rapids: MI, RBC Ministries, 1990, 1999), 5.

problem. Peter Kreeft writes, "The only long-range solution to pain, whether physical or spiritual, is to listen to what it is telling us. It is a symptom."[10] Suffering may very well be God's way to alert us that something is wrong with the world and, more importantly, with each one of us. C. S. Lewis explains, "God whispers to us in our pleasures, speaks in our conscience, but shouts in our pain: it is His megaphone to rouse a deaf world."[11]

If it is true that God is signaling a problem to us in our pain, then perhaps he is also using pain to encourage us to find the solutions in him. Suffering has a way of showing us how weak we really are, how our self-sufficiency is mostly a mirage. It humbles us to learn that there is much we cannot control in our lives. It forces us to take our eyes off our present situation and look at deeper issues. We might reevaluate our priorities, values, and goals, and take a closer look at our relationships with other people. It also has a way of directing our attention to spiritual realities, often producing in us a desire to seek after God.[12] This does not seem far-fetched at all, since it is a plain observation that most people are confused, indifferent, skeptical, or hostile towards God.

It could very well be that God's intention in creating human beings was to enter into relationship with us. God, being perfectly good, may want us to grow to moral maturity through first-hand experience of knowing evil. C. S. Lewis has this in mind when he says, "Love, in its own nature, demands the perfecting of the beloved."[13] Living in this world separated from God gives us certain kinds of experiences and knowledge that cannot be gained by creatures in any other way. Without pain and suffering we could not learn mercy, forgiveness, compassion, courage, perseverance, or patience, for example. These are all virtues that cannot be experienced in a world with no sin or evil. Suffering therefore encourages the acquisition of certain moral qualities.

By actually experiencing suffering, evil, and alienation from God, we could fully appreciate his love, justice, and mercy. We would then be in a position, when offered divine reconciliation and restoration, to choose the path that God desires for us. This possibility should cause us to be on the look-out for such clues. This life may not be all there is. God is an eternal Being and he may have in mind that human beings will experience life eternally in some way.[14] Perhaps we can look forward to a future life with no suffering. If so, then that future life would dwarf evil in this life to

---

[10] Kreeft, *Christianity for Modern Pagans*, 189.

[11] Lewis, *The Problem of Pain*, 91.

[12] De Haan, "Why Would a Good God Allow Suffering?", 15-19.

[13] Lewis, *The Problem of Pain*, 38.

[14] This is the subject of Question 3.

insignificance. This is not intended to minimize our present suffering, but to put it into perspective.

We cannot compare a temporal life of finite human suffering to an eternity filled with love, joy, meaning, and purpose if that is God's plan. Our limited human minds selfishly think that lives without pain would prove that God loves us, but this may not be the case.[15] Consider a mother who has her child immunized against measles. The child feels pain and hates it, however there is a greater good that he does not yet understand. Perhaps our life of suffering is like that, but on a much greater scale.

Milder forms of suffering

In addition to physical pain, we also experience a great deal of unhappiness, discontentment, disappointment, frustration, and anxiety in our lives. These may not be directly caused by evil; although it is likely we can trace even these more ordinary, circumstantial troubles to evil.

We are probably less happy than we think. We seek amusement and entertainment not only when we are poor and miserable, but even when we are rich and powerful. This is simple and experiential proof that wealth, power, and worldly success do not make us happy.[16] Pascal agrees: "If our condition were truly happy we should not need to divert ourselves from thinking about it."[17] A good argument can be made that the more a society advances technologically, the unhappier it becomes. We seem to have increasingly more free time, and we seek to fill it with more and more diversions that we think can satisfy us from the dreariness of our jobs. Kreeft concludes, "The society or individual which has the most diversions and amusements is not the happiest but the unhappiest."[18]

We tend to evaluate our circumstances in terms of whether or not they produce happiness, but fulfilling our conception of happiness may not be God's primary objective. Perhaps we are seeking happiness in all the wrong places, and like in the case of suffering, God wants to redirect our thinking. He might allow these other kinds of troubles for the same purpose that he permits suffering—to alert us to our separation from him and point us to a better way. C. S. Lewis described this condition like this:

> We are half-hearted creatures, fooling about with drink and sex and ambition when infinite joy is offered us, like an ignorant child who wants to go on making mud pies in a slum because he cannot imagine

---

[15] Lewis, *The Problem of Pain.*

[16] Kreeft, *Christianity for Modern Pagans,* 184.

[17] Pascal, *Pensées no. 70,* Kreeft, 169.

[18] Kreeft, *Christianity for Modern Pagans,* 169.

what is meant by the offer of a holiday at the sea. We are far too easily pleased.[19]

Indeed, perhaps we are too easily pleased with worldly pleasures. It is not so improbable to think that this is true of finite creatures who seem intent on ignoring the God who created them.

The existence of our unhappiness might very well point to an innate knowledge of happiness—a sort of collective repressed memory shared by all of humanity. Kreeft explains, "If we had no idea of happiness, we would not feel unhappy, for we would have no standard with which to measure our present state and call it lacking."[20] Kreeft wonders if perhaps we can prove a past paradise from our present unhappiness. He says that no person would be unhappy not to be a king unless he had once been a king and been dethroned. Man is unhappy to not be a king—that is, we all complain about our lives. Therefore, man must have once been this king of happiness and fallen from this state. If we never had something, we would not miss it. If we miss it, that means we once had it. Thus, we are unhappy to have one eye instead of two, but not two instead of three.[21] The happiness "we had" is not necessarily actual happiness in our present life, but a lingering remnant of our human past that is embedded deep within our hearts. We will return to this idea in Question 3.

Inequities of life

Why do bad things happen to good people and good things happen to bad people? We have all wondered about these perceived inequities in life. This also seems to be an example of something that is wrong with the world. This is a matter of justice. We intuitively expect virtuous behavior like kindness and hard work to pay off and, conversely, bad behavior such as pride, greed, and laziness to be penalized in some way.

We all long for justice, but we do not often see it in this world. Our instinctive desire for justice is part of the sense of morality we share, for the twin implications of objective morality is a duty to obey and accountability for disobedience. Accountability is necessary to fulfill justice. We all expect and want evildoers to pay a price.

As with the other problems we see in the world, we should take the longer term view of this. The existence of an all-loving, all-powerful, and all-knowing God should cause us to think that, ultimately, justice will be served. The inequities we experience in life simply give us more reasons for us to seek after God and understand what he expects of us.

---

[19] C. S. Lewis, *The Weight of Glory* (San Francisco: HarperCollins, 2001, orig. pub. 1949), 26.

[20] Kreeft, *Christianity for Modern Pagans*, 113.

[21] Ibid., 61.

CONCLUSION

What is wrong with the world?

Many of us have never realized how dreary and lifeless our existence would be without problems and difficulties.

Tim Hansel (1941-2009)
Hiker who suffered 35 years of debilitating pain from cracked vertebrae and crushed discs
You Gotta Keep Dancin'

As a Christian theist, I'm persuaded that the problem of evil, terrible as it is, does not in the end constitute a disproof of the existence of God. On the contrary, in fact, I think that Christian theism is man's last best hope of solving the problem of evil.

William Lane Craig (1949-)
Philosopher, scholar, author
The Problem of Evil[1]

Suffering is the pain that living beings feel because of evil in the world. The problem of evil is fundamentally, in the words of C. S. Lewis, the problem of pain.[2] Any true worldview needs to explain why evil and suffering exists and why there is so much of it. If we get the diagnosis wrong, then we have little hope of getting the prescription right.

Many pantheists believe that evil is not real— it is an illusion. This goes against our deepest intuitions and experiences, though. Evil is patently real and we need to face it squarely. Atheists say that human suffering disproves the existence of a benevolent God. Either God does not exist or he has lost control of the world. They say the existence of evil

---

[1] Article on www.reasonablefaith.org.
[2] C. S. Lewis, *The Problem of Pain*.

makes it impossible for an all-loving and all-powerful God to exist. An omnipotent God surely would not allow the excessive amounts of evil we observe in the world.

We have seen, however, that these challenges do not stand up to examination. First of all, atheism has no grounds to call any act or event evil without a transcendent standard of goodness to compare it against. So, it turns out that the existence of evil, paradoxically, is an argument *for* the existence of God. This does not relieve the theist of the burden to answer the atheist's challenges, but it does show that the atheist has no resources in his view to explain the existence of real evil.

Evil is the absence of good; it is not a "thing" in itself. God did not create evil, but only the potential for evil by giving human beings free will. It is us who made evil a reality by using our freedom to make immoral choices that hurt not only others, but also ourselves.

So why does God permit evil? He must think that creating humans with free will is a greater good than a world without evil. God might allow evil because it is the best way to teach people eternally valuable lessons about right and wrong, good and evil, and their personal need for him. Moreover, human beings are in no position to conclude there is "too much evil" in the world. We cannot know how much God is presently limiting suffering, nor can we know how he is using it for purposes that we cannot fully understand. It seems entirely reasonable to believe that God allows evil to give us dissatisfaction with our separation from him so that we would turn to him. In this way, evil and suffering are temporary experiences that prepare us for some sort of relationship with God.

In the end, we must look at *all* the evidence. Even if we are not fully persuaded that both God and evil can coexist in the world, we must still deal with all the other evidence that God *does* exist. God is the best explanation for the existence of the universe, life, morality, meaning, and many other things that we have examined so far in this book, as well as others still to come. Although nobody wants to endure suffering, we can be encouraged that there are plausible explanations for its beneficent purpose in a theistic universe, whereas no ultimate purpose for suffering follows from atheism or pantheism.

To this point we have only discussed intellectual explanations for why evil and suffering exist. If God really is loving and caring like we concluded earlier, we might expect God to identify with our suffering in some deep and meaningful way, and indeed he does. This will be addressed in chapters 10 and 12.

Further reading

Mere Christianity, C. S. Lewis
Not The Way It's Supposed To Be, Cornelius Plantinga
The Problem of Pain, C. S. Lewis
Unspeakable: Facing Up to the Challenge of Evil, Os Guinness

What happens after we die?

Some day we will have only one week to live. What is more real than that?

Peter Kreeft (1937-)
Scholar, philosopher, author
Christianity for Modern Pagans

We say that the hour of death cannot be forecast, but when we say this we imagine that hour as placed in an obscure and distant future. It never occurs to us that it has any connection with the day already begun or that death could arrive this same afternoon, this afternoon which is so certain and which has every hour filled in advance.

Marcel Proust (1871-1922)
Novelist, essayist
The Guermantes Way

Death never takes the wise man by surprise; he is always ready to go.

Jean de La Fontaine (1621-1695)
Poet
Fables, book VIII

Everybody thinks about their own death at some time in their life. After all, death is the most certain fact of life, perhaps the *only* certain fact. The finality and mystery of death make the possibility of an afterlife such an imperative issue for us to investigate.

The atheist says that a person ceases to exist at death. There is no afterlife, and consequently no accountability for the present life. The pantheist agrees with the atheist in denying personal immortality. Physical death simply puts an end to conscious life and returns a person to nature. Theism makes life after death not only possible, but probable, given that

God himself is eternal and has infused value, meaning, and purpose into human beings. It is not a great leap to think that there is an afterlife that extends God's plans for humans.

Most people take one of several approaches in dealing with the thought of death.[1] Some simply ignore it. They might accept it, but they do not think about it and therefore do not prepare for it. Others do think about it, but they feel hopeless and helpless. They are driven by fear of what happens after their death because they have no idea how to prepare for it. Still others put their hope in some kind of scientific "solution" to death— that man will somehow invent a way to live forever through technological advancement. The rest of us place our faith in whatever our worldview holds as ultimate reality. For many that is God—and because he is eternal, he will somehow confer immortality on humans to give us life after death. Still, most people view life after death as highly uncertain and therefore are not very confident about how to get ready for it. Peter Kreeft compares our life journey towards death to an out of control car hurtling towards an inevitable plummet over a cliff:

> We are locked in a car (our body), rushing furiously down a hill (time), through fog (ignorance), unable to see ahead, over rocks and pits (wretchedness). The doors are welded shut, the steering works only a little, and the brakes are nonexistent. Our only certainty is that all the cars sooner or later fall over the edge of the cliff (death). So what do we do? We erect billboards at the edge of the cliff, so that we do not have to look at the abyss. The billboards are called "civilization". Our "solution" is the biggest part of the problem.[2]

Kreeft observes that most of us—even those of us who believe in God— live as if death is always far off, and so we largely ignore it.

The apparent permanence of death makes it look like an insoluble problem. After all, we regularly observe that people die and then are never seen or heard from again. Who can know what really happened to them? Perhaps it will surprise you to know that there are helpful clues and good evidence to help us answer this question.

---

[1] Based on Kreeft, *Christianity for Modern Pagans,* 145-146.
[2] Ibid., 145.

CHAPTER 6

Clues to an afterlife

You don't have a soul. You are a Soul. You have a body.
> C. S. Lewis (1898-1963)
> Theologian, author
> *Mere Christianity*

Now I disappear and die; in a moment I shall be nothing, for the soul is mortal as the body.
> Friedrich Nietzsche (1844-1900)
> Atheist philosopher
> *Thus Spoke Zarathustra*

It affects our whole life to know whether the soul is mortal or immortal.
> Blaise Pascal (1623-1662)
> Mathematician, physicist, inventor, philosopher
> *Pensées, no. 164*

In this chapter we will explore reasons to believe there may be life after death by examining various clues we find in our observations and experiences of the world. In particular, we will look at the evidence for the genuine existence of souls and discuss their possible implications for an afterlife.[1] If we are simply physical beings, then when our bodies die, *we* die because we *are* our bodies. On the other hand, if we are both a material body and an immaterial soul, then when our body dies it could be true that we continue to exist indefinitely in a disembodied state, or perhaps until

---

[1] I would like to thank my friend and Biola colleague, Arnie Gentile, for his particularly helpful insights and contributions to the discussion of souls in this chapter.

we receive a new body.[2] Are souls an objective reality—something that genuinely exists—or are they simply a meaningless concept that we have invented as a way to speak poetically about our "inner" selves? This will be a major focus of the chapter.

What kind of world is this?

In chapter 2 we discussed two main approaches for explaining what kind of world we live in. One approach holds that the universe—including human beings—is composed of only physical stuff. Recall that this view is called *physicalism*, which means that humans do not have any non-physical aspects, but are purely physical in nature. In this view, everything in the universe can be explained solely through chemical, biological, and physical properties that are accessible only through scientific methods to discover their shape, size, weight, color, and other physical characteristics.

The other approach for explaining the world is to recognize the universe is composed of both physical and non-physical things. In previous chapters we discussed the reality of immaterial aspects of human beings such as, consciousness, reason, free will, language, significance, and morality. These are not physical things, but they really do exist. There are many non-physical things like this in the world, such as thoughts, knowledge, happiness, love, friendship, and virtues. These things do not extend into space, do not weigh anything, do not have a taste or a smell to them, and do not have any shape.[3] Nevertheless, they certainly seem to be real, so they must exist in a non-physical or immaterial realm. As a matter of fact, most of what is important to us is unseen and non-physical. This is a valuable insight, for it causes us to doubt physicalism and to suspect there is a more convincing explanation of the world.

The existence of mental entities

The sorts of non-physical things we just listed are called *mental* entities because they are experienced in the mind. There are at least three kinds of mental entities. One kind are *sensations*, such as our experience of colors, tastes, sounds, smells, textures, pains, and itches. Sensations are not identical to the things outside the body that stimulate or cause them. The sensations are characterized by a certain conscious feel that make us somehow aware of them within our mind.[4]

---

[2] Gary R. Habermas and J. P. Moreland, *Beyond Death: Exploring the Evidence for Immortality* (Eugene, OR: Wipf & Stock, 1998), 37.

[3] Moreland, *Scaling the Secular City*, 81.

[4] Habermas and Moreland, *Beyond Death*, 44.

Another kind of mental entity is a *feeling* or *attitude* towards or about something. Examples include thoughts, beliefs, values, hopes, desires, and emotions. When we have a feeling about something there is also a particular content of what the feeling is concerned with. Hope is a certain kind of attitude or feeling, but I can hope for many different kinds of things. For instance, I might have a hopeful expectation to go on a trip, but I could also hope to not lose my job. Although the feeling of hope is comparable in both cases, these two hopes have very different meanings because of their content. Similarly, I could fear taking an exam at school, but also fear a stranger in a dark alley. Fear is the same feeling in both instances, but there is a different quality and intensity to each. Feelings often involve a tone that is pleasant or painful, which causes some sense of appeal or distaste.[5] Since there are many different kinds of feelings with a nearly endless list of possible content, they can present very rich and diverse mental experiences.

A third kind of mental entity is *volition*, the intention to bring something about. These are acts of the will to deliberate, determine, and decide. They indicate a purposefulness to act in one way and not another. This is what we mean when we say we have free will. For example, I might choose to raise my hand, pet my dog, or go to a movie. These actions require an act of my will before I physically perform them with my body.

Mental entities can be described in terms of events and states. A mental event is a transitory occurrence of a sensation or feeling. Momentarily perceiving a rainbow is an example of a mental event. A mental state is an ongoing, conscious awareness of a sensation or feeling. Being happy or angry are examples of mental states. The mind is capable of experiencing multiple mental events and states simultaneously.

The mind and the brain

Is your mind the same thing as your brain? Some people would say yes. Physicalists generally argue that thoughts, pains, emotions, and so forth are simply physical properties and physical events of the brain and central nervous system. They point out that for every so-called mental event, a corresponding change in brain activity can be demonstrated. For example, an incident of pain or an occurrence of a thought is attended by the stimulation of neurons that are extensively interconnected through synapses.[6] This is said to prove that mental entities are identical to physical entities. If this is true, then the scientist could describe these

---

[5] Dallas Willard, *Renovation of the Heart* (Colorado Springs: NavPress, 2002), 32.
[6] Habermas and Moreland, *Beyond Death*, 43.

events solely in terms of the chemical and physical properties of the brain so that everything true of brain states would also be true of mind states, and vice versa. If this is not true, however, then physicalism must be false.

We have already suggested that mental states such as "I am happy," and mental events such as "I saw a rainbow," cannot be described exclusively in physical terms. They cannot be observed, weighed, or measured; therefore it seems that brain states/events and mind states/events cannot be identical. Let's look in more detail at the ways that mental entities differ from physical entities.

Private access to mental entities

Mental entities have the unique characteristic that the individual having them has private access to them and knows them for certain. I alone know what my thoughts or feelings are merely by paying attention to them. I can inspect them internally, but a scientist cannot inspect them at all. All he can do is monitor my brain states. Take for example the mental event of a sensation of pain. I have private access to my feeling of pain—nobody else is feeling the sensation I have when I am stuck with a needle. Likewise, I know such a sensation undeniably, which means I cannot be wrong about it, whether or not there really is a needle sticking me. Science can neither confirm nor refute this sensation. The only way a scientist can know my thoughts and feelings is if I tell him what they are.[7]

A brain surgeon may know more about my brain than I do by examining it with his scientific instruments, but he does not and cannot know my mental life as I do.[8] Picture a football in your mind. If a scientist were to open up your brain, he could not find a football. You would be having a sensory experience of a football, but no picture of a football could be found by examining your brain. Thus, the sensory event of imagining a football cannot be a physical event of the brain.[9] Therefore, your mind—the place where your mental events occur—is not your brain.

Intentionality of mental entities

Many mental entities exhibit a special characteristic called *intentionality*, which means they are *of* or *about* something other than themselves. Physical stuff can be bigger than, heavier than, softer than, or further away from other things, but it cannot be *of* or *about* anything other than itself. I can have a thought *about* my wife or a feeling *of* relief, though. These are intentions about things other than myself. Physical things are not like that; they can have no intentions.

---

[7] Ibid., 50.

[8] Moreland, *Scaling the Secular City*, 84-85.

[9] Habermas and Moreland, *Beyond Death*, 49.

The subjective nature of experience

Consciousness is the center of our self-awareness and what makes it possible for us to experience the objective world around us. It makes sense to say that *I* am active, vibrant, and alive—and not just that my body is. Philosophers Moreland and Habermas explain:

> When we pay attention to our own consciousness, we can become aware of a very basic fact presented to us: We are aware of our own self (ego, I, center of consciousness) as being distinct from our bodies and from any particular mental experience we have. I simply have a basic, direct awareness of the fact that I am not identical to my body or my mental events; rather, I am the self that *has* a body and a conscious mental life.[10]

Physicalism has no plausible explanation for consciousness. I am not merely a particular arrangement of molecules, but a *self* that *has* mental experiences of sounds, colors, tastes, thoughts, emotions, pains, and so on. There is something about *me* that exists beyond my physical body. Matter has no awareness of itself or anything else, but *I* somehow do have such an awareness.

My consciousness provides me a purely subjective vantage point. It is about me and my point of view, not the objective world outside of me. A physical-only description of the world would completely describe everything from a third-person perspective, but each of us has our own *first-person* perspective and experience.[11] *I* perceive, *I* contemplate, *I* experience, *I am*.

Personal identity through change

Are you literally the same person you were an hour ago, a year ago, or the day you were born? We have a very strong sense of personal identity that we are the same person today as we were in the past, and we will be the same person in the future. Our emotions can change, our memories can change, our beliefs can change, and our desires can change, but we always remain the same person. Only a single, enduring self can relate and unify emotions, memories, beliefs, and desires in this way. It is what makes us the *owner* of our experiences.[12] If this were not so, we could not have continuity of these mental events throughout our life.

Memories, beliefs, hopes, dreams, and even fears all presuppose unbroken personal identity over time. If we were not the same person in

---

[10] Ibid., 55.

[11] J. P. Moreland and Scott B. Rae, *Body & Soul: Human Nature & the Crisis in Ethics* (Downers Grove, IL: InterVarsity Press, 2000), 183-184.

[12] Habermas and Moreland, *Beyond Death*, 56.

the past, it is difficult to see how any of these mental entities could continue within our stream of consciousness to the present. I could not have a memory of taking a childhood camping trip if I were not the same person then as I am now. Nor could I fear anything about the future, such as going in for surgery, since I would not be the same person then as I am now. The whole concept of blame and reward presuppose sameness of persons over time, as well. Otherwise, how could *I* be punished today for a crime some *previous me* did earlier? Similarly, there could be no sensible expectation of life after death if we are not the same person prior to and following our death.

It is not our body that provides this continuity of self. The human body replaces most of its cells every seven to ten years, so we do not have anything close to the same body that we had even a decade ago. Yet, we intuitively know we are the *same* person. There must be something other than our body that provides our fundamental identity. Indeed, our identity is bound up in our mental life, in the immaterial aspects of who we are, and not in our physical properties.

Inadequate explanations for the immaterial realm

We have examined several reasons to believe that physicalism—the idea that all of reality can be explained solely in terms of chemistry, biology and physics—is not true. The existence of mental entities, and the fact that they are not identical to the physical entities that accompany them, strongly suggests that the mind is not the same thing as the brain. This conclusion is significantly strengthened by the reality of our private access to mental entities, the intentionality of mental entities, our subjective experiences through our consciousness, and our retention of personal identity through change. Everything about human beings cannot be explained exclusively in physical terms, so there must be an immaterial component to who we are as human beings.[13]

There are some people who reject physicalism, yet view mental entities as mere properties of the physical body.[14] A *property* is something that exists universally, meaning that it can be in more than one thing at a time. For example, greenness can be in the grass and a bowl of peas at the same time. Properties are also immutable, which means that they can come and go, but they do not change their inherent nature. When a leaf changes from red to green, it is the leaf that changes by losing an old property and gaining a new one. The property of redness does not change by becoming

---

[13] The opposing view to physicalism is called *dualism*, which means there is something physical and also something non-physical to our being.

[14] This view is called *property* dualism.

greenness. Properties are in the things that have them and have no causal powers to do anything.[15]

A *substance* is something that fundamentally exists by itself as a particular, individual entity that cannot be in more than one place at a time. It also remains the same thing through change. A leaf that changes from red to green is the same leaf before, during, and after the change. A substance also has the ability to do things. It can cause things to happen. A dog can bark and a leaf can fall to the ground, for instance. Therefore, dogs and leaves are examples of substances. Unlike a property, a substance is not possessed by something else in order to exist. Rather, it exists in its own right and *has* properties.[16]

In the view that mental entities are immaterial properties of the brain, there are no independent *mental* substances, only *physical* substances. Although mental states may not be identical to brain states, they are nonetheless fully dependent on the brain for their existence. They are mental conscious processes that simply happen to accompany physical neural processes. They have no autonomous, causal powers of their own. They are kind of like sparks that fly off a fire. Just as the sparks cannot exist without the fire, mental entities cannot exist without corresponding physical processes.

When I experience a thought, my brain possesses two distinct properties simultaneously. One is a physical property that can be described in chemical and electrical terms, which is caused by neurons that are stimulated within my brain. There is also a certain mental property concurrently possessed by the brain—the thought itself and its felt quality.[17] If this view were true, however, there would be no self that *has* a mental life. Rather, the brain would be the real possessor of that mental life, yet the brain, as a mere physical entity, is not conscious. We are not merely a collection of conscious experiences, though. Rather, we *are* a center of consciousness that *has* those collective experiences. It is what enables us to engage in acts of introspection in which we are aware of what is going on "inside" of us. Consciousness cannot be a mere mental property of our body. Something that is self-aware must be a substance that transcends the physical realm in a way that allows us to understand and experience reality.

Furthermore, if mental states and events were properties that come and go, they would be a series of separate, disconnected experiences that are in no sense unified in an enduring self. Personal identity would not be possible in this view. These observations run contrary to our earlier

---

[15] Moreland, *Scaling the Secular City*, 79.
[16] Habermas and Moreland, *Beyond Death*, 41-42.
[17] Ibid., 45-46.

conclusions that we are fundamentally a conscious self who is directly aware of our experiences and who also remains the same over time. Therefore, the view that mental entities are properties of the body is not an adequate explanation for the immaterial aspect of a person.

The reality of the soul

The immaterial aspects of human beings we have discovered suggest the reality of what has been traditionally called the *soul*.[18] Our soul is a mental and invisible entity which makes it possible for us to be aware of ourselves and our experiences. It is what makes each of us a conscious and living being. The soul is a *substance* that is distinct from our body.[19] We are inclined to think of substances as only being material things, but this does not have to be the case.

Every feature we are now ascribing to the soul—a concrete individual entity possessing properties, essential capacities and causal powers, and faculties of mind and spirit—are features of *me* as well. *I* am a substance with free will and causal powers because my soul is a substance, distinct from my body. *I* am an individual conscious self with private access to my inner mental life because my soul, as an immaterial substance, is the center of consciousness within me. My identity endures through time because my soul, as an enduring substance, remains the lasting essence of who *I* am. Personal identity through time is only possible, not because I have the same body, but because I have the same soul at every point in my life, even as my body decays. It is therefore not too strong to assert that *I am my soul*.

Consequently, a human being is a unity of two distinct realities—a body and a soul—which regularly interact with one another.[20] Some people may wonder how two things that are so fundamentally different from one another can have a cause and effect relationship, but it does not seem hard to believe that the non-physical and physical can interact. The existence of God, which we established in previous chapters, demonstrates this clearly. God is a transcendent, immaterial Being that brought into being and presently sustains both the physical and non-physical components of the universe. Therefore, it is not only possible, but rational to believe that physical and non-physical things can interrelate. We can

---

[18] The concept of the soul has been discussed by philosophers at least since the time of the ancient Greeks in the fourth and fifth centuries BC. Plato believed that human beings consisted of two distinct entities, body and soul. He thought the body, being of this world, is completely physical, and the soul, which is infused at birth into the body, is spiritual and immortal. Plato believed the soul represents our true self.

[19] This view is called *substance* dualism.

[20] Animals likely have souls as well, although they would be much less sophisticated than those of human beings.

easily think of examples of mutual interaction, influence, and causation between body and soul. For instance, an episode in the body such as a head injury can cause a loss of memory in the soul. Likewise, stubbing your toe can cause a painful sensation that is felt in your soul. The soul can also influence the body. For example, worry in the soul can cause an ulcer in the body and deciding to lift your arm causes your arm to raise.[21] There are thousands of potential direct and immediate interactions like this between a soul and its body.

Implications of the soul

We are not merely a physical body, but an embodied soul. There are two realms to existence, one visible (physical) and one invisible (non-physical), and human beings are privileged to be part of both. Here are two important implications of the existence of souls.

Human life has dignity beyond what we see in the body

The existence of human souls provides a powerful argument about how we should view human persons. Considering all the special capabilities of the soul, it is arguably the most important part of what makes a human being a person. Indeed, our essence as persons is our soul, which is entirely unseen. A proper view of the human soul challenges the rightness of such practices as abortion, embryonic stem cell research, and euthanasia, and also how we should value the mentally challenged and people in comas, for instance. We should take care to not assess these issues from a purely physical point of view. Lack of self-awareness or diminished capacities do not reduce the dignity and worth of the persons involved in these situations—persons with invisible souls made by God.

There may be life after death

Since the soul is a separate substance from the body, it can theoretically exist independent of its body—even though embodiment may be the soul's natural mode of existence.[22] This gives us reason to believe that the death of our body does not have to mean the death of our soul. Rather, it is possible that the soul can continue to live apart from the body. Since I *am* a soul that *has* a body, it is reasonable to think that I can

---

[21] Habermas and Moreland, *Beyond Death*, 87.

[22] Since we observe that the death of the body renders it inanimate and permanently unable to function, it is likely that the body is not capable of surviving without a soul. Indeed, some philosophers hold that the body itself is not a substance, but rather "an ensouled biological and physical structure that depends on the soul for its existence." Moreland and Rae, *Body & Soul*, 201. If this is true, then the body needs a soul, but a soul does not need a body.

survive bodily death as a soul only. This does not imply that the soul is inherently immortal, since we know only God possesses intrinsic immortality. The soul's extraordinary features certainly make it possible, though—and perhaps likely—that God has plans for human life beyond bodily death. This leads us to another intriguing clue of an afterlife.

Near death experiences

A near death experience (NDE) is a close encounter somebody has had with death and lived to tell about it. What makes some NDEs special, though, is the reported conscious experience the persons had while being in a near death state. These types of encounters are so close to death, in fact, that those reporting them often make claims of floating above their dying body, traveling down a dark tunnel, being welcomed by a being of light, hearing beautiful sounds, and even meeting deceased loved ones. Oftentimes, those who have had these experiences also report they no longer fear death.[23]

No doubt there are many suspect claims of NDEs; however it is fascinating that some NDE reports are accompanied by verifiable evidential claims. For instance, Habermas reports:

> [I]n dozens of NDE accounts, the dying person claims that, precisely during their emergency, they actually observed events that were subsequently confirmed. These observations may have occurred in the emergency room when the individual was in no condition to be observing what was going on around them. Sometimes the data are reported from a distance away from the scene and actually may not have been observable from the individual's location even if they had been healthy, with the normal use of their senses. In more evidential cases, the dying person reported their observations during extended periods of time without any heartbeat. On rare occasions, no brain activity was present in the individual either. Further, blind persons have also given accurate descriptions of their surroundings, even when they had never seen anything either before or since.[24]

Habermas goes on to relate a well-documented case involving a little girl named Katie, who had nearly drowned. She had massive brain swelling and was profoundly comatose as she lay on the emergency room operating table attached to an artificial lung machine. The attending physician suspected irreversible brain damage had occurred, which gave her little

---

[23] Gary R. Habermas, "Near Death Experiences: Evidence for an Afterlife?", *Evidence for God: 50 Arguments for Faith from the Bible, History, Philosophy, and Science* (Grand Rapids: Baker Books, 2010), William A. Dembski and Michael R. Licona editors, 24.

[24] Ibid., 25.

chance of surviving. However, to everyone's amazement, Katie made a complete recovery three days later. What the physicians and her family heard next was remarkable.

Katie was able to describe in great detail all the events of her ER visit, including what the room was like, the specific details of her resuscitation, and a physical description of the two physicians who attended to her. Katie also described an encounter she had with an angel named Elizabeth, who "took" her to visit her home during the ordeal. Katie was able to accurately describe all sorts of things from this visit, including what her siblings and parents were doing, where they were in the home, what they were wearing, what song her sister was listening to, and what meal her mom was making for dinner.[25]

Many attempts have been made to explain accounts like these in terms of natural psychological causes, such as hallucinations. These kinds of subjective approaches might be able to explain purely visionary accounts, but they do not account for cases accompanied by verified, external observations, especially at a distance from the dying body. Neither can they explain the ability of blind persons to report their surroundings.

What can we conclude from verifiable NDEs? It is difficult to determine anything about the *nature* of an afterlife for two reasons. First, since the stories are so disparate, it is not easy to find a common description of an afterlife from among them. Second, because descriptions of the afterlife are the most subjective parts of the NDE accounts, we have no means to independently verify them.

At the very least, NDEs do provide confirmatory evidence of the reality of the human soul and the possibility of its continued existence apart from the body, especially a body that is very near death. Not only this, but it appears the soul is able to somehow see and hear without a physical body. Perhaps we can go so far as to say that near death experiences are evidence of the initial moments of an afterlife, even if we cannot be sure from the experiences themselves what that afterlife is really like. Nevertheless, these modest conclusions represent a powerful clue to life beyond the present one.

---

[25] Habermas cites two books from the same author for this story. Melvin Morse (with Paul Perry), *Closer to the Light: Learning from the Near-Death Experiences of Children* (New York: Random House, 1990), 3-14 and Morse, *Transformed by the Light: The Powerful Effect of Near-Death Experiences on People's Lives* (New York: Random House, 1992), 22-23. Morse was Katie's ER physician.

Reasons to believe in life after death

We have examined in some detail the strong likelihood that the human soul exists. Furthermore, it is rational to believe that, as an immaterial substance, the soul can survive bodily death. In addition to this, we have seen evidence of verifiable near death experiences that is consistent with the existence of the soul that can live apart from the body. Together, these two findings are persuasive in suggesting the possibility of an afterlife.

There are additional reasons to believe in life after death. Here are three of them, which are based on our observation that this is a theistic universe and our understanding of what God is like. These reasons are not conclusive, but add suggestive evidence to our cumulative case for an afterlife.

The intrinsic value of human life

We have seen in previous chapters the great design, care, and concern that God has taken in creating this world. We also notice how human life stands at the pinnacle of creation in terms of complexity, intelligence, and ability. We also have considered how human life has meaning and purpose, and is subject to a moral law. All of this suggests that God bestows great intrinsic value on human beings.

In our human experience we normally think it wrong to destroy things of value. For example, in most cases, it would be wrong to demolish a fine painting because the world loses something of value as a result.[26] In a similar way, it would seem wrong for God to allow human life to be extinguished forever at bodily death. Philosopher Geddes MacGregor explains:

> If there is a Creator God who is infinitely benevolent as well as the source of all values, then he must be committed to the conservation of values. The highest values we know are experiences of the fulfillment of ideal purposes by individual persons. The existence of these values depends upon persons. God must, therefore, be the conserver of persons. Every argument for theism is an argument for the preservation of all persons whose extinction would seem to entail a failure on God's part in his benevolent purpose.[27]

This intrinsic and significant value might be reason to think that God would make human beings immortal.

---

[26] Habermas and Moreland, *Beyond Death*, 21.

[27] Geddes MacGregor, *Introduction to Religious Philosophy* (Washington, DC: University Press of America, 1981), 206.

Communion with God

An all-loving God would intend the highest good for his creatures, which would be communion with him as the most valuable and magnificent Being in existence. It certainly seems that human beings were made to be aware of and relate to God. It does not make sense that this relationship would be finite in duration, but would rather be endless, as that is a greater good. This is a further clue to the possibility of an afterlife.

Our desire for immortality

In addition to our capacities to think, to remember, to relate, to feel, to choose, and so on, we have the ability to *desire*, which means we wish or crave for things that bring us satisfaction and enjoyment. Some of our desires are short-term and relatively minor in importance, but we also have deeper desires for significant things like love, joy, meaning, and immortality.

Maybe we experience natural, innate, good desires *because* there are real objects that can fulfill them. We hunger and thirst because food and water are real and they satisfy us. Similarly, we long for love, joy, meaning, and immortality because they are real and can actually be obtained. C. S. Lewis thought along these lines when he wrote:

> Creatures are not born for desires unless satisfaction for these desires exists. A baby feels hunger; well, there is such a thing as food. A duckling wants to swim; well, there is such a thing as water. Men feel sexual desire; well, there is such a thing as sex. If I find in myself a desire which no experience in this world can satisfy, the most probable explanation is that I was made for another world.[28]

Perhaps earthly pleasures are meant, not to satisfy our need for significance and ultimate joy, but to arouse in us a desire to fulfill them more deeply in another life. It could very well be that our sense of and desire for immortality means that we were created to live forever in another place beyond this life.

Summary

Most of us hope there is life beyond the present one. Many of us even have a sense of immortality because of the deep value, meaning, and purpose we discern in the universe. In this chapter we have discovered that an afterlife is definitely possible because of the existence of our soul. In fact, the reality of the human soul and the extraordinary way in which God has fashioned it provide powerful clues that there *is* life after death.

---

[28] Lewis, *Mere Christianity*, 121.

CHAPTER 7

Back from the dead

By "resurrection" [the disciples] clearly meant that something had happened to Jesus himself. God had raised him, not merely reassured them. He was alive again.

James D. G. Dunn (1939-)
New Testament scholar, author
The Evidence for Jesus

The fact that dead people do not ordinarily rise is itself part of early Christian belief, not an objection to it. The early Christians insisted that what had happened to Jesus was precisely something new; was, indeed, the start of a whole new mode of existence, a new creation. The fact that Jesus' resurrection was, and remains, without analogy is not an objection to the early Christian claim. It is part of the claim itself...Jesus [was] raised in advance as a sign of what would later happen to everyone else.

N. T. Wright (1948-)
New Testament scholar, former bishop of Durham, author
The Resurrection of the Son of God

Although I do not deny that death embodies the chief unknown ever encountered by human beings, Jesus did experience it, and he conquered it by rising from the dead. While Jesus' resurrection does not tell us everything we may wish to know about the nature of eternal life, it does reveal enough that we need not be so fearful of death.

Gary R. Habermas (1950-)
Historian, philosopher of religion
The Risen Jesus & Future Hope

The best way to know what will happen after we die is to have it explained by somebody who speaks from the authority and experience of having died and returned to life. I am not talking about people who have had near death experiences. I am suggesting that a person who predicted his return from death—and was then brutally murdered, buried for three days, and later seen alive by hundreds of people over the course of several weeks—should cause us to stand up and take notice. If such a person really existed, then we should listen to what he says about life after death, since he would speak with impeccable authority.

Of course, I am speaking of a poor carpenter and itinerant preacher— Jesus of Nazareth—who lived in Palestine two thousand years ago. The description given above has been uniquely ascribed to this man. Nobody else in human history has led the way through death and then back again like Jesus did. What makes this distinctive event so compelling is the astonishing amount and quality of evidence for it.

Why we can trust the historical accounts of the end of Jesus' life

Jesus wrote no books, so we are dependent on his contemporaries who wrote about his life to know what he said and did. Much, but not all, of the accounts of the life of Jesus are recorded in the Christian Bible. It is clear that Jesus was a real person who was born, lived a relatively short life, and died. How can we be sure that what people wrote about him in the Bible is historically accurate?

Some people might be skeptical about the trustworthiness of the biblical authors because the claims made by Jesus and the events of his life are extraordinary. Just because Jesus was extraordinary, however, does not mean that witnesses could not reliably record what happened concerning his life. The key for us at this point in our investigation is to approach the Bible for what it claims to be in many places—an historical document that relates events of real people in real places at specific times in history.[1] There is much to be said about the historical trustworthiness of the Bible, and the next two chapters are devoted to it, but for now we want to briefly review some preliminary reasons why we can believe the Bible accurately reports the historical events about the end of Jesus' life.

Historians have ways to evaluate stories and events of the past to determine the likelihood that they really happened. They can test them on a case-by-case basis for authenticity, so we do not need to assume an error-free or even a "generally" reliable Bible in order to assess the historicity of the events surrounding the death of Jesus.[2] William Lane Craig explains,

---

[1] We will not now concern ourselves with any of the Bible's theological claims.

[2] These tests of authenticity are described in the next chapter.

"Scholars have developed a number of so-called 'criteria of authenticity' [to affirm that some event is actually historical]...In order to defend the historical credibility of some event in the life of Jesus, say, his burial, you don't need to defend the historical credibility of other events like his birth in Bethlehem, his feeding of the five thousand, his triumphal entry into Jerusalem, and so on. Specific incidents can be evaluated on their own by these criteria."[3] This authentication method provides an effective way to discern that biases, hidden agendas, or intentional deceptions have not found their way into accounts of specific events.

Virtually *all* New Testament scholars who research this area, including skeptics and critics, accept as historical facts that Jesus died by crucifixion, he was buried most likely in a private tomb, his disciples were initially despondent over these events, his tomb was discovered empty soon after his burial, his disciples believed they saw him physically alive following his death, the church was built on this belief in his resurrection,[4] the skeptics Saul and James came to believe in the resurrection, and Jesus' disciples eventually went to their deaths proclaiming this message.[5] This is not an argument from majority opinion, but rather a widespread acknowledgement of undeniable historical facts.

We must make a distinction between *evidence* and the *explanation* of that evidence. The facts of the past are accessible to the historian. Once the facts are established, the account that best explains all the facts is the one we should believe. Skeptical scholars who accept these facts try to account for them with natural—and not supernatural—explanations. The key point is that New Testament scholars, using well-established analytic methods, almost unanimously have accepted the events surrounding the end of Jesus' life as being historically certain.

Examining the historical facts

It is important to emphasize that this is an *historical* claim—that is, it is asserted that these events actually happened to a real man in a real place at a particular time in human history. Therefore, these claims can and should be evaluated using the same criteria as any other historical event.

---

[3] Craig, *On Guard*, 194-196.

[4] Resurrection differs from resuscitation, although both refer to returning to life after death. The latter means the recovery was made within minutes of death, usually by medical means. The body is in the same condition it was prior to death and will eventually die again. Resurrection, on the other hand, can occur days or years after death. The body is raised to perfection, never to die again.

[5] Gary Habermas arrived at this conclusion after conducting a bibliographical survey of over 2,200 publications on the resurrection of Jesus in English, French, and German since 1975. The empty tomb is not as widely accepted as the other facts, but is still accepted by a majority of contemporary scholars. Gary R. Habermas, *The Risen Jesus & Future Hope* (Lanham, MD, Rowman & Littlefield Publishers, 2003), 9.

We should follow the evidence where it most reasonably leads without being biased by preconceived ideas or conclusions. We will examine five of these historical facts about Jesus of Nazareth in more detail:

1. His death by crucifixion
2. His burial in a private tomb
3. The discovery of his empty tomb
4. His postmortem appearances
5. The transformation of his followers

Jesus' death by crucifixion

Roman crucifixion was a gruesome and effective means for killing people. The extremely cruel method inflicted an incredible amount of pain that always resulted in death.

Jesus' ordeal began in Jerusalem late on a Thursday evening during Jewish Passover week when he was arrested and all his followers fled. He was then put through six separate trials.[6] He was first sentenced to be beaten. Roman floggings were known to be horribly brutal. They usually consisted of thirty-nine lashes, but frequently more, using a whip embedded with sharp jagged pieces of bone and metal. When the whip struck the body of Jesus, it caused deep contusions and tears in his flesh. Research scientist and medical doctor Alexander Metherell has studied this in detail. He explains, "The back would be so shredded that part of the spine was sometimes exposed by the deep, deep cuts. The whipping would have gone all the way from the shoulders down to the back, the buttocks, and the back of the legs...We know that many people would die from this kind of beating even before they could be crucified. At the least, the victim would experience tremendous pain and go into hypovolemic shock."[7]

Jesus somehow survived this horrific torture and was then forced to carry his own one hundred pound crossbeam to the site of his crucifixion by Friday mid-morning. He was nailed to the wooden horizontal bar with seven inch spikes, most likely through his wrists. This would have crushed his median nerve, the largest nerve going to each hand, which would have caused unbearable pain.  He was then raised onto the vertical beam, where his feet were similarly nailed, causing even more agonizing pain. Metherell explains how this

---

[6] His judges were, respectively, Annas, Caiaphas, the whole Jewish Council, Pilate the first time, Herod, and Pilate a second time.

[7] Alexander Metherell, as quoted in Strobel, *Case for a Creator*, 195-196. Hypovolemic shock is an emergency condition in which severe blood and fluid loss makes the heart unable to pump enough blood to the body. This type of shock can cause many organs to stop working.

further stressed Jesus' body: "His arms would have immediately been stretched probably about six inches in length, and both shoulders would have become dislocated."[8]

Crucifixion is essentially an excruciatingly slow death by asphyxiation.[9] The slumping posture of the body on the cross puts the chest into an inhaled position. In order to exhale, the victim must lift his body by pushing it up with his feet. After exhaling, he could momentarily relax to take in another breath before having to push his body upwards again. Eventually he becomes completely exhausted and suffers cardiac arrest due to asphyxiation. Jesus endured this agonizing process for six hours, struggling to breathe and scraping his mutilated back on the wooden beam while alternately pushing himself upward and collapsing downward again. Eventually, a Roman soldier thrust a spear into Jesus' side and officially pronounced him dead around 3pm on Friday afternoon.[10] There is simply no doubt that Jesus died on the cross from suffocation and loss of blood.

Jesus' burial in a private tomb

The body of Jesus was taken down from the cross and wrapped in linen with seventy-five pounds of spices. It was then placed in a new rock-carved tomb donated by a wealthy Jewish man named Joseph of Arimathea, a member of the Jewish Council that condemned Jesus. A large, two ton stone was rolled into place to cover the entrance to the tomb and was sealed with the mark of the Roman governor. A guard unit was also posted to watch over the tomb day and night because of fear that Jesus' followers might attempt to steal his body.[11] These security measures made it clear that Jesus was indeed inside the tomb and guaranteed that no interference with the burial place would occur.

The discovery of Jesus' empty tomb

On the Sunday morning following the crucifixion and burial, women followers of Jesus discovered the stone had been rolled away up a small

---

[8] Ibid., 198.

[9] *Excruciating* literally means "out of the cross," a term coined because of the uniquely agonizing pain of being crucified.

[10] Normally, the soldiers would break the legs of a victim while he was on the cross to hasten death, since he would no longer be able to lift himself for a breath. The acceleration of death was necessary due to the late hour and the need for the bodies to be buried prior to the Sabbath, beginning at sunset on Friday. The legs were broken of the two criminals who were crucified alongside Jesus, but this was not necessary for Jesus since he was already dead.

[11] The Roman governor, Pontius Pilate, authorized the guard at the request of the Jewish authorities, but it is not clear whether the guard unit was comprised of Roman soldiers or Jewish temple guards. It hardly matters, however, since either would have been competent for this duty.

incline, the tomb was empty, and the guards had fled. The strips of linen that had wrapped Jesus' body were lying in the tomb, as well as the burial cloth that had been around his head. The cloth was folded up by itself, separate from the linen.

Both Jewish and Roman sources and traditions acknowledge the tomb was empty. In fact, the Jews admitted this very fact when they claimed that his followers stole the body of Jesus. Of course, this would have been an impossible feat with all the security measures that had been taken.

Jesus' postmortem appearances

An empty tomb is certainly intriguing, but a missing body does not, by itself, prove that a resurrection has occurred. At the same time, we do not need to actually witness a resurrection event happen before our very eyes to conclude that one has occurred. If the deceased person suddenly showed up walking, talking, eating, and allowing us to touch him, that would be evidence enough. People who have died normally do not do that, especially ones who have been dead for three days. [12]

Following his burial, Jesus made at least twelve appearances to various groups of people under all kinds of circumstances and gave many convincing proofs that he was alive. [13] His disciples at first thought they were seeing a vision of Jesus, but he assured them by eating and talking with them that he was really there in the flesh. On one occasion Jesus was seen by over five hundred people. Even the most skeptical, his disciple Thomas, worshiped Jesus as Lord and God after physically examining the wounds from his crucifixion. These experiences of Jesus' appearances convinced these observers that Jesus was alive again in flesh and blood.

Jesus did not only appear to his disciples. He also appeared to some of his most hostile critics, like his brother James. The most notable case, though, was Saul of Tarsus, a ruthless persecutor of Jesus' followers, who became one of the greatest proclaimers of his resurrection. The sheer number of eyewitnesses serves to validate the postmortem appearances of Jesus as fact. The report could easily have been refuted if it was inaccurate, but there is no evidence of this happening.

---

[12] Jesus was not in the tomb for three 24-hour periods, but rather across three days—Friday evening, all day Saturday, and Sunday morning. The Jewish custom was to reckon this period as 3 days.

[13] 1) Mary Magdalene, 2) Mary Magdalene and other Mary, 3) Peter, 4) two disciples, 5) ten apostles, 6) all apostles, 7) seven apostles, 8) all apostles, 9) more than 500 people, 10) James, 11) all apostles, 12) Paul.

The transformation of Jesus' followers

The changed lives of the early Christians provide the most compelling proof of the resurrection. Something revolutionary had to have happened to motivate this frightened, confused, and cowardly group to radically change their lives and go to their deaths proclaiming the resurrected Jesus as their central message. They abandoned numerous Jewish beliefs and traditions that had deep religious meaning to them. These beliefs and traditions were vitally important to the Jews because they contributed to their national identity that has allowed them to survive as a people group for more than 3,500 years now. Here are twelve significant changes made by these Jews who became the first Christians:

1. They held firm to their monotheism, but came to see the one Being who is God, as three distinct persons—The Father, Son [Jesus], and Holy Spirit.

2. They came to understand that the promised Messiah was God himself, coming in the form of the man Jesus.[14]

3. They also understood that the Messiah was to come twice, the first time to suffer and die for humanity and the second time to triumph over evil and establish his kingdom on Earth.

4. They began teaching that obedience to the Law was not sufficient to be saved, but that obedience must include faith in Jesus.[15]

5. They no longer offered animal sacrifices because of their understanding that Jesus was their once-for-all sacrifice for sins.

6. They no longer viewed the Temple in Jerusalem as the focal point of God's meeting with his people.

7. They began meeting for weekly worship on Sundays, rather than Saturdays, because that was the day Jesus was raised.

8. They began practicing baptism, rather than circumcision, as the outward sign of becoming a member of God's covenant family.

9. They began the regular observance of a ritual meal called *the Lord's Supper* to commemorate Jesus' dying for their sins and his demonstration of victory over death.

10. They no longer made ceremonially clean and unclean distinctions in the Jewish food laws and association with Gentiles[16] because God wanted them to see other nations as worthy of knowing him.

---

[14] The Jews had long expected a divinely anointed Redeemer whom they referred to as the *Messiah*.

[15] The Law refers to the commands God gave to Moses for the people of Israel to obey.

[16] A Gentile is a non-Jewish person.

11. They had a fervent desire to share their newfound faith, not only with their fellow Jews, but also with people of other nations.

12. They extended their sacred list of books to include twenty-seven new ones, known today as the New Testament, including the Gospels, The Acts of the Apostles, the epistles,[17] and Revelation.

These were not simply minor adjustments to their way of doing things, but monumental changes to cherished beliefs and practices. The disciples gave them up because the resurrection of Jesus produced in them a radical new way to view and live life.

The earliest Christians left their families, friends, and occupations to travel to remote lands preaching that Jesus died and came back to life. They were beaten, tortured, and murdered because of their allegiance to the risen Jesus. Nobody would willingly go to their death for what they knew was a lie. As eyewitnesses, these first believers were in a position to confirm or deny the resurrection. They saw Jesus alive again with their own eyes.[18]

Most of these eyewitnesses who were Jesus' closest followers eventually died for their faith according to church tradition. James, son of Zebedee, John's brother, was killed by the sword.[19] Andrew was crucified in Greece. Bartholomew was tortured, then beheaded in Armenia. James, son of Alphaeus, was clubbed to death in Jerusalem. Judas, son of James, (not Iscariot)[20] was crucified in Turkey or stoned to death in Persia. Matthew was speared to death in Ethiopia. Peter was crucified upside down in Rome. Philip was tortured to death in Turkey. Simon was crucified in Britain. Thomas was speared to death in India. Matthias was stoned and then beheaded in Jerusalem. James, the brother of Jesus, was stoned to death in Jerusalem. Paul was tortured, then beheaded in Rome. All but John were killed[21] because they could not deny what they witnessed with their own eyes—the resurrected Jesus.

The Christian church began shortly after Jesus appeared alive again after death. Thousands upon thousands of people abandoned their old beliefs and devoted their lives to Jesus. The church spread to Europe,

---

[17] An epistle is a letter. Twenty-one of the 27 books of the New Testament are epistles.

[18] This is the crucial difference between these apostolic martyrs and today's Islamic jihadists. The latter have been convinced by faith to die for their cause, but the original apostles were *eyewitnesses* to the very thing that produced their faith. This is an enormously significant difference. Upon threat of death for what they believed, they relied on their flesh and blood experience of the risen Christ, which they simply could not deny. Otherwise, they surely would have recanted at some point prior to their torturous deaths.

[19] This is the only account of a disciple's death that is specifically recorded in the Bible.

[20] Judas Iscariot is the disciple who betrayed Jesus and then committed suicide before Jesus was killed.

[21] John was not martyred, but rather died of old age after being exiled for his faith to the tiny island of Patmos in the Aegean Sea.

Africa, and Asia within a few decades. Because of the testimony of these early disciples and those that followed them, Christianity became the official religion of the entire Roman Empire within three hundred years.

The emergence of the Christian church is one of the strongest evidences for the resurrection of Jesus. This was a group of people who were primarily part of the lower class. They had no money or power, but this small group of men and women radically changed the entire known world. Moreover, they did this despite horrific persecution that caused many of them to be tortured and killed. Despite the persecution, the number of people who believed in Jesus and his resurrection steadily grew. Common sense would say that you run away from something that is killing other people, not embrace it—unless, of course, you are convinced that it is true and worth dying for.

Explaining the evidence

The facts about Jesus' death, burial, empty tomb, postmortem bodily appearances, and the transformation of his followers are extremely well-attested and accepted by virtually all New Testament scholars. Now they must be interpreted and explained.

The best explanation of these facts is a supernatural one—God raised Jesus from the dead. All other explanations seek to avoid a supernatural cause, but every one of them falls short because they cannot explain *all* the facts in a plausible and compelling way. Moreover, these alternate theories are no more than fanciful ideas without any first century evidence to support them. This is a crucial point. The skeptic who wants to deny the resurrection must not only provide an explanation of all the facts, but also cite credible sources to contradict the primary source evidence we already possess. Unfortunately for the skeptics, they fail on both counts. Let's examine the most popular of these naturalistic theories.

The Substitution Theory

This theory claims that it was not Jesus who died on the cross, but an imposter.[22] Several groups have advanced this theory, including Muslims, who believe that Jesus was a prophet whom God would not allow to be killed. The Qur'an says, "They declared: 'We have put to death the Messiah, Jesus Son of Mary, the apostle of God.' They did not kill him, nor did they crucify him, but they thought they did" (4:157). It is not clear who is supposed to have made the substitution or why, but the theory contradicts the evidence, nonetheless.

---

[22] Against any evidence whatsoever, some people even claim it was an unknown twin brother of Jesus!

First, Jesus was betrayed by one of his closest followers—Judas Iscariot—and was immediately taken into custody by the authorities, so there could be no mistaken identity or opportunity for a switch. Second, Jesus' strong yet calm behavior during his trials, sometimes remaining silent, would be inconceivable for a last minute substitute facing torture and execution. Third, the execution was quite public, and so a stand-in for Jesus would have been easily exposed. Fourth, Jesus' followers surely would have discovered the hoax when they wrapped his dead body and buried it. Fifth, and probably the most compelling reason, is that this theory cannot explain the empty tomb. Certainly the ruse would have been uncovered when the Jews and Romans produced the corpse of the imposter in the face of Jesus' subsequent appearances.

The Swoon Theory

This theory claims that Jesus did not die on the cross, but instead either passed out or faked his death. He was then somehow revived in the dampness of his tomb. The empty tomb and his bodily appearances are therefore explained because Jesus allegedly never died. There are three major problems with this hypothesis, though.

First, it is impossible to fake death on a cross. Surviving the gruesome beatings, being nailed to a cross, and hanging for hours in a posture that causes asphyxiation would certainly result in death, as we have already discussed. Besides this, the Roman executioners were not incompetent. They were professional and skilled killers whose own lives were on the line should they allow one of their victims to survive. Because Jesus was already dead, the Roman soldier pierced his side rather than break his legs. This piercing of the heart would have dealt the death blow if the crucifixion had not already done so.

Second, if it was possible to somehow survive all this torture *and* deceive the Roman soldiers and the crowd of spectators, how could the appearance of this tortured, emaciated survivor excite and motivate his followers? One of the facts in evidence is the complete transformation of Jesus' followers. They went from frightened and confused cowards to passionate proclaimers of Jesus' glorious resurrection. In fact, they went to their deaths declaring this very message. There is no way a bloodied and battered half-dead man who somehow managed to stagger to the door of his former followers would be embraced as the Messiah of the world and inspire them to martyrdom.

Third, the idea that Christ would fake his death and then deceitfully pass himself off as the resurrected Messiah contradicts everything else we know about his righteous character and teaching over the course of his life and ministry.

The Stolen Body Theory

This theory claims that Jesus really died and was buried, but his disciples stole his body and then lied about it. Even though this hypothesis can explain the death and empty tomb, it is not hard to see the many problems with it.

First, stealing the body would be the furthest thing from the minds of Jesus' followers. They were distraught at the death of their Master and confused about what they thought they knew about him. They were hardly in a frame of mind to concoct a story such as a fake resurrection.

Second, they had not even understood that Jesus said he would be raised from the dead. Jews expected a corporate resurrection at the end of time, not an individual resurrection before then.

Third, a small band of poor fishermen would not really be the sort to overcome or fool the soldiers who were guarding Jesus' tomb. These are the same frightened and timid guys who had fled when Jesus was arrested.

Fourth, someone who steals a corpse would not take the time to remove the burial cloths, fold them neatly, and leave them in the tomb.

Fifth, a stolen corpse is still a corpse. There would have been no postmortem appearances on this theory, yet Jesus appeared alive and in bodily form to hundreds of people. Two people who were very hostile to Jesus—Saul, later renamed Paul, and James—were converted because of their personal experience of seeing Jesus alive following his burial. This theory has no explanation for these radical conversions.

Sixth, liars do not make martyrs. If the disciples had stolen Jesus' body, and even if they decided to spend the rest of their lives proclaiming a lie that he was raised from the dead, would they really submit to a martyr's death knowing they had made up the whole thing? They certainly would have recanted their stories before the sword fell on their necks.

The Wrong Tomb Theory

This theory affirms that Jesus died, but explains the empty tomb by claiming that Jesus was never buried or his disciples went to the wrong tomb. The most obvious problem with this hypothesis is that, once Jesus' followers began declaring his resurrection around Jerusalem, the Romans or the Jews would have simply produced his decaying body from the right tomb. That would have been the end of the disturbance once and for all.

This theory suffers from additional problems. For one, it assumes the disciples would be ignorant of the location of Jesus' burial tomb. This is not credible considering their love and devotion to him after three years of very close friendship. Moreover, would Joseph of Arimathea really not know the location of the tomb he owned? The historical record even points out that some of the women "observed where he was laid" when he was buried. Furthermore, the presence of burial cloths in the empty tomb to which the disciples went indicates that they were at the correct tomb.

This theory also fails to explain Jesus' postmortem appearances because, after all, he is still dead in this view. Finally, this theory cannot explain the transformation of Jesus' disciples. No postmortem appearances means no transformation of his followers.

The Hallucination Theory

This theory claims Jesus' postmortem "appearances" were simply a mass hallucination, so Jesus did not really rise from the dead. All the supposed witnesses of the resurrection actually had the same subjective vision. As with the other naturalistic theories, this one suffers from multiple problems.

First, hallucinations are private, individual events. Hundreds of people could not share the same subjective visual perception, and especially not in twelve completely separate encounters with different groups of people in different circumstances. This is not like the case of a magic trick where many people are fooled, because those kinds of group experiences require a sense of expectation and emotional excitement. This was exactly the opposite of the disciples' state of mind. They were depressed, frightened, and confused due to the sudden and unexpected death of their beloved friend and leader. Furthermore, as noted previously, Jewish theology did not anticipate individual resurrections; rather they believed in a corporate resurrection of the righteous at the end of time. Jesus' followers were clearly not expecting him to be raised from the dead.

Second, why did the hallucinations abruptly end after forty days? The eyewitnesses did not continue to have them after Jesus left them.[23] Neither did any new believers have these visions.

Third, wouldn't any of the witnesses try to touch the risen Jesus and thereby discover the non-physical nature of their vision? In fact, the Gospels recount several such instances that demonstrate the bodily nature of Jesus' resurrection. For instance, as mentioned earlier, Jesus ate with the disciples and allowed them to touch his wounds from the crucifixion.

Fourth, hallucinations do not transform lives. People who have had hallucinations tend to forget them over time or deny them in the face of opposition. The disciples who were eyewitnesses to the resurrected Jesus, however, were beaten, tortured, and murdered while boldly preaching that Jesus died and came back to life, never recanting as a lie or hallucination what they had witnessed.

Fifth, this theory cannot explain the empty tomb. If Jesus really was not raised from the dead, then the fledgling religion could have been

---

[23] The records indicate that Jesus visibly ascended into Heaven forty days after his resurrection.

quickly crushed simply by exhuming his decaying body from the grave and thus proving to everyone that he was still dead.

No naturalistic theory is successful

All naturalistic theories of Jesus' resurrection fail. They simply cannot explain the full range of evidence. Only a resurrection explains all the evidence, so it is the simplest and most straightforward explanation. Naturalistic theories could be combined, but that only multiplies improbabilities. These theories, each by themselves, strain credulity. Combining them together would be *even more difficult* to believe. Such an approach does not follow the evidence where it leads, but rather grasps at straws to avoid a supernatural conclusion.

The resurrection of Jesus is not difficult to believe considering all the other evidence we have that this is a theistic universe. If God exists, then a miracle like a resurrection is entirely possible. Therefore, based on our reasonable conclusion that God exists and the strong historical evidence for this particular event—we have very good reasons to believe that God raised Jesus of Nazareth from the dead.

Why this matters

Jesus is not merely one among peers. He made claims of authority, mission, and identity that nobody ever did.[24] The only time in history that a resurrection can be verified, it happened to a person who predicted it would happen and who made specific claims that he was God's divine chosen messenger. God's stamp of approval must be on Jesus since it is difficult to believe that God would raise a heretic who would spawn a worldwide false religion that has now lasted for two millennia.

Therefore, it seems reasonable to believe that God's raising of Jesus validates everything that Jesus taught. In this way God uses historical truth to prove theological truth, so we should pay attention to what Jesus says. Since he went through death and returned, we should look to *him* to explain what happens after *we* die. Jesus had much to say about this. He said that he was the resurrection and the life, and that if we believed in him we would live, even though we would die in the body. This is consistent with our earlier conclusions that the human soul is likely able to survive death. Jesus went on to say that those who believe in him would *never* die, which is a promise of eternal life. In Jesus we now have the supreme authority to look to for what happens after we die.[25]

---

[24] We will discuss these in chapter 15.
[25] We will examine the nature of this afterlife in chapter 12.

CONCLUSION

What happens after we die?

Neither wealth nor fame and honor endures death; but truth does.
Peter Kreeft (1937-)
Scholar, philosopher, author
Christianity for Modern Pagans

Death is a certainty in life. The death rate per person is one hundred percent—everyone will experience it. With this kind of certainty it surely makes sense for us to take time in this life to investigate what happens after we die.

We have seen that there are good reasons to believe in the reality of the human soul, and since the soul is immaterial we have a legitimate reason to think that it will survive bodily death. This inference is justified further when we consider accounts of verifiable near death experiences. Could these be clues to an afterlife? The evidence certainly points in that direction. We also discovered more than mere clues to life after death. We learned that God has provided us an example of a man—Jesus of Nazareth—who went there and returned.

When we look at the astonishing facts surrounding the end of Jesus' life, we are confronted with a profound, life-altering decision—what do we do about Jesus? The facts of his resurrection are so clear, they are almost beyond question, which is remarkable given the relative obscurity of Jesus' life and death two thousand years ago. If the historical evidence makes it reasonable to believe that Jesus rose from the dead, then it is *not* reasonable to ignore this evidence because all other men have always remained in their graves.[1] The facts speak for themselves and Jesus

---

[1] William Lane Craig, *Reasonable Faith: Christian Truth and Apologetics* (Wheaton, IL: Crossway Books, 1984, 1994, second edition), 151.

himself predicted them and explained them—God raised him from the dead because God approved of Jesus' message to humanity.

Consequently, since this evidence has proved to be genuine, we can forgo the investigation of any other person's claim to divine authority, for they all fall far short in comparison to Jesus' claims and resurrection. The resurrection proves Jesus is who he claimed to be and therefore it is vital to our understanding of what happens after we die.

Further reading

The existence of souls

> *Beyond Death: Exploring the Evidence for Immortality,*
>   Gary R. Habermas and J. P. Moreland
> *Body & Soul: Human Nature & the Crisis in Ethics,*
>   J. P. Moreland and Scott B. Rae

The resurrection of Jesus

> *On Guard: Defending Your Faith with Reason and Precision,*
>   William Lane Craig
> *Reasonable Faith: Christian Truth and Apologetics,*
>   William Lane Craig
> *The Case for Christ*, Lee Strobel
> *The Risen Jesus and Future Hope*, Gary R. Habermas

QUESTION FOUR

Can we be sure?

Knowledge of God is not an abstract, otherworldly luxury. It is the starting point of drawing a map of reality...making it possible for us to live as we were meant to live.

Vishal Mangalwadi (1949-)
International lecturer, social reformer, political columnist
Truth and Transformation

If the human race is to know anything about God, then it must be God who takes the first step. He must draw back the curtain, remove the thick cloud and reveal himself and his will in clear and unmistakable ways...The essential fact we need to grasp is that when we talk of God's revelation, we mean that God reveals himself to us...Revelation must therefore be true and reliable, or else it is meaningless.

Brian H. Edwards (1941-)
Pastor, author, lecturer
Nothing But The Truth

To this point we have largely relied on our reason and evidence from nature and history to answer life's most important questions. We have been working on a project called *natural theology*, which is a way to study the existence of God from nature, apart from *revealed theology*, which refers to ways in which we can know about God through his more direct revelation.[1] The idea of revealed theology is that if God is there he would not be silent, and would therefore initiate communication with humanity.

We have been able to determine much about our world through natural theology. God left his mark on the world when he created it just as

---

[1] Natural theology and revealed theology also go by the names *general revelation* and *special revelation*, respectively.

an artist signs a painting to indicate that it is his creation. We have seen how God has revealed himself through the beauty, complexity, precision, and elegance of the natural world—from the microscopic to the telescopic, from the living cell to the cosmos. Through our observations and reasoning we know not only that God exists, but we also know a great deal about what he is like and much about what we as humans are really like.

We have also observed how God has revealed himself through our own consciousness, reason, free will, language, significance, and morality. We have examined a noteworthy clue of God's personal involvement in humanity—in the life, death, and resurrection of Jesus of Nazareth. There is strong evidence that this man is an emissary from God. How can we learn more about that?

Our investigation has generated several additional questions and pointed us in the direction of their answers, but we find ourselves without the necessary resources in nature alone to fully answer them. There are many things we cannot know about God simply by observing his creation, such as his nature, purposes, and expectations. It would seem that our "natural knowledge" of God forms a helpful, but incomplete picture. It certainly eliminates any excuse for us to ignore him. Therefore, we must look *beyond* nature to understand God more fully. We need to hear from God himself to tell us about who he is.

We might begin by asking how God would bridge the infinite gap between himself and us. An infinite God would have to adjust himself to the capacities of the human mind and heart in order for us to understand him, as theologian John Calvin once said. God would have to come down to our level to reveal himself by interacting with us through *human* concepts and language. Otherwise, what hope do we have of understanding a God who is beyond us in so many ways? It would be something like an ant trying to understand a human. If we were able and wanted to facilitate this, then we would have to condescend to the ant, because the reverse would be impossible.

Our first inclination might be that God would reveal himself to us in a blatant sort of way. People might prefer to see "God loves you" written in the clouds or experience a personal visit to Heaven. The skeptic assumes that God, if he exists, would try as hard as possible to make his existence obvious to us. However, this assumption ignores the possibility that a sovereign, powerful, and wise God may have other goals in mind. As we discussed earlier, God highly values man's genuine ability to choose whether or not to believe in and worship him. If God overpowered us with his presence, it would interfere with his desire to receive freely offered devotion. In fact, such an overwhelming display of God may even alienate the unbeliever, who might feel that God was forcefully imposing his will upon him. Instead of struggling desperately to get our attention, God might be restraining himself in order to give us an opportunity to learn to hate the evil in our own lives, to love truth and goodness, and to respond to him freely in faith.[2]

There is another reason that humanity may not always clearly see God. Perhaps it is not the revelation that is at fault, but *us* who routinely ignore or misunderstand it. After all, we human beings have a tendency to dismiss evidence that suggests there is an authority or power greater than ourselves, especially one to which we should be accountable. Given this disposition of humanity to ignore God, how clear does the evidence have to be before people would acknowledge God? With all this in mind, we might expect to see more subtle ways that God reveals knowledge about himself in addition to the wonder of creation. Let's consider six possible ways.

One way would be for God to appear to people individually through dreams, visions, or various physical manifestations. This way he could give a special message that he wants particular people to know.

A second way would be for God to somehow speak to us in a continuous fashion through our inner conscious life in a way that we could understand his desires and plans. The immaterial realm and the possibility of souls certainly make this kind of communication possible. These first two ways are both forms of personal witness of God directly to individual human persons, whether it is only occasionally or in an ongoing fashion.

A third way would be for God to send human spokesmen to deliver messages to large groups of people through prophetic proclamations.[3] Presumably, these prophets would hear from God in one of the first two ways, and then be directed by God to announce it to others.

A fourth way would be for God to step into humanity as a man and walk among us, teaching us about himself and how we are to live. This, in fact, is the claim made by Jesus of Nazareth.

A fifth way would be for God to perform miracles as a way to prove his existence and authenticate his message.

A sixth way would be for God to communicate to humanity through a book. Words can communicate truth to us because God made our minds to understand written and spoken language. If God's teachings were reliably recorded in written form, it would provide numerous benefits. Written words provide a very precise way to communicate a message. A book

---

[2] These insights come from John Bloom, Ph.D., lecture at Biola University, July 2006.

[3] A prophet is someone who speaks for God. Although a prophet may predict future events, he also declares God's character, promises, expectations, and judgments.

could also be reproduced in all languages and cultures and be preserved for all future generations of humans.[4] Finally, a book could be easily ignored, so it would not be an overpowering way for God to communicate.[5]

If God does speak through prophets, then he could have them write down his revelation so that all human beings in all times and places could have an opportunity to hear it and read it. It is quite interesting that nearly all worldviews that claim one or more deities also claim to have divine books. Consider these questions about a book that claims to be divine:

1. What if it corroborated everything we have come to know about the world through natural theology regarding origins, evil, suffering, and life after death?

2. What if it was confirmed through archaeology and other sources concerning what it says about people, places, times, and events?

3. What if it was transmitted through the centuries in such a way that we could be sure it contains what was originally written?

4. What if it exhibited clear marks of supernatural authorship?

5. What if it described the nature, purposes, and expectations of God?

6. What if it explained why the world has gone so wrong?

7. What if it explained how the world can be remedied?

8. What if it explained what the future of the world will be?

9. What if it revealed how we should live?

What if this possibly divine book met every one of the above criteria? The fact that it matches the world in many ways that we could verify might be sufficient reason to believe other claims it makes that we cannot directly verify through natural theology.

Our challenge is to determine if God has indeed spoken to humanity in these special ways—through personal witness, a divine Person, and a written book—and how we can be sure of it. Since a personal witness of God is a subjective individual experience, it is difficult to confirm by others in an objective way. Therefore, it seems best to first focus on whether or not a divine book exists because it would contain the kind of objective evidence we are seeking. If one does exist, then we would expect to see in it confirmation about these other methods of God's revelation.

Out of all the world's religious books, which one should we examine first? We have previously concluded that theism best explains the

---

[4] An obvious shortcoming of this approach would be illiteracy—the inability of people to read. Of course, this deficiency could be overcome through education and also oral recitation of the written words. A book would still be necessary to preserve the message.

[5] Geisler and Turek, *I Don't Have Enough Faith to Be an Atheist*, 201.

important and remarkable features of the world, so this reduces the list of candidate books to the Qur'an (Islam), the Tanakh[6] (Judaism), and the Holy Bible (Christianity). We have also previously established the extremely strong likelihood that Jesus of Nazareth was raised from the dead as a matter of historical record.[7] This extraordinary and unique event in human history simply must be accounted for.

We can use this information to further narrow the field to the Christian Bible because, whereas both Islam and Judaism deny the resurrection of Jesus as an historical fact, it is the central tenet of Christianity. Even if you are not fully convinced that Jesus was raised from the dead, the Bible is a sensible place to begin this part of our investigation for the following two reasons.

First, Judaism and Christianity are integrally related faiths from the Christian perspective. The Jewish scriptures foretell a "New Covenant" between God and his people that the Christian scriptures maintain was established by Jesus.[8] The Christian claim is that Christianity is the fulfillment of Judaism and therefore accepts its sacred book, the Tanakh, in its entirety. It therefore makes sense to first explore the Bible because, in doing so, the Tanakh is also examined and the second half of the Bible will either be confirmed or rejected as the Tanakh's fulfillment.

Second, Islam holds Jesus in very high esteem. Even though the Qur'an denies his death on a cross and his resurrection, it mentions Jesus by name 25 times. He is viewed as a prophet who was divinely chosen to spread God's message (61:6). He was a miracle worker who performed healings and raised people from the dead (5:110). He was considered to be righteous (6:85), he confirmed the Law (5:46), he brought the Gospel (57:27), and he was to be followed (3:55) and obeyed (43:63). He was taken up to Heaven by God without dying (4:158) and will return to Earth to restore justice (43:61). Since Islam honors Jesus so greatly, it would be prudent to first see what the faith named for him has to say.

Our approach will therefore be to examine the Bible to see if it is a book possibly given to humanity by God. If we find that it meets the nine criteria listed above, then that would be compelling evidence of its divine origin. It would also inform us about the other ways God may reveal himself to us.

---

[6] Tanakh is an acronym created from the first letter of the name of each of the three main sections of the book—Torah (The Law), Nevi'im (The Prophets), and Ketuvim (The Writings).

[7] We examined much of this evidence about Jesus in chapter 7. Although we learned most of our facts about the end of Jesus' life from the Bible, we were able to derive them from especially well-attested biblical passages that are believed to be historical by almost all New Testament scholars, independent of belief in an error-free or even a "generally" reliable Bible.

[8] The word *scriptures* generally refers to the sacred writings of a religion. I will often use the capitalized form *Scripture* to refer to the entire Christian Bible and the lowercase plural form when referring to parts of the Bible.

CHAPTER 8

Special delivery

While we are here on earth, it's hard for us to test what each "holy book" says about heavenly things. But where books make claims about earthly things ... aha! Here's something we can test.

David Catchpoole
Former atheist, scientist, speaker, author
Creation Ministries International

There is a reason the ancient historical accounts of the life of Jesus of Nazareth do not start with the phrase, "Once upon a time..."

Greg Koukl (1950-)
Author, speaker, teacher
Faith Is Not Wishing

As a literary historian, I am perfectly convinced that whatever else the Gospels are, they are not legends. I have read a great deal of legend and I am quite clear they are not the same sort of thing.

C. S. Lewis (1898-1963)
Theologian, author
God in the Dock

A legitimate concern about relying on any ancient document is whether or not it is trustworthy. Our first task in evaluating the trustworthiness of the Bible is to assess its historical reliability. To this end we want to examine three aspects of the Bible.

First, we want to know if what the Bible describes is supposed to be taken as history. This is important because some people charge the Bible with being legendary or mythological, not historical. If the Bible makes no claims and exhibits no evidence of narrating history, then we have no reason to trust that what it says really happened in history.

Second, we want to know if the Bible we have today really describes what the original authors wrote. This is a matter of *transmission* and *translation* of the biblical texts. If we do not have in our own language what the authors said, then there is no reason to trust what the Bible says.

Third, we want to know if the biblical authors related true facts about what they wrote. This is a matter of the *testimony* of the authors—in particular, their willingness and ability to tell us the truth about what they wrote. Even if we have all the rest, we cannot trust the Bible if we cannot trust its authors.

The Bible claims to be the words of God, but we will not begin our investigation with this assumption.[1] Instead, we will first undertake the much more modest goal of determining if we can trust the Bible as an historical document. Even though the Bible reports some extraordinary events, we cannot reject its reliability on these grounds alone. It is mistaken to think that just because a person gives an account of something he passionately believes in, he must be distorting history. Certainly a writer can be passionate and accurate at the same time. Besides, given the existence of God, extraordinary events that might be considered miracles are not only possible, but probable if God had an interest in communicating with human beings.

What is the Bible?

The word *Bible* comes from the Greek plural and Latin singular *biblia*, meaning "the books" and "the book," respectively. In a very important sense, the Bible is considered to be a single book with two parts—the Old Testament (OT) and the New Testament (NT).[2] However, we also recognize that this book was written over a fifteen hundred year period by more than forty different human authors.[3] Obviously, the text that comprises the Bible was not written in the same way a normal book would be written. Therefore, in another sense, the Bible is a collection of sixty-six different documents written over this very long time period.[4] To

---

[1] We will examine this issue in chapters 10 and 11.

[2] Testament means covenant.

[3] There are two suggested time periods for the earliest biblical books, which were written by Moses soon after the Hebrews left Egypt—the 13th and 15th centuries BC. I am persuaded by the earlier dating (about 1450 BC), but there are legitimate arguments for both time periods. See Andrew E. Hill and John H. Walton, *A Survey of the Old Testament* (Grand Rapids: Zondervan, 2000), 85-86.

[4] Thirty-nine of these books are part of the Old Testament, written between 1450-400 BC. Twenty-seven of the books are part of the New Testament, all of which were written in the first century AD. The OT is identical to the Jewish sacred scriptures—called the *Tanakh*—except it is organized a bit differently.

evaluate the historical reliability of the Bible we need to examine these separate texts written at different times by different people.

Why historical reliability is important

There are three reasons to establish the historical reliability of the Bible. First, the Bible is fundamentally one long historical narrative of God's continual interaction with human beings. There is a continuity of the story from creation to the fall of man[5] to the founding of Israel as God's holy nation, through their long succession of righteous and unrighteous actions, culminating with Jesus' inauguration of the New Covenant, the establishment of the Church, and the actions of Jesus' earliest followers to spread his message.[6] This grand narrative is comprised of hundreds of events, many of which can be checked historically.

Second, the Bible itself says that its theological doctrines are explicitly based on historical events. Pastor and author Brian Edwards explains, "The incarnation—God becoming man—is proved by the virgin birth of Christ. Redemption—the price being paid for man's rebellion to be forgiven—is obtained by the death of Christ on the cross. Reconciliation—the privilege granted to the sinner of becoming a friend of God—is gained through the resurrection and ascension of Christ."[7] If these events did not really happen, then we have no reason to believe that the theology behind them is true. Indeed, this is the specific claim of the apostle Paul when he says, "If Christ has not been raised, our preaching is useless and so is your faith" (1 Cor 15:14).[8] Judaism and Christianity are the only religions in the world that base their theological claims on historical events in this way.

Third, if the Bible can be proved to be true in areas that we can verify—such as with people, history, geography, and culture—then it gives us good reason to believe the rest of the Bible in areas that are not easily verified. This is especially true of spiritual truths that are not explicitly tied to historical events, such as the nature of God and the promised second coming of Jesus. The Bible can never be trusted on matters of doctrine if it cannot be trusted on the facts of history.

---

[5] The fall of man will be explained in chapter 12.

[6] N. T. Wright, *The Last Word: Scripture and the Authority of God—Getting Beyond the Bible Wars* (New York: HarperCollins, 2005), 121-122.

[7] Brian H. Edwards, *Nothing But The Truth* (Webster, NY: Evangelical Press, 1978, 2007), 129.

[8] Bible references are given in parentheses in this format—(Book Chapter:Verse). Note, longer book names will be abbreviated. All Bible quotations are taken from the *Holy Bible*, New International Version®. NIV®. Copyright © 1973, 1978, 1984 by International Bible Society. Used by permission of Zondervan. All rights reserved.

Does the Bible provide historical accounts?

Although the Bible contains many different literary styles, its most prominent one is historical narrative. We will look at this from two angles. First, we will see that the Bible repeatedly claims to be relating real historical events. Second, we will examine the charge that the Bible narratives are not real human history, but rather mythological accounts borrowed from pagan religions of the nations surrounding Israel.

Claims of factual truthfulness

In numerous places the Bible plainly claims to be relating true historical accounts of events that really happened in real places at particular times. For example, in the OT we often see statements that invite us to consider and appreciate the literal, historical setting of the story:

❖ "These were the sons of Israel: Reuben, Simeon, Levi, Judah, Issachar, Zebulun, Dan, Joseph, Benjamin, Naphtali, Gad and Asher" (1 Chron 2:1-2).

❖ "In the twenty-fifth year of our exile, at the beginning of the year, on the tenth of the month, in the fourteenth year after the fall of the city—on that very day the hand of the LORD was upon me and he took me there" (Eze 40:1).

❖ "In the third year of the reign of Jehoiakim king of Judah, Nebuchadnezzar king of Babylon came to Jerusalem and besieged it" (Dan 1:1).

Similarly, the NT writers make explicit claims of careful historical accounting. For example, Luke writes:

> Many have undertaken to draw up an account of the things that have been fulfilled among us, just as they were handed down to us by those who from the first were eyewitnesses and servants of the word. Therefore, since I myself have carefully investigated everything from the beginning, it seemed good also to me to write an orderly account for you, most excellent Theophilus, so that you may know the certainty of the things you have been taught (Luke 1:1-4).

Peter writes, "We did not follow cleverly devised stories when we told you about the coming of our Lord Jesus Christ in power, but we were eyewitnesses of his majesty" (2 Pet 1:16). At the end of his Gospel, John says, "This is the disciple who testifies to these things and who wrote them down. We know that his testimony is true" (John 21:24). Paul claims eyewitness testimony when he says that the risen Jesus "appeared to Peter, and then to the Twelve. After that, he appeared to more than five hundred of the brothers at the same time, most of whom are still living, though some have fallen asleep. Then he appeared to James, then to all the apostles, and last of all he appeared to me also" (1 Cor 15:5-7).

All four Gospel accounts relate the historical events of the birth, life, death, and resurrection of Jesus of Nazareth. The book of Acts describes how the early church began and expanded. Even the NT epistles, which contain more theological teaching, were written in the midst of and recount real events, such as Paul's missionary journeys and his interactions with believers and unbelievers alike.

The Bible simply and straightforwardly gives historical accounts of many events that have involved human beings, including their creation in the garden of Eden, a worldwide flood, the creation of nations after the Tower of Babel, the exodus of the Jews from Egypt, the creation of the nation of Israel, her captivity by the Assyrians and Babylonians, several episodes of the building and destruction of the Jewish Temple in Jerusalem, the coming of the Messiah, his death and resurrection, and the emergence and growth of the Christian church.

The mythology objection

Despite these sorts of historical claims in the Bible, some people have speculated that the major narrative accounts in the Bible—from creation to the resurrection of Jesus—are based on mythological stories from ancient pagan religions rather than on real historical events. When someone denounces the Bible as myth, we are supposed to understand it to mean that the Bible has no factual basis.[9]

A closer examination shows that this charge has no foundation, however. This can be seen in two ways. First, there is an enormous literary difference between mythological and historical accounts. Second, it is far more likely that polytheistic cultures would borrow from monotheism than the other way around. Let's look at these two reasons in more detail.

Literary differences

There is a qualitative difference between mythology and historical accounts. The Bible reads like history, claims to be history, and is corroborated to be history in a variety of ways.[10] This simply is not true of mythology, and is therefore the primary distinction between pagan myths and the Bible. Myths are full of colorful and legendary language that is much more elaborate than the straightforward biblical narratives. For

---

[9] The intention of these critics is to have us believe that the Bible is therefore not a revelation from God. We will address this particular issue in chapters 10 and 11.

[10] These ways will be discussed throughout this chapter and also in chapter 9.

example, the main characters in myths are often non-human (gods, goddesses, and other supernatural beings). The setting frequently involves some ancient, nebulous proto-world and often involves interplay between worlds. Equal and opposite dualities must frequently be reconciled, such as good and bad, light and darkness, and being and non-being.

Furthermore, pagan myths are heavily preoccupied with finite gods who continually argue and battle with one another, hosts of male and female deities, the divinization of the forces of nature ("Amen, the wind, initiated Creation"[11]), personification of objects ("Egyptians considered stars to be inhabitants of the underworld"[12]), personification of places ("heaven and earth are the Egyptian deities Geb and Nut"[13]), and a fascination with recurring natural phenomena such as fertility cycles, the changing of the seasons, and the motion of the stars.

These imaginative elements are not characteristic of the Bible, which is much more understated and lacks fanciful embellishment. The Bible is concerned with carefully reporting events by meticulously tying them to historical places, persons, and times; while mythical accounts are quite unconcerned with these details. It is not likely that the literary progression over time would move from the complex and fantastic mythological accounts to the simple and elegant biblical accounts. Atheist turned Christian evangelist and author Josh McDowell points out, "In the Ancient Near East, the rule is that simple accounts or traditions give rise (by accretion and embellishment) to elaborate legends, but not the reverse."[14] Simply put, the Bible reads like history and the pagan myths read like fictional accounts.

Moreover, myths make no attempt to justify themselves as being literally true or even plausibly true, whereas the Bible repeatedly does. As we will see later in this chapter and in the next, real historical accounts like we find in the Bible can be and actually are externally corroborated, but mythological accounts cannot be and, in fact, are not confirmed in this way.

The implausibility of borrowing from polytheism

Let's now consider the likelihood that the Jewish people borrowed their beliefs from polytheism. A key presupposition to skeptical theories that the Bible is based on pagan myths is the idea that the monotheistic Jews copied from the polytheistic myths and removed their references to

---

[11] Gary Greenberg, *101 Myths of the Bible: How Ancient Scribes Invented Biblical History*, (Naperville, IL: Sourcebooks, Inc., 2000), 13.

[12] Ibid., 23.

[13] Ibid., 9.

[14] Josh McDowell, *The New Evidence That Demands A Verdict* (Nashville: Thomas Nelson Publishers, 1999), 375.

multiple deities. However, it is not credible that devoted monotheists such as the Jews would adopt stories from polytheistic cultures because of the radical exclusivity of their own convictions.[15] Indeed, the evidence indicates that polytheism does not naturally evolve into monotheism.

Social anthropologist James Frazer published a "late monotheism" theory in 1912 based on Darwinian Evolution. This theory alleges that religions naturally evolve from animism to polytheism to henotheism (the belief in one supreme god among many), and eventually to monotheism.[16] This supposedly provides the necessary supporting evidence to believe the Bible was influenced by the pagan myths, implying that the faith of Israel is the result of the natural evolution of polytheism to monotheism. Is this a credible explanation? For this view to be correct, the Jews would have to be willing to adopt and revise stories infused with polytheistic beliefs, which they then refer to as true historical accounts. This view does not seem plausible given the evidence.

The fact that Israel could even *be* monotheistic in the ancient world was astonishing, considering the breadth and depth of the surrounding antagonistic cultural and religious influences. Old Testament expert James Orr observes:

> The monotheism of the Israelites is one of the first characteristics to be noted when studying the Old Testament. This is quite a feat in itself, in view of the fact that polytheism and idolatry were the modern trend. The religions of the Babylonians, the Assyrians, the Egyptians, and even Israel's Palestinian neighbors were incorrigibly corrupt and polytheistic.[17]

It is important to note that Israel was the *only* monotheistic nation in the Ancient Near East (ANE).[18] Archeologist and ancient language expert Gleason Archer writes:

> It is an incontestable fact of history that no other nation (apart from those influenced by the Hebrew faith) ever did develop a true monotheistic religion which commanded the general allegiance of its people...It remains incontrovertible that neither the Egyptians nor the

---

[15] This is not to say that Israel did not sometimes fall into idolatry by worshiping pagan idols and gods, for clearly they did at times. As a whole, however, Israel was always monotheistic and their sacred scriptures continuously reflected that belief. Even when they fell into pagan worship, they eventually repented and returned to their monotheistic roots.

[16] Norman L. Geisler, *Baker Encyclopedia of Christian Apologetics* (Grand Rapids: Baker Books, 1999), 497.

[17] James Orr, *The Problem of the Old Testament* (New York: Charles Scribner's Sons, written 1905, printed 1917), 40-41, quoted in McDowell, *The New Evidence,* 421.

[18] The Ancient Near East refers to early civilizations from the 4th millennium BC to about the 4th century BC, which lived within a region roughly corresponding to the modern Middle East.

Babylonians nor the Greeks ever embraced a monotheistic faith on a national basis.[19]

God had called his people to be different from the surrounding pagan cultures, first by promising Abraham that "all peoples on earth will be blessed through you" (Gen 12:3) and also with his instructions to Moses:

Now if you obey me fully and keep my covenant, then out of all nations you will be my treasured possession. Although the whole earth is mine, you will be for me a kingdom of priests and a holy nation. These are the words you are to speak to the Israelites...You shall have no other gods before me. You shall not make for yourself an idol in the form of anything in heaven above or on the earth beneath or in the waters below. You shall not bow down to them or worship them (Exo 19:5-20:5).

This is the resounding teaching of the Bible and it is difficult to see how one could come to hold such beliefs by starting with polytheistic myths.

Bible myth advocates fail to appreciate that monotheism and polytheism are more qualitative than quantitative concepts. Even a single deity is not necessarily a monotheistic deity. Worship is the key—if it is divided between deities then it is polytheism, even if one god is believed to be manifested in multiple gods.[20] Consequently, we find that evolution from polytheism to monotheism is not supported by experience, as we see no evidence of any polytheistic religion progressively eliminating gods until it gets to one.

Between the pantheistic religions of the East, the New Age faith prevalent in the West, and all the animistic tribes in the world, there are around two billion people who maintain some sort of belief in multiple deities today.[21] If the religious evolutionary theory is true, then why are they not eliminating deities from their list? It is because polytheism tends to add gods to their belief system, not subtract them. Archaeologist and ANE expert Ronald Youngblood concurs: "It cannot be shown that there is a universal tendency on the part of polytheistic religions to gradually reduce the number of deities until arriving at one deity...In fact, such a religion may even add *more* deities as its adherents become aware of more and more natural phenomena to deify!" [emphasis in original].[22] Indeed,

---

[19] Gleason L. Archer, Jr., *A Survey of Old Testament Introduction* (Chicago: Moody Press, 1964, 1974), 134.

[20] Carl Mosser, "Essential Christian Doctrine I" (lecture for M.A. Christian Apologetics class, Biola University, delivered July 16, 2005).

[21] Jason Mandryk, *Operation World: The Definitive Prayer Guide to Every Nation* (Colorado Springs: Biblica Publishing, 2010, seventh edition), 2.

[22] Ronald Youngblood, *The Heart of the Old Testament* (Grand Rapids: Baker Book House, 1971), 9, quoted in McDowell, *The New Evidence*, 422.

this is what we observe in Hinduism today, which worships some 330 million deities.[23]

Skeptics fail to give sufficient weight to the depth and quality of conviction of a monotheist. For the person who believes in only one Creator and Sustainer of all things—a transcendent and infinite God, distinct from creation, with no rival deities—polytheism is an abomination to be avoided at all costs. So it is with the nation of Israel, whom God called to be radically different from its pagan neighbors. Bible scholar Richard Bauckham writes:

> [Israel's] self-conscious monotheism was not merely an intellectual belief about God, but a unity of belief and praxis, involving the exclusive worship of this one God and exclusive obedience to this one God...Whereas the tendency of non-Jewish thought is to assimilate such ideas of divine uniqueness to patterns of thought in which the supreme God is the summit of a hierarchy of divinity...the tendency of Jewish thought is to accentuate the absolute distinction between God and all else as the dominant feature of the whole Jewish world-view.[24]

Biblical archaeologist G. E. Wright agrees, "The faith of Israel, even in its earliest and basic forms is so utterly different from that of the contemporary polytheisms that one simply cannot explain it fully by evolutionary or environmental categories."[25] An intensely monotheistic Israelite nation, who believed they have recorded the very words of God, would never corrupt their sacred writings with sources so obviously antithetical to those beliefs.

We may wonder why there are so many myths in so many ancient cultures that claim to explain the creation of the world, the Great Flood, and other events recounted in the Bible. It seems more likely that these events actually happened in history as the Bible affirms and that all ancient peoples either witnessed or heard about these deeds of the transcendent Creator of the world. Why should we find it surprising then, that the Egyptians, Babylonians, and other ANE cultures have echoes of these accounts woven through their pagan beliefs?

A New Testament case study

Charges of borrowing from pagan myths are not limited to the Old Testament. Critics have also suggested that the resurrection account of

---

[23] Dean Halverson, general editor, *The Illustrated Guide to World Religions* (Bloomington, MN: Bethany House Publishers, 2003), 87.

[24] Richard Bauckham, *God Crucified: Monotheism & Christology in the New Testament* (Grand Rapids: William B. Eerdmans Publishing Company, 1998), 6-16.

[25] G. E. Wright, *The Old Testament Against its Environment* (Chicago: Henry Regnery Co., 1950) 7, quoted in McDowell, *The New Evidence*, 422.

Jesus described in the New Testament is copied from similar stories of pagan cultures. For example, the story of Jesus is often compared to Osiris, a cult god of the Egyptians and later the Romans. In this myth, Osiris is murdered by his brother Seth, who then sank his body in the Nile River. Isis, the wife of Osiris, found his body and returned it to Egypt. Seth got hold of the body again, cut it into fourteen pieces, and scattered them around Egypt. Isis then recovered all the body pieces and brought Osiris back to some form of existence—not to life in the real world—but as ruler of the dead in the underworld.[26]

The Osiris myth is remarkably different from the death and resurrection of Jesus. For one, there is the obvious discrepancy that Osiris did not rise to live again in this world. For another, this myth changed its story, just as all pagan myths change over time. For example, Ptolemy, a Roman citizen of Egypt, replaced Osiris with a new god named Serapis in an effort to adapt the story to the Greek culture. Serapis was a sun god who did not die, so he certainly could not have been resurrected.[27] Contrary to the ever-changing mythical stories, the account of Jesus' resurrection has remained unchanged for 2,000 years. The really significant differences, however, are that Osiris was not an historical figure and his death and resurrection were not intended to provide salvation for humanity.

The alleged similarities between Christianity and paganism often prove to be inconsequential, superficial, or non-existent. None of the myths truly parallel the Christian resurrection account. Comparative religion scholar T. N. D. Mettinger says that these myths are far different from the reports of Jesus rising from the dead. The mythical events occurred in the unspecified and distant past and were usually related to the changing of the seasons. In contrast, Jesus' resurrection is not repeated, is not related to seasonal changes, and was sincerely believed to be an actual event by those who lived in the same generation as the historical Jesus. Moreover, there is no evidence for the death of the dying and rising gods as vicarious suffering for sins.[28] There is real, historical evidence for Jesus' resurrection, but not for any of the pagan stories. Even if there were similar stories from other cultures, we could not simply dismiss Jesus' resurrection unless we could refute the compelling evidence in its favor, which is a very difficult task.[29]

---

[26] Ronald Nash, *The Gospel and the Greeks: Did the New Testament Borrow from Pagan Thought?* (Phillipsburg, NJ: P&R Publishing, 1992, 2003), 127. Edwin M. Yamauchi as quoted in Lee Strobel, *The Case for the Real Jesus* (Grand Rapids, MI: Zondervan, 2007), 177-178.

[27] Nash, *The Gospel and the Greeks*, 126, 128.

[28] Mike Licona paraphrasing Mettinger in Strobel, *The Case for the Real Jesus,* 161. Tryggve N. D. Mettinger, *The Riddle of Resurrection: "Dying and Rising Gods" in the Ancient Near East* (Stockholm: Almquist & Wiksell International, 2001), 221.

[29] This evidence was presented in chapter 7.

The fact is that no genuine pagan resurrection account predates Christianity. Gary Habermas writes, "Not one clear case of an alleged resurrection teaching appears in any pagan text before the late second century A.D."[30] This is long after the NT documents were written and circulating widely. To the extent that pagan myths bear any resemblance to Bible stories, it is the pagan myths that have been influenced by the Bible and not vice versa.

Do we have what the biblical authors wrote?

Now that we have established that the biblical authors intended to write history, we need to determine if what we read in our Bibles today is actually what they wrote. There are two objections that are usually made about this particular aspect of reliability. The first objection is that we do not have today what the authors really wrote long ago in their original documents due to errors in copying through the centuries since then. This is an issue of *transmission*. The second objection is that the Bible we have today in our own language does not faithfully represent what was initially written in the original languages. This is an issue of *translation*. Both of these objections fail when the evidence is examined.

Transmission of the biblical texts

No original text of *any* ancient book has survived, including the Bible. All the initial documents written by the biblical authors have been lost or destroyed over the centuries. The closest we have to them are hand-written copies of the originals made by scribes over the centuries, which we refer to as *manuscripts*.[31]

Despite the very careful process used to copy biblical texts, even the best scribes occasionally made copying errors, mostly inadvertently, but sometimes deliberately to "correct," harmonize, or explain a text. These errors would in turn be propagated to other copies made in the future. Given this situation, some people think it would be impossible to recover the original text, but that is not the case. In fact, textual scholars are often able to reconstruct the original with a high degree of confidence from existing manuscripts.

Textual criticism

Textual criticism is the process by which scholars try to restore, as nearly as possible, the original text of a work that has been lost. They look

---

[30] Habermas and Moreland, *Beyond Death*,121.

[31] A manuscript is a handwritten copy of all or part of a text, which was the only means to reproduce documents until the advent of the printing press in the 15th century AD.

at all the existing copies of an original and draw conclusions about what the most likely rendering of the original should be. Their assumption is that the copyists did not all make the same mistake in the same place at the same time. Therefore, the textual critic is able to compare different hand-copied manuscripts to determine the original wording of a text.

The reliability of the reconstruction of the original is primarily dependent upon three things—the *completeness* of the copies that exist, the *number* of copies that exist, and the *time interval* between the copies and the original. Fewer gaps, more copies, and shorter intervals will yield the most accurate rendition of the original.

Suppose we were to display a short paragraph on a screen to a number of students in a classroom and then ask them to copy it to a piece of paper. Then we turn off the display so that the original paragraph is no longer available. Let's begin by assuming there are five students in the class and only two of them produce identical copies. In this case, we could not really be sure what the original paragraph was. We have four different versions and it is possible the two that are the same made the same copying mistake. However, let's now assume there are 50 students in the class. What if 20 of them have the exact same paragraph and the others substantially agree, but have a number of inverted phrases, misspellings, and an occasional new or missing word? In this scenario, because there are so many copies, it would be much easier to reconstruct the original.

Now suppose these students gave their copies to friends who also made handwritten copies, and so on. In these cases, errors in the original copies would be further propagated, with the possibility that more errors would be introduced, so we would prefer the earliest copies to minimize the amount of error transmission. Imagine also if a copied paragraph had some blank spaces where some words were missing. The copiers might leave them blank or attempt to fill them in, but in either case, there is uncertainty as to what was in the original. Although this scenario is a bit oversimplified, it is the kind of situation faced by textual critics.

Manuscript evidence

The Bible is not the only ancient document subject to textual criticism—so are secular documents. Scholars regularly give great credibility to ancient documents other than the Bible. For example, virtually no one seriously doubts the historical accuracy of Caesar's *Gallic Wars*, written about 58-50 BC or the *Dialogues* of Plato, written around 400 BC. Scholars believe that they know today what these authors originally wrote over two thousand years ago. However, the number of surviving manuscripts of these ancient secular documents is very small and the interval of time between their original writing and the earliest existing copy is very long. This is the opposite of what textual critics would prefer to be able to reconstruct the originals with confidence.

More copies provide more samples to compare, so the original reading can be discerned from texts that contain small differences. Shorter intervals provide more confidence that copying errors have not been propagated. For example, in the case of Caesar, there are only 10 existing copies and the earliest one we have was made 1,000 years after the original was written. For Plato, there are only 7 existing copies and the earliest was made over 1,300 years after the original was written. This limited level of documentary evidence is true for all classical literature as the table on the following page shows. Furthermore, in many cases the copies are incomplete. "Hundreds of books from antiquity are known to us only by name; no manuscripts remain. And even in some of the better-preserved writings, there are many significant gaps."[32]

The situation with the New Testament texts is far superior to *all* other ancient documents. There are now over 25,000 manuscript copies of portions of the NT in existence.[33] No other document of antiquity even approaches such numbers and authentication.[34] In comparison, the *Iliad* by Homer is second with only 643 manuscripts that still survive. Besides quantity, the manuscripts of the NT differ from those of the classic authors in the interval of time between the composition of the book and the date of the earliest existing manuscript. As illustrated in the following table, the earliest copies of most ancient documents appear in history a thousand years or more after the original was written. By contrast, the earliest *complete* copy of the New Testament that we have was made only about 250 years after the New Testament was written. Manuscripts of some parts have been found that were copied *less than 50 years* after the originals were written. Moreover, there are *no* gaps in the NT manuscripts. We have *everything* from *every* book, so that no speculation is necessary to fill in something that was missing.[35]

---

[32] J. Ed Komoszewski, M. James, Sawyer, and Daniel B. Wallace, *Reinventing Jesus: How Contemporary Skeptics Miss the Real Jesus and Mislead Popular Culture* (Grand Rapids: Kregel Publications, 2006), 106.

[33] This includes more than 5,700 full or partial manuscripts in Greek (these are the principal documents), over 10,000 Latin manuscripts, and in excess of 9,300 other early manuscript versions in Syriac, Coptic, Armenian, Gothic, Georgian, Ethiopic, and Arabic.

[34] This does not even count secondary witnesses to the biblical texts such as quotations made by the early church fathers in their sermons, commentaries, letters, and other writings. There are well over a million citations of the NT in the writings of the early Christians. Even if we did not possess the 25,000 biblical manuscripts, the text of the NT could still be reproduced through the writings of Christians within the first 250 years of the original NT. Komoszewski, *Reinventing Jesus*, 81.

[35] Komoszewski, *Reinventing Jesus*, 106.

AUTHOR	WORKS	DATE WRITTEN	EARLIEST COPIES	TIME GAP	# OF COPIES
Homer	*Iliad* *Odyssey*	800 BC	400 BC 1400 AD	400 yrs 2,200 yrs	643
Sophocles	*Plays*	496-406 BC	1000 AD	1,500 yrs	7
Herodotus	*History*	484-425 BC	900 AD	1,350 yrs	8
Euripides	*Plays*	480-406 BC	1100 AD	1,500 yrs	18
Thucydides	*History*	460-400 BC	900 AD	1,300 yrs	8
Aristophanes	*Plays*	446-386 BC	900 AD	1,300 yrs	11
Plato	*Dialogues*	424-348 BC	900 AD	1,300 yrs	7
Aristotle	*Philosophy*	384-322 BC	1100 AD	1,400 yrs	49
Demosthenes	*Orations*	300 BC	1100 AD	1,400 yrs	200
Caesar	*Gallic Wars*	100-44 BC	900 AD	1,000 yrs	10
Lucretius	*Poem*	53 BC	1100 AD	1,100 yrs	2
Livy	*History of Rome*	59 BC-17AD	4th century (partial) 10th century (mostly)	400 yrs 1,000 yrs	1 19
Pliny Secundus	*Natural History*	77-79 AD	850 AD	750 yrs	7
Tacitus	*Annals*	100 AD	850 AD	750 yrs	1
Matthew, Mark, Luke, John, Paul, Peter, James, Jude	*New Testament*	45-90 AD	50-125 AD (fragments) 200 AD (books) 250 AD (most of NT) 350 AD (complete NT)	**10-50 yrs** **100 yrs** **150 yrs** **250 yrs**	**25,000+**

MANUSCRIPT EVIDENCE OF ANCIENT TEXTS[36]

New Testament variants

As we noted earlier, it is common for errors to be injected into hand-copied manuscripts. This will result in a difference between a text with the

error and another that does not have the same error. Textual critics refer to these differences as *textual variants* or *variant readings*. A textual variant is simply any difference from a base text that involves spelling, word order, substitution, omission, addition, or even a rewrite of the text. A particular difference is counted as a single variant whether it is found in a single manuscript or a group of manuscripts. Textual critics only count differences in wording, regardless of how many manuscripts attest to it.[37]

---

[36] Compiled from Moreland, *Scaling the Secular City*, 135; Komoszewski, *Reinventing Jesus*, 71; http://www.christianity.co.nz/bible-3.htm; http://debate.org.uk/topics/history/bib-ur/bibmanu.htm; and http://carm.org/manuscript-evidence.
[37] A common mistake is to count textual variants as the sum of all wording differences times the number of manuscripts that exhibit those differences. Counting this way seriously exaggerates the true number of textual variants, though.

Some biblical critics complain that there are so many variant readings of the Bible that it is a hopeless cause to know the original readings. For example, liberal New Testament scholar Bart Ehrman writes, "What good is it to say that the autographs (i.e., the originals) were inspired? We don't *have* the originals! We only have error-ridden copies...There are more variations among our manuscripts than there are words in the New Testament" [emphasis in original].[38] Although this provocative statement is technically true, and is delivered in a clever way, it is terribly misleading.

Indeed, there are approximately 138,000 Greek words in the NT and there may be up to 400,000 variants among all the NT manuscripts.[39] However, we should not miss the crucial fact that the large number of variants arises *primarily* because of the large number of manuscripts we possess.[40] Textual scholars universally consider this a good situation, not a bad one. This is because the condition that causes the problem is the same one that helps to resolve it. The more manuscripts we have available, the more they will tend to contain some differences, but at the same time, the greater number of manuscripts also provides the sufficient raw materials to reconstruct the originals. In fact, the number of manuscripts is so abundant that we can be assured the original text can be found in them.[41]

The huge majority of variants are insignificant, *not at all* affecting the reconstruction of the original. For instance, over half the variants are spelling errors. Other types of trivial errors include accidental omissions of a word or phrase, the inadvertent addition of a word or phrase, the inverting of words in a phrase (e.g., Jesus Christ vs. Christ Jesus), or minor scribal "corrections" or interpretations, for instance. These errors are not only inconsequential—they are also easy to identify and correct.

Variant readings that are more significant—those that really affect the meaning of the text and that are found more abundantly in the manuscript

---

[38] Bart Ehrman, *Misquoting Jesus: The Story Behind Who Changed the Bible and Why* (New York: HarperCollins, 2005), 7, 90.

[39] Komoszewski, *Reinventing Jesus*, 54.

[40] Scholars have recognized three predominant NT Greek text "families," which each contain a large number of manuscripts and also exhibit the same pattern of preservation and variations. These texts originate in three ancient centers of Christianity. From Rome, we have the *Western Text*. From Alexandria, we have the *Alexandrian Text*, which are the oldest manuscripts. From Constantinople, we have the *Byzantine Text*, also known as the Majority Text, which as the name implies, has the most manuscripts. These three text families represent generally independent transmission histories and therefore are less likely to reproduce the same errors. All known manuscripts in all text families are at least 85% identical and most of the variations are not even translatable into English because they are merely word order or spelling differences. By comparing texts from different families, textual critics are often able to determine when and where variants were introduced.

[41] Andreas J. Köstenberger and Michael J. Kruger, *The Heresy of Orthodoxy: How Contemporary Culture's Fascination with Diversity Has Reshaped Our Understanding of Early Christianity* (Wheaton, IL: Crossway, 2010), 206, 212.

evidence—are much less than 1% of the total, according to NT textual scholar Daniel B. Wallace.[42] To put this into perspective, more than 396,000 of the variants give us *no trouble whatsoever* in reconstructing the originals. Even in the cases of the most difficult texts (from the one percent category), textual critics have an assortment of ways to resolve the conflicts. The analytical process they use is a very rigorous discipline, containing several checks and balances.[43] Wallace concludes, "The vast majority of NT scholars would say that there are absolutely no places where conjecture is necessary. Again, this is because the manuscripts are so plentiful and so early that in every instance the original NT can be reconstructed from the available evidence."[44] The result is a New Testament text today that leaves no real doubt about the historical and theological claims conveyed in the originals.

Scholars generally trust many ancient secular writings, even though the earliest manuscripts we have were written long after the original documents. If this is so, then the reliability of the New Testament is even more assured, considering it has hundreds and in most cases thousands times more manuscripts. This evidence demonstrates that the biblical text we now have is essentially what was originally recorded.

The Dead Sea Scrolls

The Dead Sea Scrolls (DSS) is a collection of ancient documents discovered between 1947 and 1956 in eleven different caves near the religious wilderness community of Qumran on the western shore of the Dead Sea, 13 miles east of Jerusalem in Israel. The first documents were discovered by a Bedouin shepherd who threw a rock into a cave to chase out one of his goats, and then investigated when he heard breaking pottery.[45] The documents were written or copied between the third century BC and first century AD by the Essenes, an ancient Jewish sect.

This extraordinary discovery includes more than 40,000 fragments from 930 manuscripts. About 80-85% of the total text is written in

---

[42] Daniel B. Wallace, "Is What We Have Now What They Wrote Then?", http://bible.org/article/what-we-have-now-what-they-wrote-then, accessed Jan 29, 2011.

[43] Some of these evaluation criteria include preferring readings that 1) best explain the origin of other variants, 2) are shorter, 3) are more difficult, and 4) are not harmonized to similar passages.

[44] Wallace, "Is What We Have Now What They Wrote Then?"

[45] The scrolls had been carefully preserved in sealed clay jars. Subsequent searches over several years after the shepherd's first discovery uncovered the rest of the scrolls.

Hebrew, the rest is Aramaic or Greek. The
documents include the Jewish Scriptures,
commentaries   on   Scripture,   and
community rules.[46] All the OT books are
represented except Esther.[47] Multiple (full
or partial) manuscripts of most OT books
were discovered, including 3 dozen copies
of the Psalms and 21 copies of Genesis.[48]
These Hebrew OT texts date from about

250-100 BC.[49] The previous oldest Hebrew manuscript was the Masoretic
Text (MT) from the Middle Ages (about AD 900).[50] With the DSS, we
now have manuscripts more than a thousand years *older* than the MT,
which puts them much closer in time to the originals.[51]

Twenty-one manuscripts of the book of Isaiah were found among the
DSS, dating from about 125 BC. Textual scholar James C. VanderKam

determined that the DSS version of Isaiah
is almost identical to the copies of Isaiah
dating   to   the   Middle   Ages.   Any
differences are minor and rarely affect the
meaning   of   the   text.[52]   Menahem
Mansoor, another textual scholar, has
similarly stated that most of the differences are spelling or grammatical
changes. Those that do not fall into this category are minor, such as an
omission or addition of a word or two, or the mixing of Hebrew letters.[53]
One such minor variant is found in Isaiah 6:3. The MT reads, "Holy, holy,
holy, is the LORD of hosts," while one of the DSS Isaiah texts reads,
"Holy, holy is the LORD of hosts." While the DSS text may be in error in
its omission of the third holy, the contents of this scroll overwhelmingly
support the MT.

---

[46] No definitive copy or part of an NT book has been discovered at Qumran, although some
scholars argue that certain fragments belong to the Gospel of Mark. The Qumran community was
wiped out around AD 66-70 when the Romans destroyed Jerusalem, so its window of opportunity to
obtain NT documents was quite short.

[47] Of course, this doesn't prove that Esther was not considered a part of the OT scriptures. It is
much more likely that a copy has not survived or has not yet been discovered. It had been thought
that Nehemiah was another OT book that was unrepresented among the scrolls until a fragment was
identified in 2008, sixty years following the initial find.

[48] James VanderKam, *The Dead Sea Scrolls Today* (Grand Rapids: Eerdmans, 2010, 2nd ed.), 48.

[49] The oldest text is a fragment from Exodus.

[50] The Codex Cairensis (AD 895) and the Aleppo Codex (AD 925).

[51] This is in addition to the Septuagint (LXX), a Greek translation of the OT made in the third
century BC. The earliest complete copies of the LXX date from the fourth century AD. Although the
LXX is extremely helpful in reconstructing the original Hebrew text, the DSS are superior because they
are copies of the *original* language, not a translation.

[52] VanderKam, *Dead Sea Scrolls*, 162.

[53] Menahem Mansoor, *The Dead Sea Scrolls* (Grand Rapids: Eerdmans, 1964), 74-75.

Considering that a thousand years separate the Isaiah copies found in the DSS from their Masoretic counterpart, it is astonishing that they are so textually close. What accounts for such a remarkable transmission achievement? The ancient Hebrews considered Scripture copying to be a sacred task, so they developed a system of detailed rules for ensuring the accuracy of their copies. The number of words and letters in each book were counted and also the middle word and letter were calculated. If a copy did not agree exactly with the original, it was destroyed and the copying began again from the beginning.[54]

The Dead Sea Scrolls are further evidence to believe that we can trust that the Bible we hold in our hands today contains the same words written by the original authors.

More examples of accurate OT transmission

Robert Dick Wilson (1856–1930) was a Bible linguist and scholar from Princeton Theological Seminary who made major contributions in verifying the reliability of the Hebrew Bible. In his quest to determine the accuracy of the original manuscripts Wilson learned 45 languages, including Hebrew, Aramaic, and Greek, as well as all the languages into which the Scriptures had been translated up to AD 600.[55] He applied his language studies to the task of proving the historical accuracy of the OT scriptures, and he discovered scores of reasons to believe them to be true.

One particular line of investigation he undertook was to trace the recording of names of foreign kings in the OT. Apparently, ancient historians were notorious for carelessly recording royal names. Wilson explains:

> Manetho[56]...about 280 B.C. wrote a work on the dynasties of Egyptian kings...Of the kings of the 31 dynasties, he gives 140 names from 22 dynasties. Of these, 49 appear on the monuments in a form in which every consonant of Manetho's spelling may possibly be recognized, and 28 more may be recognized in part. The other 63 are unrecognizable in any single syllable...Of the 27 kings of Egypt named by Josephus, only seven are spelled the same as in Manetho. Of the 41 kings of Assyria in the lists of Africanus, only one name is

---

[54] McDowell, *The New Evidence That Demands A Verdict*, 76.

[55] Amazingly, Wilson planned and executed a 45 year program for his life. Beginning at age 25, he planned to spend 15 years in language study, then 15 years studying the OT in light of these languages, and finally, 15 years publishing his findings. Among the languages he learned were Greek, Latin, French, German, Hebrew, Italian, Spanish, Portuguese, Aramaic, Syriac, Arabic, Babylonian, Ethiopic, Phoenician, Egyptian, Coptic, Persian, and Armenian.

[56] Manetho was an Egyptian historian and priest who lived during the 3rd century BC.

recognizable and it is misspelled. In Ptolemy's list of 18 kings of Babylon, only one is spelled exactly right.[57]

Wilson discovered that the OT contains the names of at least 26 foreign kings whose names have been found on extrabiblical documents contemporary with the kings. He concluded that, with few exceptions, the Hebrew renderings of the names exactly matched the foreign spellings.[58]

Wilson goes into painstaking detail, accounting for characters and consonants in each of the names. At one point he remarks, "Every one of the 22 consonants composing the names of the kings of Persia mentioned in the Bible has been transmitted correctly to us over a space of 23 or 24 hundred years. It may be added that in no other non-Persian document are they accurately transliterated."[59] In another place, commenting on five particular kings, he writes, "These names contain at least 24 consonants, and every one of them has the proper writing in our Hebrew Bibles."[60]

Wilson also found that these kings, who lived from about 2000-400 BC, each appear in the correct chronological order, both with respect to the kings of the same country and also with respect to the kings of other countries that were contemporary to them. His conclusion from these facts was this:

> No stronger evidence for the substantial accuracy of the Old Testament records could possibly be imagined than this collection of names of kings. It means that out of 56 kings of Egypt from Shishak to Darius II, and out of the numerous kings of Assyria, Babylon, Persia, Tyre, Damascus, Moab, Israel, and Judah that ruled from 2000 to 400 B.C., the writers of the Old Testament have put the names of the 40 or more that are mentioned in records of two or more of the nations, in their proper absolute and relative order of time and in their proper place. Any expert mathematician will tell you, that to do such a thing is practically impossible without a knowledge of the facts such as could be drawn alone from contemporary and reliable records.[61]

This also substantiates the traditional, older dating of these OT narrative accounts because they would never be this accurate if they were written centuries later as some critics suggest.[62] Wilson goes to great lengths to prove this as well. One area he examines is vocabulary, especially the use of foreign words. Consistent with his conclusions regarding royal names, he found that the references to foreign words in the Bible appear at exactly

---

[57] Robert Dick Wilson, *A Scientific Investigation of the Old Testament* (Philadelphia: The Sunday School Times Company, 1926, reprint by Muschamp Press, 2008), 82-83.

[58] Ibid., 72-73. In only 2 or 3 names are there spellings that cannot be explained with certainty.

[59] Ibid., 79.

[60] Ibid., 81.

[61] Ibid., 86-87.

[62] See the discussion about the *Documentary Hypothesis* in chapter 10.

the right points in the historical timeline. There are common names of Sumerian and Babylonian origin in Genesis, Egyptian words throughout the Pentateuch,[63] words of Hittite, Indian, and Assyrian origin during Solomon's time, Babylonian words during Daniel's captivity, and so on.[64]

Wilson's thorough research proves not only the great care the biblical authors took to write the truth in meticulous accuracy, but also the extraordinarily careful way in which they correctly transmitted these narratives from copy to copy down through the generations. This implies that the writers should also be trusted in other historical matters that are not so easily verified. Wilson reasons that "the probability is that since the composers are correct in the spelling of the names of the kings they are correct also in the sayings and deeds which they record concerning these kings. And this we find in general to be true where Hebrew documents and the monuments both record the great deeds of the kings."[65]

Translations of the Bible

Transmitting the Bible reliably down through the ages is only one step in the process. How does the Bible get translated from the original languages into all the languages of its present day readers? The goal of translation is to accurately, appropriately, and naturally express the written or oral thoughts and statements of one language into another language in a form as close to the original as possible. It is imperative to retain the meaning the original author intended to convey.

Method of translation

Some people think the Bible has been translated from its original language to a number of intermediate languages before it arrives in our language, so as time goes on translations get further removed from the original. This is a misconception, however, for four reasons.

First, good modern translations go from the original language— Hebrew, Aramaic, or Greek—*directly* into a reader's language, such as English for example. There are not multiple steps of translations from language to language in between.

Second, with more ancient biblical manuscripts continually being discovered, we have more accurate renderings of the originals than what older translations had, so newer translations are even closer to the original text than older ones.

---

[63] The Pentateuch is the name given to the collection of the first five books of the OT—Genesis, Exodus, Leviticus, Numbers, and Deuteronomy.

[64] Wilson, *Scientific Investigation of the OT*, 88-90.

[65] Ibid., 85.

Third, the best translations are performed by committees of dozens of highly qualified scholars who are experts in the Bible's original languages.

Fourth, translations are audited and verified by native speakers of the target language to ensure that what the Bible says in the original languages is exactly the message that is received and understood when read or heard in the target language.

Translation philosophies

No one language ever quite matches any other language in its directness or precision, the size of its vocabulary, the way its vocabulary relates to objects, events, and concepts, or its grammatical constructs such as tense, mood, voice, person, and number.[66] This makes the job of translation very challenging, though not impossible.

There are different philosophies used in Bible translation that emphasize different degrees of readability, reading level, use of cultural idioms, use of established theological terms, continuity with previous translations, and literary equivalence. This last term refers to the amount of literal correspondence between the original and translated texts. This represents a spectrum that is often described as *word-for-word* on one end and *thought-for-thought* on the other end.

Word-for-word seeks to match the individual words and word order of the original language as closely as possible to the target language. Thought-for-thought expresses the original language more in comparable thoughts, rather than words. The former is a *formal* equivalence that remains closer to the original text and therefore requires less interpretation on the part of the translator. The latter is considered to be more of a *functional* equivalence that enhances readability at the possible expense of injecting the translator's interpretation into the text.

In practice, almost no translation is exclusively one or the other, as most translations seek some kind of balance between the two. The introduction to the English Standard Version (ESV) Bible explains, "Every translation is at many points a trade-off between literal precision and readability."[67] In all cases, the goal is to retain the meaning of the original text since we want to know what the original authors intended to communicate. The meaning can be missed by adding to the original, omitting something, or translating so as to confuse the meaning or give the wrong meaning.[68] The following chart shows this translation spectrum and depicts the relative placement of the most common English translations.[69]

---

[66] Larry Walker and Raymond L. Elliot, *The Origin of the Bible*, 234-245.

[67] *The Holy Bible*, English Standard Version (Wheaton, IL: Crossway, 2001), viii.

[68] Raymond L. Elliot, "Bible Translation", *The Origin of the Bible*, 270.

[69] http://www.mardel.com/bible-translation-guide.aspx, accessed Feb 26, 2011.

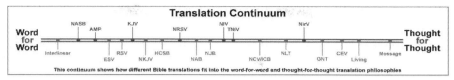

Key: NASB = New American Standard Bible
AMP = Amplified Bible
ESV = English Standard Version
RSV = Revised Standard Version
KJV = King James Version
NKJV = New King James Version
HCSB = Holman Christian Standard Bible
NRSV = New Revised Standard Version
NAB = New American Bible

NJB = New Jerusalem Bible
NIV = New International Version
TNIV = Today's New International Version
NCV = New Century Version
ICB = International Children's Bible
NLT = New Living Translation
NirV = New International Reader's Version
GNT = Good News Translation
CEV = Contemporary English Version

There is some debate about which translation philosophy is superior. Functional equivalence, also called *dynamic equivalence*, is a relatively recent theory of translation, being developed in the last fifty years or so. It had its impetus on the mission field in the explosion of Bible translations into new languages due to an increased awareness of the diversity of ethnic groups. All things considered, a greater emphasis on a literal translation[70] (formal equivalence) seems the better approach, since it remains closer to the original text and thereby properly distinguishes the tasks of translation and interpretation. There is no principal difference in the meaning of any passage in a scholarly translation of the Bible today that gives appropriate weight to formal equivalence.[71]

Have the biblical authors told us the truth?

So far we have established that the biblical authors intended to write history and that history has been reliably handed down through the centuries so that we can trust that what we read today is what those authors wrote. The last remaining aspect of our examination of biblical reliability is to determine whether or not we can trust that the authors related true facts about history.

We have already seen from Wilson's research how the OT authors recorded many true facts. We will now look at the NT. Since the events in

---

[70] Note, *literal* in this context refers only to translation, not to interpretation. It does not mean everything in the Bible is to be taken literally, since it often uses figures of speech and other symbolic language.

[71] On the other hand, we can see *some* diversity in meaning in the functionally equivalent translations, especially the more to the right we move on the translation continuum. The versions furthest to the right on the continuum are called *paraphrases*, and not *translations*. They are often made by individuals, not committees, and tend to render the original meaning of the text less accurately because of their heavy use of contemporary idioms and colorful language. Sometimes verse numbers are not used because the text has been rearranged so much.

the life of Jesus are especially significant in our study, we will limit this particular examination to the accounts of Jesus. There are two common objections about this aspect of NT reliability. The first is that its authors did not really know Jesus, so they were *unable* to tell us the truth. The other objection is that its authors had a theological agenda, so they were *unwilling* to tell us the truth. In either case, the authors did not give us the true facts. However, an examination of the evidence reveals that both of these objections are without merit.

Ability to tell us the truth

We normally put a great deal of stock in eyewitness testimony—and for good reason. Seeing is believing, as they say, and eyewitnesses tell us what they saw with their own eyes. There are four important criteria to consider when evaluating the truth of eyewitness testimony.

The first is the vantage point of the witness in relation to the event. The closer the witness was to the actual event and the more involved he was in it, the greater his credibility in reporting what was seen and heard.

The second is the interval of time between the event and the witness' reporting of the event. The shorter the interval, the less likely the witness' memory will have become clouded about the details of the event.

The third is the significance of the event to the witness. We should consider if the event affected the witness in some important way or if it was of little consequence to him. A life-changing event will be easier to remember accurately since its effects have impacted the witness' life.

The fourth is the number of witnesses testifying to the event. The more witness testimonies the better we can fill in the details of the whole picture and also corroborate overlapping observations.

Of course, we do not always rely exclusively on eyewitnesses. We also generally trust carefully researched accounts of past events, such as a biographer today might write of some person alive today or who lived at some time in the past. Hopefully though, *the biographer* has relied on eyewitness accounts or other primary sources to get the facts right.

Early and proximate sources

The sources which report the events in the life of Jesus are very near to that time and place. Being his earliest followers, they were in a position to know what happened. All the NT books were written in the first century by eyewitnesses to the events or close associates of the eyewitnesses. The Gospels written by Matthew, Mark, Luke, and John were likely completed around AD 40-65, which is only 7 to 32 years after Jesus' earthly life.[72]

---

[72] John A.T. Robinson, *Redating the New Testament* (Eugene, OR: Wipf and Stock, 1976, 2000).

Most of the other NT books were completed by AD 70.[73] Luke wrote Acts around AD 62. Paul wrote all his letters around AD 48-66. Peter wrote his letters about AD 62-67. James wrote around AD 49 and Jude around AD 65. The Book of Hebrews was written around AD 70.

In comparison, the Greek historian Plutarch[74] wrote his biography of Alexander the Great 400 to 450 years after the events, yet it is considered to be accurate, so 7 to 32 years for the NT books is extraordinarily short by ancient documentary standards. Even so, some people think that one to three decades is simply too long a time to be able to accurately recall all the events in the kind of detail conveyed by the Gospels. There are three reasons to believe this was quite possible, though.

First, even in our own experience we can accurately recall events from many years ago, often back to our childhood. This is especially true for events that had a huge emotional impact on us. For example, many people remember in considerable detail the events of 9/11. How much easier is it to remember something that radically changed your own life?

Second, the recollections of the NT authors were not just *individual* memories, but *collective* ones. These were momentous events that forever changed the lives of thousands of people. There were hundreds of eyewitnesses and the stories were constantly being retold. This repetition of the stories provided a check and balance on the accuracy of the apostles' writings.[75]

Third, Jewish oral transmission of sacred traditions was highly developed and reliable. The stories about Jesus were being exchanged almost immediately following his resurrection. In fact, several of the key passages in the NT came from very early oral traditions, some of which date to within two years of the crucifixion.[76] These creeds, therefore, represent the earliest sources for the life of Jesus.[77]

It is extremely difficult to create a legend from an historical figure in such a short interval of time. There were simply too many eyewitnesses to the events alive at the time who would refute the Gospels as being false,

---

[73] Scholars are divided on when John wrote his Gospel, letters, and Revelation. Some say around AD 85-90, but others place them prior to AD 70, when the Jerusalem Temple was destroyed, or even prior to AD 66, when the Romans began their siege on Jerusalem. The earlier dates give strong weight to the fact that John never mentions the Jewish War, nor the destruction of the Temple and, in fact, speaks about Jerusalem in the present as if it was intact, and not destroyed. This seems like a very reasonable assumption, especially in light of 4 Ezra, a non-biblical Jewish religious book written after AD 70, which contains extensive reflections of the after-effects of the destruction.

[74] Plutarch was a Greek historian and biographer who lived in the first and second century AD.

[75] Komoszewski, *Reinventing Jesus*, 33-34.

[76] For example, Rom 1:3-4, Rom 4:25, Rom 10:9-10, 1 Cor 11:23-26, 1 Cor 15:3-7, Phil 2:6-11, Col 1:15-18, 1 Tim 3:16, 1 Tim 6:13, and 2 Tim 2:8.

[77] Gary R. Habermas, *The Historical Jesus: Ancient Evidence for the Life of Christ* (Joplin, MO: College Press Publishing Company, 2003, 6th printing), 143-154. A creed is an often recited statement of religious belief.

but we see no evidence of this. It would be like someone today claiming that Billy Graham was the president of the United States in 1985. This assertion would be immediately rejected, and the testimony would certainly not live on for centuries and cultivate billions of followers.[78] There was simply not enough time for legendary influences to erase or alter the core historical facts. The NT authors were in a position to know and communicate what really happened, and, in fact, this is their specific claim in several places as noted earlier.

We hold eyewitness testimony in high regard in our courts today. If we can believe Plutarch and dozens of other ancient writers who were not eyewitnesses to the accounts they reported, how can we dismiss the New Testament authors as being unable to give us true accounts of Jesus?

Multiple attestation

There are multiple, independent witnesses to the events of Jesus' life. Two of the Gospel writers, Matthew and John, were direct disciples of Jesus, specifically chosen by him. They walked, talked, and ate with him for three years. Mark was a personal associate of Peter, who was also a disciple of Jesus. Paul had a personal encounter with Jesus and was a contemporary of the apostles. Luke, an associate of Paul, states how he carefully related eyewitness accounts. James was the brother of Jesus.

For the most part, these witnesses represent independent sources. Although Matthew and Luke may have used Mark as a source, they each contain material not found in any other Gospel. With John's independent Gospel and the independent accounts of Paul, Peter, and James, we have at least seven corroborating views of Jesus. These accounts provide just the sort of picture we would expect of seven reliable eyewitnesses—solid agreement on the important facts of the historical events, accompanied by varying details from the unique perspective of each witness.

Multiple, independent accounts that provide eyewitness or primary source testimony is strong evidence that cannot be ignored or discounted. The more witnesses we have, the more reason we have to believe a story, especially when the details are confirmed among the accounts.

Willingness to tell us the truth

The NT authors were certainly *able* to tell us the truth, but it is possible they were *unwilling* to tell us the truth. Perhaps they were overly biased or had a particular agenda and therefore made up things that were not true. Maybe they deliberately lied in order to make a legend out of Jesus. Skeptics are quick to make such challenges, but the evidence

---

[78] There are an estimated 2.2 billion followers of Christ today. Mandryk, *Operation World*, 2.

indicates otherwise. Let's examine five reasons to believe that the NT authors were willing to tell the truth.

Embarrassing details

The criterion of embarrassment refers to incidents that would have been awkward or counterproductive for the early Christian church. The NT writers would have no motive to include embarrassing material because it would make them look bad in the eyes of their readers. Therefore, the inclusion of such material is a sign of willingness to tell the truth no matter the consequences.

For example, it was embarrassing to report that women discovered the empty tomb of Jesus. Women were not considered to be reliable witnesses in Israel at that time, yet all four Gospels state that it was women who first found the tomb empty. The authors had every reason to ignore this fact and say that men found the empty tomb because that would have been accepted more easily by others. Their claim that it was women only makes sense if it were true. The NT is filled with unfavorable portrayals of Jesus and his disciples. Here are some more examples of these embarrassing details:

1. Jesus had an unremarkable background as a poor, uneducated carpenter from the obscure town of Nazareth (Mark 6:1-3).

2. Jesus was sinless, yet he submitted to baptism by John the Baptist for the forgiveness of sins (Mark 1:4, 9).

3. Jesus said he was not able to do major miracles in his home town of Nazareth (Mark 6:4-5).

4. Jesus' brothers, future leaders of the faith, did not believe in him for a long time (John 7:5).

5. One of Jesus' disciples, Matthew, was a tax collector, a profession despised by the Jews (Luke 5:27).

6. Jesus once referred to Peter as Satan (Matt 16:23).

7. Jesus got so angry that he physically cleared the Temple in Jerusalem (John 2:13-16).

8. Jesus referred to Gentiles as "little dogs" not worthy of God's blessings (Mark 7:24-30).

9. Jesus was seemingly lax about certain parts of the Law, such as touching lepers and the dead, and healing on the Sabbath (Mark 1:40-41, Mark 5:41, Mark 3:1-5).

10. Jesus asked a man why he called Jesus good when only God was good (Mark 10:18).

11. Jesus was accused of being demon possessed (John 7:20).

12. Jesus did not know when he would return (Mark 13:32).

13. Jesus' disciples misunderstood many of his teachings (Mark 9:32).

14. Many of Jesus' disciples turned away and no longer followed him (John 6:66).

15. Jesus was betrayed by one of his own disciples (Mark 14:10).

16. Jesus' disciples kept falling asleep instead of praying for him as he had asked on the night of his arrest (Mark 14:32-42).

17. Jesus' disciples all fled when he was arrested (Mark 14:50).

18. Peter denied Jesus three times on the night of his arrest (Mark 14:66-72).

19. Jesus was beaten and then executed by crucifixion (Mark 15:15).

20. On the cross, Jesus commended the care of his mother into the hands of his disciple John, rather than James, his still unbelieving brother (John 19:25-27).

21. Jesus was buried in the tomb of a man who was a member of the Jewish Council who condemned him (Mark 15:42-46).

22. Jesus' disciples were very slow to believe that he had been resurrected (John 20:25).

23. The greatest persecutor of Christians, Saul, became their greatest missionary (Acts 8:1-3).

If someone wanted to manufacture a legend of a divine Jesus, he certainly wouldn't include stories that painted such an unflattering picture of Jesus and his followers. There are good explanations for these embarrassing events, but why would the authors put such obstacles to belief in the minds of their readers if they were simply making up the whole thing? The presence of these depictions argues for the truthfulness of the accounts.[79] In contrast, we see in the apocryphal gospels[80] of the second, third, and fourth centuries, the tendency to omit these kinds of troubling details and instead emphasize Jesus' divine qualities and miracles.[81]

---

[79] Examples of this principle from the OT include Abraham having a child with his wife's maidservant, Moses' murder of an Egyptian, the enslavement of the Hebrews in Egypt, their forty years of wandering in the wilderness due to their rebellion, Moses' need to receive the Ten Commandments a second time because he destroyed the first tablets in anger at the Israelites' idolatry, God not permitting Moses to enter the Promised Land, the Israelites' failure to drive out all the Canaanites, David's adultery with Bathsheba and arranging for her husband's death, Israel's exiles to Assyria and Babylon, and the destruction of the Jewish Temple. Many others could be cited.

[80] The term "apocryphal gospels" is used to describe Gospel-like books that were written later than the first century AD by Jews or Christians who were not contemporaries of Jesus. These books provide some insights into early Christian history, but they often contain imaginative and unorthodox elements and were therefore not considered to be Scripture by the early Church.

[81] Robert Stein, "Criteria for the Gospel's Authenticity", *Contending with Christianity's Critics*, 93.

Lack of embellishment

Another sign of willingness to tell the truth is the straightforward recounting of events without exaggeration. The following description of Jesus' crucifixion is typical of all four Gospels:

> A certain man from Cyrene, Simon, the father of Alexander and Rufus, was passing by on his way in from the country, and they forced him to carry the cross. They brought Jesus to the place called Golgotha (which means "the place of the skull"). Then they offered him wine mixed with myrrh, but he did not take it. And they crucified him. Dividing up his clothes, they cast lots to see what each would get. It was nine in the morning when they crucified him. The written notice of the charge against him read: THE KING OF THE JEWS (Mark 15:21-26).

This deeply disturbing and sorrowful event lacks embellishment of any kind. The worst part of it is related by the simple phrase, "they crucified him." It is a straightforward description of an event much like we would expect an objective eyewitness to relate. Consider also the extraordinarily profound event of Jesus' resurrection. Here is how it is described in Luke:

> On the first day of the week, very early in the morning, the women took the spices they had prepared and went to the tomb. They found the stone rolled away from the tomb, but when they entered, they did not find the body of the Lord Jesus. While they were wondering about this, suddenly two men in clothes that gleamed like lightning stood beside them. In their fright the women bowed down with their faces to the ground, but the men said to them, "Why do you look for the living among the dead? He is not here; he has risen!" (Luke 24:1-6).

Notice that this incident also lacks elaborate and sensational description, which would be clear signs of fabrication. Information that is stated simply and matter-of-factly resonates truth more than that which contains fancy adornments. There are no bold declarations of the theological significance of this event. William Lane Craig explains, "The resurrection is not witnessed or described, and there is no reflection on Jesus' triumph over sin and death, no use of Christological titles, no quotation of fulfilled prophecy, no description of the Risen Lord."[82] Instead, we read in the accounts the simple facts of the matter. By contrast, consider the following account from the non-biblical Gospel of Peter,[83] written in the late second century:

---

[82] Craig, *Reasonable Faith* (third edition, 2008), 367.

[83] Obviously, this book was not written by the apostle Peter, since it was penned more than 100 years after his death. It was common practice in ancient times to ascribe authorship of a work to an admired individual, which is what happened in this case. Such works are referred to as *pseudepigraphal,* from the Greek meaning "falsely attributed."

[34]Early in the morning, as the Sabbath dawned, <u>a crowd came from Jerusalem and the surrounding area</u> to see the sealed crypt. [35]But during the night on which the Lord's day dawned, while the soldiers stood guard two on their watch, <u>a great voice came from the sky.</u> [36]<u>They saw the skies open and two men descend from there</u>; they were very bright and drew near to the tomb. [37]<u>The stone cast before the entrance rolled away by itself</u> and moved to one side; the tomb was open and both young men entered. [38]When the solders [sic] saw these things, they woke up the centurion and <u>the elders—for they were also there on guard.</u> [39]As they were explaining what they had seen, they saw three men emerge from the tomb, two of them supporting the other, <u>with a cross following behind them.</u> [40]<u>The heads of the two reached up to the sky</u>, but the head of the one they were leading went up above the skies. [41]And they heard a voice from the skies, "Have you preached to those who are asleep?" [42]And <u>a reply came from the cross, "Yes."</u>[84]

Notice how this account parallels the account in the Gospel of Luke in some ways, but contains several elaborations. First, there is a crowd from the whole area who comes to the tomb. The soldiers are said to have heard a voice from Heaven, seen two men descending from there, and witnessed the stone rolling away on its own. There are (presumably Jewish) elders also guarding the tomb through the night. Then we read about two giant men and Jesus, whose heads reach up to sky, and also a walking, talking cross. These are indications of embellishment, which suggest an unwillingness of this author to tell the truth. This is how a legend is created.

This stands in stark contrast to the NT authors, who showed considerable restraint in their desire to describe the events as truthfully as they could. In fact, the letters of the earliest church leaders—James, Peter, John, and Paul—never argue for the truth of the resurrection of Jesus. They simply *assume* their readers accept it as fact because the event was so well-known and well-attested in the day. Their references to it are done more in passing as they make other points of doctrine or practice.

Dissimilar ideas and terms

The inclusion of ideas and terms that were not common in Judaism or the early church indicates a willingness on the part of the authors to tell the truth. Writers have a natural tendency to "write back" into an historical account something they would seek to legitimize. If a saying or teaching is not found in Judaism prior to Jesus, then there is good reason to think it began with Jesus. Likewise, if the early church did not repeat it or use it,

---

[84] Translated by Bart D. Ehrman, *Lost Scriptures* (New York: Oxford University Press, 2003), 33.

then they obviously did not invent it.[85] Dissimilarity therefore shows that the authors were interested in conveying truth, no matter what.

One good example of this involves the use of the title "Son of Man" by Jesus in the Gospels. This is Jesus' favorite title for himself, which is used 82 times in the Gospel accounts. However, it is found in only one place in the OT in the same sense that Jesus used it (Dan 7:13). It is found only four times in the rest of the NT, and only in one case is it used as a title for Jesus.[86] Because of its scant usage before and after the life of Jesus, it is highly unlikely that this title could have been a legendary development of the early church. Rather, it suggests that the title "Son of Man" was faithfully retained in the texts because that is how Jesus really referred to himself.[87] Here are some other examples of dissimilarity:

1. Jesus rejected fasting, which conflicts with the Jewish practice of the day and that of the early church.

2. Jesus referred to the Father as *Abba* in prayer.

3. Jesus frequently used parables, which are not found in the rest of the NT.

4. Jesus claimed authority to extend the meaning of Mosaic laws against murder and adultery to also refer to anger and lust, respectively.

These ideas, which are dissimilar to Judaism and early Christianity, are evidence for their authenticity in the NT.

Early linguistic traditions

This criterion refers to the inclusion of pre-Christian expressions in descriptions of events. The closer an incident is reported in contemporary style and idioms, the more we can trust that it is an early account and therefore authentic. For example, the following Aramaic expressions were attributed directly to Jesus in the Gospel of Mark:[88]

1. *Boanerges*, which means "Sons of Thunder" (3:17)

2. *Talitha cumi*, which means "Little girl, I say to you, arise" (5:41)

3. *Ephphatha*, which means "Be opened" (7:34)

4. *Amen*, which means "Truly" (8:12, 9:1)

---

[85] Komoszewski, *Reinventing Jesus*, 39-40.

[86] Acts 7:56, Heb 2:6, Rev 1:13, and Rev 14:14. Furthermore, it is found only three times in Christian literature outside the Bible within the Church's first 120 years.

[87] Stein, *Contending with Christianity's Critics*, 95-96. We will discuss the meaning of this term in chapter 15.

[88] It is widely considered that Aramaic was the common language of Palestine in Jesus' day before it was supplanted by Greek soon afterwards.

5. *Abba*, which means "dear Father" (14:36)
6. *Eloi eloi lama sabachthani*, which means "My God, my God, why have you forsaken me?" (15:34)

It would have been far easier to relate these phrases in Greek when the accounts were later written down, but in the interests of authenticity the original sayings were retained.

Another example of this is Mark's account that the empty tomb was discovered by the women "on the first day of the week." The earliest Christian traditions referred to this day as "the third day." The fact that Mark uses the older phrasing suggests that the empty tomb story is not a late developing legend. This is further confirmed by the fact that the phrase "the first day of the week" is very awkward in the Greek, but is very natural when translated back into Aramaic. Thus it would have been far easier for Mark to use the more common "third day" reckoning.[89] That he did not indicates a desire to faithfully relate the true facts.

Willingness to die

Perhaps the clearest evidence that the NT authors' have told us the truth is that they were willing to die for believing what they wrote. If they had made it all up, surely they would have recanted their elaborate hoax before suffering a martyr's death. We have already addressed this previously in our discussion of evidence for Jesus' resurrection, so we will not repeat it here except to say that it is hard to fathom that anyone would willingly go to their death for what they *knew* to be a lie.

Other signs of truthfulness

It is a mark of authenticity when an antagonistic source expresses agreement regarding a person or an event in a case where it is contrary to his best interest to do so. When one's critic or enemy admits something that makes him look bad, then it is strong evidence that the claim is true. We find several examples of these cases surrounding Jesus.

The miracles of Jesus

Jesus worked many miracles during his brief ministry in Palestine. It is interesting to observe that those who opposed him did not deny his miracle working. Instead, they attributed his miracles to Satan. "Then they brought him a demon-possessed man who was blind and mute, and Jesus healed him, so that he could both talk and see. All the people were

---

[89] Craig, *Reasonable Faith*, third edition, 366.

astonished and said, 'Could this be the Son of David?' But when the Pharisees heard this, they said, 'It is only by Beelzebub, the prince of demons, that this fellow drives out demons'" (Matt 12:22-24). This acknowledges that Jesus really did do miracles. His enemies could not deny them, so instead they questioned how Jesus was able to do them.

The empty tomb

When the tomb of Jesus was reported by the disciples to be empty, the Jewish authorities claimed his body had been stolen:

> Some of the guards went into the city and reported to the chief priests everything that had happened. When the chief priests had met with the elders and devised a plan, they gave the soldiers a large sum of money, telling them, "You are to say, 'His disciples came during the night and stole him away while we were asleep.' If this report gets to the governor, we will satisfy him and keep you out of trouble." So the soldiers took the money and did as they were instructed. This story has been widely circulated among the Jews to this day" (Matt 28:11-15).

This is a remarkable admission because it acknowledges that the tomb was really empty. Of course they had to accuse the disciples of stealing the body since they themselves could not produce it. Moreover, Matthew makes the point that this same story continued to be circulated even to the time of his writing. This means the Jews were saying this for many years without ever producing any evidence to support their claim.

Once hostile critics

Jesus was not popular with many people, both while he lived and after his death. In the Bible we find the astonishing conversion of two of his harshest critics. One of them was James, the brother of Jesus.[90] Early in the Gospels, we learn that Jesus' brothers did not follow him. "Even his own brothers did not believe in him" (John 7:5). This is not really surprising. We can all imagine how we might react if one of our own siblings was thought to be a sinless, miracle-working, awe-inspiring, divine messiah-figure. This unbelief among the brothers would have included James, whom we do not hear anything more about until the early church arose following Jesus' resurrection.

It is church tradition that James became the leader of the first Jerusalem church. This is borne out by a few references in the NT. We find that he is among the "apostles and elders" in an important council in Jerusalem, where he spoke last and made the final judgment (Acts 15:13). Paul tells of another time when he and others "went to see James, and all

---

[90] Jesus had at least four brothers—James, Joseph, Simon and Judas (Matt 13:55).

the elders were present" (Acts 21:18). Paul tells of yet another occasion when he met with James: "I saw none of the other apostles—only James, the Lord's brother" (Gal 1:19). It is this James who is thought to have written the NT book of James, where he calls himself a "slave of the Lord Jesus Christ" (Jas 1:1).[91] James was stoned to death for his faith in AD 62.[92] What can explain this complete reversal in James' attitude towards Jesus—from jealous and mocking sibling to devoted follower and martyr? There is only one reasonable explanation, which the apostle Paul gives when he says that the resurrected Jesus "appeared to James" (1 Cor 15:7).

Paul's story is clearly depicted in the NT. He first appears in Acts 7, when he was present at the stoning of the martyr Stephen: "Saul was there, giving approval to his death" (Acts 8:1).[93] That began a great persecution of the church: "Saul began to destroy the church. Going from house to house, he dragged off men and women and put them in prison" (Acts 8:3). He later honestly admitted, "I persecuted the church of God" (1 Cor 15:9). As he "was still breathing out murderous threats against the Lord's disciples" (Acts 9:1), Saul had an encounter with the risen Jesus on the road to Damascus. He immediately began preaching that Jesus is Savior and Lord: "Saul spent several days with the disciples in Damascus. At once he began to preach in the synagogues that Jesus is the Son of God" (Acts 9:19-20). Just as with James, a dramatic encounter with the risen Jesus turned Paul from an antagonistic murderer of Christians to the first and greatest Christian missionary to the Gentile world. He wrote almost half the books of the New Testament before he was eventually martyred for his devotion to Jesus at the hands of Emperor Nero around AD 63-68.

Summary

The biblical narratives are written as history and are supposed to be read as history. We can also trust that the Bible we have today contains what the original authors wrote. The biblical texts have been reliably transmitted to us down through the centuries and have been accurately translated into the languages of its readers today. Finally, we know that the biblical authors were both willing and able to tell us what really happened. They were in a position to know and wanted us to know the truth. These facts allow us to conclude with confidence that the Bible is a historically reliable document.

---

[91] The writer of the Book of Jude is also thought to be one of Christ's four brothers (Jude is a form of the name Judas). He begins his book with this statement: "Jude, a servant of Jesus Christ and a brother of James..." Although less prominent than James, Jude was also formerly one of Jesus' critics (John 7:5), who subsequently became his disciple.

[92] Flavius Josephus, *Jewish Antiquities,* 20.197, translated by Paul L. Maier, *Josephus: The Essential Writings* (Grand Rapids: Kregel Publications, 1988), 276.

[93] Saul is the apostle Paul's pre-Christian name (Acts 13:9).

CHAPTER 9

History speaks

Most people want to know whether or not the New Testament is historically true before they can begin to think about believing its theological message. If they doubt the historical truth of the New Testament, that is the end of the matter.

Paul Barnett (1935-)
Historian, New Testament scholar
Is The New Testament Reliable?

The truth of Christianity is bound up with the truth of certain historical facts, such that if those facts should be disproved, so would Christianity. But at the same time, this makes Christianity unique because, unlike most other world religions, we now have a means of verifying its truth by historical evidence.

William Lane Craig (1949-)
Philosopher, scholar, author
Reasonable Faith

We have seen that the biblical authors intended to write true historical accounts, they were willing and able to tell us the truth, and we actually have today what they wrote. In this chapter, we will put the biblical writers to more tests by looking for evidence outside the Bible that corroborates the historical accounts we find inside the Bible. We find this evidence from two main sources—secular literature and archaeology.

Corroboration through ancient secular literature

There is a considerable amount of ancient secular literature that confirms various facts in the biblical accounts. We will also refer to some of this in the next section that discusses archaeology, but in this section we will examine what some ancient secular writings have to say specifically about Jesus and some aspects of early Christianity.

A secular portrait of Jesus and Christianity

Some people believe that Jesus of Nazareth was not a real person who lived two thousand years ago in Palestine. We have already examined many accounts concerning Jesus in the NT. This is remarkably strong evidence for the historicity of Jesus, but there is also a substantial amount of data outside the Bible that Jesus was a real person who lived in the early first century AD. Not only do many early extrabiblical sources speak about Jesus, they paint a picture of him and early Christianity remarkably similar to what the NT tells us. Let's review some of these first century and early second century secular sources.[1]

Thallus

Thallus (c. AD 52-55) was a Samaritan historian who wrote a three-volume history of the Mediterranean world from the Trojan War (12th century BC) to his own time. Most of his work has been lost, but fortunately some of it was preserved by Sextus Julius Africanus in his *History of the World*, written around AD 217-221.

Writing about the crucifixion of Jesus and the darkness that covered the land during that event, Africanus writes, "On the whole world there pressed a most fearful darkness; and the rocks were rent by an earthquake, and many places in Judea and other districts were thrown down. This darkness Thallus, in the third book of his *History*, calls, as appears to me without reason, an eclipse of the sun."[2]

Africanus implies that Thallus associates the darkness to Jesus' crucifixion, but we are not told if Thallus mentions Jesus specifically. At the very least, he does describe a widespread darkness in Judea which he explains as an eclipse. Africanus doubts him on the reason for the darkness, probably because an eclipse could not occur during a full moon as was the case during the Jewish Passover season. If this brief statement by Thallus does indeed refer to Jesus' crucifixion, then it affirms three facts in the NT:

1. An account of the crucifixion was known in the Mediterranean region by the middle of the first century AD, less than 20 years after the event.

---

[1] Much of the information in this section is based on Habermas, *The Historical Jesus*, 187-201.

[2] Julius Africanus, *Extant Writings*, XVIII in the *Ante-Nicene Fathers*, edited by Alexander Roberts and James Donaldson (Grand Rapids: Eerdmans, 1973), vol. VI, 130.

2. There was a widespread darkness in the land around the time of the crucifixion.
3. Unbelievers offered naturalistic explanations for supernatural events.

Josephus

Flavius Josephus (AD 37-97), was a Jewish historian working for the Romans. His two major works include *The Antiquities* and *The Jewish War*, written around AD 90-95. His two direct references to Jesus are the earliest by a non-Christian author. His first reference is brief. He says, "Convening the judges of the Sanhedrin, he brought before them a man named James, the brother of Jesus, who was called the Christ."[3] The second reference is longer:

> At this time there was a wise man called Jesus, and his conduct was good, and he was known to be virtuous. Many people among the Jews and the other nations became his disciples. Pilate condemned him to be crucified, and to die. But those who had become his disciples did not abandon his discipleship. They reported that he had appeared to them three days after his crucifixion, and that he was alive. Accordingly, he was perhaps the Messiah, concerning whom the prophets have reported wonders. And the tribe of the Christians, so named after him, has not disappeared to this day.[4]

Josephus affirms eleven facts from the NT in these two references:

1. Jesus was known as a wise and virtuous man.
2. He had many Jewish and Gentile disciples.
3. Pilate condemned him to death.
4. His method of execution was crucifixion.
5. His disciples reported seeing him alive after he had died.
6. This occurred three days after his crucifixion.
7. Consequently, his disciples continued to proclaim his teachings.
8. Perhaps he was the Messiah foretold in the Jewish scriptures.
9. Christians have not disappeared to his present day.
10. Jesus was the brother of James.
11. Jesus was called the Christ (also Messiah).

---

[3] Josephus, *Antiquities*, 20.197, Maier, 276. The Sanhedrin was the ruling Jewish Council in Jerusalem.
[4] Ibid., 20.63, 264-265.

Tacitus

Cornelius Tacitus (c. AD 55-120) was a Roman historian who lived during the reign of six Roman emperors. His two greatest works are the *Annals,* which cover the period from AD 14-68, and the *Histories,* which cover the period from AD 68-96. Tacitus recorded one reference to Christ and two to early Christianity, one each in his major works. He wrote the following in regards to the great fire in Rome under Nero:

> But all human efforts, all the lavish gifts of the emperor, and the propitiations of the gods, did not banish the sinister belief that the conflagration was the result of an order. Consequently, to get rid of the report, Nero fastened the guilt and inflicted the most exquisite tortures on a class hated for their abominations, called Christians by the populace. Christus, from whom the name had its origin, suffered the extreme penalty during the reign of Tiberius at the hands of one of our procurators, Pontius Pilatus, and a most mischievous superstition, thus checked for the moment, again broke out not only in Judaea, the first source of the evil, but even in Rome, where all things hideous and shameful from every part of the world find their center and become popular. Accordingly, an arrest was first made of all who pleaded guilty; then, upon their information, an immense multitude was convicted, not so much of the crime of firing the city, as of hatred against mankind. Mockery of every sort was added to their deaths. Covered with the skins of beasts, they were torn by dogs and perished, or were nailed to crosses, or were doomed to the flames and burnt, to serve as a nightly illumination, when daylight had expired. Nero offered his gardens for the spectacle, and was exhibiting a show in the circus, while he mingled with the people in the dress of a charioteer or stood aloft on a car. Hence, even for criminals who deserved extreme and exemplary punishment, there arose a feeling of compassion; for it was not, as it seemed, for the public good, but to glut one man's cruelty, that they were being destroyed.[5]

This account implicitly or explicitly confirms eleven separate facts reported in the NT:

1. Christians were named for their founder, Christus (Latin).
2. Christ was put to death by the Roman procurator Pontius Pilatus.
3. This happened during the reign of Tiberius (AD 14-37).
4. His death ended the alleged "superstition" for a short time.
5. This superstition "broke out" again, especially in Judea where it originated.
6. The followers of Christus took the teaching to Rome.

---

[5] Tacitus, *The Annals,* 15.44.

7. Christians were hated for their so-called "abominations."
8. These Christians were arrested after pleading guilty.
9. Many of them were convicted for allegedly hating mankind.
10. The Christians were mocked.
11. The Christians were tortured and killed.

Tacitus seems to be indirectly, although perhaps not intentionally, referring to the resurrection when he says that the movement "broke out" again after Jesus had died.

Pliny the Younger

Pliny the Younger (c. AD 61–112) was a Roman author and also governor of Bithynia in Asia Minor.[6] Pliny was confronted with a problem of how to deal with the Christians and sought advice from the Roman Emperor Trajan. Here are excerpts of that letter:

> I have never been present at an examination of Christians. So, I do not know the nature or the extent of the punishments usually dealt out to them, nor the grounds for starting an investigation and how far it should be carried...For the moment this is the line I have taken with all persons brought before me on the charge of being Christians. I have asked them in person if they are Christians; if they admit it, I repeat the question a second and a third time, with a warning of the punishment awaiting them. If they persist, I order them to be led away for punishment; for whatever the nature of their admission, I am convinced that their stubbornness and unshakeable obstinacy ought to be punished. There have been others similarly fanatical who are Roman citizens; I have entered them on the list of persons to be sent to Rome for punishment....

> I considered that I should dismiss any who denied that they were or ever had been Christians, once they had repeated after me a formula of invocation to the gods and had made offerings of wine and incense to your statue (which I had ordered to be brought into court for this purpose along with images of the gods), and furthermore had used the name of Christ. Real Christians (I understand) can never be induced to do these things....

> They declared that the sum total of their guilt or error amounted to no more than this: they had met regularly before dawn on a fixed day to chant verses alternately among themselves in honor of Christ as if to a god, and also to bind themselves by oath, not for any criminal purpose, but to abstain from theft, robbery and adultery, to commit no breach of

---

[6] He is the nephew and adopted son of the natural historian known as Pliny the Elder.

trust and not to refuse to return a deposit upon demand. After this ceremony it had been their custom to disperse and later to take food of an ordinary harmless kind. But they had in fact given this up since my edict, issued on your instructions which banned all political societies. This made me decide it was all the more necessary to extract the truth from two slave women (whom they call "deaconesses") by torture. I found nothing but a degenerate sort of cult carried to extravagant lengths...I have therefore postponed any further examination and hastened to consult you...[7]

This letter by Pliny substantiates thirteen facts about early Christianity:

1. Christians were punished and tortured for their faith.
2. Some professing Christians recanted their faith.
3. "Real" Christians could not be induced to recant.
4. Roman citizens were becoming Christians.
5. Christians met regularly on a fixed day (probably Sunday).
6. They often met pre-dawn.
7. They sang songs in honor of Christ when they met.
8. Christ was worshiped as deity.
9. They committed to living virtuous lives free from theft and adultery, and they could be trusted.
10. The Christians claimed they had committed no crimes.
11. Taking food of "an ordinary kind" is likely a reference to Christian communion.
12. There were recognized positions in the church ("deaconesses").
13. Christians were considered to be fanatics, part of a "degenerate cult carried to extravagant lengths."

Emperor Trajan

Marcus Ulpius Nerva Traianus (AD 53-117), commonly known as Trajan, was Roman Emperor from AD 98-117. Trajan responded to Pliny's letter as follows:

The method you have pursued, my dear Pliny, in sifting the cases of those denounced to you as Christians is extremely proper. It is not possible to lay down any general rule which can be applied as the fixed standard in all cases of this nature. No search should be made for these people; when they are denounced and found guilty they must be punished; with the restriction, however, that when the party denies

---

[7] Pliny, *Letters*, translated by William Melmoth, revised by W.M.L. Hutchinson (Cambridge: Harvard University Press, 1935), vol. II, X:96.

himself to be a Christian, and shall give proof that he is not by worshipping the gods he shall be pardoned on the ground of repentance even though he may have formerly incurred suspicion. Information without the accuser's name inscribed must not be admitted in evidence against anyone, as it is introducing a very dangerous precedent, and by no means agreeable to the spirit of the age.[8]

Trajan replies that Pliny is correct that confessing Christians who persisted in their faith must be punished. This corroborates, from a Roman Emperor no less, the NT assertion that Christians were persecuted for their faith.

Suetonius

Gaius Suetonius Tranquillas (c. AD 71-135) was the chief secretary to Emperor Hadrian (reigned AD 117-138). He makes a couple of references to Christ. The first is "Because the Jews at Rome caused continuous disturbances at the instigation of Chrestus, he expelled them from the city."[9] The second reference confirms what Tacitus wrote about Nero's treatment of Christians: "After the great fire at Rome...punishments were also inflicted on the Christians, a sect professing a new and mischievous religious belief."[10] Suetonius confirms four facts from the NT:

1. Jews were expelled from Rome.
2. The reason for the expulsion was the teachings of Chrestus.
3. The term "Christians" identified the group.
4. Christians were punished for their faith.

Summary

There are other secular sources from the second century AD that give much the same picture. Habermas lists a total of 45 ancient sources for the life of Jesus, which include 19 early creeds, 4 archaeological, 17 non-Christian, and 5 non-NT Christian sources. From this data he found 129 facts concerning the life, person, teachings, death, and resurrection of Jesus, plus the disciples' earliest beliefs.[11] Consequently, using only secular sources, we have a remarkably accurate sketch of the key aspects of Jesus' life and the beliefs, practices, and persecution of the early church.

---

[8] Ibid., X:97.

[9] Suetonius, *Life of the Emperor Claudius*, 25.4. *Chrestus* was a common misspelling of the name of Christ in those days. Note its similarity to *Christus*, referenced by Tacitus as the leader followed by Christians and from whom they derived their name.

[10] Suetonius, *Life of the Emperor Nero*, 16.

[11] Habermas, *The Historical Jesus*, 250.

Secular verification of other biblical events

The corroboration of NT facts extends beyond Jesus and the early Christians. There are many areas of intersection between biblical and secular accounts.[12] Here is a brief survey, covering the 66 years from the time around Jesus' birth until about three decades following his death and resurrection.[13]

Date	Event	Biblical Account	Extrabiblical Account
6 BC	King Herod and the killing of the boys	When Herod...gave orders to kill all the boys in Bethlehem and its vicinity who were two years old and under... (Matt 2:16)	"When [Augustus] heard that Herod king of the Jews had ordered all the boys in Syria under the age of two to be put to death and that the king's son was among those killed, he said "I'd rather be Herod's pig than Herod's son." (Macrobius, *Saturnalia* 2:4:11)
4 BC	Archelaus, ruler of Judea	When he [Joseph] heard that Archelaus was reigning in Judea in place of his father Herod... (Matt 2:22)	[Augustus] gave half the kingdom to Archelaus with the title of ethnarch. (Josephus, *Jewish War*, 2.94)
AD 6-7	Roman census	This was the first census that took place while Quirinius was governor of Syria. (Luke 2:2)	Quirinius was sent by Caesar to take a census. (Josephus, *Jewish Antiquities*, 17.355)
AD 6-7	Revolt of Judas	Judas the Galilean appeared in the days of the census and led a band of people in revolt. (Acts 5:37)	Galilean...Judas incited his countrymen to revolt...[over] paying tribute to the Romans. (*Jewish War*, 2.118)
AD 28	Emperor, prefect, tetrachs, high priests	In the fifteenth year of the reign of Tiberius Caesar—when Pontius Pilate was governor of Judea, Herod tetrarch of Galilee, his brother Philip tetrarch of Iturea and Traconitis, and Lysanias tetrarch of Abilene— during the high priesthood of Annas and Caiaphas... (Luke 3:1-2)	Pilate being sent by Tiberius as procurator to Judea... (*Jewish War*, 2.169) Herod Antipas and Philip were administering their tetrachies. (*Antiquities*, 18.26) ...Abilene, which had been governed by Lysanias... (*Antiquities*, 19.212) Gratus deposed Ananus from the high priesthood and made three more changes before appointing Joseph Caiaphas to the office. (*Antiquities*, 18.26)

[12] Most of the following thoughts come from Paul Barnett, *Is The New Testament Reliable?* (Downers Grove: IL, InterVarsity Press, 2003), 170-175.

[13] There is a small amount of overlap from the previous section.

Date	Event	Biblical Account	Extrabiblical Account
AD 33	Execution of Jesus	Pilate...had Jesus flogged, and handed him over to be crucified. (Mark 15:15)	Christus...suffered the extreme penalty...at the hands of Pontius Pilate. (Tacitus, *Annals*, 15.44)
AD 36	Aretus IV, king of the Nabateans	In Damascus the governor under King Aretas had the city of the Damascenes guarded in order to arrest me. (2 Cor 11:32)	A quarrel...arose between Aretus king of Petra, and Herod [Antipas who] had taken the daughter of Aretas as his wife. (*Antiquities*, 18.109)
AD 44	Death of Agrippa I	...The people of Tyre and Sidon; they now joined together and sought an audience with him...They asked for peace...Herod, wearing his royal robes, sat on his throne and delivered a public address to the people. They shouted, "This is the voice of a god, not of a man." Immediately, because Herod did not give praise to God, an angel of the Lord struck him down, and he was eaten by worms and died. (Acts 12:20-23)	Clad in a garment woven completely of silver...he entered the theatre at daybreak. There the silver, illuminated by the touch of the first rays of the sun...inspired awe...His flatterers addressed him as a god...The king did not rebuke him...[he] felt a stab of pain in his heart...After five days...he departed this life. (*Antiquities*, 19:344-349)
AD 45-46	Famine	Agabus...predicted that a severe famine would spread over the entire Roman world. This happened during the reign of Claudius. (Acts 11:28)	It was in the administration of Tiberius Alexander that the great famine occurred in Judaea. (*Antiquities*, 20.101)
AD 49	Claudius' expulsion of Jews from Rome	There he met a Jew named Aquila, a native of Pontus, who had recently come from Italy with his wife Priscilla, because Claudius had ordered all the Jews to leave Rome. (Acts 18:2)	Since the Jews constantly made disturbances at the instigation of Chrestus, he [Claudius] expelled them from Rome. (Suetonius, *Life of Claudius*, 25.4)
AD 52	Felix, Roman procurator, and his wife Drusilla	Several days later Felix came with his wife Drusilla, who was a Jewess. He sent for Paul and listened to him as he spoke about faith in Christ Jesus. (Acts 24:24)	Claudius now sent Felix...to take charge of Judea...Felix fell in love with...Drusilla... They married... (*Antiquities*, 20.131-143)
AD 57	James, brother of Jesus	When we arrived at Jerusalem...Paul and the rest of us went to see James, and all the elders were present. (Acts 21:17-18)	Convening the judges of the Sanhedrin, he brought before them a man named James, the brother of Jesus who was called the Christ. (*Anitquities*, 20.197)

Date	Event	Biblical Account	Extrabiblical Account
AD 57	The Egyptian prophet	"Aren't you the Egyptian who started a revolt and led four thousand terrorists out into the desert some time ago?" (Acts 21:38)	The Egyptian false prophet...appeared in the country, collected a following of about thirty thousand dupes, and led them...from the desert to the mount of Olives. (*Jewish War*, 2.261)
AD 60	Pharisees and Sadducees	A dispute broke out between the Pharisees and the Sadducees, and the assembly was divided. The Sadducees say that there is no resurrection, and that there are neither angels nor spirits, but the Pharisees acknowledge them all. (Acts 23-7-8)	The Pharisees regard observance of their doctrine and commandments as of most importance, and they believe that souls have power to survive death and receive rewards or punishments...The Sadducees teach that the soul dies along with the body and they observe no tradition apart from the [written] laws. (*Anitquities*, 18.1)
AD 60	Festus, Roman procurator	When two years had passed, Felix was succeeded by Porcius Festus. (Acts 24:27)	When Porcius Festus was sent by Nero as successor to Felix... (*Antiquities*, 20.182)
AD 60	King Agrippa II and Bernice	A few days later King Agrippa and Bernice arrived at Caesarea to pay their respects to Festus. (Acts 25:13)	Agrippa, who, with his wife, were later buried in the eruption of Mount Vesuvius. Bernice, another sister of Agrippa the Younger, was rumored to have had a liaison with her brother. (*Antiquities*, 20.182)

Corroboration through archaeology

Archaeology is the study of past human societies, primarily through the recovery and analysis of things they have left behind, such as buildings, memorials, statues, carvings, inscriptions, pottery, implements, coins, bones, and so on. Some have called it the study of "durable rubbish." Archaeology has consistently and repeatedly confirmed the historical reliability of the Bible. There have been thousands of archaeological finds in the Middle East that support what the Bible has recorded and there have been no finds that contradict what the Bible has said. In fact, this intersection of archaeology and the Bible is so prolific that it has a dedicated trade journal—*Biblical Archaeological Review*. There is so

much evidence in this area that many books have been written about it as well. Let's examine only a few of the thousands of examples of archaeological confirmation of people, places, and events from both the OT and the NT.

Archaeology and the Old Testament

The Gilgamesh Epic

The story of a worldwide flood is widespread amongst dozens of ancient cultures. Native global flood stories are documented as history or legend in almost every region on Earth. Ancient civilizations in China, Babylonia, Persia, Wales, Greece, Siberia, India, North America, Hawaii, Scandinavia, Sumatra, Peru, Polynesia, Australia, and Africa all have their own versions of a great flood. What is particularly interesting is that a large majority of them agree with the Bible in the important details of the story. For instance, nearly all the stories claim that the Earth was completely destroyed by water and animals and humans were saved in a ship. Many cultures agree that God sent the flood because of mankind's wickedness and that he chose a particular family to save.

The best known extrabiblical account is the Mesopotamian flood story in the Gilgamesh Epic. Gilgamesh was a real king of the Uruk Dynasty circa 2500 BC.[14] The Gilgamesh Epic, discovered in 1853, is a collection of poems and stories recorded on twelve stone tablets in cuneiform script.[15] The eleventh tablet, containing a story of a worldwide flood, dates to the seventh century BC (other parts of the epic date to the third millennium BC). Although  the Gilgamesh flood story is clearly polytheistic, it nevertheless contains numerous parallels to the biblical account in Genesis 6-9. Biblical archaeologist Alfred Hoerth lists fourteen parallels shared by Noah's Flood and the Gilgamesh Flood:[16]

1. The flood was divinely planned.
2. The flood was connected with the defection of the human race from God (or the gods).

---

[14] Uruk was an ancient Sumerian city, situated east of the present-day Euphrates river.

[15] Cuneiform script is one of the earliest known forms of writing and consists of pictographs rather than alphabetic characters.

[16] Alfred J. Hoerth, *Archaeology & The Old Testament* (Grand Rapids: Baker Academic, 1998), 195-196.

3. A divine revelation to the hero of the deluge tells of an imminent disaster that no one else knows about.
4. A ship is built, pitched inside and out.
5. The family of the hero is saved.
6. The living creatures that are to be saved are put aboard.
7. A storm brings on the flood.
8. Everyone not on the ship is destroyed.
9. The duration of the flood is specified.
10. The ship lands on a mountain.
11. Birds are sent out to see whether the water has receded.
12. Sacrifice is offered to and accepted by the deity.
13. The hero receives a special blessing.
14. There is reference to the possibility of no future flood.

It is difficult to see how so many similar stories could arise in so many ancient cultures if they were not, in fact, based on a true event. It makes sense that all cultures would have a creation story, but why a flood story? The widespread popularity of flood stories is good evidence for the historicity of the event.

The Ebla Tablets

The Ebla tablets are a collection of thousands of clay tablets, found in 1974 in the palace archives of the ancient city of Ebla, near the modern-day village of Mardikh in northwest Syria. They are written in both Sumerian and the local language (referred to today as Eblaite), and date to the period between 2500-2250 BC. These tablets corroborate a number of names, places, and events mentioned in the OT.

The Eblaite language is quite similar to biblical Hebrew. In fact, it seems to come from the same linguistic family. The similarity of names on the tablets and their counterparts in the biblical narratives is remarkable. For example, the tablets contain many references to familiar names from the OT, including Abraham, Esau, Saul, David, Israel, and Eber.[17] Many biblical cities are also mentioned in the tablets, such as Ashtaroth, Sinai, Hazor, Gaza, Lachish, Megiddo, Gaza, Joppa, Ur, Damascus, Sodom, Gomorrah, and Jerusalem. The reference to Jerusalem predates the

---

[17] E.M. Blaiklock and R.K. Harrison, *The New International Dictionary of Biblical Archaeology* (Grand Rapids: Zondervan, 1983). 441. The tablets do not necessarily refer to the actual biblical persons, but rather demonstrate that those names were commonly used in ancient times.

previous oldest reference to this city by almost a thousand years. Sodom and Gomorrah were previously thought by biblical skeptics to be legendary and not real cities. The tablets include the first known references to the "Canaanites," who were the occupants of the Promised Land driven out by the nascent Israel nation. The tablets also refer to the Sumerian deities Dagon, Baal, and Chemosh, which are referenced in the OT as well.[18]

Another important discovery recounted in the tablets relates to Genesis 14, where the story is told of a war between several kings. Five kingdoms had rebelled against Kedorlaomer, king of Elam, so Kedorlaomer formed a coalition with some other kingdoms and attacked the five who had joined forces. Both the Bible and the tablets lists the same five kingdoms in the same order—Sodom, Gomorrah, Admah, Zeboiim, and Zoar.[19]

Another interesting feature of the tablets is that they say the heavens, Earth, Sun, and Moon were created by a God, which corresponds to Genesis 1. Even more striking was the discovery of a creation hymn in the tablets. In fact, three different versions of the Eblaite "creation hymn" were discovered. One of these hymns was translated by Ebla archaeologist Giovanni Pettinato as follows: "Lord of heaven and earth: the earth was not, you created it, the light of day was not, you created it, the morning light you had not [yet] made exist."[20] Pettinato made the following remarks about this extraordinary find: "These words echoing the first chapter of Genesis have not been taken from the Bible but rather from a literary text found in three copies in the royal library of Ebla of 2500 B.C."[21] Even the polytheistic Eblaites had a concept of God as Lord of Heaven and Earth. This suggests that the biblical creation account was very likely known and exchanged among ancient cultures. Ebla has provided a rich source of corroboration of OT people, places, events, and ideas.

The Amarna Letters

In 1887, about 350 clay tablets were found at Amarna, the modern site of the ancient Egyptian capital of Akhetaten. The tablets are written in the Babylonian language using cuneiform characters. Most of the letters are dated to the reigns of Amenhotep III (also known as Amenophis, 1386-1350 BC) and Amenhotep IV (Akhenaten, 1350-1334 BC). They contain

---

[18] Ibid., 441.

[19] Hoerth, *Archaeology & The Old Testament*, 73.

[20] Giovanni Pettinato, *The Archives of Ebla: An Empire Inscribed in Clay* (Garden City, New York: Doubleday & Company, 1981), 244.

[21] Ibid.

correspondence describing the state of international affairs between Egypt
and the major powers in Babylon, Assyria, Syria, and Palestine.

 The Bible describes the journey of Jacob's
family to Egypt to escape famine, followed by
their enslavement there and huge increase in
numbers over a period of 430 years before a
mass exodus to the Promised Land, later referred
to as Israel (Gen 45-50, Exo 1-40).[22] The
Amarna letters contain evidence that the
Hebrews were at one time a significant presence in Egypt. Robert Dick
Wilson explains, "The fact that there are more than one hundred
explanations in Hebrew of Babylonian words in the Amarna letters shows
that Hebrew was understood at the court of the Egyptian kings, Amenophis
III and IV. This confirms the biblical account of the residence of Israelites
in Egypt before the time of Moses."[23]

The Merneptah Stele

The Merneptah Stele[24] contains an inscription by the Ancient
Egyptian king Merneptah, who reigned from 1213-1203 BC. It was
discovered in 1896 in the modern-day city of Luxor. The
stele describes the king's military victories in Africa and
the Near East and is noteworthy for being the earliest
extra-biblical reference to the nation of Israel yet
discovered.

The mention of Israel is short—"Israel is laid waste,
its seed is not"—but the reference is significant because
it shows that the nation of Israel was important enough to
be named among other major city-states of the late 13th
century. This corroborates the biblical account that Israel
was a major presence in Canaan at that time (Josh 1-24).

The Tel Dan Stele

The Tel[25] Dan Stele is a black basalt stele which was erected by the
Syrian king Hazael commemorating his victory over Israel in the mid-

---

[22] Exo 12:40 says that the Israelite people lived in Egypt 430 years. Exo 12:37 states there were
600,000 Israelite men, not counting women and children, at the time of their exodus.

[23] Wilson, *Scientific Investigation of the OT*, 178.

[24] A *stele* (also *stela*) is a stone or wooden slab erected for commemorative purposes. It is
usually decorated with important names and titles, which are either inscribed, carved in relief, or
painted onto the slab.

[25] A *tel* (also *tell*) is a mound that contains the archaeological remains of an ancient town or
city. It consists of multiple layers of ruins that accumulated as the city was successively razed by
conquering armies over the years.

ninth century BC. It was discovered in 1993 in northern Israel. The stele contains an Aramaic inscription that says, "[I killed Jeho]ram son of [Ahab] king of Israel, and I killed [Ahaz]iahu son of [Jehoram kin]g of the House of David."[26] This is in reference to the battle at Ramoth Gilead,

 recounted in the Bible: "Ahaziah went with Joram son of Ahab to war against Hazael king of Aram at Ramoth Gilead. The Arameans wounded Joram; so King Joram returned to Jezreel to recover from the wounds the Arameans had inflicted on him at Ramoth in his battle with Hazael king of Aram. Then Ahaziah son of Jehoram king of Judah went down to Jezreel to see Joram son of Ahab, because he had been wounded" (2 Kings 8:28-29).

This inscription is noteworthy, not only for its confirmation of particular events and people described in the Bible, but also for its reference to "the House of David." This makes it the first extrabiblical evidence for the fact that King David ruled in Israel.

The Moabite Stone

The Moabite Stone, also called the Mesha Stele, was discovered in Palestine in 1868. It has an inscription in ancient Moabite from about 840 BC that reads in part, "I am Mesha, son of Chemosh...king of Moab...As for King Omri of Israel, he humbled Moab many years, for Chemosh was angry at his land. And his son [Ahab] followed him and he also said, 'I will humble Moab.' In my time he spoke thus, but I have triumphed over him and over his house."[27]

This confirms a number of biblical claims. First, Mesha was king of Moab. Second, Omri was king of Israel. Third, Moab paid tribute to Israel during the reign of Ahab. Fourth, Moab broke free from Israel. "Now Mesha king of Moab raised sheep, and he had to supply the king of Israel with a hundred thousand lambs and with the wool of a hundred thousand rams. But after Ahab died, the king of Moab rebelled against the king of Israel" (2 Kings 3:4-5).

In fact, the Moabite Stone inscription fits so well with the biblical narrative that it actually fills in some missing details. The Bible says that David conquered Moab, that Solomon held Moab, and that Moab broke

---

[26] Israel Finkelstein and Neil Asher Silberman, *The Bible Unearthed: Archaeology's New Vision of Ancient Israel and the Origin of its Sacred Texts* (New York: The Free Press, 2001), 129. Note, the brackets indicate the archaeologists' best guess of text missing from the inscription.

[27] Hoerth, *Archaeology & The Old Testament*, 308.

away from Israel when the kingdom divided.[28] The next biblical reference to Moab (the one cited above) mentions Ahab receiving tribute from Moab, without giving an explanation of how Moab came to be under Israel's reign again. The Moabite Stone explains this by saying that King Omri of Israel had conquered Moab in the intervening time.[29]

The Black Obelisk of Shalmaneser

Shalmaneser III was King of Assyria from 859-824 BC. He left several editions of his royal annals that recorded his military campaigns, the last of which is engraved on the Black Obelisk, discovered in 1846 in modern-day Iraq at the ancient site of Calah, which was located south of Nineveh on the Tigris river. Calah is mentioned in Genesis 10:11-12 as one of many cities built after the Great Flood. In all, various Assyrian records mention contacts with ten Hebrew kings: Omri, Ahab, Jehu, Menahem, Pekah, Hoshea, Azariah, Ahaz, Hezekiah, and Manasseh.[30]

The Black Obelisk (c. 825 BC) names Jehu and depicts him prostrate before Shalmaneser.[31] It reads, "The tribute of Jehu, son of Omri:[32] I received from him silver, gold, a golden bowl, a golden vase with pointed bottom, golden tumblers, golden buckets, tin, a staff for a king [and] spears."

Jehu reigned over the northern kingdom of Israel from 841-814 BC (2 Kings 9:1-13). Since the inscription does not say that Shalmaneser defeated Jehu in battle, it is likely that Jehu ended up paying tribute to Shalmaneser to save his kingdom.

The Taylor Prism

The Taylor Prism is a six-sided, 15 inch tall, baked clay prism found in 1830 at the location of ancient Nineveh, the capital of the Assyrian Empire. This prism describes the military campaigns of King Sennacherib of Assyria, including his invasion of Judah (the southern kingdom of

---

[28] After the death of King Solomon, his sons were unable to reach an agreement to keep the kingdom united. In 922 BC, the nation of Israel was divided into two—the southern kingdom of Judah and the northern kingdom of Israel.

[29] Hoerth, *Archaeology & The Old Testament*, 309-310.

[30] Wilson, *Scientific Investigation of the OT*, 81.

[31] This is the earliest surviving picture of an ancient Israelite.

[32] Assyria often called Israel the "land or house of Omri." The use here indicates only that Jehu was an Israelite. Hoerth, *Archaeology & the OT*, 321-322.

divided Israel) in 701 BC. Part of the inscription related to this attack says, "As to Hezekiah, the Jew, he did not submit to my yoke, I laid siege to forty-six of his strong cities, walled forts, and the countless small villages in their vicinity and conquered them...Himself I made a prisoner in Jerusalem, his royal residence, like a bird in a cage."[33] The Bible describes the account like this:

> In the fourteenth year of King Hezekiah's reign, Sennacherib king of Assyria attacked all the fortified cities of Judah and captured them. So Hezekiah king of Judah sent this message to the king of Assyria at Lachish: 'I have done wrong. Withdraw from me, and I will pay whatever you demand of me.' The king of Assyria exacted from Hezekiah king of Judah three hundred talents of silver and thirty talents of gold. So Hezekiah gave him all the silver that was found in the temple of the LORD and in the treasuries of the royal palace (2 Kings 18:13-15).

The Bible goes on to explain how Sennacherib's army surrounded Jerusalem and threatened the whole city. Hezekiah was indeed like a caged bird, but he prayed to God, who delivered Jerusalem from Sennacherib. Although the prism, not surprisingly, omits the Assyrian army's failure to take Jerusalem,[34] its account of the events up to that point are in complete agreement with what the Bible describes.

The Cyrus Cylinder

The Cyrus Cylinder, nine inches long and made of baked clay, was discovered in the ruins of Babylon (now Iraq) in 1879. It records how Cyrus II, King of Persia, conquered Babylon (in 539 BC) without a battle and also his decree to allow Babylonian captives to return to their homelands to worship their own gods. This decree included the Jews, who were captives of Babylon at that time.[35] Here is part of the inscription: "I am Cyrus, king of the universe, the great

king, the powerful king, king of Babylon, king of Sumer and Akkad, king of the four quarters of the world...I collected together all of their people and returned them to their settlements...May all the gods whom I have placed within their sanctuaries and resettled in their sacred cities, address a

---

[33] Ibid., 348.

[34] Defeats or failures of one's own army are rarely recorded in ancient documents.

[35] Bill T. Arnold and Bryan E. Beyer, *Encountering the Old Testament* (Grand Rapids: Baker Books, 1999), 257-258.

daily prayer in my favor… and may they recommend me to him, to Marduk my lord." This repatriation of the Jews to Israel by decree of Cyrus is also recounted in the Bible:

> In the first year of Cyrus king of Persia, in order to fulfill the word of the LORD spoken by Jeremiah, the LORD moved the heart of Cyrus king of Persia to make a proclamation throughout his realm and to put it in writing: This is what Cyrus king of Persia says: "The LORD, the God of heaven, has given me all the kingdoms of the earth and he has appointed me to build a temple for him at Jerusalem in Judah. Anyone of his people among you—may his God be with him, and let him go up to Jerusalem in Judah and build the temple of the LORD, the God of Israel, the God who is in Jerusalem. And the people of any place where survivors may now be living are to provide him with silver and gold, with goods and livestock, and with freewill offerings for the temple of God in Jerusalem" (Ezra 1:1-4).[36]

This biblical passage had been doubted for years, since it was assumed that no pagan king would refer to the gods of any of his conquered nations in this way, nor would he allow the people he defeated to return to their homes to rebuild their temples. Yet once again the Bible is vindicated in a claim once thought to be inconceivable.

Archaeology and the New Testament

Jerusalem pools

Jesus once encountered a man who had been lame for thirty-eight years and healed him at the Pool of Bethesda in Jerusalem (John 5:1-15). The Bible gives a brief description and location of the pool: "Now there is in Jerusalem near the Sheep Gate a pool, which in Aramaic is called Bethesda and which is surrounded by five covered colonnades" (John 5:2). In the 19th century, archaeologists discovered the remains of a pool in Jerusalem that exactly matches the name and description in John's Gospel.

On another occasion, Jesus healed a man who had been blind from birth. After healing him, Jesus told him to "Go and wash in the Pool of Siloam" (John 9:7). This is the same pool referred to in 2 Kings 20:20 that describes one of King Hezekiah's great achievements, the digging of a tunnel to bring water from the Gihon Spring into a pool within the walls of

---

[36] While Cyrus gave credit to the Babylonian god Marduk for his restoration of the temples of other deities to their "sacred cities," the Jews viewed Cyrus as the agent of the biblical God.

the city.[37] In 2004, archaeologists were checking the area near the traditional Pool of Siloam for a public works project when they discovered some large stone steps. Further excavations uncovered several flights of steps and a pool that were in use during the first century AD.[38] Scholars now believe that this pool—and not the one nearby—is the actual Pool of Siloam. Much more of the pool remains to be excavated.

The Roman census

Some critics have challenged Luke's claim of an empire-wide census that forced the parents of Jesus, Joseph and Mary, to go to Bethlehem, where Jesus was then born. "In those days Caesar Augustus issued a decree that a census should be taken of the entire Roman world. This was the first census that took place while Quirinius was governor of Syria. And everyone went to his own town to register" (Luke 2:1-3). The challengers doubted three things about Luke's claim. They said that Rome would *not* issue a census decree like this, the empire would *not* require citizens to return to their place of birth to register and pay their taxes, and Quirinius was *not* the governor of Syria at this time. Again we find that archeology has shown that Luke's account is accurate. Let's examine the three criticisms in order.

First, an ancient Latin inscription called the Titulus Venetus has been discovered that indicates a census took place in Syria and Judea about AD 5-6. It implies that this was typical of those held throughout the Roman Empire from the time of Augustus (23 BC) through the third century AD.[39] Letters of Pliny, a Roman governor of Bithynia, reveal that the Roman Empire regularly took a census. There is clear evidence of this around the years 28 and 8 BC, and AD 6, 20, 34, 48, 62, and 76.[40]

Second, an Egyptian papyrus dated AD 104 orders all people in the region to return to their place of birth to pay taxes and register for a census. Sir William M. Ramsay, one of the greatest archaeologists of modern times, was once among the critics who were not "disposed to accept as a regular Roman principle this rule that the census must be taken of each individual at his original and proper home."[41] However, after much

---

[37] Incidentally, this feat, which occurred about 701 BC, is documented in an ancient inscription found on the tunnel wall in 1880.

[38] This dating was made based on certain pottery and coins discovered during the excavation.

[39] Habermas, *The Historical Jesus*, 172.

[40] John McRay, *Archaeology & the New Testament* (Grand Rapids: Baker Academic, 2009), 155.

[41] William M. Ramsay, *The Bearing of Recent Discovery on the Trustworthiness of the New Testament* (London: Hodder & Stoughton, 1915), 261.

research, he concluded that this "was the customary Roman method of making the census."[42] He explains the reason for this as follows:

> The order to return to the home was an economic measure intended to ensure that the supply of food should be maintained for the Empire by keeping a sufficient number of cultivators on the land. It was also a device for keeping up the value of the vast Imperial estates all over the East...The Imperial government aimed at preventing the cultivators from leaving the land in too great numbers and they took advantage of the census to compel return to the home once in fourteen years.[43]

Third, we know for certain that Quirinius was governor of Syria in AD 6,[44] however Luke is saying that he was governor at the time around Jesus' birth (5-4 BC).[45] There are two possible ways to resolve this. One way is to translate Luke 2:2 as "This census was before the one made when Quirinius was governor of Syria," which is a legitimate translation.[46] In this case Luke would not be interpreted as claiming that Quirinius was governor of Syria at the time Jesus was born. However, as Ramsay discovered, there is another way to explain this.

The evidence is somewhat fragmented, but we know that Quirinius had a series of government assignments in Syria from 11-2 BC. He was a consul in Rome in 12 BC, where he was preparing to command an army to fight the Roman Empire's war in Syria. This war was fought from 10-8 BC, followed by two years of reorganization of the region.[47] Ramsay discovered an inscription in Antioch, Syria which reveals that Quirinius was the chief magistrate of that city in 8 BC.[48] Since he was away fighting a war at this time, this was likely a shared post. In fact, the inscription lists Quirinius as a *duumvir*, which means he was one of two men who exercised joint authority, each with different duties. While Quirinius was

---

[42] Ibid., 262.

[43] Ibid., 260-261.

[44] Roman historians Tacitus, Suetonius, and Dio Cassius, and Jewish historian Josephus all wrote of Quirinius. Quirinius conducted another census during this time period in AD 6 as noted in the Titulus Venetus. This second census is also referred to in passing by Luke (Acts 5:37), which explains why Luke referred to the earlier one as the *"first* census while Quirinius was governor of Syria" (Luke 2:2).

[45] Jesus was probably born in late 5 BC or early 4 BC. King Herod, who tried to kill the baby Jesus (Matt 2:13-19), is known to have died in the spring of 4 BC. The present calendar dating system was developed by the monk Dionysius Exiguus in AD 533. Dionysius had intended that historical time should be made to pivot at the birth of Jesus, with the first year AD (*Anno Domini* means "year of the Lord") marking Jesus' first year of earthly life. However, Dionysius miscalculated Jesus' birth date by several years. This happened because he had relied on a statement by Clement of Alexandria that Jesus was born in the twenty-eighth year of the reign of Emperor Augustus, however he failed to take into account that Augustus first ruled under his given name of Octavian before the Roman Senate conferred on him the name of Caesar Augustus.

[46] The Greek word for "first" (*protos*) can be translated as "prior to" or "before."

[47] Ramsay, *Bearing of Recent Discovery*, 281, 290.

[48] Ibid., 286.

engaged in the war, the other magistrate was likely attending to the administrative duties of the province. In this way both men operated as co-governors of the two Eastern provinces of Syria and Galatia, according to Ramsay.[49]

This also helps to explain another minor problem. Tertullian, an early church father writing around AD 200, reports that Sentius Saturninus was governor of Syria at the time of Jesus' birth. We know that the period from 7-6 BC was a transition period between the rule of two successive governors of Syria: Saturninus ruling from 9-7/6 BC and Varus from 7/6-4 BC.[50] It is entirely possible that Quirinius, having just returned as a war hero, either continued or was reappointed as co-governor during this transition time to conduct the census taxation. Ramsay further confirms this with the observation, "When Quirinius in A.D. 6 returned to administer Syria, this would naturally lead to the expression in his epitaph 'legatus of Syria *again*'" [emphasis added].[51] This general outline of Quirinius' role and influence in Syria is also corroborated by a coin discovered with his name, placing him as proconsul of Syria and Cilicia during the time we would refer to as 11-4 BC.[52]

Although this evidence is not decisive, the research of Ramsay and others has shown that it is very possible that Quirinius was the governor of Syria at the time around Jesus' birth, just as Luke has told us. We also discovered that a combined census and taxation was relatively common in the Roman Empire and there is specific evidence of it occurring in Judea. Furthermore, citizens were required to return to their home town in order to register.

This matter of the Roman census is a good example of how we should view Luke as an historian. He is so accurate and precise in so many places that we should give him the benefit of the doubt when we find some apparent inconsistency. As we have seen, careful archaeological study has shown the critics to be wrong, and Luke to once again be vindicated. Luke has earned the right to be considered a trustworthy primary source of first century history. *His* historical claims should be used to verify *other* finds, and not vice versa.

---

[49] Ibid., 287.

[50] Emil Schürer, *The History of the Jewish People in the Age of Jesus Christ*, Volume 1 (Edinburgh: T&T Clark Ltd, 1973, first published 1885, revised and edited by Vermes, Millar, and Black), 257.

[51] Ramsay, *Bearing of Recent Discovery*, 293.

[52] McRay, *Archaeology & the NT*, 154.

Roman method of crucifixion

Some skeptics have claimed the Romans executioners used ropes, and not nails, to attach the legs of condemned men to their crosses. However, archaeology has proven the Bible to be accurate even in this detail. An ossuary (bone box) was discovered in 1968 in Jerusalem, with the name Yohanan ben Hagkol engraved on the side of it. Inside were the remains of a crucified man—about five feet six inches in height and about 24-28 years old—dated to the mid-first century AD.[53] These are the only known remains of a man crucified in Roman Palestine.

A seven inch long nail had been driven through the side of his heel bone. The remains of an olive wood plank placed on the outside of his foot were also found, evidently to prevent the victim from pulling his foot off the nail. Part of the cross itself was still attached to the nail on the inside of his foot.[54] There were also nail marks found between the radius and ulna bones in the lower arm and both legs were broken. The radius bone was scratched and worn smooth, probably caused by scraping on the cross as the victim repeatedly raised and lowered himself.[55]

The Bible refers to Jesus being nailed to the cross (John 20:25)[56] and to crucifixion victims having their legs broken to hasten their death (John 19:31-32).[57] This discovery confirms details in the Bible about crucifixion, both its actual usage in the first century and its method.

Luke's meticulous accuracy

Luke, the author of the Acts of the Apostles and the Gospel that bears his name, was very meticulous about recording the names and titles of officials in various locations throughout Palestine and Asia. This is especially impressive, given how much titles varied from place to place.

Notice, for example, the historical detail that Luke offers when he announced the commencement of John the Baptist's ministry: "In the fifteenth year of the reign of Tiberius Caesar—when Pontius Pilate was governor of Judea, Herod tetrarch of Galilee, his brother Philip tetrarch of Iturea and Traconitis, and Lysanias tetrarch of Abilene—during the high

---

[53] Ibid., 204.

[54] The accompanying picture shows a reconstructed model on the left and the actual artifact on the right.

[55] Habermas, *The Historical Jesus*, 174.

[56] Tacitus also mentions Christians being "nailed to crosses" in *Annals,* 15.44.

[57] Although Jesus' legs were not broken since he had already died (John 19:33).

priesthood of Annas and Caiaphas, the word of God came to John son of Zechariah in the desert" (Luke 3:1-2). Luke gives exact times, names, and titles—just the sort of thing we would expect a careful historian to do.

Pontius Pilate was the Roman governor who sentenced Jesus to death. He reigned from AD 26-36. His name and title were confirmed, exactly as Luke described, when a limestone block was found in 1961 bearing the Latin inscription, "Pontius Pilatus, Prefect of Judaea." Coins have also been discovered, dated to AD 29-31, minted to honor Pontius Pilate. Josephus also

mentions "Pilate, having been sent by Tiberius as procurator of Judea..."[58]

Some have questioned Luke's accuracy regarding Lysanius being the tetrarch of Abilene around AD 28. At one time, only one Lysanius was known in Roman records, a regional ruler some fifty years earlier. However, the discovery of an inscription found on a temple from the time of Tiberius, the Roman emperor from AD 14-37, reinforced the credibility of Luke's Gospel account yet again. The inscription named Lysanias as the Tetrarch of Abila near Damascus, just as Luke had written. This is also confirmed by Josephus: "Claudius now confirmed Agrippa as king and added to his domain Judea and Samaria as well—all the lands formerly ruled by his grandfather, Herod—but also Abilene, which had been governed by Lysanias."[59]

Josephus also corroborates the names and titles of the tetrarchs Herod and Philip and also the Jewish high priests Annas and Caiaphas.[60] Caiaphas served as high priest from AD 18-36. In 1990, an ornate first century ossuary was discovered in Jerusalem bearing the inscription, "Yehosef bar Kayafa," which means "Joseph, son of Caiaphas." In the box were the remains of six people, including a 60-year-old man who was most likely Caiaphas.[61]

Luke also correctly described Philippi as a Roman colony whose officials were called *stratagoi* ("magistrates", Acts 16:38). He refers to city officials at Thessalonica as *politarchs* (Acts 17:6-8). A stone inscription discovered at Thessalonica in the 19th century has confirmed this title. He calls officials in Ephesus *asiarchs* (Acts 19:31), the exact title

---

[58] Josephus, *Antiquities,* 18.55, Maier, 263.

[59] Ibid., 19.212, 271.

[60] Ibid., 18.26, 262.

[61] Randall Price, *The Stones Cry Out: What Archaeology Reveals About the Truth of the Bible* (Eugene, OR: Harvest House Publishers, 1997), 305.

of those we now know controlled religious affairs. He says, in Malta, that Publius was the *protos,* the chief official in charge of the island (Acts 28:7).[62]

Dating events of Paul's ministry

In Acts (13:7-12), Luke tells a story of Paul and Barnabas sailing to Cyprus and coming to the city of Paphos on their first missionary journey. There they met the proconsul, Sergius Paulus, who became a Christian as a

result of their preaching and miracle working. In 1877, an inscription was found near Paphos, bearing Sergius Paulus' name and title of proconsul. Ten years later, his name was also found on a memorial stone in Rome. The stone records that in AD 47 he was appointed as the keeper of a channel on the Tiber River. He held this office when he returned to Rome after his three years as governor of Cyprus. This places his conversion, and Paul's presence in Cyprus, around AD 44.

Archaeology has helped establish the dates of other events of Paul's ministry. According to Acts 18:11, Paul had been in Corinth for eighteen months before being brought before Gallio in court: "While Gallio was proconsul of Achaia, the Jews made a united attack on Paul and brought him into court" (Acts 18:12). In 1885, archaeologists discovered a stone at

Delphi, Greece with an inscription of a letter from Emperor Claudius that gives the name and title of Gallio as "Lucius Junius Gallio, my friend, and the proconsul of Achaia." This shows yet again the accuracy of Luke in getting names and titles correct, and also helps to date other events in the life of Paul.

This inscription is dated to AD 52. Since Gallio is known to have assumed office in the early summer of AD 51, Paul would have arrived in Corinth in early AD 50.[63] This date can also be confirmed from the other direction. Luke writes, "Paul left Athens and went to Corinth. There he met a Jew named Aquila, a native of Pontus, who had recently come from Italy with his wife Priscilla, because Claudius had ordered all the Jews to leave Rome" (Acts 18:1-2). The Roman historian Suetonius, chief secretary of Emperor Hadrian (AD 117-138), confirms this expulsion by

---

[62] Edwards, *Nothing But The Truth,* 370.
[63] McRay, *Archaeology & the NT,* 226-227.

writing that Claudius banished all the Jews from Rome because they "caused continuous disturbances at the instigation of Chrestus."[64] Suetonius notes that these riots within the Jewish community of Rome occurred during the year AD 49.[65] This fits exactly with the picture of Paul arriving in Corinth in early AD 50, after Aquila and Priscilla had "recently come from Italy" because of the expulsion.

Using Paul's arrival date in Corinth, scholars can work backwards to determine the dates of other events. For example, the Jerusalem Council (Acts 15),[66] which preceded Paul's second missionary journey that took him to Corinth, would have taken place around AD 48-49. Paul said this visit to Jerusalem occurred 14 years after his conversion (Gal 2:1),[67] which would place that event somewhere around AD 34-35. This is very close to the presumed dates for Jesus' death and resurrection, which shows how early Paul's conversion was.

The latter years of Paul's ministry can also be determined through extra-biblical sources. At the end of his third missionary journey, Paul left Greece and set sail for Jerusalem (Acts 20:16), where he was arrested "for teaching against the Jews" (Acts 21:27-36). He was transferred to Caesarea,[68] where he remained in custody of the Roman governor Felix for two years (Acts 24:24-27). At that time, Porcius Festus, whose arrival in Judea is dated at AD 60, replaced Felix. Luke is very specific that Festus heard Paul's case within two weeks of his arrival (Acts 25:1-6). Festus decided to send Paul to Rome to be tried by Caesar. This means that Paul set out for Rome in AD 60 and arrived sometime early the next year after a shipwreck detoured him (Acts 27-28). This is where Luke ends his book, but his very last statement says that Paul remained in Rome for two years. Early church historical accounts indicate that Paul was released by Caesar, traveled for 2-3 years, and was eventually arrested and imprisoned again in Rome, probably in AD 63-64. Paul wrote five of his thirteen letters while in Roman prisons.[69] We know Paul was martyred in Rome under Nero. Since Nero died in AD 68, Paul was killed between AD 63-68.[70]

---

[64] Suetonius, *Life of the Emperor Claudius*, 25.4, as quoted in Habermas, *The Historical Jesus*, 191. Note, *Chrestus* is a variant spelling of Christ.

[65] The Jews were allowed to return to Rome five years later, at the beginning of Emperor Nero's reign in AD 54.

[66] This was the first known church council, which was convened to determine what, if any, aspects of the Mosaic Law non-Jewish converts had to comply with.

[67] Paul actually says "Fourteen years later." Many scholars believe this refers to "later than Paul's conversion," which is the temporal reference point in the passage beginning in Galatians 1.

[68] Caesarea is an ancient port city in Israel, about forty miles northwest of Jerusalem.

[69] While under house arrest in Rome, Paul was able to conduct a limited ministry (Phil 1:12-14, 4:22). There, he wrote Ephesians, Philippians, Colossians, and Philemon during his first imprisonment and 2 Timothy during the second one. Note, 1 Timothy and Titus were written between Paul's two imprisonments.

[70] Eusebius, *Church History*, 2:25, as quoted in Barnett, *New Testament Reliability*, 38.

Summary

There is a vast array of external evidence that corroborates the historical accuracy of the biblical accounts. When all the evidence is weighed it is simply more credible to believe that the Bible is what it claims to be—real depictions of history that we can rely on today. This is not to say that there are no open questions or unexplained details in the biblical accounts. In fact, to some extent we should expect this with true historical accounts. Any loose ends merely point to the sincere motives of the writers. They were not trying to contrive a "story" where everything fits together seamlessly, but rather they were simply reporting events as truthfully as they could.

We find that the biblical authors have a proven track record of historical reliability. When the details they give about people, titles, times, places, events, and customs can be independently checked, they have been discovered to be extraordinarily accurate and never proven wrong. When historians are found to be reliable in so many details that are independently verifiable, we should be willing to grant them the benefit of the doubt in details that cannot be readily verified.

CHAPTER 10

Divine fingerprints

In the Christian structure, would it be unlikely that this personal God who is there and made man in his own image as a verbalizer, in such a way that he can communicate horizontally to other men on the basis of propositions and language—is it unthinkable or even surprising that this personal God could or would communicate to man on the basis of propositions? The answer is no...Indeed, it is what one would expect.

Francis Schaeffer (1912-1984)
Theologian, philosopher
He Is There and He Is Not Silent

It is unthinkable that the God who knows best and has plans should either keep them all to himself or allow his plans to be so jumbled in the process of communication that they become unrecognizable.

Brian H. Edwards (1941-)
Pastor, author, lecturer
Nothing But The Truth

The curious thing about the God of the Bible is how unlike us He is. His wisdom confuses us; His purity frightens us. He makes moral demands we can't live up to, then threatens retribution if we don't obey. Instead of being at our beck and call, He defies manipulation. In His economy, the weak and humble prevail and the last become first.

Greg Koukl (1950-)
Author, speaker, teacher
Faith Is Not Wishing

Now that we have established the historical accuracy of the Bible we must determine whether or not it is really from God. After all, there are many ancient books that are considered to be historically reliable, but we do not normally consider them to be divine. For example, the books *Jewish Antiquities* and *The Jewish War* by the first century writer Flavius Josephus are well regarded as generally accurate, but merely human, historical accounts.

The Bible claims to contain the very words of God in hundreds of places. For example: "God spoke all these words" (Exodus 20:1) and "It is not the word of men, but the word of God" (1 Thes 2:13). We do not need to believe the Bible is divine simply because it says so, however. That would be circular reasoning—assuming the very thing we seek to prove. Besides, other books make similar claims. For instance, the Qur'an, Hindu Vedas, and the Book of Mormon all claim to be of divine origin. Nevertheless, it is significant that the Bible does *claim* to be from God. We would not need to bother investigating the issue any further if it did not.

How can it be that both God and humans were the authors of the Bible? Christians describe this process as *biblical inspiration*.[1] Primarily, this means that the Bible has been breathed out by God: "All Scripture is God-breathed" (2 Tim 3:16). Secondly, God used human prophets as his writing instrument: "For prophecy never had its origin in the human will, but prophets, though human, spoke from God as they were carried along by the Holy Spirit" (2 Pet 1:21). This was not a mere dictation process, where the prophets simply transcribed what was spoken by God.[2] Rather, God superintended the human authors so that, using their own individual personalities and writing styles, they composed and recorded exactly what God intended them to write in the original manuscripts.[3] In this way, the words of the biblical text are attributed equally to the voice of the writers and to the voice of God, equating their words with God's words: "They have been entrusted with the very words of God" (Rom 3:2).

To know whether or not the Bible contains the very words of God we need to examine the evidence. This book is either given by God to men or it is merely a book by men about God. If it is only from men, then it will be marked by human limitations.[4] On the other hand, if it is divine, then it will exhibit signs of supernatural origin. If God has indeed

---

[1] The idea of biblical inspiration does not refer to the Bible's literary quality or its ability to motivate us, but rather to its character as divine revelation. The entire Bible is inspired, not just certain parts, according to Christianity.

[2] This is the claim of Joseph Smith for the Book of Mormon and Muhammad for the Qur'an. In fact, Qur'an means "the recitation." The word *qur'an* appears about 70 times in the Qur'an itself.

[3] God did not allow human error to influence the writing, as he oversaw the human authors' work.

[4] Greg Koukl, "The Bible: Has God Spoken?", Ambassador Basic Curriculum, Stand To Reason, 2002.

spoken through the Bible, then it will exhibit characteristics or "fingerprints" of God that could not have been caused by mere men. Here are eight marks of the Bible's supernatural origin:[5]

1. Supernatural orientation
2. Supernatural unity
3. Supernatural insight
4. Supernatural impact
5. Supernatural survival
6. Supernatural events
7. Supernatural predictions
8. Supernatural testimony

No other book exhibits even *one* of these marks more than the Bible. When we consider all eight marks together—plus its claims of divine origin *and* its impeccable credentials of historical accuracy—the cumulative evidence for its supernatural origin becomes hard to deny. In this chapter we will examine the first five of these characteristics and we will look at the last three in the next chapter.

Supernatural orientation

The Bible is truly unique among ancient and modern literature in its relentless spotlight on God as the central character in one long, continuous drama. This story reveals God's nature, purposes, and expectations in the context of his regular interactions with human beings. From beginning to end, the Bible features a divine focal point to get its readers to lift their eyes from themselves to a much grander and more profound view of reality with God at the center. English professor Leland Ryken explains:

> The God-centeredness and supernatural orientation of the Bible make it stand out. God is the leading character or actor in the Bible in a way that is without parallel in other literature. Furthermore, although ancient literature presupposes the existence of a supernatural world with otherworldly scenes and characters, the Bible is more consistent in portraying the interpenetration of a divine world into the ordinary realm of earthly life.[6]

The Bible presents a distinctive picture of a theistic universe created by a sovereign and loving God who is deeply involved and concerned with his

---

[5] I borrowed the idea of supernatural marks 2 through 7 from Koukl, "The Bible: Has God Spoken?"

[6] Leland Ryken, "The Bible as Literature", *The Origin of the Bible* (Carol Stream, IL: Tyndale House Publishers, 2003), F.F. Bruce, J.I. Packer, Philip Comfort, Carl F.H. Henry editors, 120.

creation. This is consistent with the Bible's self-claims of divine revelation—that the Creator God *intended* to communicate with his creation through the written word. In fact, the Bible makes stronger claims of inspiration and authority than any other work of literature. It claims to be God's direct communication to humanity some fifteen hundred times. No other religious book makes claims of this magnitude. It is not surprising, then, that the Bible is unique in how it intermingles historical and literary writing with theological teaching. The Bible has the unmistakable marks of supernatural orientation.

Supernatural unity

The Bible was written over a fifteen hundred year period by more than forty different human authors. The books of the Bible are written in numerous styles and genres, including history, poetry, song, teaching, law, prophecy, parable, and allegory. They were written in three different languages—Hebrew, Aramaic, and Greek. The authors came from all kinds of backgrounds and status in life—leaders and servants, educated and uneducated, wealthy and poor, skilled and unskilled. They wrote under a wide variety of circumstances—wandering in the wilderness, fighting for their survival, running for their lives, suffering in captivity, exile, and slavery, traveling the world, reminiscing, teaching, enjoying family and friends. They wrote from many different states of mind—uncertainty, fear, despair, doubt, grief, rebellion, humility, peace, contentment, joy, and hope. They wrote to individuals, groups, nations, and the world. They addressed hundreds of profound and controversial topics such as God, man, salvation, origins, meaning, morality, destiny, evil, and suffering.

What is remarkable about the Bible is that it exhibits tremendous unity throughout all of its pages, *in spite of* these incredibly diverse origins. The Bible is not merely a compilation of many stories. It is  actually a single powerful story of God's purposes and actions of creation, providence, judgment, and redemption. There is a uniform purpose, plan, and message woven throughout the entire Bible from its beginning to its end—God's revelation of himself to humanity and his constant pursuit of individuals and nations. Man continually rebels against the Creator and God responds by sending his Son Jesus to reconcile man to God. This was foretold repeatedly in the OT and dramatically fulfilled in the NT.

Ryken describes it like this: "The overall framework of the Bible is that of a story. It begins with the creation of the world and ends with the consummation of history and the recreation of the world. The plot conflict is a prolonged spiritual battle between good and evil. The central character is God, and every creature and nation interacts with this mighty protagonist. Every story, poem, or proverb in the Bible fits into this overarching story."[7] Yet this unified message was not fully understood by any single human biblical author. Each one added a small part which, when included in the whole, showed what God has been doing throughout human history and is planning to do in times still to come.

Imagine if you were one of forty people gathered today from many different backgrounds and were asked to write about even one controversial subject, let alone dozens of them. What are the chances that you and the other thirty-nine people, writing independently, would produce a unified, harmonious document without contradictions?[8] There is little to no chance it would happen. Even if each of you shared a common background or were told to write from a particular perspective, the resulting document would still not be in complete agreement.

The Bible tells one marvelous, continuous story with one central message, which means the multitude of human writers had to be inspired by a single, divine Author. It is the only thing that can explain such amazing harmony amidst such incredible diversity. The Bible has the unmistakable marks of supernatural unity.

Supernatural insight

The Bible addresses the most profound questions that humans can ask, such as the ones we have been asking in this book. It describes God as the very kind of Creator that we have concluded must exist—one who is necessary, eternal, unique, distinct from the universe, timeless, immaterial,  sovereign, self-sufficient, good, powerful, intelligent, rational, creative, loving, caring, and personal. The Bible does more than affirm God's naturally revealed attributes, though. It also describes his nature as triune—three co-eternal and co-equal persons in one Being—the Father,

---

[7] Ibid., 150.

[8] Some people allege that there are contradictions in the Bible—either self-contradictions or contradictions with science or history—which, if true, would diminish its unity. Careful examination shows that this charge is untrue, however. There is no room to examine this further here, but the reader is encouraged to consult some of the many good resources that address this issue. Here are a few of them: Norman Geisler and Thomas Howe, *When Critics Ask: A Popular Handbook on Bible Difficulties* (Grand Rapids: Baker Books, 1992-2003), Gleason L. Archer Jr., *Encyclopedia of Bible Difficulties* (Grand Rapids: Zondervan, 1982), John Haley, *Alleged Discrepancies of the Bible* (New Kensington, PA: Whitaker House, 1992), and John Wenham, *Easter Enigma: Are the Resurrection Accounts in Conflict?* (Eugene, OR: Wipf and Stock, 1992).

the Son, and the Holy Spirit.[9] It explains God's plans and purposes in creation, as well. God desires close relationship with human beings and is working out a remarkable plan to accomplish that.

Good and evil

The Bible takes good and evil seriously—acknowledging the reality of both, while also explaining them both. Man can be both noble and cruel. We can be noble and good because we are made in God's likeness. This means that we have certain characteristics and abilities in common with God.[10] For example, we have a keen self-awareness of ourselves as distinct persons with our own private thoughts, beliefs, and desires. We have a will of our own—the ability to make choices and take deliberate action. If this were not true, then we would not really be personal beings. As reflections of God, we are able to appreciate truth, beauty, and goodness. We are rational creatures—we can seek and discover truth, and we can think and reason through challenging intellectual problems. We have the capacity for advanced language and communication, and we are able to imagine the future. We are highly creative, being able to design and innovate. We also have a moral conscience, knowing right from wrong.

As God's image bearers, we are emotional beings, able to experience a wide range of higher-order and complex feelings such as love, joy, gratitude, anger, compassion, optimism, disappointment, anticipation, and remorse. We are also relational, which means we are capable and desirous of deep relationships with other persons, including God. In fact, we were designed to be able to comprehend God and relate to him on a personal level, including the capacity to worship him. We are spiritual beings with an immortal soul that will live forever. We are God's representatives on Earth, created to reflect and display his character. To be made in God's image is an extraordinary honor that, out of all the creatures in the universe, has been given only to humanity. This confers great intrinsic value, dignity, and worth to every member of the human race.

Man is also cruel and evil—not only the murderers and rapists—but *all* of us. We each have misused the freedom God gave us and have acted contrary to God's ways. Our fallen nature is corrupt, perverse, and sinful

---

[9] This will be discussed more in chapter 12, as well as many of the other supernatural insights previewed in this section.

[10] These characteristics and abilities that we have in common with God are *immaterial*—not physical—because God does not have a body. The immaterial aspects of a person are referred to as his soul, which we discussed in chapter 6. Additionally, being God's image bearers does not mean that we share all of his attributes. He will always be the infinite God and we will always be finite human beings. Examples of God's *incommunicable* attributes—those characteristics that are unique to him, and are not also characteristics of us—include self-existence, sovereignty, omnipresence, omnipotence, omniscience, triunity, among others.

throughout our being. Our disposition is naturally hostile to God and enslaved to sin. At its very core, sin is godlessness. It is the deliberate and willful exclusion of God from our life. More specifically, sin is any deed, thought, desire, emotion, attitude, or word that displeases God and deserves blame.

Sin is both overstepping a line and failing to reach another.[11] We overstep a line when we break God's laws. We would be mistaken to think that this is simply a matter of trying to do more good than bad because we become guilty in God's eyes with a single transgression. We fail to reach a line when we do not love God as we should. God wants us to seek satisfaction and joy in him, but instead we make inferior choices. We choose to live apart from him and settle for trivial pursuits. We love created things more than the Creator, which is idolatry.

Sin not only disrupts the harmony that God intended in creation, it also resists the divine restoration of that harmony, including man's relationship with God. Sin impedes the close personal relationship and communion that God seeks with us. It is going our own way, rebelling against God. It creates separation from him, not relationship with him.[12]

The penalty and remedy for sin

The Bible says that sin is real, and it is the root cause of the evil and suffering we experience in this world. The solution to this problem is not denial of our guilt, but divine forgiveness—through Jesus Christ.

The penalty for sin is death. Spiritual death is the penalty *in this life* for sin—living apart from God. The penalty *after this life* is that spiritual death is extended forever—*eternal* separation from God. However, God has made a way to remedy this situation. He sent his son, Jesus—the second person of the triune God—to be born in human flesh. Jesus lived a sinless life of obedience to God the Father, died a tortuous death by crucifixion, and was raised to life on the third day. Jesus took on himself the suffering necessary to pay the penalty for our sins, and in doing this, he bore God the Father's wrath against sin. He stood in our place and represented us, and God the Father counts Jesus' payment for sin as our own.

If we believe this about Jesus, trust in his provision, and follow him as Lord and Savior, then we have eternal spiritual life. This was God's plan to demonstrate both his love and justice towards humanity. Because God loves us, he wants to redeem us. Because God is just, he must deal with our sin, so he sent Jesus to die to earn our salvation.

---

[11] Cornelius Plantinga Jr., *Not the Way It's Supposed to Be: A Breviary of Sin* (Grand Rapids, Eerdmans, 1995), 5.

[12] Ibid.

To really drive this point home, journalist Fred Heeren asks us to consider: "If [the Creator] wanted to communicate to us the seriousness of breaking His moral law, how could He show us more forcefully than by demanding that the most valuable thing in the universe be forfeited as a penalty? And if He wanted to tell us how much He loves us, how could He do so more dramatically than by dying for us?"[13]

Many difficult teachings

We might expect some of these insights to be unusual, difficult to understand or accept, and even inexplicable at times—if they truly were divine in origin. Perhaps we would even find some of them offensive to our human sensibilities. This is all the more reason to believe that they come from God. The mind of man is too feeble and self-serving to conceive many of the ideas we find in the Bible. Consider the following challenging and sometimes startling biblical teachings:[14]

1. This world is not primarily about us human beings, but about God.
2. God is triune—three Persons in one Being.
3. God is zealous for his name, fame, and glory, yet this does not make him vain since he is supremely and infinitely valuable.
4. God is completely sovereign, but man has genuine free will.
5. God permits evil, but uses it for his good purposes.
6. God, the Creator of all, enters into covenants with human beings.
7. God gives us his words, not through a process of dictation, but by speaking through human beings.
8. God uses weak people and nations to accomplish his purposes.
9. God created a nation, Israel, for the purpose of making himself known to the whole world.
10. God is like a loving father to his people.
11. God cares deeply for the lowly, needy, and oppressed people of the world.
12. God is completely loving, but he is also completely just—all sin must be punished.
13. Doing good works will not get us to Heaven.
14. Sin is the problem that plagues all of creation and Jesus is the only one who solves the problem.

---

[13] Fred Heeren, *Show Me God: What the Message from Space is Telling Us About God* (Olathe, KS: Day Star Publications, 2004, 2nd revised edition), 397.

[14] These teachings will be further discussed in chapter 12.

15. Every human being has fallen short of giving God the worship he deserves.

16. Blood sacrifice is required to pay for mankind's sins.

17. God freely offers forgiveness to sinners.

18. Jesus is a single person with two separate and distinct natures— one divine and the other human.

19. God, in the person of Jesus, humbled himself by leaving Heaven to become a man to die in place of his creatures to save us from our sins.

20. Jesus first came to Earth under the lowliest of conditions—as a baby, born in a stable to poor parents, visited by shepherds, and forced to flee Israel under threat of death.

21. Jesus endured cruel torture and execution by crucifixion even though he committed no crime and was, in fact, sinless.

22. Jesus was raised to life after three days to demonstrate his victory over death.

23. The merits of Jesus' sacrifice pays for the sins of those who place their trust in him.

24. God offers personal relationship between himself and believers.

25. Man must be born again spiritually to be able to relate to God.

26. God describes this relationship as a marriage where he is the husband and we are the bride.

27. We become part of God's family through faith in and obedience to Jesus.

28. Heart change is fundamentally more important than behavioral change, and only God can truly motivate and empower it.

29. We are to love our enemies, do good to those who hate us, bless those who curse us, and pray for those who mistreat us.

30. True believers should expect to be persecuted.

31. Jesus will return one day in glorious triumph over sin and death.

32. There will be a Final Judgment where every one of us will be held to account for everything we have ever done.

33. Those who have rejected God's offer of forgiveness and reconciliation will be separated from him forever in Hell.

34. God promises believers new bodies, hearts, and minds in Heaven and that he will dwell with them forever.

35. The future Heaven will be a completely restored Earth with no more sin.

Indeed, there are some hard teachings in the Bible—both hard to comprehend and hard to accept. The apostle Peter himself admitted this when he said that many things Paul wrote were difficult to understand, and people distort them to their own destruction (2 Peter 3:15-16). Pastor and theologian John Piper writes of the Bible:

> If everything were easy and straightforward, no controversy at all, nothing complex, nothing apparently out of sync with my little human brain and its ability to discern contradictions, then I bet there would be a question here like, "If this is really God's word, why is it so simple? Why isn't it more complex? If this is really God's word, why wouldn't it cause some difficulties among us humans?"[15]

No other book in the world—sacred or not—gives the kinds of explanations the Bible gives. The Bible's answers to life's toughest questions resonate with the deepest intuitions we have about ourselves and our world.[16] It is sophisticated and profound enough to satisfy the most intellectual minds, yet it is also simple and clear enough to be understood by a child. The Bible has the unmistakable marks of supernatural insight.

Supernatural impact

The Bible explains how God supernaturally changes lives because we are incapable of changing ourselves in any real and lasting way. He changes us as we obey what he has written in Scripture. God does this through a process of soul transformation. With our cooperation, he will gradually change our desires, motivations, attitudes, emotions, thoughts, words, and actions to become like Jesus—and this will have a radical effect on the world.

Personal change

Since we are all born as sinners with a corrupt nature that is separated from God and in active rebellion against him, we require a remarkable transformation to become like Jesus. No self-help strategy can achieve this. That is why the Bible teaches that this transformation begins only with a divinely empowered new birth—a spiritual birth. Before we know Jesus, we are spiritually dead, but we become spiritually alive through God's work in us. This kind of change is God's purpose for us, and it is he who motivates and empowers it.

---

[15] John Piper, "Why Can't We Get Any Straight Answers from Christianity?", The Christian Post, http://www.christianpost.com/article/20101116/why-cant-we-get-any-straight-answers-from-christianity/, accessed Nov 19, 2010.
[16] Koukl, "The Bible: Has God Spoken?"

This spiritual rebirth begins a life-long process of spiritual formation—or, more accurately, *reformation*. We learn to love differently, think differently, and act differently. Spiritual reformation is the process of transforming our soul to be in alignment with God's intended design as he has revealed in the Bible. In particular, the believer cooperates with God's work within him to become more like Jesus.

The Bible is more than just a book. It is "sharper than any double-edged sword, it penetrates even to dividing soul and spirit, joints and marrow; it judges the thoughts and attitudes of the heart" (Heb 4:12). It "is useful for teaching, rebuking, correcting and training in righteousness" (2 Tim 3:16). The Bible is unique among books. It is the only book that reads us,[17] providing a true assessment of what is wrong with us and supplying the teaching necessary for the only kind of personal transformation that really works and actually lasts.

World change

Jesus demands radical transformation of his followers, demonstrated by radical obedience to his commands carried out in radical urgency, resulting in radical impact in the world. This impact transcends all human boundaries—temporal, geographical, economical, political, and cultural. When people genuinely and consistently obey the teachings of the Bible, something dramatic happens to individuals and entire cultures.

The influence of biblical thought and the outworking of biblical faith have had such a massive and profound effect on the world that it is nearly impossible to conceive what life would be like without it.[18] People may be amazed to discover how many of our present institutions and values reflect a Judeo-Christian origin, rooted in biblical teaching. Christians did not plan to change the world; the dramatic changes largely occurred as a consequence of their transformed lives.

The ancient Greek and Roman societies had virtually no concept of compassion to suffering human beings. Life had little value to them. They viewed helping a sick person as a sign of human weakness. Christianity put an end to the widespread practices of human sacrifice, infanticide, child abandonment, abortion, and suicide. Human charity and compassion

---

[17] Hans-Ruedi Weber, *The Book That Reads Me* (Consul Oecumenique, 1995).

[18] For a more thorough discussion of this topic, I highly recommend Alvin J. Schmidt, *How Christianity Changed the World* (Grand Rapids: Zondervan, 2004), formerly published with the title *Under the Influence: How Christianity Transformed Civilization*.

are distinctly Christian innovations that sprung directly from the teachings of Jesus. Christians invented and established hospitals, mental asylums, orphanages, rescue missions, institutions for the poor, blind, and aged, and the field of medical nursing. They created charitable organizations such as The Red Cross, Salvation Army, YMCA, The United Way, and many others. They fed the hungry, gave a drink to the thirsty, clothed the naked, provided shelter for the homeless, and taught the illiterate to read and write. In fact, many spoken languages were converted to a written form just so the Bible could be translated into them. Christians demonstrated love and lived as if people mattered.

The Bible's influence significantly contributed to the liberties and rights that currently exist in free societies of the West. This includes such values as personal responsibility, personal freedom, and the equality of individuals. Political, economic, and religious freedom can only exist where the individual has freedom. The model of democratic government, the U.S. Constitution, was founded on biblical principles. The separation and balance of powers in the three government branches were created because of the founders' understanding that man is inherently sinful and corrupt. The abolition of slavery in the Western world was a Christian achievement driven by the understanding that all people are made in God's image and therefore have extraordinary worth and dignity.

Because of the teachings of Jesus, women in much of the world today, especially in the West, enjoy more privileges and rights than ever before in history. Christians also impacted the East by working to ban the evil practices of widow burning in India and foot binding in China. They promoted the institution of monogamous marriage and family as the only means to produce a strong society with equal rights for women and the proper nurture for children.

Christians also pioneered education for children of both sexes, public schools, compulsory education for children, kindergarten, graded school levels, and education for the deaf and blind. The whole concept of universities had its origins in Christianity, growing out of Christian monasteries. Beginning with Harvard, Christians established nearly every one of the first 123 colleges founded in America for Christian purposes.

The biblical belief in the rationality of God and the fact that he is separate from his creation made modern science possible. Before that the Greek pantheistic belief held that God and the universe were intertwined, which meant that attempts to discover natural laws were an insult to the gods. Because Christians believed the universe to be the rational and orderly creation of God, they developed the scientific methods of inductive reasoning and experimentation to discover how it operated. Incredible advances were made in the fields of biology, astronomy, physics, chemistry, and medicine because the sincere biblical convictions of scientists motivated and influenced their scientific efforts. Among these were da Vinci, Copernicus, Kepler, Galileo, Newton, Pascal, Boyle, Faraday, and Mendel.

The Bible has also significantly affected the world's best art, literature, architecture, and music. Artists such as Michelangelo, Raphael, and Rembrandt; writers such as Dante, Chaucer, and Milton; and composers such as Bach, Handel, Mozart, Beethoven, Mendelssohn, Haydn, and Brahms; and many others were inspired by Jesus Christ to create their works for the glory of God.

Perhaps the most influential invention in all of history was the printing press, built by Gutenberg around AD 1440 so he could print the Bible for mass distribution. The Bible was the first book ever printed in Europe. Finally, there is the world's modern calendar, which literally splits human history into two halves—B.C. and A.D.—to honor Jesus Christ. Every time we read or write a date we are reminded that the birth of Jesus is the central event around which all of history pivots.

This world would be a much colder, darker, harsher place if Jesus had never been born and the Bible had never been written. This is another compelling testimony to the truths contained in the Bible. It has undeniably been the driving force in transforming civilization during the last two thousand years. No other religion, philosophy, movement, or nation has changed the world for the better as much as biblical faith has.[19] The Bible is God's prescription to transform lives. For millennia it has renewed people by giving them hope, courage, purpose, wisdom, guidance, and power. It has pointed them to truth and formed an anchor for their lives.[20] The Bible has the unmistakable marks of supernatural impact.

Supernatural survival

The Bible has demonstrated supernatural survival throughout its history. This is not only because the Bible is very old—3,500 years—but even more significantly, because it has survived intact *despite* thousands of years of relentless attempts to alter, discredit, restrict, ban, and destroy it. Here are some examples, dating back more than 2,500 years.

Attempts to destroy the Bible

Jehoiakim, king of Judah from 608-597 BC, burned the scroll of the prophet Jeremiah, which contained God's words pronouncing judgment on

---

[19] Certainly there have been evils perpetrated in the name of Christianity such as the Crusades, the Inquisition, and the enslavement of indigenous peoples, but these were contrary to the teachings of Jesus.

[20] Norman L. Geisler, from Strobel, *The Case For Faith*, 128.

Judah for its wickedness unless they repented. "Whenever Jehudi had read three or four columns of the scroll, the king cut them off with a scribe's knife and threw them into the firepot, until the entire scroll was burned in the fire" (Jer 36:23).

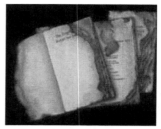

Antiochus Epiphanes, ruler of the Seleucid Empire from 175-163 BC, burned the Bible and killed its followers. "The books of the law which they [the officials of Antiochus] found they tore to pieces and burned with fire. Where the book of the covenant was found in the possession of any one, or if any one adhered to the law, the decree of the king condemned him to death" (*The Apocrypha*, 1 Maccabees 1:56-57).

In AD 303, the Roman Emperor Diocletian issued an edict to stop Christians from worshipping Jesus Christ and ordered the destruction of all their scriptures. He had churches burned to the ground and Christians thrown into prison, beaten, and killed. This was the last and most severe persecution of Christians in the Roman Empire. Despite more than two and a half centuries of brutal persecution and attempts to destroy the Bible, the Roman Empire eventually itself became Christian and the Bible was revered.[21]

Attempts to restrict and ban the Bible

There have been attempts even within the Christian Church to restrict the accessibility of the Bible. Many Roman Catholic popes have issued decrees forbidding Bible reading in the common language of the people, condemning Bible societies, and banning its possession and translation under penalty of death. They insisted that only their Latin translation, the Vulgate, was authoritative and that the Catholic Church was solely responsible for its interpretation. This effectively kept the Bible from being read by the masses since most people could not read Latin. In 1199, Pope Innocent III had French Bibles burned and forbade the people to possess any copies of it. In 1234, Pope Gregory IX ordered the people to surrender their Bibles for burning. In 1600, Pope Ferdinand II commanded that ten thousand Bibles be burned.

In 1383, John Wycliffe was charged with heresy for translating the Bible into the common language. Although he died before he was

---

[21] The Roman Emperor Constantine issued the Edict of Milan in AD 313, which proclaimed religious tolerance of Christians throughout the empire. In AD 380, the Roman Emperor Theodosius issued the Edict of Thessalonica, which established Christianity as the official state religion of the Roman Empire.

convicted, the Church burned his translated Bibles and exhumed his body 43 years after his death to burn his remains as well. In the 16th century, William Tyndale translated the Bible from the original Hebrew and Greek into vernacular English. His Bibles were accused of containing many errors and propaganda, and in 1526 they were ceremoniously burned, as was he after being strangled to death. In 1844, Pope Gregory XVI condemned Bible societies and also "the publication, dissemination, reading, and possession of vernacular translations."

The twentieth century brought some of the most anti-Christian and cruel government regimes the world has ever seen. Totalitarian dictatorships arose in Russia, Germany, China, North Korea, Cambodia, and other places, resulting in the worst genocides in human history— approximately 152 million people murdered by their own atheistic governments between 1917 and 2007.[22] One of the primary goals of each of these regimes was to eradicate the Bible and Christian belief.

The Soviet Union, following the Russian revolution under Vladimir Lenin in 1917, was the first nation to attempt to systematically eliminate organized religion and establish atheism as the basis of its society. This included the severe persecution of Christians and the restriction of the Bible. When Lenin died in 1924, Joseph Stalin continued what Lenin had started. Stalin's persecution campaigns are often referred to as "Russia's national Holocaust." Some 20 million Christians were imprisoned or died in the system of prison camps known as *gulags*, made famous by the writings of Aleksandr Solzhenitsyn. In total, the atheistic government of Russia murdered nearly 62 million of its own citizens from 1917 to 1987.[23]

Communist supporters in modern Russia still revere Lenin, but he was not successful in eliminating the Bible. Contemporary Russian Communist party leader Gennady Zyuganov remarks, "Lenin is one of the greatest politicians and thinkers of our time. It is impossible to turn him into a brand, simply because every prominent library in the world has the full collection of his works. The only book that is more popular is the Bible."[24]

Under Adolph Hitler, the German Nazi party rewrote Bible passages, changing the Ten Commandments and eliminating all mention of the special role of the Jewish people. According to Hitler's version, Jesus was an advocate of Aryan ideas. In 1933, Hitler tried to nationalize every church and ordered the arrest of any clergyman who did not comply. What the Hitler government envisioned for Germany was clearly set out in a

---

[22] Vox Day, *The Irrational Atheist* (Dallas: BenBella Books, 2008), 241.

[23] Ibid.

[24] RT (Russia Today), a global multilingual television news network based in Russia, interview with Gennady Zyuganov, April 22, 2010, http://rt.com/politics/interviews/bible-more-popular-lenin/, accessed Nov 15, 2010.

thirty-point program for the "National Reich Church." Here are three of the thirty articles: [25]

❖ Article 5: The National Reich Church is determined to exterminate irrevocably and by every means the strange and foreign Christian faiths imported into Germany in the ill-omened year 800.

❖ Article 13: The National Reich Church demands immediate cessation of the publishing and dissemination of the Bible in Germany.

❖ Article 14: The National Reich Church has to take severe measures in order to prevent the Bible and other Christian publications being imported into Germany.

Today, Hitler and his Nazi party are long gone, but the Bible is alive and well in Germany.

In Mao Tse-tung's so-called "Great Leap Forward," one of the goals was to obliterate Christianity and the Bible from China. This atheistic regime murdered over 76 million of its own people.[26] Liu Zhenying (aka Brother Yun), a Chinese pastor persecuted in the brutal Chinese regime, writes, "China became a Communist nation in 1949. Within a few years all missionaries were expelled, church buildings were closed, and thousands of Chinese pastors were imprisoned. Many lost their lives."[27] When he was 16 in the year 1974, Yun asked his mother if there were any words of Jesus left that he could read for himself. She replied, "No. All his words are gone. There is nothing left of his teaching." Yun explained that the Cultural Revolution had eliminated all the Bibles. At one point he asked some other Christians what a Bible looked like, but no one knew. One person had seen some hand copied Scripture portions and song sheets, but never a whole Bible. Only a few old believers could recall seeing Bibles many years before.[28]

Even though persecution of Christians continues today in China, the Cultural Revolution ultimately failed. Today there are somewhere between 90-120 million Christians in China, with about 10 million new believers being added each year. Author Paul Hattaway explains, "Surely the authorities in China have long been confused and amazed at how the church continues to grow and flourish despite their most brutal attempts to crush, seduce, and deceive believers...Somehow, in a way only God could

---

[25] William L. Shirer, *The Rise and Fall of the Third Reich: A History of Nazi Germany* (New York: Simon & Schuster, 1960), 240.

[26] Day, *The Irrational Atheist*, 241.

[27] Brother Yun and Paul Hattaway, *The Heavenly Man* (London: Monarch Books, 2002), 20.

[28] Ibid., 26.

do, the church in China had not merely survived the brutality of the past thirty years, but had actually grown and flourished!"[29]

Although China is officially still an atheistic nation today and the Chinese government places restrictions on the distribution of the Bible, the Bible is thriving there. In 2007, Austin Ramzy wrote an article in TIME  magazine called "China's New Bestseller: The Bible."[30] Ramzy says that Amity Printing, a Bible publisher based in Nanjing has printed 41 million Bibles for Chinese believers and is thought to be one of the largest Bible production facilities in the world. It even exports some of its Bibles to other parts of Asia, Africa, and central Europe. For a country whose religious oppression still greatly exceeds its religious tolerance, the widespread availability of the Bible in China is remarkable.

Attempts to discredit the Bible

Attacks on the Bible have not been limited to attempts at physical destruction or restriction. History is filled with skeptics and atheists who set out to discredit and disprove the Bible in the name of textual criticism and academic scholarship. We have already discussed and refuted the tactic to identify alleged parallels between Bible stories and pagan myths in order to raise doubts about the Bible's divine origin.[31]

Another common practice is to question the authorship and dating of biblical books, so they would appear less trustworthy. Modern biblical studies are customarily divided into two branches. "Lower" or textual criticism addresses issues surrounding the Bible's canon,[32] existing manuscripts, and variant readings. The other branch, called "higher" criticism, analyzes the date, unity, and authorship of the texts. It seeks to investigate and interpret their literary structure and the assumptions and biases of its writers.[33] Both branches are essential to proper understanding of the origin of biblical texts, however higher criticism is frequently used by skeptics to try to discredit the reliability of the Bible.

---

[29] Paul Hattaway, *Back to Jerusalem* (Waynesboro, GA: Gabriel Publishing, 2003), 2, 13-14.

[30] Austin Ramzy, "China's New Bestseller: The Bible", TIME magazine, December 17, 2007, available at http://www.time.com/time/world/article/0,8599,1695279,00.html#ixzz15gF9CtnI, accessed Nov 17, 2010.

[31] See chapter 8.

[32] The canon refers to the list of books considered to be divinely inspired and therefore authoritative. "Canon" (Greek *kanon*) means a measuring stick.

[33] The word "higher" is an academic term, used in this context to mean a higher-level perspective than mere words and sentences. It does not intend to convey an idea of superiority.

The higher critics often concentrate their efforts on questioning the origin of the first five books of the Bible, called the Pentateuch, traditionally believed to have been written by Moses around 1450-1400 BC.[34] By challenging these foundational biblical texts they seek to prove that the whole OT is unreliable, and since Jesus referred to these texts, he also cannot be trusted.

According to these higher critics, the Pentateuch consists of four completely diverse documents, written not by Moses, but by different authors.[35] In addition, they were not written in the fifteenth century BC, but supposedly in the ninth, seventh, sixth and fifth centuries BC. They further conclude that these different works disagree with one another in important respects, which casts further doubt on their reliability. Interestingly, the higher critics do not know who, how, why, or when these documents were really written and edited, as their methods and conclusions are highly speculative. Robert Dick Wilson did much to discredit this view in the early twentieth century.[36] Although some contemporary skeptics have embraced this line of reasoning, most mainstream biblical scholars reject it today.[37] The attempts of the higher critics to cloud the OT in questions and doubts have not been successful.

Another infamous attempt to discredit the Bible centers around the Gospels—in particular the events of Jesus' life. The Jesus Seminar was a group of about 150 biblical scholars and laymen founded in 1985 by Robert Funk and John Dominic Crossan. Their methodology was to vote using colored beads to decide their collective view of the historicity of about 500 deeds and sayings of Jesus of Nazareth. The color of the bead represented how sure the voter was that a saying or act was or was not authentic.[38] The Seminar concluded that of the various statements in the Gospels attributed to Jesus, only about 18% of them were likely uttered by

---

[34] The higher critics also aim their skepticism at the NT, questioning the authorship and dating of all the NT books.

[35] They designate these four documents as the Jahwist, the Elohist, the Deuteronomist, and the Priestly code, referring to them as J, E, D, and P, respectively. This theory is referred to as the *Documentary Hypothesis*.

[36] Wilson, *Scientific Investigation of the OT*. Some of his work was discussed in chapter 8.

[37] For example: Gleason L. Archer, *A Survey of Old Testament Introduction* (Chicago: Moody Bible Institute, 1994), Gordon J. Wenham, *Word Biblical Commentary, Vol. 1, Genesis 1-15* (Thomas Nelson, 1987), Kenneth A. Kitchen, *Ancient Orient and the Old Testament* (Tyndale Press, 1966), Umberto Cassuto, *The Documentary Hypothesis and the Composition of the Pentateuch* (Jerusalem: Shalem Press, 1961).

[38] A red bead indicated the voter believed Jesus did say the passage quoted, or something very much like the passage (worth 3 points). A pink bead indicated the voter believed Jesus probably said something like the passage (worth 2 points). A gray bead indicated the voter believed Jesus did not say the passage, but it contains Jesus' ideas (worth 1 point). A black bead indicated the voter believed Jesus did not say the passage (worth no points). The consensus position was determined by the average weighted score, rather than by simple majority; so the really extreme skeptics had more say in the final score.

Jesus himself. They concluded that the Gospel of John was almost entirely inauthentic. The Jesus Seminar has been severely criticized by a wide number of scholars regarding its method, assumptions, and conclusions.[39]

Some of these discrediting attacks have back-fired on the skeptics themselves, resulting in their own conversion to Christianity. William Ramsay, the renowned archaeologist we mentioned in chapter 9, went to Asia Minor in 1880 for the purpose of proving the Bible to be historically inaccurate. He took particular interest in Luke's accounts in his Gospel and in the Acts of the Apostles, which contains numerous geographical and historical references. As Ramsay meticulously examined the ancient artifacts, he realized that the evidence supported Luke's accounts down to the smallest details. Luke had mentioned governors that no historian had ever heard of, but Ramsay's team confirmed they existed. Ramsay found that Luke was accurate in naming 32 countries, 54 cities, and 9 islands, without a single error.

Ramsay became so overwhelmed with the evidence he eventually converted to Christianity. At the end of his excavation, he wrote, "I began with a mind unfavorable to it...but more recently I found myself brought into contact with the Book of Acts as an authority for the topography, antiquities, and society of Asia Minor. It was gradually borne upon me that in various details the narrative showed marvelous truth."[40] He also concluded, "Luke is a historian of the first rank; not merely are his statements of fact trustworthy...this author should be placed along with the very greatest historians."[41]

Attempts to add to the Bible

Others have tried to change the Bible by altering and diluting it with other so-called Gospels that have been recently discovered. The Gospel of Thomas, the Gospel of Philip, and the Gospel of Truth, found in the Nag Hammadi library in Upper Egypt in 1945, are some well-known examples of such lost-and-found ancient manuscripts. The idea that lost books of the Bible may exist raises questions about the current canon of Scripture. If

---

[39] For example: Michael J. Wilkins and J. P. Moreland (general editors), *Jesus Under Fire: Modern Scholarship Reinvents the Historical Jesus* (Grand Rapids: Zondervan, 1995), Ben Witherington III. *The Jesus Quest: The Third Search for the Jew of Nazareth* (Downers Grove, IL: InterVarsity Press, 1997), Gary R. Habermas, *The Historical Jesus: Ancient Evidence for the Life of Christ* (Joplin, MO: College Press, 2003), Craig A. Evans, *Fabricating Jesus: How Modern Scholars Distort the Gospels* (Downers Grove, IL: InterVarsity Press, 2006), J. Ed Komoszewski, M. James, Sawyer, and Daniel B. Wallace, *Reinventing Jesus: How Contemporary Skeptics Miss the Real Jesus and Mislead Popular Culture* (Grand Rapids: Kregel Publications, 2006), N. T. Wright, *The Challenge of Jesus: Rediscovering Who Jesus Was and Is* (Downers Grove, IL: InterVarsity Press, 1999).

[40] William M. Ramsay, *St. Paul the Traveler and Roman Citizen* (Grand Rapids: Kregel, 2001, from the 15th edition published by Hodder & Stoughton, London, 1925), 19.

[41] Ramsay, *Bearing of Recent Discovery*, 222.

the Bible is incomplete, how can we really trust what we have? Furthermore, since many of the statements and teachings in these lost books contradict what is in the Bible, they are supposed to cause us to question the trustworthiness of what we read in Scripture today.

Of course, this whole approach begs the question[42] by assuming that these books are supposed to be in the Bible in the first place. However, there is no good reason to believe this—*whether or not* the Bible is from God. If the Bible were merely a human book, we should still allow the early Christian church leaders to decide which books *they* considered to be representative of *their* beliefs. They rightfully should have the final word on what is included because it is their faith that is at stake. Any books they rejected were never part of their Bible to begin with. It is clear they rejected these books primarily because of their late date (late-second to fourth centuries AD) and also their disharmony with the Bible. On the other hand, if the Bible really is divinely inspired, then we should think that God would not lose books of the Bible that he intended to be included. Surely, almighty God could guarantee that no portion of it could ever be lost.[43]

The so-called lost books are not missing from the Bible because they were accidentally forgotten or misplaced. They are missing because early church leaders explicitly rejected and discarded them with good reason.[44] When liberal scholars who deny God's inspiration of the Bible try to add or delete from the Bible, they are not "discovering" the real Scriptures. Rather they are inventing their own alternate view of the Bible to reflect what they want to believe about spiritual truth. In that case, they are no longer talking about the historic Christian faith, but a considerable departure from it and an outright contradiction of it.

All attempts to eliminate the Bible have failed

No other book in history has been subjected to such intensive and continuous attacks. There have been many deliberate and powerful attempts to destroy the existence, authenticity, availability, and influence of the Bible; however, all of these attempts have ultimately failed.

We saw earlier how the biblical documents are the best-preserved historical documents of the ancient world. It should make us wonder why the NT manuscript evidence is hundreds of times better than *any* other

---

[42] *Begging the question* means arguing in a circle or using circular reasoning.

[43] Greg Koukl, "No Lost Books of the Bible", Stand To Reason, http://www.str.org/site/News2?page=NewsArticle&id=5473, accessed Mar 9, 2011.

[44] The criteria used by the early Church to accept any particular book as being divinely inspired included: 1) Apostolicity—was it early, did it have apostolic authority, and was it not a forgery? 2) Catholicity—was it widely read and used in the universal Church? 3) Orthodoxy—was it consistent with teachings of other books already accepted as authentic?

ancient document, or why OT manuscripts are nearly identical to copies made a thousand years earlier. This is evidence of God's supernatural preservation of his words to humanity. Indeed, Jesus said that his words would never pass away (Matt 24:35).

The Bible remains the bestselling, most distributed, most read, and most studied book of all-time. It is impossible to know how many Bibles have been printed throughout history. Estimates of six billion have been suggested. One list of the most popular books of the last

fifty years claims the Bible is the most read book, selling 3.9 billion copies, which is two and half times the other nine books on the list *combined.*[45] The other nine books were all written in the twentieth century. How should we explain that the world's most admired book is *more than two thousand years old?*

The Bible has been translated in whole or in part into nearly five thousand different languages around the world.[46] This has made the Bible the most widely distributed and accessible book in history.

Despite all the vain attempts over the centuries to alter, discredit, restrict, ban, or destroy it, the Bible remains intact and as influential as ever. If it were not a book from God, then it would have been destroyed long ago. The Bible bears the unmistakable marks of supernatural survival.

---

[45] The other nine books are *Quotations from the Works of Mao Tse-tung* (820 million), *Harry Potter* (400 million), *Lord of the Rings* (103 million), *The Alchemist* (65 million), *The Da Vinci Code* (57 million), *Twilight - The Saga* (43 million), *Gone With the Wind* (33 million), *Think and Grow Rich* (30 million), *Diary of Anne Frank* (27 million). http://witneybookfestival.wordpress.com/2011/02/27/, accessed Mar 3, 2011. I have seen different lists like this with various titles, but I have never seen such a list that did *not* show the Bible at the top by the same kind of margin that we see here.

[46] Wycliffe Bible Translators, http://www.wycliffe.org/about/statistics.aspx, accessed Nov 10, 2010.

CHAPTER 11

Divine signature

Since we know that God exists, miracles are possible...For if there is a God who can act, there can be acts of God.

Norman Geisler (1932-)
Theologian, philosopher, author
I Don't Have Enough Faith to Be an Atheist

Miracles are a retelling in small letters of the very same story which is written across the whole world in letters too large for some of us to see.

C. S. Lewis (1898-1963)
Theologian, author
God in the Dock

To declare a thing shall come to pass long before it is in being, and to bring it to pass, this or nothing is the work of God.

Justin Martyr (AD 103–165)
Early Christian scholar
The First Apology

The literal fulfillment of a prophecy is the seal of its divine origin.

Herbert Lockyer (1886-1984)
Pastor, author
All the Messianic Prophecies of the Bible

If supernatural *orientation*, *unity*, *insight*, *impact*, and *survival* are divine fingerprints—substantial clues to the divine origin of the Bible—then supernatural *events*, *predictions*, and *testimony* represent a full-fledged divine signature. These three marks are powerful indicators of divine authorship of the Bible.

Supernatural events

Miracle is an overused word today. Some people call a sixty yard touchdown pass with one second remaining on the clock a miracle. Some think it is a miracle to see an image of Mary, the mother of Jesus, in a tortilla. Others find it miraculous when an illusionist appears to levitate a person or a psychic tells someone their future. Certainly many of us have referred to the birth of a baby as a miracle. However, a miracle is something more than a highly improbable or wonderful event. When we speak of a miracle, we are referring to a dramatic and unusual supernatural act of God.

Objections to miracles

Some people think that miracles are violations of the laws of nature, and since natural laws are constant and cannot be violated, miracles therefore cannot occur. In this view, miracles are simply defined as being impossible, but this begs the question by assuming the conclusion. Clearly, this way of reasoning about miracles is not correct.

David Hume was an 18th century philosopher who argued against the possibility of miracles in a more subtle way.[1] He observed that a miracle is by definition a rare occurrence, whereas natural law is by definition a description of a regular occurrence. He went on to claim that since regular events are much more common, the evidence for them is much greater than for miracles. Since a wise man always bases his belief on the greater evidence, he should therefore never believe in a miracle.[2]

Hume makes a fundamental mistake in reasoning, however. We shouldn't add up the evidence for all regular events and compare that to the amount of evidence for rare events. Hume's logic would rule out belief in *any* unusual or rare event, such as Alexander the Great conquering the world, Usain Bolt setting a new world record in the 100 meter sprint, Neil Armstrong walking on the Moon, the woman next door winning the lottery, or even the origin of the universe. According to Hume's view, we should disbelieve these events simply because they are rare occurrences, but this is obviously fallacious.

The issue is not how often an event occurs—whether commonly or rarely—but how good the evidence is for the event. Miracle stories are historical claims whose merits must be evaluated on a case-by-case basis. Not all miracle claims are true, but even if many miracle stories are false we cannot therefore conclude that *all* miracles are false. We need to look

---

[1] David Hume, *An Enquiry Concerning Human Understanding* (1777).
[2] Geisler and Turek, *I Don't Have Enough Faith to Be an Atheist*, 205-207.

at each claim independently and weigh *its* specific evidence to judge its credibility.

The possibility of miracles

God's existence makes miracles possible. Given the fact that God exists, miracles are not hard to believe at all. Since God is all-powerful, miraculous events are no more difficult for him than ordinary events. In fact, we might *expect* miracles if God had an interest in communicating with human beings and desired that we be able to recognize some message as coming from him.[3] We can therefore reasonably base our beliefs about him on their occurrence.[4]

Let's return to the idea that a miracle is a violation of the laws of nature. The laws of nature are really only our best understanding of how God normally governs the natural world. They are not some kind of impersonal cosmic mechanism that runs the world independent of God.[5] God created the universe and the rules by which it functions and he continually sustains it. We discover scientific laws through observation and experimentation and sometimes we make mistakes or see anomalies. Miracles look to us like exceptions to natural laws. They may be surprising and dramatic, but they do not *violate* the laws of nature. Let's consider an illustration.

Picture a vase falling off a table. Due to the law of gravity, we would expect the vase to continue falling to the floor. The fall of the vase is a natural and predictable event as long as no other factors are at work. Suppose however, that you are standing next to the table and catch the vase. Has the law of gravity been violated? No, the law of gravity does not account for the action of a person who freely chooses to interfere with the fall of the vase. The law of gravity is not violated, but remains fully in effect whether or not you choose  to catch the vase.[6] Likewise, God is a transcendent personal agent who can act in nature to change its regular patterns.

---

[3] R. Douglas Geivett and Gary R. Habermas, *In Defense of Miracles* (Downers Grove, IL: InterVarsity Press, 1997), 191.

[4] Miracles are an interesting phenomenon because they enable us to argue from God to miracles and also from miracles to God. If we already believe in God, then miracles are obviously possible and not hard to believe. However, if one does not believe in God, but sees good evidence for miracles (e.g. the resurrection of Jesus), then belief in God is justified.

[5] Vern S. Poythress, *Redeeming Science: A God-Centered Approach* (Wheaton, IL: Crossway Books, 2006), 28.

[6] I borrowed this illustration from Doug Powell, *Holman QuickSource Guide to Christian Apologetics* (Nashville: Holman, 2006), 204-205.

The purpose of miracles

Why might God use miracles? In times past when long-distance messages were sent by hand, a king would place his seal on his message to be a sign to the recipient that the message was genuine. The seal needed to be unusual, easily recognizable, and something only the king had. God might use a similar system to authenticate his messages. He could use miracles because they are unusual, easily recognizable, and only God can do them. God could use miracles, then, to tell the world which book or which person speaks for him.[7] We see from Scripture that a miracle is an event in which God temporarily makes an exception to the natural order of things to show that he is acting. Miracles have five distinct characteristics:[8]

1. They are exceptions to how nature usually works.
2. They are temporary since subsequent events follow natural laws.
3. They are caused by the power of God alone.
4. Their message is absent of error and immorality.
5. They occur for a purpose.[9]

The Bible relates many events that have no adequate explanation other than a supernatural one. Here are three examples (notice the purpose in each case):

Parting of the Red Sea to display God's glory

> Raise your staff and stretch out your hand over the sea to divide the water so that the Israelites can go through the sea on dry ground. I will harden the hearts of the Egyptians so that they will go in after them. And I will gain glory through Pharaoh and all his army, through his chariots and his horsemen. The Egyptians will know that I am the LORD when I gain glory through Pharaoh, his chariots and his horsemen (Exo 14:16-18).

Raising of Lazarus from the dead to display God's glory

> Jesus, once more deeply moved, came to the tomb. It was a cave with a stone laid across the entrance. 'Take away the stone,' he said. 'But, Lord,' said Martha, the sister of the dead man, 'by this time there is a bad odor, for he has been there four days.' Then Jesus said, 'Did I not tell you that if you believed, you would see the glory of God?' So they took away the stone. Then Jesus looked up and said, 'Father, I thank you that you have heard me. I knew that you always hear me, but I said this for the benefit of the people standing here, that they may believe

---

[7] Geisler and Turek, *I Don't Have Enough Faith to Be an Atheist*, 201.

[8] Geivett and Habermas, *In Defense of Miracles*, 62-64.

[9] This is consistent with God's character as a purposeful planner and designer.

that you sent me.' When he had said this, Jesus called in a loud voice, 'Lazarus, come out!' The dead man came out, his hands and feet wrapped with strips of linen, and a cloth around his face. Jesus said to them, 'Take off the grave clothes and let him go'" (John 11:38-44).

Healing of a paralytic to authenticate Jesus' claim to be the Son of Man

Jesus stepped into a boat, crossed over and came to his own town. Some men brought to him a paralytic, lying on a mat. When Jesus saw their faith, he said to the paralytic, 'Take heart, son; your sins are forgiven.' At this, some of the teachers of the law said to themselves, 'This fellow is blaspheming!' Knowing their thoughts, Jesus said, 'Why do you entertain evil thoughts in your hearts? Which is easier: to say, `Your sins are forgiven,' or to say, `Get up and walk'? But so that you may know that the Son of Man has authority on earth to forgive sins. . . .' Then he said to the paralytic, 'Get up, take your mat and go home.' And the man got up and went home. When the crowd saw this, they were filled with awe; and they praised God, who had given such authority to men (Matt 9:1-8).

Confirmation of miracles

It is not possible to independently verify all the miracle stories in the Bible, but it *is* significant that the Bible relates many stories of this nature. We would expect that a divine book that shows God's action in the world would contain stories of God's miraculous interventions. This is similar to our expectation that the Bible would claim to be God's words if it was, in fact, divine. In the same way, we would expect to see miracles described in the Bible if God were the author. This is suggestive, but not conclusive, evidence. Is there any way we can substantiate miracle claims?

Miracles, like all truth claims, can be substantiated with good evidence. In fact, the *quality* of evidence for a miracle claim is centrally important. It simply does not matter that an event is rare or improbable if sufficient evidence is present. William Lane Craig explains, "That dead men do not rise is a generally observed pattern in our experience. But at most it only shows that a resurrection is naturally impossible. That's a matter of science. But it doesn't show that such a naturally impossible event has not in fact occurred. That is a matter of history...If the historical evidence makes it reasonable to believe Jesus rose from the dead, then it is illegitimate to suppress this evidence because all other men have always remained in their graves."[10]

Miracles are not only possible; miracles are real because the greatest one of all is plain to see. The creation of the universe out of nothing has

---

[10] Craig, *Reasonable Faith*, second edition, 151. We previously examined this evidence in chapter 7.

already occurred. In fact, we have seen that miracles are actually *necessary*, for there must be a supernatural explanation for the origin of the universe. So, if Genesis 1:1 is true—"In the beginning, God created the heavens and the earth"—then every other miracle in the Bible is easy to believe.[11] We have already seen evidence and made reasonable inferences that a God very much like what the Bible describes must have created the entire universe out of nothing and created life from non-life. A God who did this can also easily do things like:

- ❖ Part the Red Sea
- ❖ Raise the dead
- ❖ Heal diseases instantly
- ❖ Walk on water
- ❖ Turn water into wine
- ❖ Feed thousands with a few loaves of bread

These miracles, and many others, are simple tasks for an all-powerful God who designed and created the universe. In fact, we find in the Bible hundreds of miracles related to nature, healing, exorcism, and resurrection. We would expect just this sort of thing from a loving and caring God who has a purpose for his creation. The Bible has the unmistakable marks of supernatural events.

Supernatural predictions

A sure sign of divine authorship is the ability to accurately predict what is going to happen in the future. We recognize that human beings are not able to do this with any degree of accuracy or consistency. It especially strengthens the indication of a divine source if the predictions are specific and predate the events by a long period of time. This sort of ability is what the Bible itself claims about God. "I am God, and there is no other; I am God, and there is none like me. I make known the end from the beginning, from ancient times, what is still to come" (Isa 46:9-10). "I told you these things long ago; before they happened I announced them to you" (Isa 48:5).

Not surprisingly then, the Bible contains many detailed and accurate predictions of the future that have already been fulfilled.[12] We are able to

---

[11] Geisler and Turek, *I Don't Have Enough Faith to Be an Atheist*, 203.

[12] J. Barton Payne lists 1,239 prophecies in the OT and 578 in the NT, for a total of 1,817— *Encyclopedia of Biblical Prophecy* (Grand Rapids: Baker Book House, 1997). Hugh Ross estimates that there are some 2,500 prophecies in the Bible, about 2,000 of which already have been fulfilled— Reasons To Believe, http://www.reasons.org/fulfilled-prophecy-evidence-reliability-bible, accessed Nov 17, 2010.

confirm many of the Bible's predictions using the records of history and discoveries of archaeology. The Bible has made approximately two thousand predictions, but we will look at only six of them in some detail to see how they have been fulfilled:

1. The destruction of the city of Tyre
2. The rise of five successive world kingdoms
3. The rise and fall of Alexander the Great
4. The coming of the Messiah
5. The destruction of Jerusalem and the Jewish Temple
6. Christ's resurrection from the dead

An interesting feature of biblical prophecies is that the prophets probably wrote more than they fully understood. They most likely did not know how their prophecies would come to pass, when they would occur, or even what their significance was.[13]

The destruction of the city of Tyre

Around 590-580 BC, the prophet Ezekiel predicted the ruin of the city of Tyre, the cosmopolitan center of the Ancient Near East, famous for its wealth and beauty. In Ezekiel's day, Tyre existed in two parts, one on the coast of the mainland in modern day Lebanon and the other on an island a half a mile from shore. Here is the passage from Ezekiel 26:1-21, with the verse numbers included so we can more easily refer to them.

1   In the eleventh year, on the first day of the month, the word of the LORD came to me:

2   Son of man, because Tyre has said of Jerusalem, "Aha! The gate to the nations is broken, and its doors have swung open to me; now that she lies in ruins I will prosper,"

3   therefore this is what the Sovereign LORD says: I am against you, O Tyre, and I will bring many nations against you, like the sea casting up its waves.

4   They will destroy the walls of Tyre and pull down her towers; I will scrape away her rubble and make her a bare rock.

5   Out in the sea she will become a place to spread fishnets, for I have spoken, declares the Sovereign LORD. She will become plunder for the nations,

6   and her settlements on the mainland will be ravaged by the sword. Then they will know that I am the LORD.

---

[13] Edwards, *Nothing But The Truth*, 164.

7 For this is what the Sovereign LORD says: From the north I am going to bring against Tyre Nebuchadnezzar king of Babylon, king of kings, with horses and chariots, with horsemen and a great army.

8 He will ravage your settlements on the mainland with the sword; he will set up siege works against you, build a ramp up to your walls and raise his shields against you.

9 He will direct the blows of his battering rams against your walls and demolish your towers with his weapons.

10 His horses will be so many that they will cover you with dust. Your walls will tremble at the noise of the war horses, wagons and chariots when he enters your gates as men enter a city whose walls have been broken through.

11 The hoofs of his horses will trample all your streets; he will kill your people with the sword, and your strong pillars will fall to the ground.

12 They will plunder your wealth and loot your merchandise; they will break down your walls and demolish your fine houses and throw your stones, timber and rubble into the sea.

13 I will put an end to your noisy songs, and the music of your harps will be heard no more.

14 I will make you a bare rock, and you will become a place to spread fishnets. You will never be rebuilt, for I the LORD have spoken, declares the Sovereign LORD.

15 This is what the Sovereign LORD says to Tyre: Will not the coastlands tremble at the sound of your fall, when the wounded groan and the slaughter takes place in you?

16 Then all the princes of the coast will step down from their thrones and lay aside their robes and take off their embroidered garments. Clothed with terror, they will sit on the ground, trembling every moment, appalled at you.

17 Then they will take up a lament concerning you and say to you: "How you are destroyed, O city of renown, peopled by men of the sea! You were a power on the seas, you and your citizens; you put your terror on all who lived there.

18 Now the coastlands tremble on the day of your fall; the islands in the sea are terrified at your collapse."

19 This is what the Sovereign LORD says: When I make you a desolate city, like cities no longer inhabited, and when I bring the ocean depths over you and its vast waters cover you,

20 then I will bring you down with those who go down to the pit, to the people of long ago. I will make you dwell in the earth below, as in ancient ruins, with those who go down to the pit, and you will not return or take your place in the land of the living.

21   I will bring you to a horrible end and you will be no more. You will be
     sought, but you will never again be found, declares the Sovereign
     LORD.

Notice how the city of Tyre is personified in this passage. The city is
addressed using personal pronouns fifty-five times in only twenty-one
verses (you, your, her, she). The significance of this is that God viewed the
city as more than a mere cluster of people and buildings, but rather as a
vibrant, living entity that had widespread influence in the world. Tyre was
perfect in beauty and splendor, and did business with many nations
because of her great wealth and industry. Tyre "satisfied many peoples"
and "enriched the kings of the earth" (Eze 27:33).

The next thing we notice in the prophecy is that "many nations" will
come against the city in waves like the ocean (verses 3-6). Ezekiel is
describing a gradual process of one nation after another slowly bringing
the city to complete destruction.[14]

We know from history that Nebuchadnezzar, king of Babylon,
destroyed the mainland part of the city in 572 BC (verses 7-11). Notice the
shift in the passage beginning in verse 12, referring to the attackers as
"they" instead of "he." This signals the end of the prophecy regarding
Nebuchadnezzar (he) and now refers to unspecified other nations (they),
which was first mentioned in verse 3 (many nations).

Almost 250 years later, in 332 BC, Alexander the Great attacked and
destroyed the island part of the city. Whereas Nebuchadnezzar was unable
to plunder the city of her wealth because its citizens had smuggled it to the
island (Eze 29:18), Alexander succeeded in looting Tyre. To accomplish
his attack Alexander built a 200 foot wide causeway from the mainland to
the island using the city's rubble from Nebuchadnezzar's earlier attack
(verse 12).

Interestingly, the Bible has a prophecy within a prophecy. The
prophet Isaiah foretold in 700 BC that Tyre would be partially restored to
prominence after being destroyed.[15] He first acknowledges that "Tyre is
destroyed" and that "The LORD Almighty planned it, to bring down her
pride in all her splendor and to humble all who are renowned on the earth"
(Isa 23:1, 9). Then he writes:

> At that time Tyre will be forgotten for seventy years, the span of a
> king's life. But at the end of these seventy years, it will happen to Tyre
> as in the song of the prostitute: "Take up a harp, walk through the city,
> you forgotten prostitute; play the harp well, sing many a song, so that
> you will be remembered." At the end of seventy years, the LORD will
> deal with Tyre. She will return to her lucrative prostitution and will ply

---

[14] The total duration of the process is not specified.
[15] This prophecy predates Ezekiel's prophecy about Tyre by over 100 years.

her trade with all the kingdoms on the face of the earth. Yet her profit and her earnings will be set apart for the LORD; they will not be stored up or hoarded. Her profits will go to those who live before the LORD, for abundant food and fine clothes (Isa 23:15-18).

In 274 BC, fifty-eight years after Alexander's demolition of Tyre, the rebuilt city was given independent status by Ptolemy II. This resulted in a relatively brief period of prosperity in fulfillment of Isaiah's prophecy. Destruction continued after that in various attacks. In AD 638 the Arabs conquered Tyre. The Muslims completely destroyed the city in 1291.

History has recorded that many nations ultimately came against Tyre—the Persians, Macedonians, Ptolemies, Seleucids, Romans, and Arabs. This fits the description of "waves" of nations foretold by Ezekiel. "All the inhabitants of the coastlands were appalled" at Tyre because she had "come to a dreadful end and shall be no more forever" (Eze 27:35-36). Tyre remained devastated for six hundred years following the last attack, until its recent development by Lebanon as a tourist attraction. Modern-day Tyre has a population of a little over one hundred thousand people.

Verse 14 says of Tyre, "You will never be rebuilt" and verse 21 says "You will be no more" and "You will never again be found." Given that Tyre still exists today, can we really say that these statements are true? Notice it says "*you* will never be rebuilt, *you* will be no more, and *you* will never be found again" not "*the city* will never be rebuilt," and so on.[16] God is not as much concerned in this prophecy with the buildings or presence of people in the city as he is with its flourishing, prosperity, prominence, and influence.[17] Tyre has never regained her former glory in these areas. She is nothing close to the "person" she was in the sixth century BC.[18] This biblical prophecy exhibits amazing accuracy in numerous details over twenty-seven centuries.

The rise of five successive world kingdoms

The prophet Daniel foretold the rise of five successive kingdoms in the world. This is found in chapter two of the book of Daniel, which was written around 535-530 BC. Daniel lived in Jerusalem, but was taken to Babylon as a slave when King Nebuchadnezzar conquered the city. Daniel

---

[16] For example, this is in sharp distinction to other prophecies Ezekiel made against Ammon, Moab, Seir, Edom, and Philistia, immediately before this prophecy against Tyre (Eze 25). God did not refer to them using personal pronouns, but spoke directly of their complete destruction. We do not see those nations today.

[17] Recall that Isaiah said that God would "bring down her pride" (Isa 23:9).

[18] Paul Ferguson, *"Ezekiel 26:1-14: A Proof Text For Inerrancy or Fallibility of The Old Testament?"*, http://www.biblearchaeology.org/post/2009/12/07/Ezekiel-261-14-A-Proof-Text-For-Inerrancy-or-Fallibility-of-The-Old-Testament.aspx, accessed Oct 3, 2010.

was a godly man of wisdom and much ability and was trained in the king's court to serve the king.

One night, King Nebuchadnezzar had a dream about a large statue that was dazzling and awesome. It had a head of gold, a chest and arms of silver, a belly and thighs of bronze, and legs of iron and clay. A rock was cut out of the statue and smashed all the parts of the statue. All the pieces of the statue were swept away by the wind without leaving a trace, leaving only the rock. This dream frightened Nebuchadnezzar. He desperately wanted the wise men in his court to tell him his dream and what it meant, but none of them could even say what his dream was. They complained, "There is not a man on earth who can meet the king's demand." The king threatened to kill all the wise men in the land, but Daniel requested that he be given a chance to tell the king's dream and also to interpret it. Daniel then asked God to reveal it to him, and God revealed both the dream and its meaning to Daniel.

Daniel went before the king to explain the dream. He told the king that no wise man could show the king what he asked, but there is a God in Heaven who reveals mysteries. He explained that the dream was a vision of the future. He said the different parts of the statue represented different kingdoms that would rule the world. The gold represented the Babylonian Empire currently ruled by Nebuchadnezzar. After that, another kingdom inferior to the first would rise, signified by the silver. After that, a third kingdom of bronze would arise. Then there would be a fourth kingdom, strong as iron, and it would crush all things. Finally, the God who is in Heaven will set up a kingdom that shall never be destroyed.

The king then said to Daniel, "Truly, your God is God of gods and Lord of kings. He is a revealer of mysteries for you have been able to reveal this mystery." Then the king gave Daniel high honors and many great gifts, and he made him a ruler over the whole province of Babylon. It is amazing that God would reveal Nebuchadnezzar's dream to Daniel, but that is not the most remarkable part of this story.

Today, we can look back in history and see that Daniel's prophecy was fulfilled exactly. All five kingdoms prophesied by Daniel came to power over the next six centuries, just as he foretold. After Babylon (626-539 BC), the silver kingdom called the Medo-Persian Empire arose, ruled by Cyrus the Great (539-330 BC). After that kingdom, the bronze kingdom called the Greek Empire arose, ruled by Alexander the Great (356-323 BC).[19] After that kingdom, the iron kingdom called the Roman Empire arose. This was led by the Roman general Pompey (63 BC) and the first Roman Emperor Julius Caesar (44 BC).

---

[19] Daniel actually names the Media-Persian and Greek empires in Dan 8:20-21 and 11:2-4.

During the Roman Empire the rock, representing the kingdom of God, was announced by Jesus Christ (AD 30). Jesus' central message was the proclamation that the kingdom of God had come: "The kingdom of God is near; repent and believe the good news" (Mark 1:15). Two thousand years later, this kingdom is still increasing.[20] Remember that Daniel said this kingdom would *never* be destroyed. All of this came true exactly as Daniel prophesied.

The rise and fall of Alexander the Great

Another prophecy was given to Daniel in the third year of the reign of Cyrus, King of Persia (535 BC):

> Now then, I tell you the truth: Three more kings will appear in Persia, and then a fourth, who will be far richer than all the others. When he has gained power by his wealth, he will stir up everyone against the kingdom of Greece. Then a mighty king will appear, who will rule with great power and do as he pleases. After he has appeared, his empire will be broken up and parceled out toward the four winds of heaven. It will not go to his descendants, nor will it have the power he exercised, because his empire will be uprooted and given to others (Dan 11:2-4).

The "mighty king" who arose to meet this challenge by the Persian king seems to be Alexander the Great, who had such great power that he created one of the largest empires in ancient history. However, his reign came to an early end and his kingdom was split across four of his surviving generals. None of these new rulers were Alexander's descendents, nor did any of them have the power Alexander once had, thus fulfilling Daniel's prophecy.

Daniel had a second vision of Alexander's rise and fall. He saw a goat with a prominent horn between his eyes come from the west, crossing the whole Earth without touching the ground. He came toward the two-horned ram Daniel had seen standing beside a canal and charged at him in a great rage. Daniel saw him attack the ram furiously, striking the ram and shattering his two horns. The ram was powerless to stand against the goat, which knocked him to the ground and trampled on him, and no one could rescue the ram from his power. The goat became very great. At the height of his power his large horn was broken off, and in its place four prominent horns grew up toward the four winds of Heaven (Dan 8:5-8). Daniel was then visited by an angel, who interpreted the vision for him. He said, "The two-horned ram that you saw represents the kings of Media and Persia. The shaggy goat is the king of Greece, and the large horn between his eyes

---

[20] There are more professing Christians today than at any time in history (2.2 billion or 32% of the world's current population). Mandryk, *Operation World*, 2.

is the first king. The four horns that replaced the one that was broken off represent four kingdoms that will emerge from his nation but will not have the same power" (Dan 8:20-22).

This vision corroborates the other vision Daniel had about Nebuchadnezzar's dream and also matches the historical record exactly. God proclaimed through Daniel what would happen on the world stage nearly 200 years before it occurred.

The coming of the Messiah

The Old Testament contains many prophecies regarding the coming of a Messiah who would save the world from its sins. The NT reveals that the Messiah was Jesus of Nazareth, also known as Jesus Christ.[21] By some accounts there are over three hundred predictions in the Old Testament about the coming of Christ.[22] These are incredible predictions that were literally fulfilled in the life of one man, even though he had no direct control over the vast majority of them. These prophecies were written 400 to 1,500 years in advance of their fulfillment. We will briefly examine forty-five of these prophecies.

All parts of the Bible point to Christ in one way or another, whether it is through direct prophecies, symbolic prophecies, or types.[23] Jesus himself proclaimed this when he said, "You study the Scriptures diligently because you think that in them you have eternal life. These are the very Scriptures that testify about me" (John 5:39). Pastor and author Herbert Lockyer describes it like this: "As the whole of Scripture is the *mirror* of the Messiah, we can expect his image to be indirectly, as well as directly, forecast and foreshadowed in its sacred pages."[24] Often only in hindsight can we see this ancient picture of Christ with great clarity.

Jesus referred to this partial clarity and partial obscurity of himself in the Bible while talking with two men on the road to Emmaus following his resurrection. "He said to them, 'How foolish you are, and how slow of heart to believe all that the prophets have spoken! Did not the Christ have to suffer these things and then enter his glory?' And beginning with Moses and all the Prophets, he explained to them what was said in all the Scriptures concerning himself" (Luke 24:25-27). When looking back at the events through the lens of history the earlier indirect prophecies and types of Jesus often become very clear. Their cumulative weight, including the

---

[21] Christ is not Jesus' last name, but a title that means the Anointed One, the Messiah.

[22] Herbert Lockyer, *All the Messianic Prophecies of the Bible* (Grand Rapids: Zondervan, 1973).

[23] A type is a person, event, or circumstance which is intended to represent another, more important, future reality. For example, Adam is a type of Christ because Adam is the head of creation and Christ is the head of the Church. Likewise, Noah's Ark is a type of Christ because it signifies redemption of all of mankind. There are many types of Christ throughout the OT.

[24] Lockyer, *Messianic Prophecies*, 212.

detail and accuracy of the direct prophecies, present a remarkable portrait of Jesus Christ throughout the pages of the Bible.

In addition to the events themselves, the OT predicted with astonishing accuracy *when* these events would unfold. The prophet Daniel predicted more than five hundred years in advance that a sequence of four specific events would occur. First, the city and Temple of Jerusalem would be rebuilt. Second, the Messiah would come. Third, the Messiah would be "cut off," that is he would die. Fourth, the city and the Temple would be destroyed. These prophecies were recorded in Daniel 9:24-26:

> Seventy 'sevens' are decreed for your people and your holy city to finish transgression, to put an end to sin, to atone for wickedness, to bring in everlasting righteousness, to seal up vision and prophecy and to anoint the most holy. Know and understand this: From the issuing of the decree to restore and rebuild Jerusalem until the Anointed One, the ruler, comes, there will be seven 'sevens,' and sixty-two 'sevens.' It will be rebuilt with streets and a trench, but in times of trouble. After the sixty-two 'sevens,' the Anointed One will be cut off and will have nothing. The people of the ruler who will come will destroy the city and the sanctuary. The end will come like a flood: War will continue until the end, and desolations have been decreed.

To understand this prophecy we need to realize that the Hebrew word translated as "week" (*shabuwa*) means a period of seven (days or years). In this case it is intended to mean seven years, so that each "week" is seven years. The reference to the Anointed One is the Messiah, who will come before Jerusalem and the Temple are destroyed ("The people of the ruler who will come will destroy the city and the sanctuary"), which occurred in AD 70 by the Romans. At the time Daniel wrote this (around 530 BC), Jerusalem was already in ruins from Babylonian attacks. He predicted that Jerusalem would be rebuilt before it was destroyed  again ("the decree to restore and rebuild Jerusalem"), which also marks the beginning of the seventy "weeks" of years. These two events bound the time for the Messiah to come and die ("the Anointed One will be cut off and will have nothing").

The question we need to answer is when this window of time begins. The Bible records four royal decrees referring to the restoration of Jerusalem, but the one that best fits Daniel's prophecy was made by the

Persian King Artaxerxes to Nehemiah (Neh 2:1-9).[25] Artaxerxes assumed his throne in 465 BC and this decree was made in the month of Nisan of the twentieth year of his reign (Neh 2:1). Assuming the first day of the month, the decree occurred March 5, 444 BC using our modern calendar.

To calculate the arrival date of the Messiah, the sixty-nine weeks of years must be added to the date of the decree. To do this, we reckon years in the traditional prophetic way, using 360-day years instead of 365¼ day solar years.[26] We convert the sixty-nine weeks to years (69 x 7 = 483 years) and then to days (483 x 360 = 173,880 days). Adding 173,880 days to the date of the decree and accounting for 115 leap years and no year zero, we get a date of AD March 30, 33. This would be Palm Sunday, the date of Jesus' triumphal entry into Jerusalem.[27] This calculation yields a date consistent with the time frame that most scholars believe Jesus began and ended his ministry.[28]

This is one of the most amazing prophecies imaginable. Not only does the Bible predict many details of the coming Messiah (see the following table), but it also predicts the precise time in history when this would happen. Listed below are forty-five prophecies of the coming Messiah, with their OT and NT references.[29]

#	Messianic Prophecy	Declared (OT)	Fulfilled (NT)
1.	He would come as a child.	Isa 9:6	Luke 2:5-7
2.	He would come from the tribe of Judah.	Gen 49:10	Matt 1:2-3
3.	He would come from the family of David.	Jer 23:5-6	Matt 1:6
4.	He would be born in Bethlehem.	Mic 5:2	Luke 2:4-7
5.	He would be the reason for Herod's killing of the infants.	Jer 31:15	Matt 2:16-18
6.	He would be taken to Egypt.	Hos 11:1	Matt 2:13
7.	He would be heralded by a messenger of the Lord.	Isa 40:3-5	Matt 3:1-3
8.	He would begin his ministry 483 years from the decree to rebuild Jerusalem.	Dan 9:25	Luke 3:23

[25] The other three decrees were made by Cyrus (2 Chron 36:22-23), Darius (Ezra 5:3-17), and Artaxerxes to Ezra (Ezra 7:11-26).

[26] See Revelation 11:2-3 for an example that uses this method.

[27] Harold W. Hoehner, *Chronological Aspects of the Life of Christ* (Grand Rapids, MI: Zondervan, 1973, 1977), 115-139. See also D.A. Carson, Douglas J. Moo, and Leon Morris, *An Introduction to the New Testament* (Grand Rapids: Zondervan. 1992), 54-55.

[28] The start of Christ's ministry was most likely the year AD 29 because Luke tells us that John the Baptist began his ministry in the fifteenth year of the reign of Tiberius Caesar (Luke 3:1-2). Since Tiberius began to reign in AD 14, this sets AD 28 or 29 as the beginning of John's ministry. Christ's ministry began shortly after John's and lasted about 3½ years.

[29] Sometimes prophecies and their fulfillments are stated in more than one place in the Bible, but multiple locations are not listed here for the purpose of brevity.

#	Messianic Prophecy	Declared (OT)	Fulfilled (NT)
9.	He would be anointed by the Holy Spirit.	Isa 11:2	Acts 10:38
10.	He would begin his ministry in Capernaum.	Isa 9:1-2	Matt 4:12-13
11.	He would minister in Galilee.	Isa 9:1	Mark 1:28
12.	He would perform miracles.	Isa 35:5-6	Luke 7:21-22
13.	He would heal people from sickness and disease.	Isa 53:4	Matt 8:16
14.	He would preach good news.	Isa 61:1	Luke 4:18
15.	He would speak in parables.	Psa 78:2	Matt 13:33-35
16.	His message would not be believed.	Isa 6:10	John 12:37
17.	He would be zealous for God's house.	Psa 69:9	John 2:13-17
18.	He would be worshiped.	Dan 7:13-14	Matt 14:33
19.	He would be called the Son of Man.	Dan 7:13	Matt 12:8
20.	He would enter Jerusalem as a king on a donkey.	Zech 9:9	Matt 21:1-9
21.	He would be despised.	Isa 53:3	Matt 27:27-31
22.	He would be hated without a reason.	Psa 69:4	John 15:25
23.	He would be rejected by Jews.	Psa 118:22	Luke 20:17-19
24.	He would be betrayed by a friend.	Psa 41:9	Matt 26:49
25.	He would be betrayed for thirty pieces of silver.	Zech 11:12	Matt 26:14-16
26.	The betrayer would try to return the thirty pieces of silver but would be refused and then throw them on the floor of the temple.	Zech 11:13	Matt 27:5
27.	He would be arrested and taken away.	Lam 4:20	Matt 26:47-55
28.	He would be forsaken and deserted by his disciples.	Zech 13:7	Mark 14:50
29.	He would be beaten.	Isa 53:5	Matt 27:26
30.	He would be disfigured.	Isa 52:14	Mark 15:19
31.	He would be silent before his accusers.	Isa 53:7	Mark 14:61
32.	He would be judged and killed.	Isa 53:8	John 19:16
33.	He would die as a criminal and with criminals.	Isa 53:12	Mark 15:27
34.	He would have his hands and feet pierced.	Psa 22:16	Luke 23:33
35.	He would be mocked.	Psa 22:6-8	Matt 27:39-44
36.	He would cry out asking God why he had forsaken him.	Psa 22:1	Matt 27:46
37.	He would pray for his persecutors.	Isa 53:12	Luke 23:34
38.	He would be given gall and vinegar to drink.	Psa 69:21	John 19:28-29

#	Messianic Prophecy	Declared (OT)	Fulfilled (NT)
39.	He would commit his spirit into the hands of God.	Psa 31:5	Luke 23:46
40.	He would have no broken bones.	Psa 34:20	John 19:33
41.	He would have his clothing divided and lots cast for them.	Psa 22:18	John 19:23-24
42.	He would be buried in a rich man's tomb.	Isa 53:9	Matt 27:57-60
43.	He would see no bodily decay after death.	Psa 16:10	Acts 2:31
44.	He would be raised from the dead.	Isa 53:11	Acts 2:32
45.	He would ascend into heaven.	Psa 68:18	Eph 4:8-10

Every one of these predictions was fulfilled in the life of Jesus of Nazareth, even though he had no human control over most of them. The probability that all these events would happen in the life of one person is staggering.[30]

Let's first consider *only seven* of these prophecies: Jesus would come from the family of David, be born in Bethlehem, begin his ministry 483 years from the decree to rebuild Jerusalem, be betrayed for thirty pieces of silver, be judged and killed, have his hands and feet pierced, and be buried in a rich man's tomb. The odds of one person fulfilling these seven prophecies is a very, very small fraction of a percentage point—about 1 in 10^{24}—which is one trillion trillionth.[31] Here is an illustration to help us visualize this.

Suppose that we emptied the water from all the oceans on our planet and filled them with a trillion trillion silver dollars.[32] We then randomly  mark one of these silver dollars by painting it blue. Now we blindfold a man and tell him that he must pick only one silver dollar from anywhere in these oceans without looking. What chance would he have of getting the one silver dollar that we marked? It is the same chance that seven of the prophecies written of the Messiah would come true in any one man.

Now let's consider the likelihood of one person fulfilling all forty-five of the prophecies listed above. Using fairly conservative probabilities for each of these prophecies, when they are multiplied such that they *all*

---

[30] The probability of multiple events occurring successively is the product of their individual probabilities, provided that the events are independent of one another. For example, if we have three independent probabilities of 1 in 10, 1 in 100, and 1 in 10, we multiply 1/10 * 1/100 * 1/10 to get an overall probability of 1/10,000 or one in ten thousand, represented as 10^4.

[31] The probabilities used are 10^3, 10^3, 10^4, 10^4, 10^3, 10^3, and 10^4, respectively.

[32] All the earth's oceans hold approximately 362 billion billion gallons of water. It takes about 2,800 silver dollars to fill a gallon.

would happen in the same person, the probability is 1 in 10^{152}, which is a one followed by one hundred fifty-two zeros:

1 in 100,000,000,000,000,000,000,000,000,000,000,000,000,000,000,000,
000,000,000,000,000,000,000,000,000,000,000,000,000,000,000,000,000,
000,000,000,000,000,000,000,000,000,000,000,000,000,000,000,000,000

This number is incomprehensible. The most liberal estimate of the number of human beings that have ever lived is only one hundred billion (10^{11}). The probability that Christ fulfilled these forty-five prophecies is one billion trillion trillion trillion trillion trillion trillion trillion trillion trillion trillion trillion times that! Keep in mind that this is only forty-five of the more than three hundred prophecies of Christ. The odds are so staggering that it is impossible to compare them with anything tangible that we can relate to. Here are some examples of very large real-world quantities that we know of, even though they still pale in comparison:

- ❖ The number of cells in the human body is about 10^{14}
- ❖ The number of seconds in the history of the universe is about 10^{17}
- ❖ The width of the universe is about 10^{27} inches (100 billion light years)
- ❖ The number of electrons in the universe is around 10^{79}

We cannot even conceive of anything real with numbers large enough to compare to these probabilities about Jesus. It is quite evident that Jesus did not fulfill these prophecies by accident.

The destruction of Jerusalem and the Jewish Temple

Recall earlier how Daniel had predicted the destruction of Jerusalem and its Temple. Jesus did likewise. Here is his prediction of the destruction of the Jewish Temple: "As Jesus was leaving the temple, one of his disciples said to him, 'Look, Teacher! What massive stones! What magnificent buildings!' 'Do you see all these great buildings?' replied Jesus. 'Not one stone here will be left on another; every one will be thrown down'" (Mark 13:1-2, cf. Matt 24:1-2, Luke 21:5-6). He also predicted the destruction of the whole city of Jerusalem:

When you see Jerusalem being surrounded by armies, you will know that its desolation is near. Then let those who are in Judea flee to the mountains, let those in the city get out, and let those in the country not enter the city. For this is the time of punishment in fulfillment of all that has been written. How dreadful it will be in those days for pregnant women and nursing mothers! There will be great distress in the land and wrath against this people. They will fall by the sword and

will be taken as prisoners to all the nations. Jerusalem will be trampled
on by the Gentiles" (Luke 21:20-24).

Less than thirty-five years later, in the year AD 66, the Jews rebelled
against their Roman conquerors in Judea. The Roman Emperor Nero
dispatched troops to restore order. By the year 70, the Romans began a
systematic assault on Jerusalem, culminating in the burning and
destruction of the Temple and the city. Our only first-hand account of this
Roman attack comes from the Jewish historian Josephus Flavius, a Jew
who had surrendered to the Romans. Josephus wrote a long account of the
siege in considerable detail. Here are some excerpts:

> The missiles shot by the catapults, stone-throwers, and "quick-firers"
> flew all over the temple, killing priests and worshipers at the very altar
> itself...The area around the temple became a mass of ruins.

> ...The Roman troops set the gates on fire, and the flames spread
> quickly to the porticoes. When the Jews saw the circle of fire
> surrounding them, they lost all spirit and stood gaping at the flames,
> without trying to put them out. Through the whole day and the
> following night the fire continued to burn.

> ...The soldiers rushed on, hurling their torches into the sanctuary. The
> rebels now were helpless, and made no attempt at defense, for on every
> side was slaughter and flight, civilians being butchered the most.
> Around the altar were heaps of corpses, while streams of blood flowed
> down the steps of the sanctuary.

> ...While the temple was in flames, the victors stole everything they
> could lay their hands on, and slaughtered all who were caught. No pity
> was shown to any age or rank, old men or children, the laity or
> priests—all were massacred. As the flames roared up, and since the
> temple stood on a hill, it seemed as if the whole city were ablaze. The
> noise was deafening, with war cries of the legions, howls of the rebels
> surrounded by fire and sword, and the shrieks of the people. The
> ground was hidden by corpses, and the soldiers had to climb over heaps
> of bodies in pursuit of the fugitives...The Romans now set fire to all
> the surrounding buildings, the remains of the porticoes and gates, and
> the treasury chambers.

> ...[Titus] then gave his troops permission to burn and sack the city, and
> flames soon consumed the Archives, the Acra, the council chamber,
> and many homes...Pouring into the streets [of the upper city], they
> massacred everyone they found, burning the houses with all who had
> taken shelter in them. So great was the slaughter that in many places
> the flames were put out by streams of blood. Towards evening the
> butchery ceased, but all night the flames spread, and when dawn broke,

all Jerusalem was in flames…[Titus] later destroyed the rest of the city and razed the walls.[33]

Josephus summarizes the whole affair with this statement: "Caesar ordered the entire city and the temple smashed to the ground."[34] The unthinkable had happened—the majestic and glorious Jewish capital city and Temple had been totally destroyed, just as Jesus and Daniel had foretold.

Christ's resurrection from the dead

Jesus prophesied his own resurrection from the dead on a number of occasions. "He then began to teach them [his disciples] that the Son of Man must suffer many things and be rejected by the elders, chief priests and teachers of the law, and that he must be killed and after three days rise again" (Mark 8:31). About a week later, Jesus said, "The Son of Man is going to be betrayed into the hands of men. They will kill him, and after three days he will rise" (Mark 9:31). And then again at a later time:

> They were on their way up to Jerusalem, with Jesus leading the way, and the disciples were astonished, while those who followed were afraid. Again he took the Twelve aside and told them what was going to happen to him. "We are going up to Jerusalem," he said, "and the Son of Man will be betrayed to the chief priests and teachers of the law. They will condemn him to death and will hand him over to the Gentiles, who will mock him and spit on him, flog him and kill him. Three days later he will rise" (Mark 10:32-34).

The disciples never understood this prophecy of Jesus until after his resurrection. In fact, Peter naively admonished Jesus on the occasion of the first prediction: "Peter took him aside and began to rebuke him" (Mark 8:32). On the second occasion, the Bible says plainly, "But they did not understand what he meant and were afraid to ask him about it" (Mark 9:32).

Even *following* the resurrection, some of his followers still did not understand. They said, "About Jesus of Nazareth, he was a prophet, powerful in word and deed before God and all the people. The chief priests and our rulers handed him over to be sentenced to death, and they crucified him; but we had hoped that he was the one who was going to redeem Israel" (Luke 24:19-21).

The disciples most likely had these reactions because the Jews did not think of the Son of Man as a suffering Messiah who would come to die, but rather who would triumph over their present enemies. Neither did they

---

[33] Flavius Josephus, *The Jewish War*, volumes 5-6, translated by Maier, *The Essential Writings*, 329-366.

[34] Ibid., 7.1, 369.

believe in any kind of individual resurrection, but rather a corporate resurrection at the end of time.

We examined the historical evidence for Christ's resurrection in chapter 7, so we will not repeat it here. The evidence clearly shows that Jesus died by crucifixion, was buried, his tomb was found empty, he appeared alive to hundreds of people, the lives of his disciples were completely transformed, and the Christian church, which is still alive and growing today, emerged as a direct result of this event.

Some people might object that, unlike the other biblical prophecies we have examined, this prophecy by Jesus was clearly written down *after* the predicted event had occurred.[35] Should we therefore not consider it a real prophecy, since it is simply reporting what was known to have already happened? I do not think so. This objection overlooks the criteria of embarrassment when assessing an historical account.[36] By including this prophecy in their Gospel accounts, the disciples admitted they lacked understanding of what Jesus told them and they looked foolish as a result. The only reason they would include such an embarrassing account in the Gospels is because it actually happened that way—Christ really did predict his resurrection from the dead. Moreover, the OT also predicted the Messiah would be raised from the dead (Psa 16:10, Isa 53:11).

The power of prophecy

Fulfilled prophecies may be the surest sign of divine authorship since they are so astounding and obviously beyond human capability. The prophecies we have examined are merely the tip of the iceberg. We could multiply these with hundreds of additional examples. The fulfilled predictions in the Bible are simply astonishing. No other book in the world has multiple, detailed predictions that have been fulfilled accurately—it is the only book that is supernaturally confirmed this way. The Bible has the unmistakable marks of supernatural predictions.

Supernatural testimony

The apostle Paul said that if Jesus was not raised from the dead, then the Christian faith is a lie and not worth believing (1 Cor 15:16-19). We have seen that the evidence for the resurrection of Jesus is remarkably strong, so we are warranted in believing that it happened. Since God raised Jesus from the dead, then we should listen to what Jesus teaches,[37] and he

---

[35] These events happened about 33 AD and Mark wrote his Gospel around AD 45-60.

[36] We discussed this in chapter 8.

[37] This also is the claim of the Bible. God the Father said of Jesus, "This is my Son, whom I love. Listen to him!" (Mark 9:7).

believed and taught that the Bible came from God. He repeatedly quoted it and accepted its accuracy and authority without question.

The Old Testament

At the time that Jesus walked the Earth the only part of the Bible that was written down was the Old Testament. When he would talk about the "Scriptures," he was referring to the OT. Here are some of the things that Jesus had to say about these scriptures:

1. "It is written: 'Man does not live on bread alone, but on every word that comes from the mouth of God'" (Matt 4:4, referencing Deut 8:3).

2. "You nullify the word of God for the sake of your tradition" (Matt 15:6).

3. "You are in error because you do not know the Scriptures or the power of God" (Matt 22:29).

4. "The scripture cannot be broken" (John 10:35).

5. "The scriptures must be fulfilled" (Mark 14:49).

6. "Not the smallest letter, not the least stroke of a pen, will by any means disappear from the Law until everything is accomplished" (Matt 5:18).

7. "You study the Scriptures diligently because you think that in them you have eternal life. These are the very Scriptures that testify about me" (John 5:39).

8. "If you believed Moses, you would believe me, for he wrote about me" (John 5:46).

9. "Everything must be fulfilled that is written about me in the Law of Moses, the Prophets and the Psalms" (Luke 24:44).

10. "This generation will be held responsible for the blood of all the prophets that has been shed since the beginning of the world, from the blood of Abel to the blood of Zechariah" (Luke 11:51).

When Jesus refers to the blood of all the prophets, he is tacitly authenticating the entire OT canon, from the first martyr mentioned in Gen 4:3-15 (Abel) to the last one listed in 2 Chron 24:19-22 (Zechariah).[38] Similarly, when he refers to "the Law of Moses, the Prophets and the Psalms," he is referring to the entire OT.

When Jesus says that we should live "on every word that comes from the mouth of God," he is claiming the Bible is inspired by God. Likewise,

---

[38] At that time, the traditional ordering was to place the book of Chronicles last in the OT canon.

when he says that "the scripture cannot be broken," he is making a claim that the scriptures are without error—they can be relied upon in every respect.

Jesus quoted extensively from the Old Testament. He did this not only to authenticate the historicity of the OT scriptures, but also to teach his followers. Here are a few examples:

1. He referred to God's creation of the world as "the beginning" (Mark 13:19, Gen 1).
2. He quoted from the creation story to make the point that marriage is sacred (Matt 19:4-5, Gen 1:27, 2:24).
3. He taught his own eternal self-existence by saying that he existed before Abraham (John 8:56-58, Gen 15-25).
4. Jesus compared the suddenness of the Flood in Noah's time to the coming of the day when he would return (Matt 24:37-39, Gen 6-8).
5. He referred to the story of Lot and the devastation of Sodom and Gomorrah also as an example of sudden destruction and judgment (Luke 17:28-29, Gen 19).
6. He taught of Heaven and Hell by saying the believers will take their places at the feast with Abraham, Isaac and Jacob in the kingdom of Heaven (Matt 8:11-12, Gen 25-35).
7. He referred to Moses' burning bush encounter as a real event to teach about resurrection (Luke 20:37, Exo 3).
8. He taught about eternal life by comparing the manna in the wilderness to the true bread from Heaven (John 6:30-51, Exo 16).
9. He compared his own crucifixion to Moses lifting up the snake on a pole so that those who looked upon it could live (John 3:14-15, Num 21:4-8).
10. He compared the three days and nights that Jonah spent in the belly of a great fish to the time he would spend in the grave (Matt 12:40-41, Jonah 1-2).

Jesus clearly taught that the scriptures were from God, that they could be trusted, and that they were true and accurate histories containing spiritual messages to be learned. If the stories were false, then he would have been basing his entire ministry on a lie, which is not consistent with the character of Jesus.

The New Testament

The New Testament was not written until after Jesus was raised from the dead and ascended into Heaven; however, he foretold that it would be written. Jesus said that the Holy Spirit would be the one who would remind his disciples what to write: Jesus said, "The Advocate, the Holy Spirit, whom the Father will send in my name, will teach you all things and will remind you of everything I have said to you" (John 14:26). Jesus also said that the Holy Spirit would teach them even *more* things: "I have much more to say to you, more than you can now bear. But when he, the Spirit of truth, comes, he will guide you into all truth" (John 16:12-13). Peter confirmed this new written revelation later when he wrote, "For prophecy never had its origin in the human will, but prophets, though human, spoke from God as they were carried along by the Holy Spirit" (2 Pet 1:21).

Jesus predicted that his words would be eternal. He said, "Heaven and earth will pass away, but my words will never pass away" (Matt 24:35). He also specifically confirmed the validity of the last book in the NT when he said to John in a vision, "Blessed is he who keeps the words of the prophecy in this book" (Rev 22:7)[39] and also "I, Jesus, have sent my angel to give you this testimony for the churches" (Rev 22:16).

Jesus clearly and repeatedly authenticated both the Old and New Testaments. The Bible not only claims to be of divine origin, but it is directly validated as divine by the one who God raised from the dead. If we believe what Jesus taught, then we must also believe the Bible is God's Word. The Bible has the unmistakable marks of supernatural testimony.

Summary

The Bible is able to substantiate its claims of divine authorship. God has indeed revealed himself to humanity in a book—the Holy Bible—and has given us sufficient proof that he is its author through clear signs of supernatural orientation, unity, insight, impact, survival, events, predictions, and testimony. No other book is divinely authenticated in this way!

Most of what we know we have learned from a reliable authority who gives us accurate information. Spiritual truth works the same way. When dealing with profound life issues such as we are in this book, we would like to rely on an authority with flawless credentials, and of course, that can only be God himself as the Creator of everything.

---

[39] Some people think this statement may apply to the entire NT, since this was the last NT book written and all of the other books had been circulating among believers for many years by this time. However, the more conservative conclusion is to apply this statement only to the Book of Revelation.

CHAPTER 12

The voice of truth

In the Judeo-Christian position...we find that there is someone there to speak, and that he has told us about two areas. He has spoken first about himself, not exhaustively, but truly; and second, he has spoken about history and about the cosmos, not exhaustively, but truly.

Francis Schaeffer (1912-1984)
Theologian, philosopher
He Is There and He Is Not Silent

What a book the Bible is, what a miracle, what strength is given with it to man. It is like a mould cast of the world and man and human nature, everything is there, and a law for everything for all the ages. And what mysteries are solved and revealed.

Fyodor Dostoyevsky (1821-1881)
Novelist and essayist
Brothers Karamazov

Christianity explains not only freedom, but also the other dimensions of human personality that derive from freedom: creativity, originality, moral responsibility, and even love. The whole range of human personality is accounted for only by the Christian worldview because it begins with a personal God.

Nancy Pearcey (1952-)
Worldview scholar, author
Total Truth

We have come to many fascinating conclusions about our natural world through reason, experience, history, and science. The most important of these conclusions is that the theistic worldview best explains all the data. Atheism, pantheism, and all other worldviews simply do not have enough explanatory power or scope to account for everything we know about the world.

A supernatural Creator—whom we refer to as God—is responsible for origins, explains the evil and suffering in the world, and makes sense of life after death. We have also discovered a sacred book—the Christian Bible—that exhibits the hallmarks of supernatural origin. We have also seen a vitally important intersection between this book and the historical event of the resurrection of Jesus of Nazareth, who is *the* central focus of the Christian worldview.

We now will look more closely at how the Bible confirms and further develops all that we have learned in our examination of nature in our first three questions.[1] The Bible not only corroborates everything we have observed about the world through nature, it actually extends our knowledge of it through deeper insights. This is because the Bible, which contains the very words of the God who created everything, gives the decisive meaning of all things.

What God is like

The universe is real, but it is not ultimate—God is the only ultimate reality. This section will provide a brief description of God and his main attributes.

God has always existed

God is *eternal*, which refers to both his endless past and his endless future. "Before the mountains were born or you brought forth the whole world, from everlasting to everlasting you are God" (Psa 90:2). God made a very profound declaration to Moses on Mt. Sinai when Moses asked God his name. God replied, "I AM WHO I AM. This is what you are to say to the Israelites: 'I AM has sent me to you'" (Exo 3:14). When God says "I AM," he is making a claim of necessary, self-existence. He never began to exist—he simply *is* and always has *been*.

As an eternal and necessary being, God must be *independent* and *self-sufficient*, not in need of anything outside himself. Paul explained to the Greek philosophers in Athens, "The God who made the world and everything in it is the Lord of heaven and earth and does not live in temples built by human hands. And he is not served by human hands, as if he needed anything" (Acts 17:24-25).

God is *timeless*—he existed before time began, he created time, and he presently exists in some sense outside of time. "We declare God's

---

[1] The descriptions that follow are frequently repeated in many places in the Bible. I will most often only show one or two references for each due to space limitations.

wisdom, a mystery that has been hidden and that God destined for our glory before time began" (1 Cor 2:7). Even though God was timeless without creation, he stepped into time at the moment of creation and now interacts with human beings in time.

God is *immaterial*, which means he has no physical substance. The Bible teaches that there is another form of existence—a spiritual, non-physical, invisible realm where God exists, as do angels whom he created. John says plainly, "God is spirit" (John 4:24). Paul also affirms this when he rejoices, "Now to the King eternal, immortal, invisible, the only God, be honor and glory for ever and ever" (1 Tim 1:17).

God is triune

The Bible describes God's most fundamental nature as triune, which means three in one. The doctrine of the Trinity teaches that within the one Being who is God, there exist three co-equal and co-eternal persons—the Father, the Son, and the Holy Spirit. There is only one God and he is tri-personal. He is not one person, he does not exist in three different modes, nor does he exist as a hierarchy of gods. Neither is Jesus a created being or the Holy Spirit an impersonal force. God is one Being, revealed in three distinct Persons. Let's look at how the Bible describes God as three in one.

There is no greater reality about God unmistakably taught in Scripture than he is One—he is God *alone*. Probably the clearest and most direct teaching is the Hebrew *Shema* in Deut 6:4: "Hear, O Israel: The LORD our God, the LORD is one." There are plenty of other passages that affirm monotheism. In Isa 44:8, God proclaims, "Is there any God besides me? No, there is no other Rock; I know not one." The first two of the Ten Commandments forbade Israelites from worshipping any other gods because none of them are real. The New Testament affirms this as well. Paul says, "There is only one God" (Rom 3:30). This belief in monotheism means that exclusive worship and obedience belong to one God only.

It is truly astonishing that early Jewish Christians accepted the Trinity since it required belief in a non-unitarian concept of God. These early Christians were deeply monotheistic, yet they had no problem worshipping Jesus alongside God the Father. This is because Jesus exhibited a clear self-understanding of his deity,[2] performed divine acts, and fulfilled prophecies of divinity. Matthew relates the conversation between an angel and Mary: "The virgin will be with child and will give birth to a son, and they will call him Immanuel—which means, 'God with us'" (Matt 1:23). Jesus and the NT writers also provide confirmation that the Holy Spirit is divine. The Holy Spirit is ascribed the divine attributes of eternality (Heb 9:14), omnipresence (John 14:16-17; Acts 1:8), omniscience (1 Cor 2:10-

---

[2] This will be discussed in chapter 15.

11), and omnipotence (Luke 1:35; Rom 15:19). What is more, it is clear from Scripture that the three persons of the Trinity are distinct from one other, so they are not simply one person performing three different roles. For instance, Jesus told his followers to make disciples, "baptizing them in the name of the Father and of the Son and of the Holy Spirit" (Matt 28:19).[3] Since the Bible declares that God is one being, but also names three persons as being divine, we conclude that God is triune—three Persons existing in one Being.

God is truth

Truth is what is real about the world. Since God is the ultimate reality and the source of all things, he literally *is* the truth by which we compare everything. We are not saying only that God speaks the truth, although he does do that. We are saying more fundamentally that he is, by his very nature as the only necessary and eternal thing in existence, *truth itself.*

God the Father is Truth. Jesus affirms, "Now this is eternal life: that they know you, the only true God" (John 17:3). God the Son is Truth. Jesus also declares, "I am the way and the truth and the life" (John 14:6). God the Holy Spirit is Truth. Jesus also says, "I will ask the Father, and he will give you another Counselor to be with you forever—the Spirit of truth" (John 14:16).

Jesus came to testify to the truth. The Roman governor Pontius Pilate said to him at his trial, "You are a king, then!" and Jesus answered, "You are right in saying I am a king. In fact, for this reason I was born, and for this I came into the world, to testify to the truth. Everyone on the side of truth listens to me" (John 18:37).

God's Word is truth. Jesus prayed to the Father, "Sanctify them by the truth; your word is truth" (John 17:17). Jesus claimed this same authority with his teaching. He said to the Jews who had believed him, "If you hold to my teaching, you are really my disciples. Then you will know the truth, and the truth will set you free" (John 8:31-32).

All of this means that we can completely depend on God. He cannot lie: "It is impossible for God to lie" (Heb 6:18). We can always trust his promises: "The LORD is trustworthy in all he promises and faithful in all he does" (Psa 145:13). His judgments are true. In his vision of Heaven, John heard a great multitude shouting, "Salvation and glory and power belong to our God, for true and just are his judgments" (Rev 19:1-2).

---

[3] The OT gives us some clues of a plurality of divine persons. For example, God makes several self-references in the plural. "Then I heard the voice of the Lord saying, 'Whom shall I send? And who will go for us?'" (Isa 6:8). There are also some direct references to a triunity in God, that is, references to the LORD, the Messiah, and God's Spirit as separate divine persons. For example, in Isa 48:16, the Messiah says, "Come near me and listen to this: From the first announcement I have not spoken in secret; at the time it happens, I am there. And now the Sovereign LORD has sent me, with his Spirit."

God is maximally great

To be maximally great means to have the highest possible degree of excellence in every virtuous quality and a complete lack of non-virtuous qualities. It is conceptually impossible for a being to have any more excellence—it is perfection.[4] Let's look at some of these attributes of God.

God is *holy*. Isaiah recounts a vision he had about a song the angels were singing around the throne of God: "They were calling to one another: 'Holy, holy, holy is the LORD Almighty; the whole earth is full of His glory'" (Isa 6:3). The song is the repetition of a single word—holy. The Bible mentions only God's holiness three times in succession; never any of his other attributes. This is done to elevate it to the highest degree, meaning that we should think of this as the principal description of God.[5]

The primary meaning of *holy* is "separate." God is utterly different than his creation, including us human beings. He is infinite and faultless and creation is finite and flawed. Holiness is one way the Bible's expresses God's maximal greatness. Pastor and author R. C. Sproul refers to this as God's transcendence. He explains, "When we speak of the transcendence of God, we are talking about that sense in which God is above and beyond us. Transcendence describes his supreme and absolute greatness...It points to the infinite distance that separates him from every creature."[6]

When we experience the holy presence of God, we have an immediate and overwhelming awareness of ourselves as created beings. When Isaiah had his vision of God in Heaven, he exclaimed, "Woe to me! I am ruined! For I am a man of unclean lips, and I live among a people of unclean lips, and my eyes have seen the King, the LORD Almighty" (Isa 6:5). Sproul comments, "When we meet the Absolute, we know immediately that we are not absolute. When we meet the Infinite, we become acutely conscious that we are finite. When we meet the Eternal, we know we are temporal. To meet God is a powerful study in contrasts."[7]

God is *all-glorious*. The glory of God is the magnitude of his importance, the greatness of his presence and majesty, the demonstration of his power, and the beauty of his many perfections.[8] It is the expression of his goodness and all his other fundamental, eternal qualities. "Yours, O LORD, is the greatness and the power and the glory and the majesty and the

---

[4] For example, maximal knowledge means knowing all and only true propositions. It is impossible for a being to know more than this. Maximal power means being able to do everything that is possible to do. It is impossible for a being to be able to do more than this. Maximal goodness means to always do the right thing. It is impossible for a being to be more righteous than this.

[5] R. C. Sproul, *The Holiness of God* (Wheaton, IL: Tyndale House Publishers, 1998), 24-25.

[6] Ibid., 38.

[7] Ibid., 44.

[8] John Piper, *Desiring God: Meditations of a Christian Hedonist* (Sisters, OR: Multnomah Publishers, 1996), 42-43.

splendor, for everything in heaven and earth is yours. Yours, O LORD, is the kingdom; you are exalted as head over all" (1 Chron 29:11).

God's glory is manifest in the whole world. David cries out, "The heavens declare the glory of God; the skies proclaim the work of his hands" (Psa 19:1). All the world will know of God's glory. Habakkuk foretells, "The earth will be filled with the knowledge of the glory of the LORD, as the waters cover the sea" (Hab 2:14). God is the supreme treasure in the universe. His beauty is beyond comparison. David expresses this desire of his heart: "One thing I ask of the LORD, this is what I seek: that I may dwell in the house of the LORD all the days of my life, to gaze upon the beauty of the LORD" (Psa 27:4).

In previous chapters we concluded that God was extremely powerful since he was able to create something as vast and complex as the universe out of nothing. The Bible says that God is *all-powerful* (omnipotent). God declares, "I am the Alpha and the Omega, who is, and who was, and who is to come, the Almighty'" (Rev 1:8). This means that God has the ability to do whatever he wills.[9] He is able to bring about everything he declares, including what he says about man and final judgment.

We also said earlier that God must be exceedingly intelligent to be able to design the complexities and intricacies of the entire universe. The Bible says that God is not merely really intelligent, but *all-knowing* (omniscient). "Great is our Lord and mighty in power; his understanding has no limit" (Psa 147:5). God eternally, perfectly, and exhaustively knows all things which can be known—past, present, and future. A consequence of omniscience is that God knows how best to attain his desired goals. Man cannot hide from God because God knows everything, including our every thought and every action. David acknowledges, "O LORD, you have searched me and you know me. You know when I sit and when I rise; you perceive my thoughts from afar. You discern my going out and my lying down; you are familiar with all my ways. Before a word is on my tongue you know it completely, O LORD" (Psa 139:1-4).

God is *all-present*, which means he is present everywhere at once in the universe (omnipresent).[10] He rhetorically asks, "Am I only a God nearby and not a God far away? Who can hide in secret places so that I cannot see them? Do not I fill heaven and earth?" (Jer 23:23-24). He is

---

[9] God's will is limited by his nature, so he cannot do anything contrary to his nature, such as make a mistake, commit a sin, or ignore our sin. Neither can God do something absurd or self-contradictory, like make a rock too heavy for him to lift.

[10] God's omnipresence is to be distinguished from pantheism, which holds that God is in everything and everything is in God, and also animism, which holds that spirits inhabit inanimate objects and natural phenomena. Contra pantheism, God is entirely distinct from his creation. Contra animism, God is not divided into separate spirits, nor does he "inhabit" objects. Instead, God, as the immaterial Creator of everything, is actively present at every material point in the universe, while retaining his distinctiveness from the universe.

fully present and causally active in every part of the universe at every moment in time.[11] A consequence of omnipresence is that God is there in the midst of our joys, our sufferings, and also our sinful actions.

God is *sovereign*. To be sovereign means to be the supreme authority within a given sphere. In the case of God, he is the absolute ruler of the entire universe. David declares, "The earth is the LORD's, and everything in it, the world, and all who live in it" (Psa 24:1). Job says, "In his hand is the life of every creature and the breath of all mankind" (Job 12:10). God himself claims, "Everything under heaven belongs to me" (Job 41:11).

God has the power and knowledge to maintain complete control over everything that happens and he is completely free to act as he wills, in keeping with his own nature. The psalmist proclaims, "Our God is in heaven; he does whatever pleases him" (Psa 115:3) and "The LORD has established his throne in heaven, and his kingdom rules over all" (Psa 103:19). Everything that happens everywhere to every creature is under the sovereignty of God. God has no obligations to anyone or anything other than himself. No human being or force of nature can impose anything upon God.

God's sovereignty also means that he is the *only* truly autonomous being in existence since he is governed in no way by anyone else or any external force. He has full and final authority over the universe. Through his infinite knowledge and power he supervises all of human history. He permits and prevents what he pleases. His plans will always prevail because his intentions can never be ultimately frustrated by mere human beings. Job says, "I know that you can do all things; no plan of yours can be thwarted" (Job 42:2). God himself declares, "My purpose will stand, and I will do all that I please" (Isa 46:10).

God is *all-good*. His very nature is moral perfection. David exclaims, "The LORD is righteous in all his ways" (Psa 145:17). Habakkuk says, "Your eyes are too pure to look on evil; you cannot tolerate wrongdoing" (Hab 1:13). Part of God's goodness is being just. "God is a righteous judge" (Psa 7:11). His justice demands that sin be punished. Nahum remarks, "The LORD will not leave the guilty unpunished" (Nah 1:3). God's good nature is also expressed in the goodness of creation. God is the source of all good things, which he freely bestows on creation. David rejoices, "Praise the LORD, my soul, and forget not all his benefits—who forgives all your sins and heals all your diseases, who redeems your life from the pit and crowns you with love and compassion, who satisfies your desires with good things" (Psa 103:2-5). God is a fountain of blessing to his creation.

---

[11] Moreland and Craig, *Philosophical Foundations for a Christian Worldview*, 510.

God is *all-loving*. Scripture from beginning to end teaches that God loves all people. At every turn, God demonstrates his universal love for all of humanity. John tells us, "God loves the world" (John 3:16) and the psalmist writes, "The LORD is compassionate and gracious, slow to anger, abounding in love" (Psa 103:8). Indeed, God's very nature is love; it is part of his essence. "Whoever does not love does not know God, because God is love" (1 John 4:8).

God has a special heart for the oppressed and downtrodden in the world. David says, "The LORD is close to the brokenhearted and saves those who are crushed in spirit" (Psa 34:18). "He raises the poor from the dust and lifts the needy from the ash heap" (1 Sam 2:8). He is "a father to the fatherless, a defender of widows" (Psa 68:5).

God loves everyone with a redemptive kind of love, that is, with a heart to rescue them from eternal condemnation. The psalmist prays, "May your unfailing love come to me, O LORD, your salvation according to your promise" (Psa 119:41). David celebrates, "He rescued me because he delighted in me" (Psa 18:19). God demonstrates his redemptive love through extraordinary patience. Moses writes, "The LORD is slow to anger, abounding in love and forgiving sin and rebellion" (Num 14:18). God's loving nature is expressed in his grace, mercy, compassion, patience, and forgiveness. Love does whatever is in one's power to do for the best interests of someone else. John explains, "This is how we know what love is: Jesus Christ laid down his life for us" (1 John 3:16). God has met our *greatest* need—offering to rescue us from the ultimate loss of eternal life without him.

How many beings like this can there be? God is *unique*—there is no other being in existence like him. God asks us, "To whom will you compare me? Or who is my equal?" (Isa 40:25).

God is personal

God is personal in the sense that he has consciousness, thoughts, feelings, desires, free will, and engages in social relationships.

God thinks, chooses, and has intelligence, so we know he has a mind. Since we observe so much order in the universe and we experience our own ability to reason, we also know that God is rational. He says to Israel, "Come now, let us reason together" (Isa 1:18).

God has intentions. He has plans and purposes, and he is working to fulfill them. "The plans of the LORD stand firm forever, the purposes of his heart through all generations" (Psa 33:11). God is orchestrating human history toward a particular end, namely that he would be worshiped forever by people from every ethnic group. In the midst of his vision of Heaven, John writes, "After this I looked and there before me was a great multitude that no one could count, from every nation, tribe, people and language, standing before the throne and in front of the Lamb.[12] They were wearing white robes and were holding palm branches in their hands. And they cried out in a loud voice: 'Salvation belongs to our God, who sits on the throne, and to the Lamb'" (Rev 7:9-10).

God is also relational. Love is expressed in relationship with another, so to show love God gives himself to humanity—the pinnacle of his creation. Jesus says, "Here I am! I stand at the door and knock. If anyone hears my voice and opens the door, I will come in and eat with him, and he with me" (Rev 3:20). Since God perfectly loves by his nature, and love is expressed in relationship with another, how can we say that God was in relationship prior to creation? God expressed his love within himself, among the three persons of the Trinity. He has always enjoyed an eternal, perfectly harmonious relationship as a tri-personal God (John 17:24).

God communicates with humanity. We discussed earlier a number of possible ways that God might reveal himself, and, we discover that he has, in fact, spoken to mankind in a variety of ways. Here are several of them:

1. God has shown himself to all people through his creation. "What may be known about God is plain to them, because God has made it plain to them. For since the creation of the world God's invisible qualities—his eternal power and divine nature—have been clearly seen, being understood from what has been made, so that men are without excuse" (Rom 1:19-20).

2. God has appeared to people individually through dreams, visions, and various physical manifestations. "God does speak—now one way, now another—though man may not perceive it. In a dream, in a vision of the night, when deep sleep falls on men as they slumber in their beds, he may speak in their ears" (Job 33:14-16).

3. God has spoken through angelic messengers. "I, Jesus, have sent my angel to give you this testimony for the churches" (Rev 22:16).

4. God speaks to all people through the human conscience. We all have a moral intuition about right and wrong. "The requirements of the law are written on their hearts, their consciences also bearing witness, and their thoughts now accusing, now even defending them" (Rom 2:15).

5. God uses a special means to speak to those who have a true belief in him. The Bible describes this as God indwelling believers. The relationship between God and believer is so intimate that Scripture describes it as God being *in* the believer and the believer being *in* God. "God lives in us...We know that we live in him and he in us,

---

[12] Christ is referred to as a Lamb because he was the perfect sacrificial offering for humanity.

because he has given us of his Spirit" (1 John 4:11-13). The Holy Spirit is the divine Person most often described as inwardly leading and guiding believers. "The Spirit himself testifies with our spirit that we are God's children" (Rom 8:16).

6. God has sent dozens of prophets to deliver messages to the world through prophetic proclamations. "In the past God spoke to our forefathers through the prophets at many times and in various ways" (Heb 1:1).

7. God the Son stepped into humanity as a man named Jesus to walk among us, teaching us about himself and how we are to live. "The Word [Jesus] became flesh and made his dwelling among us" (John 1:14).

8. God performs miracles as a way to prove his existence and authenticate his message. "Jesus of Nazareth was a man accredited by God to you by miracles, wonders and signs, which God did among you through him" (Acts 2:22).

9. God has given us a sacred book—the Bible—as a way to specifically communicate his purposes, plans, precepts, and promises. "The law from your mouth is more precious to me than thousands of pieces of silver and gold" (Psa 119:72).

God is a personal being and he created us as personal beings. All of these various ways of communication demonstrate God's intense interest in relating with us on a very personal level.

Where everything came from

Everything that exists owes its existence to God who created the universe and all that is in it at some time in the finite past.

God created the universe

The universe is a creation made out of nothing by a transcendent and eternal being who is more powerful and wise than we can imagine. The very first verse of the Bible makes it clear who we owe our origin to: "In the beginning God created the heavens and the earth" (Gen 1:1). The phrase "the heavens and the earth" is the Hebrew way of denoting the entire universe—all of creation. Additionally, because God created "in the beginning," we know that the universe itself is not eternal, but something made by God.

God merely spoke and the universe was formed. "By the word of the LORD the heavens were made, their starry host by the breath of his mouth" (Psa 33:6). Paul writes, "God...calls into being things that were not" (Rom

4:17). Since God created everything, by inference we conclude that nothing other than God himself preceded it, so the universe was "created out of nothing."[13] "The universe was formed at God's command, so that what is seen was not made out of what was visible" (Heb 11:3). God created from his incredible power and intelligence. Jeremiah says that God "made the earth by his power; he founded the world by his wisdom and stretched out the heavens by his understanding" (Jer 51:15).

The universe is immense in size, and it was all created by God. Isaiah explains that God "stretches out the heavens like a canopy, and spreads them out like a tent to live in" (Isa 40:22). While it is impossible for us to observe, much less count, the trillions upon trillions of stars in the universe, the Bible tells us that God has a name for every one of them because he created them all. The psalmist says that God "determines the number of the stars and calls them each by name" (Psa 147:4).

The staggering vastness of the universe says something about us and about God. On the one hand, it shows us how tiny we are as human beings. On the other, it reveals how enormous God is. Looking at the universe should give us a sense of the difference between us and God. Just as we use telescopes to magnify massive stars to make them look as they really are, we should magnify God through worship to make him look like he really is—the infinite and magnificent Creator of the universe.[14]

Since the universe's origin is due to a supernatural cause, we should suspect that its continuation is also supernatural. Indeed, the Bible reveals that God, through Jesus, is presently sustaining the universe. It does not continue to exist on its own, but only because God actively sustains it. "The Son is the radiance of God's glory and the exact representation of his being, sustaining all things by his powerful word" (Heb 1:3).

God created life

God's creation of life is described in the first chapter of the Bible, following his creation of the universe.[15] First, God created plant life. God said, "Let the land produce vegetation: seed-bearing plants and trees on the land that bear fruit with seed in it, according to their various kinds" (Gen 1:11). Then God created the animal kingdom. He said, "Let the water teem with living creatures, and let birds fly above the earth across the expanse of the sky" (Gen 1:20) and "Let the land produce living creatures

---

[13] This is often expressed by the Latin phrase *creatio ex nihilo*.

[14] I owe this analogy to John Piper.

[15] The biblical creation story parallels what we know from science very closely, far more than the creation myths of other religions. We see in science and the Bible a singular creation event of the whole universe and then life creation in stages, beginning with plants, then animals, and finally man. Note, the Bible does not say how much time elapsed between God's creation of the universe (stars and planets) and creation of life on planet Earth.

according to their kinds: livestock, creatures that move along the ground, and wild animals, each according to its kind" (Gen 1:24).

Finally, God created humans. "The LORD God formed the man from the dust of the ground and breathed into his nostrils the breath of life, and the man became a living being" (Gen 2:7). God placed the first man, Adam, in a garden to work it and take care of it, thereby demonstrating the goodness of work. God also had Adam name all the animals, thereby demonstrating man's role as ruler and caretaker of the Earth. God told him to fill the earth and subdue it, and to rule over the fish of the sea, the birds of the air, and every creature that moves on the ground (Gen 1:28).

God did not plan for man to live without a mate. God said, "It is not good for the man to be alone. I will make a helper suitable for him" (Gen 2:18). So God created the first woman, Eve (Gen 2:21-22). Then we read, "For this reason a man will leave his father and mother and be united to his wife, and they will become one flesh" (Gen 2:24). We should not miss the significance of this. In this act, God created the sacred institution of marriage, which we read elsewhere in Scripture is a reflection of God's relationship with his people. Isaiah explains, "As a bridegroom rejoices over his bride, so will your God rejoice over you" (Isa 62:5). God takes his relationship with humanity so seriously that he views rebellion from him as an act of prostitution and adultery. He warns Israel, "I will scatter you like chaff driven by the desert wind. This is your lot, the portion I have decreed for you, because you have forgotten me and trusted in false gods. I will pull up your skirts over your face that your shame may be seen—your adulteries and lustful neighings, your shameless prostitution!" (Jer 13:24-27).

Man is special and of great value to God—the masterpiece of his creation. Job wonders, "What is man that you make so much of him, that you give him so much attention?" (Job 7:17). Paul says that "we are God's workmanship" (Eph 2:10). Indeed, God formed man—and not animals—in his own image; therefore we have great value and worth to him. "God created man in his own image" (Gen 1:27).[16] This makes human beings qualitatively different from animals, especially in the areas of value, meaning, purpose, morality, intelligence, and ability. The Creator has something special in mind for humanity.

God's purpose in creation

The ultimate goal of the universe is to show the glory of God, that is, his greatness, power, beauty, majesty, and perfection. It is the reason for everything that exists, including each of us. God made it all for his glory. David writes, "Ascribe to the LORD the glory due his name; worship the

---

[16] We discussed what it means to be made in God's image in chapter 10.

LORD in the splendor of his holiness" (Psa 29:2). God says, "Bring my sons from afar and my daughters from the ends of the earth—everyone who is called by my name, whom I created for my glory, whom I formed and made" (Isa 43:6-7).

God's glory is profoundly important to him and he seeks to magnify his glory and worth in all that he does. "O LORD, our Lord, how majestic is your name in all the earth! You have set your glory above the heavens" (Psa 8:1). God created mankind "for the display of His splendor" (Isa 60:21) and, in particular, he seeks to be "glorified in his holy people and to be marveled at among all those who have believed" (2 Thes 1:9-10). God is zealous for his glory. He says, "I will not yield my glory to another" (Isa 48:11) or "my praise to idols" (Isa 42:8), and "I will show the holiness of my great name" (Eze 36:23).[17]

What is wrong with the world

We find no scarcity of references to evil and suffering in the Bible. The Bible does not deny their existence in the least. The Bible provides several key teachings that actually explain why evil and suffering exist and why God allows them to continue.

Human free will

Being God's image bearer means, among other things, that we have genuine freedom to choose. Free will is our ability to make real choices without coercion. Free will is the only real basis to express true love. Coerced or compelled "love" is not genuine and, so, is meaningless. This explains why God places so much value on human free will—so that we can express genuine love and worship towards him.

God holds people morally responsible for their free choices. This is amply demonstrated in hundreds of places in Scripture where we are commanded to do right or suffer the consequences. Every command in Scripture presumes our freedom and ability to obey it, and every appeal or offer made to us by God assumes that we can freely accept or reject it. Jesus says, "These are the Scriptures that testify about me, yet you refuse to come to me to have life" (John 5:39-40).

There can be no responsibility where there is no ability to respond, so genuine responsibility requires real freedom to choose. This is sometimes described by the phrase "*ought implies can.*" In other words, if we *ought* to do something, then we must be *able* to do it, otherwise we cannot be held accountable for it. Genuine praise and blame are only possible if there is true responsibility. To be authentically responsible means that we justly

---

[17] This will be discussed further in chapter 13.

reap praise and reward for behaving rightly, and blame and punishment for behaving badly. Without free will—if our behavior were deterministically caused—then there would be no basis for our own responsibility or to receive praise or blame for our actions.

The state of man

We have regrettably used our free will badly, choosing to ignore God and even to rebel against him. This began with the very first man and woman in the Garden of Eden. God commanded Adam and Eve not to eat the fruit from a particular tree, but they disobeyed. This event is referred to as the fall of man or simply "the Fall" because man lost his innocence and became spiritually separated from God. Before the Fall, Adam was sinless and good. After God created man Scripture records, "God saw all that he had made, and it was very good" (Gen 1:31). He was innocent because he had committed no sins. However, in the Fall he became a sinner which corrupted his nature. "He boasts about the cravings of his heart; he blesses the greedy and reviles the LORD. In his pride the wicked man does not seek him; in all his thoughts there is no room for God" (Psa 10:3-4).

Since we are all descended from Adam, we each inherit his corrupt nature from the Fall. Paul explains, "As through the disobedience of the one man the many were made sinners" (Rom 5:19). We become corrupt from the moment we are conceived. David laments, "Surely I was sinful at birth, sinful from the time my mother conceived me" (Psa 51:5). This corrupt nature inclines us toward evil. "The LORD saw how great man's wickedness on the earth had become, and that every inclination of the thoughts of his heart was only evil all the time" (Gen 6:5). In fact, every human being is unable to keep from committing sins. We are all born spiritually dead, separated from God and corrupt in our nature (Eph 2:1-3). Once we know right from wrong, we cannot help but do wrong. We cannot *not* sin. Paul tells us the bad news: "Just as sin entered the world through one man, and death through sin, and in this way death came to all men, because all sinned" (Rom 5:12). Because Adam's original sin leads all people to sin, we all are condemned. "The result of one trespass was condemnation for all men" (Rom 5:18).

This is not the way the world normally views the situation, however. People often deny their own sin. David bemoans the situation: "An oracle is within my heart concerning the sinfulness of the wicked: There is no fear of God before his eyes. For in his own eyes he flatters himself too much to detect or hate his sin" (Psa 36:1-2). Peter Kreeft explains:

> The world judges what is natural and normal to man empirically, from observing his present state. This is the world's base line. Christianity begins with a completely different base line and therefore judges

everything differently. Its assumption is that what we see is not normal but abnormal; not natural but unnatural, inhuman, fallen. The reason it judges so differently is that it judges human experience by divine revelation, while the world judges divine revelation by human experience.[18]

Evil exists because we *choose* to do evil. Man's sinful choices cause the suffering we experience in this world. This explains both moral evil and natural evil. Moral evil is the result of man's sins against one another. The Bible says that moral evil has also caused natural evil. When Adam and Eve first sinned, God said, "Cursed is the ground because of you" (Gen 3:17). Referring to this, Paul writes, "The creation was subjected to frustration...We know that the whole creation has been groaning as in the pains of childbirth right up to the present time" (Rom 8:20-22).

Disease and disaster are therefore symptoms of a deeper problem—the human race's rebellion against the Creator—and so the harmony and tranquility God created on the Earth were destroyed. Physical and spiritual death became a part of human existence and life became hard and painful. Every sorrow, grief, and agony is a reminder of our human predicament.[19] We need to see clearly that human suffering and death are the result of rebellion, both that of the first humans in the Garden of Eden *and also our own*. We are all guilty and need to realize it. "The wages of sin is death" (Rom 6:23). When we understand this connection, we will begin to hate sin as much as God does.

Man's real purpose

God's main purpose for man is to know him. He explains, "Let not the wise man boast of his wisdom or the strong man boast of his strength or the rich man boast of his riches, but let him who boasts boast about this: that he understands and knows me, that I am the LORD, who exercises kindness, justice and righteousness on earth, for in these I delight" (Jer 9:23-24). This incomparable good will, in fact, lead us to the greatest possible happiness. There is nothing man can pursue that is better than knowing the Creator of the universe. When we know him truly, we will also love him and worship him, which glorifies him and brings us great joy. When we freely direct our worship to God he is glorified. David exclaims, "O God, you are my God, earnestly I seek you; my soul thirsts for you, my body longs for you, in a dry and weary land where there is no water" (Psa 63:1).

---

[18] Kreeft, *Christianity for Modern Pagans*, 70.
[19] De Haan, "Why Would a Good God Allow Suffering?", 9.

God's eternal perspective

We often look at evil and suffering from our own temporal perspective and cannot understand how it makes any sense. However, God takes a much longer view of things—he always has eternity in view. The Bible describes our earthly life as a temporary assignment in which we are being tested.[20] Our real rewards are in the next life, not this one. "What is your life? You are a mist that appears for a little while and then vanishes" (Jam 4:14). Paul urges us to "set our minds on things above, not on earthly things" (Col 3:2).

God uses temptations, trials, and suffering to both reveal and develop our character. Paul says, "We rejoice in our sufferings, because we know that suffering produces perseverance; perseverance, character; and character, hope" (Rom 5:3-4). James teaches, "Consider it pure joy, my brothers, whenever you face trials of many kinds, because you know that the testing of your faith develops perseverance. Perseverance must finish its work so that you may be mature and complete, not lacking anything" (Jas 1:2-4).

God permits suffering in our lives so that we would have a level of discontentment with this present life. This dissatisfaction we all experience should draw us closer to God, who is the source of all goodness. Ultimate peace and joy come only through him. God has designed this life so that we would press through our suffering to come to know and enjoy him— now and in the next life. We should therefore look at our suffering in light of eternity. Whatever we suffer in this life will not compare to a life that will continue into the future with no end and no suffering. Paul puts suffering into perspective when he says, "I consider that our present sufferings are not worth comparing with the glory that will be revealed in us" (Rom 8:18).

God's identification with evil and suffering

God is not distant and detached from human suffering because he entered into it himself. We find the greatest evidence of God's concern for us by looking at Jesus Christ. Jesus was the only truly innocent and righteous person in all of history, yet he suffered more than anyone else who ever lived.[21] Bible teacher and author Kurt De Haan remarks, "God loved our suffering world so much that He sent His Son to agonize and die

---

[20] Rick Warren, *The Purpose Driven Life: What On Earth Am I Here For?* (Grand Rapids, Zondervan, 2002), 42.

[21] Christ's sufferings go beyond his torturous execution, for he bore the enormous burden of humanity's horrific sin and experienced, for a time, terrible wrath and alienation from God the Father for that reason (Matt 27:45-46). The physical pain was immense, but the spiritual pain was far worse.

for us, to free us from being sentenced to eternal sorrow."[22] This echoes what Paul said: "God demonstrates his own love for us in this: While we were still sinners, Christ died for us" (Rom 5:8). Jesus had an eternal perspective about his great sacrifice: "Let us fix our eyes on Jesus, the author and perfecter of our faith, who for the joy set before him endured the cross, scorning its shame, and sat down at the right hand of the throne of God" (Heb 12:2).

We should stop and reflect on the profound significance of this. *The greatest evil the world has ever seen also produced the greatest good the world has ever seen.* Jesus Christ's death on the Cross, a so-called "gratuitous" evil with no apparent purpose, brought about the greatest possible good for humanity—the possibility of humanity's complete reconciliation with God. This fact alone should teach us that we cannot properly judge any given instance of suffering, for we cannot possibly know its eternal ramifications.

Because of Jesus we can avoid the most terrible pain imaginable—the pain of being separated from God forever. We desperately want complete and satisfying answers for evil and suffering. Instead, God offers himself and declares that it is enough for us. If we will trust him we do not need full explanations. It is enough to know that our pain and suffering are not meaningless. It is enough to know that God still rules the universe and that he cares deeply about every single one of us.[23]

Jesus not only has provided eternal life through his suffering, but that very suffering also makes it possible for him to understand ours: "We do not have a high priest [Jesus] who is unable to sympathize with our weaknesses, but we have one who has been tempted in every way, just as we are—yet was without sin. Let us then approach the throne of grace with confidence, so that we may receive mercy and find grace to help us in our time of need" (Heb 4:15-16).

God's plan for evil and suffering

One of the most important implications of a perfectly designed universe is that a good God would *do something* about all the evil in the world.[24] Instead, people often *blame* God for all the evil and suffering we see, but what exactly is the accusation against him? He does not cause it; it is *our* fault. Despite this, God uses it for good and eternal purposes, he entered into it through Jesus, and he will ultimately end it. Greg Koukl writes about the price God paid in sending Jesus to suffer and die for us: "Our dilemma should not be why God allows evil. Instead, our wonder

---

[22] De Haan, "Why Would a Good God Allow Suffering?", 32.
[23] Ibid.
[24] Heeren, *Show Me God*, 266.

should be why He would pay such an incredible price to rescue us at all when we have rebelled so completely against Him."[25]

God will not let evil and suffering persist forever. He is being patient with us, waiting for more people to turn to him. Peter explains, "He is patient with you, not wanting anyone to perish, but everyone to come to repentance" (2 Pet 3:9). God will deal with evil and suffering in two primary ways at the end of the age.

First, he will judge every act of evil ever committed. Paul says, "We must all appear before the judgment seat of Christ, that each one may receive what is due him for the things done while in the body, whether good or bad" (2 Cor 5:10). God's omniscience guarantees that he knows everything we will ever think, say, and do; so the accounting will be complete and correct. "Nothing in all creation is hidden from God's sight. Everything is uncovered and laid bare before the eyes of him to whom we must give account" (Heb 4:13).[26]

Second, God will vanquish evil once and for all. Jesus is ultimately the solution to *all* evil—both moral and natural evil. Jesus is the solution to moral evil because he took the punishment that evildoers deserve and paid for it by his own death. And he will sit in judgment of evildoers who refuse to turn away from their evil ways and devote their lives to him. Jesus is also the solution to natural evil. In his resurrection we see his body restored to a glorious state. God will restore all creation to a glorious state, as well. There will be no more evil, suffering, or decay. John describes the result of this great news: "Now the dwelling of God is with men, and he will live with them. They will be his people, and God himself will be with them and be their God. He will wipe every tear from their eyes. There will be no more death or mourning or crying or pain, for the old order of things has passed away" (Rev 21:3-4).

What happens after we die

Our life has purpose. Death is not the permanent end of our existence. The Bible describes our present life as temporary, followed by an entirely different kind of life. Two distinctive characteristics mark this afterlife—immortality and accountability.

First, the next life is eternal—while this life ends in bodily death for everyone, the next one will never end. Ultimate value, meaning, and purpose are possible *because* our lives are immortal. Heeren notes, "Our

---

[25] Gregory Koukl, *Faith Is Not Wishing: 13 Essays for Christian Thinkers* (Signal Hill: CA, Stand to Reason, 2011), 56.

[26] The sins of Christ-followers will be paid for by Christ's death on the cross, so they will not be condemned. Unbelievers will be condemned to Hell for their unpaid sins, which includes their rebellion from God.

lives aren't pointless; we don't live only to have all memory of us snuffed out in a few generations and throughout eternity. Rather, we find access to eternity through the One who exists outside of time. This is the one relationship that can give our lives lasting value."[27] We all have an innate sense of this immortality because God has "set eternity in the hearts of men; yet they cannot fathom what God has done from beginning to end" (Ecc 3:11).

Second, where and how we spend the next life will depend on what we did in this life. God's justice will ultimately be done and he will hold us accountable after we die: "Man is destined to die once, and after that to face judgment" (Heb 9:27).

Reality of the soul

The universe includes both a physical and non-physical realm. Paul urges us to "fix our eyes not on what is seen, but on what is unseen, since what is seen is temporary, but what is unseen is eternal" (2 Cor 4:18). The non-physical or spiritual realm is invisible and includes God and his angels. Some of these angels have rebelled against God and are now called demons. They presently fight against God by influencing human beings to do evil. Paul explains, "Our struggle is not against flesh and blood, but against the rulers, against the authorities, against the powers of this dark world and against the spiritual forces of evil in the heavenly realms" (Eph 6:12). God has temporarily permitted the chief of these demons, Satan, to have limited authority in this world. Peter tells us that "our enemy the devil prowls around like a roaring lion looking for someone to devour" (1 Pet 5:8).

We previously discussed the existence of the human soul, which is immaterial and thus invisible. We also find that the Bible speaks about the life of a person being not primarily in his body, but in his soul. Jesus warns, "Do not be afraid of those who kill the body but cannot kill the soul. Rather, be afraid of the One who can destroy both soul and body in hell" (Matt 10:28). We are spiritual beings with an immortal soul that will live forever. Our soul is what makes us God's image bearer. It is from our soul that we love and worship God. David exults, "My soul will boast in the LORD" (Psa 34:2). It is also the aspect of us that sins because that is where we conceive and choose to do it, even though we often use our bodies to act it out. Micah asks, "Shall I offer my firstborn for my transgression, the fruit of my body for the sin of my soul?" (Mic 6:7).

Paul strongly implied the existence of the soul when he said that if he died now, he would leave his body and be with Christ: "For to me, to live is Christ and to die is gain. If I am to go on living in the body, this will

---

[27] Heeren, *Show Me God*, 397.

mean fruitful labor for me. Yet what shall I choose? I do not know! I am torn between the two: I desire to depart and be with Christ, which is better by far; but it is more necessary for you that I remain in the body" (Phil 1:21-24).[28] The only way to leave our body and still "be" in any sense is if *we* are really a soul.

Although our souls represent the essence of who we are as persons, our physical bodies are also a crucial aspect of who we are. Some people might think a disembodied soul is more natural and desirable, but the Bible portrays it as unnatural and undesirable. We are unified beings—body and soul—that is why the bodily resurrection of the dead is so important in God's redemptive plan. We will never be all that God intended for us to be until our bodies and souls are again joined in resurrection.[29] And lest we think we should spend eternity with weak and ailing bodies, which are all too common in our old age in this life, Paul describes our resurrected bodies as being imperishable, glorious, and powerful (1 Cor 15:42-44). Paul exhorts us to look forward to this resurrection: "We wait eagerly for our adoption as sons, the redemption of our bodies" (Rom 8:23). We are a body-soul unity that has an eternal destiny in God's plan for the world.

Eternal life

Eternal life does not refer only to a quantity of life—that we live forever. This is evident from the fact that Scripture teaches that both believers and unbelievers will live forever; however, unbelievers do not have eternal *life*. Matthew says that "they will go away to eternal punishment, but the righteous to eternal life" (Matt 25:46). In this passage, eternal life is opposed to eternal punishment. Only true believers have eternal life because eternal life is only found in Jesus Christ, who "is the true God and eternal life" (1 John 5:20). John also says, "God has given us eternal life, and this life is in his Son. He who has the Son has life; he who does not have the Son of God does not have life" (1 John 5:11-12).

Therefore, eternal life is not merely endless existence; it is also a quality of life that enjoys a special relationship with God. Jesus prayed to the Father, "Now this is eternal life: that they may know you, the only true God, and Jesus Christ, whom you have sent" (John 17:3). Jesus compares this to drinking from a fountain of living water: "Everyone who drinks this water will be thirsty again, but whoever drinks the water I give him will never thirst. Indeed, the water I give him will become in him a spring of

---

[28] In this passage Paul twice refers to remaining in the body, which means to continue living in this world. He contrasts this "remaining in the body" with "departing to be with Christ." By this contrast, Paul is saying that to die and be with Christ now is to be without a body and, by inference, be with him in soul only.

[29] Randy Alcorn, *Heaven* (Wheaton, IL: Tyndale House Publishers, 2004), 111.

water welling up to eternal life" (John 4:13-14). We all need this living water because our lives are dry and barren apart from God. Eternal life means that we will forever experience all the many and varied blessings of God while in a saving, personal relationship with him. Jesus says, "I have come that they may have life, and have it to the full" (John 10:10).

Heaven

Heaven is the place where Christ-followers will experience eternal life. It is where life's value, meaning, and purpose are ultimately fulfilled. To experience the perfection of Heaven, we must be restored from the effects of the Fall. Heaven will only be filled with lovers and followers of God. This is only possible through the work of Jesus Christ on the cross, whose sacrifice redeems broken sinners who put their trust in him and provides them access to a relationship with God.

This is the central message of biblical Christianity—the possibility of human beings approaching God through the work of Christ.[30] "People who would be happy in heaven if Christ were not there, will not be there," writes John Piper, "The gospel is not a way to get people to heaven; it is a way to get people to God...If we don't want God above all things, we have not been converted by the gospel."[31] If we do not genuinely love and worship Christ, then Heaven is not our final destination.

Hell

Hell is necessary in a universe where ultimate justice is done; otherwise evil would never be held to account. Our choices in this life do matter; they have meaning. Everyone deserves Hell because we have all rebelled against God. Hell is where people who reject Christ's offer of mercy and forgiveness will be "punished with everlasting destruction and shut out from the presence of the Lord and from the majesty of his power" (2 Thes 1:9). Hell is described in the Bible as a place of "everlasting burning" (Isa 33:14) and "utter darkness" (Jude 13). These descriptions figuratively depict the terrible tragedy of life apart from God. The image of fire is a symbol of judgment and destruction. The references to darkness refer to the agony and utter hopelessness of separation from God. Hell is also described as "a place of torment" (Luke 16:28), with "weeping and gnashing of teeth" (Matt 8:12), in which there will be "torment forever and no rest day or night" (Rev 14:11).

Hell is not a place where God actively tortures people forever. Rather, the everlasting, conscious torment is *relational* in nature, which is caused

[30] Francis A. Schaeffer, *How Should We Then Live?* (Wheaton, IL: Crossway Books, 1976), 245.

[31] John Piper, *God is the Gospel: Meditations on God's Love as the Gift of Himself* (Wheaton, IL: Crossway Books, 2005), 47.

by the condemned person's eternal banishment from Heaven.[32] Those in Hell are shut out from the presence of God and are deprived of eternal joy with him in Heaven. Hell is therefore the ultimate, everlasting separation from the source of life and hope, which is God. Philosopher Dallas Willard observes, "The fact that only God can take away our aloneness by his presence explains why the ultimate suffering and punishment is separation from the presence of God."[33] This is truly the greatest loss possible.

Future restoration

Scripture teaches that when Christ returns there will be an entirely renewed creation—a new Heaven and a new Earth—and that is where we will live with God. John paints the picture for us:

> Then I saw a new heaven and a new earth, for the first heaven and the first earth had passed away, and there was no longer any sea. I saw the Holy City, the new Jerusalem, coming down out of heaven from God, prepared as a bride beautifully dressed for her husband. And I heard a loud voice from the throne saying, "Now the dwelling of God is with men, and he will live with them" (Rev 21:1-3).

The prophet Isaiah also foretold, "Behold, I will create new heavens and a new earth. The former things will not be remembered" (Isa 65:17, cf. Isa 66:22). Peter also writes, "keeping with his promise we are looking forward to a new heaven and a new earth, the home of righteousness" (2 Pet 3:13). This represents a new kind of unification of Heaven and Earth where God will dwell with man. The present fallen creation will be restored when all things are renewed (Matt 19:28).

Author Randy Alcorn says the fact that God would come down to the new Earth to live with us fits perfectly with his original plan. In the beginning, God could have taken Adam and Eve up to Heaven to visit him in his world. Instead, he came down to walk with them in their world in the Garden of Eden:[34] "Then the man and his wife heard the sound of the LORD God as he was walking in the garden" (Gen 3:8). Jesus says of anyone who would be his disciple, "My Father will love him, and we will come to him and make our home with him" (John 14:23). This is God's ultimate plan—not that we would be taken up to live with him in Heaven, but that he would come down to live with us on Earth—Heaven on Earth. Heaven will be God dwelling with us, resurrected people on a completely renewed and restored Earth.

---

[32] Habermas and Moreland, *Beyond Death*, 303.

[33] Dallas Willard, *Hearing God: Developing a Conversational Relationship with God* (Downers Grove, IL: InterVarsity Press, 1999), 44.

[34] Alcorn, *Heaven*, 45.

God will give believers renewed, physical, resurrected bodies to live in the new Heaven. There will be continuity of our current bodies in this life with our resurrected bodies in the next life. They will be the same bodies God created for us, but they will be raised to greater perfection than we have experienced in this life. They will be free from the curse of sin and have special qualities that we never before experienced.

How we can be sure

We have previously examined the evidence why we can believe that the Bible is historically accurate and divine in origin. This provides us good reason to trust what the Bible says. We can be sure of what it teaches. Now we will examine what the Bible itself claims about how we can know God.

Knowing God through his creation

The Bible says we can know God through the wonder of the created universe. "The heavens declare the glory of God; the skies proclaim the work of his hands" (Psa 19:1). Not only can we know God in this way, but God has made this so clear to people that we have no excuse but to see him in creation (Rom 1:19-20).

Knowing God through his Word

The Bible says we can know God through the Bible. God said to Moses, "Write this on a scroll as something to be remembered" (Exo 17:14). God also said, "Write down the revelation and make it plain on tablets" (Hab 2:2). God gave us all the words of the Bible and they are useful and valuable to us. Paul  explains, "All Scripture is God-breathed and is useful for teaching, rebuking, correcting and training in righteousness, so that the man of God may be thoroughly equipped for every good work" (2 Tim 3:16-17).

God's Word is so real and life changing that it describes itself as living and active. "The word of God is living and active. Sharper than any double-edged sword, it penetrates even to dividing soul and spirit, joints and marrow; it judges the thoughts and attitudes of the heart" (Heb 4:12). David says:

> The law of the LORD is perfect, reviving the soul. The statutes of the LORD are trustworthy, making wise the simple. The precepts of the LORD are right, giving joy to the heart. The commands of the LORD are radiant, giving light to the eyes. The fear of the LORD is pure,

enduring forever. The ordinances of the LORD are sure and altogether righteous. They are more precious than gold, than much pure gold; they are sweeter than honey, than honey from the comb (Psa 19:7-10).

We know God's nature, purposes, plans, promises, and commands through the Bible. The psalmist writes:

> Oh, how I love your law! I meditate on it all day long. Your commands make me wiser than my enemies, for they are ever with me. I have more insight than all my teachers, for I meditate on your statutes. I have more understanding than the elders, for I obey your precepts. I have kept my feet from every evil path so that I might obey your word. I have not departed from your laws, for you yourself have taught me. How sweet are your words to my taste, sweeter than honey to my mouth! I gain understanding from your precepts; therefore I hate every wrong path (Psa 119:97-104).

God's Word accomplishes his purposes. He says it "will not return to me empty, but will accomplish what I desire and achieve the purpose for which I sent it" (Isa 55:11). Jesus said to a group of Jewish believers, "If you hold to my teaching, you are really my disciples. Then you will know the truth, and the truth will set you free" (John 8:31-32). Jesus also equated Scripture with the very food we eat. He said, "It is written: 'Man does not live on bread alone, but on every word that comes from the mouth of God'" (Matt 4:4).

Knowing God through his Son

The Bible says we can also know God through Jesus Christ, who is God in the flesh. "The Son is the radiance of God's glory and the exact representation of his being" (Heb 1:3). Paul says that the God who declared, "Let light shine out of darkness," also made his light shine in our hearts to give us the light of the knowledge of the glory of God in the face of Christ (2 Cor 4:6).

Knowing God through Christ is the most valuable knowledge we can ever have. Paul exclaims, "I consider everything a loss compared to the surpassing greatness of knowing Christ Jesus my Lord" (Phil 3:8) and "My purpose is that they may be encouraged in heart and united in love, so that they may have the full riches of complete understanding, in order that they may know the mystery of God, namely, Christ, in whom are hidden all the treasures of wisdom and knowledge" (Col 2:2-3).

Knowing God through personal experience

The biblical concept of knowing is more than intellectual assent to facts. There is a difference between *knowing about* God and *knowing him as* God. When another person is involved, knowing includes the idea of relating intimately to that person. In the biblical view, to know God is to have a one-on-one relationship with him. To live like this is to see God, not with our eyes, but with our heart. Paul writes:

> I pray that out of his glorious riches he may strengthen you with power through his Spirit in your inner being, so that Christ may dwell in your hearts through faith. And I pray that you, being rooted and established in love, may have power, together with all the saints,[35] to grasp how wide and long and high and deep is the love of Christ, and to know this love that surpasses knowledge—that you may be filled to the measure of all the fullness of God (Eph 3:16-19).

We can subjectively know God through a direct understanding of him as a personal Being who is holy, good, beautiful, and glorious. This inspires a deep, reverential awe and desire for God, but there is also an awareness that God is nearby, working in our lives to change our thoughts, desires, motivations, and behavior. This dual experience of God's transcendence and God's immanence results in an increasing love *for*, enjoyment *of*, and satisfaction *in* him as our ultimate treasure and greatest good.[36]

Knowing God through his Holy Spirit

Knowing God in an experiential way only happens through the inner testimony of God himself. Paul says that unbelievers "are darkened in their understanding and separated from the life of God because of the ignorance that is in them due to the hardening of their hearts" (Eph 4:18). John Piper explains, "No amount of reasoning or historical argument alone can produce spiritual sight in the blind. This is the limit of thinking...No logical argument for the lordship of Christ will bring about submission, apart from the work of the Holy Spirit."[37] The Holy Spirit is the one who opens the heart of the unbeliever to the truth of the gospel and enables him to respond positively in faith. On one occasion Luke reports, "One of those listening was a woman named Lydia...who was a worshiper of God. The Lord opened her heart to respond to Paul's message" (Acts 16:14).

The Holy Spirit overcomes our inability to know God due to the Fall by a direct work on our heart so that we are *able* to respond. This work of the Spirit is sufficient to enable us to desire God, to understand the truth of the gospel, and to exercise saving faith. Paul says that "no one can say, 'Jesus is Lord,' except by the Holy Spirit" (1 Cor 12:3).

---

[35] Paul often uses the word *saints* to refer to believers in Christ.

[36] More will be said about this in Question 5.

[37] John Piper, *Think: The Life of the Mind and the Love of God* (Wheaton, IL: Crossway, 2010), 76-77, 126.

This means that, fundamentally, we do not know God through facts and evidence, but through the self-authenticating witness of God's Holy Spirit in our own hearts. William Lane Craig explains that a person "does not need supplementary arguments and evidence in order to know and to know with confidence that he is in fact experiencing the Spirit of God."[38] God is drawing all people to himself in this way. Paul explains, "The grace of God that brings salvation has appeared to all men" (Tit 2:11). Craig concludes, "Therefore, when a person refuses to come to Christ, it is never just because of intellectual difficulties: at root, he refuses to come because he willingly ignores and rejects the drawing of God's Spirit on his heart."[39]

This is both a comforting and humbling thought. It comforts us because ultimately we do not have to investigate and understand all the available evidence to have knowledge of God. We do not need to be intellectually gifted to come to God. In fact, we can come to him with no external arguments or evidence at all. Rather, the Holy Spirit draws us, persuades us, and testifies to us of the truth of God's Word. This also humbles us though, because ultimately we cannot come to God under our own power—power of motivation, power of intellect, or power of will. We come to God because he works in us and we simply respond to that with belief and trust. However, we *must* respond, for we have no excuse not to do so (Rom 1:20).

So why have we spent so many pages laying out all the intellectual reasons to believe that Christianity is true? Hopefully you have not thought this has been a waste of time, because the role of argument, evidence, and reason—although not primary—can play an important role in knowing God and growing in that knowledge. Many unbelievers often have intellectual problems with Christianity. These barriers sometimes need to be removed in order for the gospel to penetrate their hearts. The Holy Spirit will often use argument, evidence, and reason to persuade the unbeliever to consider Christianity seriously. Believers also find that sound reasons for their faith, while not serving as the basis for belief, do reinforce and confirm the Spirit's witness for belief. Since there is a subjective element to this internal testimony, having objective evidence provides assurance of the subjective experience.[40]

---

[38] Craig, *Reasonable Faith*, third edition, 43.

[39] Ibid., 47.

[40] This provides a reliable way to discern inauthentic claims to an internal witness of God. Many religions claim such a subjective witness. Mormonism and Islam are two examples.

Can we be sure?

The best data we have concerning the big bang are exactly what I would have predicted, had I nothing to go on but the five books of Moses, the Psalms, the Bible as a whole.

Arno Penzias (1933-)
Physicist, cosmologist, Nobel laureate
Interview with The New York Times (1978)

We have three things coming together: God, the infinite-personal God, who made the universe; and man, whom he made to live in that universe; and the Bible, which he has given us to tell us about that universe. Are we surprised that there is a unity between them? Why should we be surprised?

Francis Schaeffer (1912-1984)
Theologian, philosopher
He Is There and He Is Not Silent

While all of God's creation serves to reveal him in some way, he has willed that the clearest and most authoritative knowledge of him this side of heaven come through his written Word, the Bible.

John Piper (1946-)
Pastor, author
Think: The Life of the Mind and the Love of God

We have covered a lot of ground in answering this question. This was deliberate because it is vital to increase our confidence in the answers to our big life questions. If we want to live our lives based on the truth, then we need to be sure we actually have the truth. In the introduction to this question, we pondered the consequences of a sacred book that could satisfactorily answer these questions:

1. What if it corroborated everything we have come to know about the world through natural theology regarding origins, evil, suffering, and life after death?

2. What if it was confirmed through archaeology and other sources concerning what it says about people, places, times, and events?

3. What if it was transmitted through the centuries in such a way that we could be sure it contains what was originally written?

4. What if it exhibited clear marks of supernatural authorship?

5. What if it described the nature, purposes, and expectations of God?

6. What if it explained why the world has gone so wrong?

7. What if it explained how the world can be remedied?

8. What if it explained what the future of the world will be?

9. What if it revealed how we should live?

We have examined the Christian Bible in depth and discovered it to be capable of answering all of these questions in a compelling manner.[1] The Bible not only addresses all the big questions in life, it also proves to be a very reliable guide in all the areas we can directly verify. Most importantly, it exhibits the hallmarks of divine origin. This is a truly astonishing discovery because the consequences are profound. Since God is the sovereign Creator of the universe, he is the ultimate authority in the universe. This means that what the Bible says has a serious claim on our lives.

The Christian claims are extraordinary, but we have equally extraordinary reasons to believe they are true. In other words, we are so well justified in these beliefs that we can claim to *know* they are true.

God's desire is that humanity would have this knowledge of reality so that we would properly, but freely, respond to it. God has provided two main sources of this knowledge. The first source is often called *general revelation*, which refers to creation itself. The mere existence of the universe, the great design and beauty we observe in the created order, the moral conscience we each possess, and our deep longing for  meaning and purpose are all examples in creation that testify to the existence of God. This should motivate us to seek more information. This

---

[1] The last question in the list will be covered in more depth in Question 5.

leads us to the second source, which is often called *special revelation*. This refers to a book of knowledge that God has given us called the Bible.

We have seen several ways the Bible proves itself to be supernatural in origin. Since the Bible is divine in origin, we can trust that it does not contain errors. It is correct in its affirmations about the natural world and we should be able to verify this through history, archaeology, cosmology, and other investigative disciplines. Indeed we have, because the Bible corroborates everything we have concluded about the natural world through reason, experience, history, and science. The Bible is also correct in its affirmations about the spiritual world. Therefore, we can *know* religious truth—that God has made himself known to humanity.

Further reading

Reliability of the Bible

> *Archaeology & the New Testament,* John McRay
> *Archaeology & the Old Testament,* Alfred J. Hoerth
> *Christ and the Bible,* John Wenham
> *Easter Enigma: Are the Resurrection Accounts in Conflict?,* John Wenham
> *Is The New Testament Reliable?,* Paul Barnett
> *Jesus and the Eyewitnesses,* Richard Bauckham
> *Nothing But The Truth,* Brian H. Edwards
> *On the Reliability of the Old Testament*, K.A. Kitchen
> *Reasonable Faith: Christian Truth and Apologetics,* William Lane Craig
> *Reinventing Jesus: How Contemporary Skeptics Miss the Real Jesus and Mislead Popular Culture,* Komoszewski, Sawyer, and Wallace
> *The Gospel and the Greeks: Did the New Testament Borrow from Pagan Thought?,* Ronald Nash
> *The Heresy of Orthodoxy* Andreas J. Köstenberger and Michael J. Kruger
> *The Historical Reliability of the Gospels,* Craig Blomberg
> *The New Evidence That Demands a Verdict,* Josh McDowell
> *The Origin of the Bible,* F.F. Bruce (editor)

The historical Jesus

> *Fabricating Jesus: How Modern Scholars Distort the Gospels ,* Craig A. Evans
> *Jesus Under Fire: Modern Scholarship Reinvents the Historical Jesus,* Michael J. Wilkins and J. P. Moreland
> *The Challenge of Jesus: Rediscovering Who Jesus Was and Is,* N. T. Wright
> *The Historical Jesus,* Gary Habermas
> *The Jesus Quest: The Third Search for the Jew of Nazareth,* Ben Witherington III

How should we live?

There is a way that seems right to a man, but in the end it leads to death.
Solomon (c. 1011-931 BC)
King of Israel
Proverbs 14:12

If we do not create reality, but God does, then the more reality we know, the more we must adjust our minds and our lives to that reality.
John Piper (1946-)
Pastor, author
Think: The Life of the Mind and the Love of God

Wisdom is the right use of knowledge. To know is not to be wise. Many men know a great deal, and are all the greater fools for it. There is no fool so great a fool as a knowing fool. But to know how to use knowledge is to have wisdom.
Charles Spurgeon (1834-1892)
The "Prince of Preachers"

Give me understanding that I may live.
David (c. 1040–970 BC)
King of Israel
Psalm 119:144

Everything we have discussed so far has helped lay the foundation to answer this last important question. How should we live our lives in light of all the truths we have learned in our journey to answer life's most important questions? After all, we only have one life and we do not want to waste it. We all want to live our lives in a way that is filled with value, meaning, purpose, joy, and hope; but there seems to be so many different ideas about how to do that. The kind of world we live in has great bearing on answering this question correctly.

If there is no God, as atheists believe, then we are merely a random, cosmic accident and are doomed to complete and utter destruction after living a mere three to four score years on this hopeless planet. There is nothing to live for, except what we can muster from pure willpower out of our miserable, insignificant lives. *We* are the highest being and our own end in the universe. There is no *real* value, meaning, purpose, joy, or hope in this mortal life, so we manufacture them simply to get by. We live our lives creating our own moral code as we go, believing we are innocent and blameless because we are "better than the next person." We think that we will ultimately escape any serious accountability or judgment unless we get caught by human authorities doing something that society considers to be unacceptable.

If we are all part of one big divine impersonal Oneness, as pantheists would have us believe, the picture is not much different. We live our lives trying to convince ourselves that the physical world is a mere illusion. In the absence of any transcendent moral code to guide our lives, we make it up as we go, while "self-actualizing" ourselves to discover some vague divine spark within. We spend our lives trying to know and satisfy ourselves above all else. We fabricate value, meaning, purpose, joy, and hope if we want to feel that we have them in any sense at all.

Thankfully, those views do not represent the kind of universe in which we actually find ourselves. Instead, this is a theistic world, infused with transcendent meaning and moral significance. God has not left us to grope in the darkness. We do not *invent* value, meaning, purpose, joy, and hope—rather we *discover* them because they are part of the very fabric of the universe, being rooted in the ultimate reality of God himself. Moreover, to our delight, we find them to be much deeper, richer, and more rewarding than we could ever imagine...*forever.*

How do we live our lives with the understanding that a powerful and loving triune God rules the universe and wants these things for us? We first need to recognize that we live always in the full view of God, the Creator and Sustainer of everything who sees all. With that understanding, we need to live a life of genuine and deep faith in God, while following the Divine One who came to Earth as a man to show us how to live.

CHAPTER 13

An audience of one

If we listen to the pseudo-scientists and assume our ancestors were monkeys, then we shall behave like monkeys. On the other hand if we appreciate that we are created in the image of God, then we shall understand that we are accountable to God and that we shall one day stand before him. All this inevitably affects the way we live.

Brian H. Edwards (1941-)
Pastor, author, lecturer
Nothing But The Truth

May the Living God, who is the portion and rest of the saints, make these our carnal minds so spiritual, and our earthly hearts so heavenly, that loving him, and delighting in him, may be the work of our lives.

Richard Baxter (1615-1691)
Puritan pastor
The Saints' Everlasting Rest

Think about it. If this is a theistic universe created by a sovereign, powerful, holy, and loving God, who is beautiful and majestic beyond all comprehension, who created everything for a specific purpose, and who is orchestrating history to his appointed ends, then how wise is it for us to live as if that is not true or that it does not matter? This would be extremely foolish, and yet this is how most people in the world choose to live their lives—as if the God revealed in nature and the Bible simply were not there.

Sure, many people are "religious," but this is not about some make-believe, man-made spirituality. Hopefully, having come this far, you have seen through the deadly error of religious pluralism. People can believe something sincerely, but be dead wrong in their beliefs. In that case, what has their belief gotten them? Nothing. It is no virtue to call something as serious as the reality of God, human sinfulness, and eternal life a matter of mere personal opinion.

The whole point of this book has been to get us to reflect systematically, thoughtfully, and critically about the most important questions in life, so that once we have discovered the truth we can live our lives according to it. As we have seen, all but one of the world's religions and worldviews make grave errors about how the world really is and consequently do not lead their supporters to the triune God of the universe.

The conclusions we have reached in this book have astounding implications. They should cause us to reorient *everything* in our lives. *All* other things fade to insignificance compared to the existence of a loving Creator God who has a plan and purpose for us.

Living Coram Deo

Coram Deo is a Latin phrase that means "before the face of God." It refers to something that takes place in the presence of God. Since God is omnipresent in the universe, *everything* takes place in his presence. He knows the thoughts and actions of every person who has ever lived, including mine and yours at this very moment. There is no escaping his attention. We all live before an audience of One.

It makes sense that we should live our lives with this understanding that God sees all of it, down to the last detail. In fact, this is the only rational response to what we have discovered in our investigation of the universe. R. C. Sproul explains, "To live *coram Deo* is to live our entire life in the presence of God, under the authority of God, and to the glory of God."[1] This captures the essence of what God wants for each of us, as individuals made in his image and for his purposes.

This idea completely invalidates the popular notion that life is compartmentalized into the sacred and the secular—that we need to separate the so-called "spiritual" parts from the public parts of our lives, as if there is no connection between the two. This is nonsense, for how can a person's beliefs, values, and character be set aside whenever he leaves his personal realm and enters a public arena? Surely the God who created the universe is intensely interested in every aspect of our lives, the private as well as the public. Nothing escapes his gaze or interest. If God exists, then *all* of life is religious.

Coram Deo means that whatever we do in our career as a teacher, farmer, salesman, homemaker, attorney, politician, missionary (or anything else), and whatever we do in an ordinary daily activity like eating

---

[1] R. C. Sproul, Ligonier Ministries, http://www.ligonier.org/blog/what-does-coram-deo-mean/, accessed Dec 12, 2010.

a meal, reading a book, going to a movie, talking to a friend, or praying, it is *all* done before the face of God. It all matters to him, and so it matters not only what we do, but also what our motivations, attitudes, and methods are. John Piper explains:

> If all the universe and everything in it exist by the design of an infinite, personal God, to make his manifold glory known and loved, then to treat any subject without reference to God's glory is... insurrection...Without a spiritual wakefulness to divine purposes and connections in all things, we will not know things for what they truly are...To see reality in the fullness of truth, we must see it in relation to God, who created it, and sustains it, and gives it all its properties, relations, and designs.[2]

To appreciate this and embrace it and to live and breathe it is to live *coram Deo*.

Finding our total satisfaction in God

Living *coram Deo* is not a reluctant and unhappy admission that God is sovereign, constantly watching us and directing our lives so that we had better continually watch what we do. Rather, it is to recognize that there is no higher goal in life than loving, honoring, and enjoying God.

As human beings, we often think we are self-sufficient and in control, but we are not. We have no say in our own birth or our own death. The Bible says that our life is a mist that appears for a little while and then vanishes. Without God's life-giving provisions and preservation of the universe moment-to-moment we would all instantly perish.

We need God, but not only for physical life. We all have a longing for value, meaning, and purpose in our lives and we spend our lives seeking it, whether consciously or not. Our search only culminates properly when we see God as the answer, for that is his intended purpose and design for creatures made in his very image. "The goal of our life is not people. It is God," says priest and author Henri Nouwen.[3]

Living the good life

There are many strategies and methods contending for our allegiance today for living "the good life." Most of them involve the pursuit of pleasure in some fashion. The points of distinction between the many alternatives are the diverse answers to these two simple questions: *"What is the object of my pleasure?"* and *"How do I best attain that pleasure?"*

---

[2] Piper, *Think: The Life of the Mind*, 168-169.
[3] Henri J. M. Nouwen, *The Way of the Heart: Connecting with God through Prayer, Wisdom, and Silence* (New York: Ballantine Books, 1981), 32.

The usual answer to the first question is ourselves. Personal pleasure is primary; therefore we make life choices that maximize our own self-gratification. We often seek fulfillment of this goal—the answer to the second question—in things like money, power, status, security, sex, physical appearance, amusement, and the like. These vain pursuits are all inferior choices that waste our lives.

Our desires for enjoyment, pleasure, and self-gratification are not inherently bad; rather they are badly misdirected, for they should be satisfied in God. The object of our pleasure must be the triune God alone. We are to find our ultimate joy in God himself. John Piper says that the longing to be happy is a universal, and not sinful, human experience. We should not try to deny or resist this longing to be happy. Instead, we should seek to intensify and nourish it by finding it in God.[4] Since God is all-glorious, only he can satisfy the deep cravings of our souls. The psalmist captures this idea when he declares, "As the deer pants for streams of water, so my soul pants for you, O God. My soul thirsts for God, for the living God. When can I go and meet with God?" (Psa 42:1-2).

Glorifying God

The Bible often speaks of "glorifying God" and "giving God glory." To glorify God does not mean to make him more glorious because that is impossible. He is all-glorious in and of himself, completely independent of his creation. Rather, God is glorified when his magnificence and splendor, power and wisdom, love and mercy, truth and beauty, and greatness and goodness are displayed, acknowledged, admired, and praised:

> Great is the LORD and most worthy of praise; his greatness no one can fathom. One generation will commend your works to another; they will tell of your mighty acts. They will speak of the glorious splendor of your majesty, and I will meditate on your wonderful works. They will tell of the power of your awesome works, and I will proclaim your great deeds. They will celebrate your abundant goodness and joyfully sing of your righteousness (Psa 145:3-7).

God glorifies himself in his revelation to man because these characteristics of God are on display for everyone to admire and enjoy. We see this in creation as all of it declares God's glory (Psa 19:1). "You are worthy, our Lord and God, to receive glory and honor and power, for you created all things, and by your will they were created and have their being" (Rev 4:11). We also see God's glory in his Son, Jesus Christ. "The Son is the radiance of God's glory" (Heb 1:3).

---

[4] Piper, *Desiring God*, 23.

We glorify God when we recognize God's glory for what it is intrinsically and value it above everything else. This is the chief end of man—the very reason for our existence—to exalt God's glory. "I will extol the LORD at all times; his praise will always be on my lips. My soul will boast in the LORD; let the afflicted hear and rejoice. Glorify the LORD with me; let us exalt his name together" (Psa 34:1-3). Since God created man to glorify him, it is our *duty* to do so, and we should do so in *everything* we do: "Whatever you do, do it all for the glory of God" (1 Cor 10:31).[5]

We glorify God when we find no more superior satisfaction in all of creation than in God himself. Piper writes that "God is most glorified in us when we are most satisfied in Him…God's pursuit of praise from us and our pursuit of pleasure in Him are the same pursuit."[6] This is because the *most* enduring joy and contentment are found in God himself—not in his creation, which is where most people look for pleasure. The Bible invites us to taste and see that God is good, for blessed is the person who takes refuge in him (Psa 34:8). It is no coincidence that our response to God in this manner also glorifies him. God receives pleasure from our praise and exaltation of him, that is, when we give him honor and glory.

It would be a mistake to think that God is vain for loving his glory, however. Vanity is a *misconceived* sense of self-worth—it is placing more value on oneself than is rightfully due. As the only perfect, all-glorious, morally excellent, totally self-sufficient Being in existence, it is impossible for God to place too much value on himself. If God thought of something more highly than himself, *that* thing would be more valuable and glorious than he, but that is impossible. God is the most glorious being in existence and therefore supremely valuable—above all other things. When we human beings exalt ourselves we are both mistaken and sinful. However, for God this is virtuous since it is both true and loving of God to do so. If God should deny the infinite worth of his own glory, he would no longer be God. This would be idolatry—which God hates—because it would imply that there is something more worthy than himself that he should value. Of course, this is impossible for God because he has infinite value, so he cannot be vain for loving his own glory.[7]

Having a relationship with God

We were made by God and for God, so that he could love us and we could love him. God made us to be in a close personal relationship with him. We can imagine what this is like from the things we do in

---

[5] Man's problem, however, is that he has fallen far short of this standard. "All have sinned and fall short of the glory of God" (Rom 3:23), which is why we need God to save us.

[6] Piper, *Desiring God*, 50.

[7] Ibid., 47-49.

relationships we have with other people. We know their likes and dislikes, recognize their voice, think about them, spend time with them, walk and talk with them, and so on. It is the same with God.

The awe-inspiring majesty and glory of an eternal, all-powerful God who transcends the universe can make it difficult even to conceive of being in some kind of individual relationship with him. This indeed can be a frightening thought. This is only possible, though, because God desires it and he makes it possible by taking the first step towards us. There is probably no greater evidence of God's desire for personal relationship with human beings than when Scripture tells us that God loves us: "How great is the love the Father has lavished on us" (1 John 3:1). And he wants us to love him: "Love the Lord your God with all your heart and with all your soul and with all your mind" (Matt 22:37).

The most intimate of all human relationships is marriage, and Scripture describes the love relationship between God and those who love him as that of husband and wife.[8] Isaiah explains, "As a bridegroom rejoices over his bride, so will your God rejoice over you" (Isa 62:5). The Lord declares, "I will betroth you to me forever; I will betroth you in righteousness and justice, in love and compassion. I will betroth you in faithfulness, and you will acknowledge the LORD" (Hos 2:19-20). Scripture pictures the final consummation of all things as a wedding between Christ and his Church: "The wedding of the Lamb has come, and his bride has made herself ready" (Rev 19:7).

Jesus Christ is the particular focus of our relationship with God. When we believe in him, he fills us with an inexpressible and glorious joy because we are receiving the goal of our faith, the salvation of our souls, which is eternal life with him. Nothing compares to knowing Christ. Paul makes the choice clear: "Whatever was to my profit I now consider loss for the sake of Christ. What is more, I consider everything a loss compared to the surpassing greatness of knowing Christ Jesus my Lord" (Phil 3:7-8). Christ is such a treasure that even death is not to be feared because it brings us into his presence. Paul also says, "To live is Christ and to die is gain" (Phil 1:21). This joy is what God gives us as a result of our relationship with him—it is not something we can manufacture on our own. Jesus *wants* this relationship with us. He metaphorically speaks about dining with us when he says, "Here I am! I stand at the door and knock. If anyone hears my voice and opens the door, I will come in and eat with him, and he with me" (Rev 3:20). This is an invitation to intimacy with God, and is open to everyone.

---

[8] This is why human marital union is so sacred—it is a covenant promise that reflects God's relationship with his people.

CHAPTER 14

A reasonable faith

If we are honest with truth, reason will lead us to faith.

Peter Kreeft (1937-)
Scholar, philosopher, author
Christianity for Modern Pagans

For me, having lived much of my life as an atheist, the last thing I want is a naive faith built on a paper-thin foundation of wishful thinking or makebelieve. I need a faith that's consistent with reason, not contradictory to it; I want beliefs that are grounded in reality, not detached from it.

Lee Strobel (1952-)
Former atheist, journalist, pastor, author
The Case for Faith

Faith is a rational response to the evidence of God's self-revelation in nature, human history, the Scriptures and his resurrected Son Jesus Christ.

W. Bingham Hunter (1943-)
Professor of Bible Exposition
The God Who Hears

We have come this far and have not yet discussed the place of faith in our lives. Some people have an unfavorable view of faith. They would say that faith is a merely a feeling, nothing more than wishful thinking. Some critics are more hostile, accusing those with faith of irrational belief in things that are logically impossible—a total divorce of reason and faith. It is a crutch for weak-minded people, they say. Richard Dawkins says that "Faith is the great cop-out, the great excuse to evade the need to think and evaluate evidence. Faith is belief in spite of, even perhaps because of, the lack of evidence."[1] Is this an accurate view of faith? Does it really oppose common sense? For some people faith may be an inner feeling they invent in order to believe in something that is unbelievable, but it does not have to be that way. We do not need to choose between having faith and using reason.

Nobody has the answers to every question, so everybody lives by faith to some degree—even atheists.[2] The real issue is *what* we place our faith in and *why*. We will see that faith does not have to be a blind leap in the dark; on the contrary, it can be eminently reasonable.

What is faith?

The dictionary defines faith as: "Confidence in or dependence on a person, statement, or thing as trustworthy. It is belief without certain proof." Faith has four important elements. First, faith is *personal*. We each decide for ourselves to exercise faith. Second, we place our faith in something specific, not something vague or abstract. There should always be a clear *object* of faith. Third, we actually come to *trust* this faith object. Fourth, we have sufficient *reason* to trust in the object of faith. Therefore, faith that is worthwhile is personal active trust in some object because it has demonstrated its reliability.

Faith is required where we lack certainty. We do not have faith that we exist or that two plus two equals four. We have no doubts about these facts. We need faith to act when we are not certain. We need faith because we are limited beings.[3] Our knowledge is neither exhaustive nor infallible. We need to fill the gap between the probable and the proven through a step of faith, which is active trust. Faith is what gets us from some level of belief to a willingness to act on that belief.

We all exercise faith everyday in all kinds of circumstances. When we drive through an intersection we have faith that cars traveling in the crossing direction will stop at their red light. When we schedule a lunch appointment we show faith that our friend will meet us there. When we take medication we have faith that it will heal us. When we get on an airplane we have faith that we will arrive safely at our destination. Are we *certain* of the outcomes of these simple activities? No, faith in these things may fail us at times. Our faith is only as good as the object in which we

---

[1] Richard Dawkins, Lecture from "The Nullifidian" (Dec 94), http://richarddawkins.net/articles/89, accessed Feb 19, 2011.

[2] Atheists have faith that the universe came from nothing, that life came from non-life, that humans evolved from a single-celled life form, that there is no ultimate morality or accountability in the universe, and so on.

[3] This is why God does not need faith. He has exhaustive knowledge and therefore he has certainty in all things.

place it. So why do we do these sorts of things by faith? We have a goal in mind. We want to accomplish something and we need to act, but because we do not have complete knowledge we take steps of faith. We *know* enough about these things to cause us to *believe* that *acting* in these specific ways will be beneficial to us.

We would not take these steps of faith without the knowledge that leads us in that direction. This is why knowledge is necessary for faith. Faith that cannot be confirmed by evidence is irrational and unwarranted. It requires a "blind leap." However, faith based on knowledge *is* rational and warranted. We have a lot of experiential knowledge that people stop at red lights, that our friends show up for lunch, that medicine improves our health, and that airplanes get us safely to where we want to go. We have seen evidence that these actions will yield their desired results, so we continue doing them.

Faith of the most profound kind is the faith we have in God. In fact, the most important thing about a person is what he or she believes about God.[4] We live our whole lives by faith in many things, so it would be completely arbitrary and foolish to exclude faith in God. Although the objects of faith are radically different between ordinary things and God, the basic components are the same.

An authentic step of faith in God starts with *knowledge*, grows into *conviction*, turns into *trust*, and results in *action*. Faith includes knowledge because we cannot trust in a God about whom we know nothing. It includes conviction because we must accept the truth about God. It includes trust, for having faith is not merely being convinced of facts about God; it also requires being committed to him. Finally, faith in God causes us to take action as a result of our conviction and trust; otherwise it is useless.

Knowledge of God

The Bible repeatedly emphasizes the importance of having knowledge of God. Knowledge and truth are mentioned over fifteen hundred times in the Bible. Here are a few examples of how much God values knowledge:

❖ The lack of knowledge leads to ruin: "My people are destroyed from lack of <u>knowledge</u>" (Hos 4:6).

---

[4] A.W. Tozer, *The Knowledge of the Holy* (New York: HarperCollins, 1961), 1.

❖ Passion for God without knowledge can be misguided: "I can testify about them that they are zealous for God, but their zeal is not based on <u>knowledge</u>" (Rom 10:2).

❖ God has given us knowledge about himself in Christ: "For God…made his light shine in our hearts to give us the light of the <u>knowledge</u> of the glory of God in the face of Christ" (2 Cor 4:6).

❖ This knowledge of God is universal: "For the earth will be filled with the <u>knowledge</u> of the glory of the LORD, as the waters cover the sea" (Hab 2:14).

❖ We should strive to personally know God: "Let him who boasts boast…that he understands and <u>knows</u> me, that I am the LORD" (Jer 9:24).

❖ And this knowledge should be increasing: "Grow in the grace and <u>knowledge</u> of our Lord and Savior Jesus Christ" (2 Pet 3:18).

God provides evidence for this knowledge. The pattern throughout the Bible is that we can know about God *because* of his acts towards human beings. Here are some examples:

❖ Moses asked God why the Jews should listen to him. God replied that he would do miracles so that they would "<u>know</u> there is a God in Israel"; then they could exercise trust in him (Exo 4:1-5).

❖ Moses said that all the miraculous signs and wonders that God showed the Israelites were done so that they "might <u>know</u> that the LORD is God" (Deut 4:34-35).

❖ Joshua said that God dried up the Jordan river just like he did the Red Sea so that "all the peoples of the earth might <u>know</u> that the hand of the LORD is powerful and so that you might always fear the LORD your God" (Josh 4:23-24).

❖ Elijah announced to the false prophets that God sent fire from Heaven so that they would "<u>know</u> that the LORD is God" (1 Kings 18:20-39).

❖ Jesus healed the paralytic so that those watching would "<u>know</u> that the Son of Man has authority to forgive sins" (Mark 2:6-12).

❖ Peter gives a long list of evidence and then concludes that the whole house of Israel should <u>know</u> for certain that God made Jesus both Lord and Christ (Acts 2:22-36).

❖ Paul claims that we <u>know</u> that Jesus will judge the world because God raised him from the dead (Acts 17:31).

All of these examples (and many more) are intended by God to be evidence that leads us to knowledge of him so that we may act in faith.

Faith in God therefore depends on divine testimony. Throughout the Bible, God intends our trust to rest on belief in what he has revealed. Therefore, since faith is based on the testimony of God, who cannot lie, it is completely trustworthy.

Verifiable faith

A unique feature of Christianity is that its religious claims are rooted in history.[5] The Bible could have been written as a list of ideas to believe and commands to perform, perhaps arranged topically for easy reference, but it wasn't. Instead, it was written as a record of God's continuous interaction with humanity. In this context of thousands of historical events, God teaches us many spiritual truths. In this way, God associates religious claims—which are not easily verified—with historical claims—many of which can be verified. Historical truth proves spiritual truth.

We have looked at a lot of evidence that God is real and has acted in the world and in human history. We have seen evidence from creation, evidence of a divine book, and evidence of Jesus Christ being raised from the dead. In fact, Christianity appeals to facts of history to provide proof that it is true. It is a faith based on knowledge. This means that we can *know* that Christianity is true; it does not require a blind leap of faith. If certain things happened in the physical world in the past, then we have reason to believe certain spiritual truths today. Historical truth proves spiritual truth.

Jesus said to Nicodemus, "I have spoken to you of earthly things and you do not believe. How then will you believe if I speak of heavenly things?" (John 3:12). Jesus performed his miracles so that we would believe that he came from God the Father. We mentioned earlier a story about Jesus preaching in a town when some men brought him a paralyzed man. Jesus saw the faith of the paralyzed man and forgave his sins. Knowing that his audience questioned his ability to forgive sins, Jesus proved his authority to do that by healing the paralyzed man (Matt 9:1-8). Anyone can say they have all authority on Earth, but not everyone can prove it—only God can. Jesus used something in the physical world to prove something in the spiritual world. Historical truth proves spiritual truth.

The apostle Paul made this same kind of appeal to historical facts as a means to discredit the entire Christian faith. He wrote, "If Christ has not been raised, your faith is futile" (1 Cor 15:17). Paul is saying that our faith is useless if Christ was not resurrected from the dead. Why does he say this? He is inviting us to put our faith to the test. If Christ was not raised then we shouldn't believe *anything* he said, but if he was raised then we

---

[5] This is also true of Judaism.

should believe *everything* he said. Three verses later (v20), Paul says "Christ has indeed been raised from the dead." We have already looked at the evidence for this in detail, so we know Paul is correct. Historical truth proves spiritual truth.

We do not want to miss this critical point. In the first century, Christians did not primarily come with a new idea to believe, but with *news* of something that had *happened.*[6] A man claiming to be divine predicted his resurrection from the dead and then it came to pass! Jesus gave them something they could see in the physical realm to substantiate claims he was making about something they could not see in the spiritual realm.

This should not surprise us. We should expect that the God who created everything with design and purpose would have the knowledge we need and the desire to give it to us. This is exactly what the Bible teaches: "This is what the LORD says, he who made the earth, the LORD who formed it and established it—the LORD is his name: 'Call to me and I will answer you and tell you great and unsearchable things you do not know'" (Jer 33:2-3).

A rational step, not a blind leap

Biblical faith is therefore a reasonable faith. God does not ask us to believe against all reason and experience; rather we can really *know* God. He has given us very good reasons to believe and he desires us to pursue this knowledge. Based on what we know about God we realize that we can trust him in those things that we do not see. God gives us evidence in the visible realm in order for us to have faith in the invisible realm.

For the Christian there is a rational *step* of faith, but no blind *leap* of faith. There is harmony between our spiritual convictions and the facts of our world as we have seen. Faith in the God of the Bible is not a blind leap into thin air, but rather a leap onto a solid rock—the rock of Jesus Christ. John 3:16 says, "For God so loved the world that he gave his one and only Son, that whoever believes in him shall not perish but have eternal life." This is not religious wishful thinking. This is *knowledge* given by God to human beings that Jesus Christ can save us. Faith is responding to this knowledge in a step of active trust. God has given us enough knowledge to lead us to a joyful and reasonable faith.

---

[6] John Piper, "This Is Why We Are Here!", Desiring God Ministries, http://www.desiringgod.org /resource-library/taste-see-articles/this-is-why-we-are-here/print, accessed Mar 19, 2011.

Faith in what?

God calls us to a life of faith. The Bible says that without faith it is impossible to please God (Heb 11:6). In what, specifically, are we to have faith? The Bible says much about who God is and what he is doing in the world. We must study the Bible to know and understand what he has revealed, and then trust him for all the things that he has not clearly revealed, including what will happen in our own earthly life. Here are some areas where God calls us to express our faith:

1. Faith in the identity of God
2. Faith in the character of God
3. Faith in the sovereignty of God
4. Faith in the abilities of God
5. Faith in the declarations of God
6. Faith in the purposes of God
7. Faith in the promises of God
8. Faith in the ways of God
9. Faith in the salvation of God
10. Faith in the Son of God

God has shown himself to humanity in all these areas—not exhaustively, but truly, as Francis Schaeffer once said. God points us in the right direction in each of these areas and tells us to trust him.

A response is required

God has done everything necessary for us to believe and trust in him. He has revealed himself to humanity in many ways so that we can have knowledge of him. The Holy Spirit calls each one of us to have faith in God by convincing us of the truth of the gospel, making this truth appealing to us, and enabling us to receive Christ by faith. God has initiated everything. All that we need to do is respond to him, but *we do need to respond*. Ultimately, this is an invitation that every individual must personally accept or reject. To avoid a deliberate choice is to reject God's offer. Our response is four-fold—believe, repent, trust, and obey.

First, we need to believe. Previously we said that faith includes knowledge. Scripture speaks of several truths about who Jesus is and what he has done that we must believe in order to be saved. We need to believe that Jesus is the Christ, the Messiah, the Anointed One, who saves sinners (1 John 5:1). We need to believe that Jesus is the eternal divine Son of God (1 John 4:15), that he came to Earth as a man of flesh and blood (1 John

4:2-3), and that he died and rose from the dead (Rom 10:9). We need to believe that Jesus is the only way to be saved (Acts 4:12) and that he demands exclusive loyalty and discipleship (Luke 14:26-27).

Second, we need to repent, which means to change our hearts, minds, and wills from living our lives indifferent to or against God to living *for* God. It means changing our mind about sinning. Repentance includes admission of and sorrow for our own sin and the resolution to live according to God's ways.

Third, we place our full trust in God. This is the personal subjective act of our will to take the step of faith that saves. This step of trust includes submission to Jesus Christ, which means a commitment to surrender all to him and to obey him.

Fourth, we begin to obey Christ. Faith must result in action, otherwise it is useless. Jesus came to teach us how to live in God's world and we need to obey his teachings.[7]

This four-fold response is not a one-time event, but a life-long journey. Daily we believe, repent, trust, and obey. By its very nature, faith in God is a brand new way to live life. It is to be lived out every day in every part of our lives. Faith may ebb and flow and sometimes falter. Perseverance is the key. We dare not get complacent or become stagnant. If we fall down, then we need to get back up. If we fall away, then we need to return to Jesus.

---

[7] This will be discussed further in the next chapter.

CHAPTER 15

Follow the leader

For by [Jesus] all things were created: things in heaven and on earth, visible and invisible, whether thrones or powers or rulers or authorities; all things were created by him and for him.

Paul (c. AD 5-67)
Apostle, missionary, teacher, author
Colossians 1:16

All the natural world was created through and for Jesus. This is a spectacular statement. Every scholar who devotes himself to observing the world should think long and hard about the words "All things were created...for Christ."

John Piper (1946-)
Pastor, author
Think: The Life of the Mind and the Love of God

See to it that no one takes you captive through hollow and deceptive philosophy, which depends on human tradition and the basic principles of this world rather than on Christ.

Paul (c. AD 5-67)
Apostle, missionary, teacher, author
Colossians 2:8

Jesus is the central figure in the Bible, not only in that his death accomplished our forgiveness but also in that his life gave us a pattern to follow.

Thomas E. Schmidt
Professor of New Testament
Trying To Be Good

After all the questions, evidence, analysis, and discussion, everything comes down to Jesus of Nazareth—a poor carpenter who lived in Palestine two thousand years ago and had a brief three-year ministry as an itinerant preacher. He had few possessions, never led an army, never held an office, never published anything, and never travelled very far from home. His life came to an abrupt end while he was in his mid-thirties. He was falsely accused by those who despised him. He endured several mock trials and then a brutal flogging. He was finally executed as a criminal, even though his judge found that he committed no crime.[1] This is a presumably insignificant life and a strange end for someone that commands our attention two thousand years later. What is so special about Jesus? Why does it all come down to *this* man?

We previously made much of the fact that Jesus was raised from the dead. We know that resurrections are unnatural occurrences and this one was unique in history because Jesus was transformed and never died again. What is the significance of *this* particular event? In order to interpret an event properly, we must understand its context for only then can we understand its meaning. Especially in the case of a miracle like a resurrection it is important to know *who* this resurrected person was and *why* it happened. In order to answer these questions we need to look more closely at the life and ministry of Jesus, including his self-understanding.

Who was Jesus of Nazareth?

The Bible tells the story of Peter and some other followers of Jesus who were going around Jerusalem healing and preaching in his name. This made many of the Jewish authorities furious to the point of wanting to put Peter and his friends to death. While they were discussing this issue at the Jewish Council, a respected Jewish leader and teacher named Gamaliel stood up and addressed the Council. He said:

> Men of Israel, consider carefully what you intend to do to these men. Some time ago Theudas appeared, claiming to be somebody, and about four hundred men rallied to him. He was killed, all his followers were dispersed, and it all came to nothing. After him, Judas the Galilean appeared in the days of the census and led a band of people in revolt. He too was killed, and all his followers were scattered. Therefore, in the present case I advise you: Leave these men alone! Let them go! For if their purpose or activity is of human origin, it will fail. But if it is from God, you will not be able to stop these men; you will only find yourselves fighting against God (Acts 5:12-39).

---

[1] Based on a sermon by James Allan Francis, *The Real Jesus and Other* Sermons (Philadelphia: Judson Press, 1926), 123-124.

Gamaliel was very perceptive and amazingly prophetic, for the teaching and preaching about Jesus *did* come to something. Two millennia later, it is going stronger than ever. Today, nobody has heard of Theudas or Judas the Galilean[2] or the many other Jewish revolutionaries who came after them, but Jesus is known in every corner of the Earth. Jesus has been the most widely recognized and most influential person in the world for nearly two thousand years since Gamaliel issued his warning. His influence on human civilization is incalculable.

The life of Jesus

Jesus lived a remarkable and unique life that set him worlds apart from any other religious leader who has ever lived. According to the Bible Jesus never sinned. "In him is no sin" (1 John 3:5). No other religious leader claimed to be sinless nor was considered to be sinless.

The crowds were repeatedly amazed at the powerful teaching of Jesus. They wondered, "How did this man get such learning without having studied?" (John 7:15). His own disciples were equally astounded at his words (Mark 10:24). One of his most provocative teachings was that his death would save men from their sins. No other religious leader made claims such as this.

Jesus performed many extraordinary miracles that exhibited his power over demons, sickness, nature, and death. He healed blind, deaf, paralyzed, and leprous people, and many others. He fed thousands of people with a few loaves and a few fish, he walked on water, calmed a storm by his words, and turned water into wine. He raised people from the dead, including the daughter of Jairus, the son of the widow at Nain, and a close friend, Lazarus. Jesus appealed to his miracles as evidence of who he was. He said, "Believe me when I say that I am in the Father and the Father is in me; or at least believe on the evidence of the miracles themselves" (John 14:11). Other world religious leaders either discouraged miracles or were unable to perform them.

Jesus fulfilled many OT prophecies as we discussed in chapter 11. The Messiah was to be a Jew, from the tribe of Judah and the family of David, born in Bethlehem, despised and rejected by the Jewish people. He would be guiltless, yet die as a result of a judicial proceeding before the destruction of the second temple in AD 70. All these and many other prophecies were uniquely fulfilled only in Jesus. Jesus himself made prophecies that were fulfilled, such as his own resurrection from the dead, the destruction of Jerusalem and the Jewish Temple, and the future persecution of his disciples.

---

[2] Except for this passing reference by Gamaliel.

The identity of Jesus

Jesus is so revered that most of the world's religions have something good to say about him. They make room in their beliefs for Jesus, but they put him somewhere in the margins. He is special in *some* way, but not in a *supreme* way, so they say. They make many claims about him: Jesus was one of many sons of God, a sinless prophet, a spiritual model, a social reformer, a great teacher, or a miracle worker. However, Jesus says none of these things about himself. He claimed to be the one and only Son of God, which other religions unanimously deny. It is a complete disservice to Christ to think highly of him and ignore all he said about himself. If someone does not believe what he said, then why pay tribute to him at all?

Christianity is not based primarily on the *teachings* of Jesus, but on the *person* of Jesus. The identity of Jesus is the central issue. One time Jesus asked Peter, "Who do you say I am?" Peter answered, "You are the Christ, the Son of the living God." Jesus replied, "Blessed are you, Simon son of Jonah, for this was not revealed to you by man, but by my Father in heaven" (Matt 16:15-17). Jesus was not only the Messiah, but God in the flesh. This was proclaimed even before he was born, when an angel announced to his father Joseph: "The virgin will be with child and will give birth to a son, and they will call him Immanuel—which means, 'God with us'" (Matt 1:23).

Jesus' disciples worshiped him as God. After Jesus walked on water and calmed a storm Scripture says, "Those who were in the boat worshiped him, saying, 'Truly you are the Son of God'" (Matt 14:33). Upon seeing the risen Christ, Thomas acknowledged Jesus as, "My Lord and my God" (John 20:28). "Following Jesus' resurrection, the disciples worshiped him" (Matt 28:17). Jesus always accepted this worship.

John refers to Christ as "God the One and Only, who is at the Father's side" (John 1:18). Both Peter and Paul spoke of Jesus as "our God and Savior" (2 Pet 1:1; Tit 2:13). Even demons referred to Jesus as God. Jesus "was met by a demon-possessed man from the town…When he saw Jesus, he cried out and fell at his feet, shouting at the top of his voice, 'What do you want with me, Jesus, Son of the Most High God?'" (Luke 8:27-28).

Jesus himself claimed to be God. His frequent self-references as "the Son of Man" are directly tied to the divine figure prophesied in Daniel:

> In my vision at night I looked, and there before me was one like a son of man, coming with the clouds of heaven. He approached the Ancient of Days and was led into his presence. He was given authority, glory and sovereign power; all peoples, nations and men of every language worshiped him. His dominion is an everlasting dominion that will not pass away, and his kingdom is one that will never be destroyed (Dan 7:13-14).

Only God comes on the clouds of Heaven. Only God has all authority, glory, and power. Only God is worshiped by all people and nations. Only God has an everlasting dominion that will never be destroyed. It could not be more apparent that Christ's claim to be the Son of Man is a claim to be God himself. Jesus made this connection clear at his trial when the high priest asked him, "Are you the Christ, the Son of the Blessed One?" Referring to this passage in Daniel, Jesus replied, "I am, and you will see the Son of Man sitting at the right hand of the Mighty One and coming on the clouds of heaven." At this, the high priest tore his clothes in outrage and accused Jesus of blasphemy (Mark 14:61-64).

Jesus' enemies killed him because he claimed to be God. "For this reason the Jews tried all the harder to kill him...he was even calling God his own Father, making himself equal with God" (John 5:18). When the chief priests asked Jesus, "Are you then the Son of God?" he replied, "You are right in saying I am" (Luke 22:70). On another occasion Jesus said, "Before Abraham was born, I am." At this they picked up stones to stone him (John 8:58-59). The Jews wanted to stone him for blasphemy because they recognized this was a claim to being God himself: "We are not stoning you for any of these, but for blasphemy, because you, a mere man, claim to be God" (John 10:33). Jesus claimed to be the eternal, self-existent Creator of the universe, whose name "I AM" was first revealed to Moses (Exo 3:14).

Jesus had a clear divine self-understanding as Messiah, Prophet, Priest, Savior, King, and God. He described himself in many different ways during his ministry, including the following:

1. The Son of God (Matt 26:63-64)
2. The Son of Man (Matt 16:13)
3. One with the Father (John 10:30)
4. The Fulfiller of the Law (Matt 5:17)
5. The Lord of the Sabbath (Matt 12:8)
6. The One who Forgives Sin (Mark 2:10)
7. The Bread of Life (John 6:35)
8. The Good Shepherd (John 10:11)
9. The True Vine (John 15:1)
10. The Resurrection and the Life (John 11:25)
11. The Great Physician (Mark 2:17)
12. The Giver of Living Water (John 4:10)
13. The Healer (Luke 18:42)
14. The Light of the World (John 8:12)

15. The Judge of the World (John 5:22-23)

16. The Giver of Eternal Life (John 10:28)

17. The Door of Salvation (John 10:9)

18. The Faithful and True Witness (Rev 3:14)

19. The Ruler of God's Creation (Rev 3:14)

20. The Way, the Truth, and the Life (John 14:6)

21. The First and the Last (Rev 1:17)

22. The Living One (Rev 1:18)

23. The Beginning and the End (Rev 22:13)

24. The Bright Morning Star (Rev 22:16)

25. The Savior (John 3:14-16)

26. The Messiah (John 4:25-26)

27. The Great "I AM" (John 8:58)

The identity of Jesus is the central issue of Christianity. He is God himself—the King of kings and Lord of lords. He created the world and reigns over it now and forever, and he will judge all men in a time of his own choosing.

The mission of Jesus

Jesus, the Son of God, is God the Father's great revelation to humanity. "In the past God spoke to our forefathers through the prophets at many times and in various ways, but in these last days he has spoken to us by his Son, whom he appointed heir of all things" (Heb 1:1-2).

Jesus presented a clear mission of why he came. He announced that people needed to repent because the kingdom of God was near and *he* was the only way to enter it (John 8:24, 10:9, 14:6). Jesus would sacrifice his life to save people from their sins and the response of each person to Jesus would determine where they would spend eternity. "Salvation is found in no one else, for there is no other name under heaven given to men by which we must be saved" (Acts 4:12). This was the message and mission of Jesus. He said to Pilate at his trial, "For this reason I was born, and for this I came into the world, to testify to the truth. Everyone on the side of truth listens to me" (John 18:37).

The mission of Jesus to come to Earth as the only means to save humanity is inexplicable if it is not true. If Jesus were merely one among many ways to be saved, then there is no reason he would come to suffer and die. Why endure *that* if there are other ways to God?

The authority of Jesus

Jesus claimed unprecedented authority in his ministry, which was unlike that of any other world religion founder. He claimed this authority in many different ways:

1. *Authority over God's Law.* Jesus claimed to not only fulfill the Law, but also to extend it. "You have heard that it was said to the people long ago, 'Do not murder, and anyone who murders will be subject to judgment.' But I tell you that anyone who is angry with his brother will be subject to judgment" (Matt 5:21-22). "You have heard that it was said, 'Do not commit adultery.' But I tell you that anyone who looks at a woman lustfully has already committed adultery with her in his heart" (Matt 5:27-28).

2. *Authority to forgive sin.* "'So that you may know that the Son of Man has authority on earth to forgive sins.' Then he said to the paralytic, 'Get up, take your mat and go home'" (Matt 9:6).

3. *Authority to judge sin.* "The Father judges no one, but has entrusted all judgment to the Son" (John 5:22).

4. *Authority over demons.* "With authority and power he gives orders to evil spirits and they come out!" (Luke 4:36).

5. *Authority over disease.* "He called his twelve disciples to him and gave them authority to...heal every disease and sickness" (Matt 10:1).

6. *Authority over death.* "I lay down my life—only to take it up again. No one takes it from me, but I lay it down of my own accord. I have authority to lay it down and authority to take it up again" (John 10:17-18).

7. *Authority over all things.* Jesus said, "All authority in heaven and on earth has been given to me" (Matt 28:18).

The resurrection of Jesus

The man Jesus of Nazareth lived a sinless life of incredible teaching, miracles, and prophecy, while demonstrating unparalleled divine identity, mission, and authority. He predicted he would die and be raised from the dead, and then it happened. This proves beyond question that Jesus is exactly who he claimed to be.

This is why the resurrection of Jesus Christ is the very foundation of Christianity. The apostle Paul said, "If Christ has not been raised, our preaching is useless and so is your faith" (1 Cor 15:14). This singular, spectacular event in history is so important because it confirms many spiritual truths that are expressed in the Bible. This claim is unique among all the world's religions. Here are ten of these spiritual truths that, according to the Bible, are explicitly tied to and proven by the resurrection of Jesus:

1. *It proves the power of God.* The resurrection was an incredible demonstration of the awesome power of God. "I pray that you will begin to understand the incredible greatness of his power for us who believe him. This is the same mighty power that raised Christ from the dead" (Eph 1:19-20).

2. *It proves Jesus was the Son of God.* Through the resurrection, Christ demonstrated that he is not on an equal level with Abraham, Muhammad, Buddha, Confucius, or any other world religious leader. He is absolutely unique. "Jesus Christ our Lord was shown to be the Son of God when God powerfully raised him from the dead by means of the Holy Spirit" (Rom 1:4).

3. *It proves that Jesus will live forever.* Jesus' resurrection demonstrated his victory over death. Death and the grave hold no power over him. "For we know that since Christ was raised from the dead, he cannot die again; death no longer has mastery over him" (Rom 6:9).

4. *It proves that Jesus will reign forever.* The resurrection led to Christ's present heavenly reign as Lord of all the Earth. "God exalted him to the highest place and gave him the name that is above every name, that at the name of Jesus every knee should bow, in heaven and on earth and under the earth, and every tongue confess that Jesus Christ is Lord, to the glory of God the Father" (Phil 2:9-11).

5. *It proves that Jesus will judge the world.* The resurrection is indisputable proof that the message about Jesus as Judge and Savior is true. "For [God] has set a day when he will judge the world with justice by the man he has appointed. He has given proof of this to all men by raising him from the dead" (Acts 17:31).

6. *It proves that followers of Christ are forgiven.* The resurrection guarantees believers present forgiveness of their sins and right standing before God. "If Christ has not been raised, your faith is futile; you are still in your sins" (1 Cor 15:17).

7. *It proves that followers of Christ can have new life in Christ.* Because Christ is alive, we too can experience his resurrection life. "We were therefore buried with him through baptism into death in order that, just as Christ was raised from the dead through the glory of the Father, we too may live a new life. If we have been united with him like this in his death, we will certainly also be united with him in his resurrection" (Rom 6:4-5).

8. *It proves that all people will be raised from the dead.* Life on this Earth is not all there is. The Bible teaches and the resurrection confirms that Christ will raise the whole human race. Those who do not belong to him through faith will be raised to eternal condemnation and those who have devoted themselves to him will be raised to eternal glory. "By his power God raised the Lord from the dead, and he will raise us also" (1 Cor 6:14).

9. *It proves that followers of Christ will receive transformed bodies.* The hope of the Christian faith is not the mere immortality of the soul, but also the resurrection of the body. Our bodies will be supernaturally released from their graves and will be made perfect and eternal, just as Christ's was. "So will it be with the resurrection of the dead. The body that is sown is perishable, it is raised imperishable; it is sown in dishonor, it is raised in glory; it is sown in weakness, it is raised in power; it is sown a natural body, it is raised a spiritual body" (1 Cor 15:42-44).

10. *It proves that creation will be restored.* Just as our bodies will be raised imperishable for the glory of God, so the Earth itself will be made new and fit for the habitation of risen and glorified persons. "The creation itself will be liberated from its bondage to decay and brought into the glorious freedom of the children of God" (Rom 8:21).

The resurrection of Christ serves as the supreme proof of God's plan to redeem and restore all of creation. It forms the very basis of salvation: "If you confess with your mouth, 'Jesus is Lord,' and believe in your heart that God raised him from the dead, you will be saved" (Rom 10:9). The resurrection gives firm assurance for faith in Christ here and now and offers us a sure and certain hope for the future.

How should we respond to Jesus?

The resurrection of Jesus sheds special light on his claims and demands. The same God who raised Jesus from the dead is also the one who said we must listen to Jesus. On one occasion, Peter, James and John were with Jesus and experienced this: "A bright cloud covered them, and a voice from the cloud said, 'This is my Son, whom I love; with him I am well pleased. Listen to him!'" (Matt 17:5).

Since everything in the universe was created by Jesus and for Jesus, he has complete authority to make demands on his creation. Jesus taught that we demonstrate our love for him when we obey him: "If you love me, you will obey what I command" (John 14:15). The commands that Jesus gave throughout his ministry are universal in their application—he expects *all* human beings to obey them. This is because Jesus is the one to whom all people will have to give an account of their lives. "We must all appear before the judgment seat of Christ" (2 Cor 5:10). Here are some of the demands that Jesus personally places on all human beings:[3]

1. *Come to me (John 7:37).* All human beings are in a desperate situation under the wrath of God due to our sins and only Jesus can rescue us. Jesus paid the penalty on our behalf, but only for those who come to him.

2. *Believe in me (John 3:16-18).* Whoever believes in Jesus shall not perish but have eternal life. We need to believe who Jesus is and what he has done to save us. The belief that Jesus requires is not a blind leap in the dark; it is based on evidence that is rooted in history—the facts of his birth, life, death, and resurrection.

3. *Repent (Matt 4:17).* To repent is to turn from our sin and turn to Jesus. We experience a change of mind so that we see Jesus as true, good, beautiful, and worthy of all of our praise and devotion.

4. *Trust me (John 14:1-6).* Jesus alone is the way, the truth, and the life, so he provides the only way for us to know God. We should not let our hearts be troubled, but place our full trust in him. He will satisfy our thirst and hunger for an abundant and meaningful life.

5. *Love me (John 14:21-24).* Jesus came to restore human beings to the kind of relationship with God for which we were created. The most important thing he has to say about that restored relationship is that we were meant to love God with all our being—all our heart, soul, mind, and strength. To love God we must know him as he is revealed in Jesus. Jesus said that our love for him must exceed the love we have for our own spouse, son, daughter, mother, and father.

---

[3] This list is loosely based on John Piper, *What Jesus Demands from the World* (Wheaton, IL: Crossway Books, 2006).

6. *Rejoice in me (John 16:22).* Jesus came into the world with good news and that news is worth rejoicing over. Seeing and savoring Jesus as the greatest treasure in existence is the reason we were created. Jesus *himself* is our great reward, nothing less. Jesus does not ask that we abandon our pursuit of pleasure and joy, but instead to find their fulfillment in him. We are to be completely enthralled with Jesus.

7. *Listen to me (Matt 7:21-27).* We should listen to what Jesus has to say because of who he is and what he has done. His words have authority and power because they are the words of God. Jesus speaks *from* God the Father and *as* God the Son. He speaks words of eternal life that awaken faith in those who will listen. Jesus said that if we do not put into practice what we hear from him then we are like a foolish man who builds his house on sand.

8. *Abide in me (John 15:4-8).* The only way we can live a truly good life is to stay close to Jesus, like a branch attached to its vine. We abide in Jesus when we continue to believe moment-by-moment that we are loved by him and when we trust and depend on him in all things. He provides us peace in the confusion, anxieties, and tribulations of life. The storm rages, but we are at rest in Jesus.

9. *Follow me (Matt 4:19).* Jesus' commands are for a lifetime. He does not demand a one-time decision to come, believe, repent, trust, love, rejoice, listen, and abide. If we do not continue to obey these commands throughout our lives, then we are not a true disciple of Jesus. This is an all-day, every-day, life-long calling.

10. *Imitate me (John 13:15).* The goal of our faith is to become like Jesus. Our discipleship must be intentional. We must view Jesus as the Master Teacher and ourselves as his devoted students. He has set the example for us and we are to pattern our lives after his in love, humility, gentleness, mercy, compassion, kindness, service, and sacrifice.

11. *Feed on my words (Matt 4:4).* Jesus expects us to know and understand the Bible in its entirety because it is our infallible guide to faith and life. God's words to us in Scripture are a more important source of sustenance to us than food, for they nurture our spiritual needs in a way that benefits us eternally, rather than merely providing temporary relief from physical hunger.

12. *Hate your sin (Mark 9:43-47).* It is astonishing how many Christians deal with their sin casually. Jesus demands otherwise.

We are to fight for a pure heart with the same urgency as tearing out an eye or cutting off a hand. We are to stop sinning.

13. *Be vigilant (Matt 13:18-23).* Jesus warned that the zeal of many of his followers would grow cold and they would drift away from the faith, either because of tribulation or the pleasures of life. Jesus constantly warns us to be alert and to watch. He is calling us to serious personal vigilance.

14. *Seek first my kingdom (Matt 6:33).* God's kingdom is that sphere where he rules and his will is done, which is all of creation. We are to seek that aspect of his kingdom which is already present. We are to pray and work for it to take over all aspects of the personal, social, and political order where it is now excluded.[4]

15. *Love one another (John 13:34).* Jesus demonstrated his love by leaving the glory of Heaven to die for us. In doing this, he set an example for us to follow. We love another person when we desire the best for them—regardless of whether we feel they deserve it or not—and then do all that is in our power to accomplish that. We are to love all people, not only our family and friends, but also strangers and even our enemies.

16. *Tell others about me (Matt 28:19-20).* We have an obligation to spread the good news of Jesus to everyone in the world. This includes our near neighbors as well as those in the furthest corners of the Earth. This demand reveals God's heart that people from every segment of human society would experience the supreme and eternal joy and blessing of knowing God through Jesus.

17. *Deny yourself (Matt 5:38-42).* Turning to Jesus is essentially turning from self-centeredness to God-centeredness. We should not be concerned when we are interrupted, insulted, or offended, or when our freedom, status, or power are restricted. Jesus calls us to surrender our personal rights in favor of his purposes and plans. He demands that instead of retaliating, we do good to those who wrong us. Patience, self-denial, and sacrifice are the marks of his disciples.

18. *Take up your cross (Mark 8:34).* Following Jesus means joining him in what he was sent to do. He calls us to follow him in his sufferings because a life of joyful suffering for his sake shows that he is more valuable than all the earthly rewards the world lives for.

---

[4] Dallas Willard, *The Divine Conspiracy: Rediscovering Our Hidden Life in God* (San Francisco: HarperCollins, 1997), 26.

Suffering for Christ is temporary, however, because joy in him will be eternal.

19. *Sell everything you have and give to the poor (Luke 18:22).* This life should not mean anything to us compared to the surpassing greatness of knowing Christ. Jesus taught that we must be so willing to be his disciple that we would leave everything to follow him. We are to use what God has given us to help and serve others.

20. *Expect trials, betrayal, and martyrdom (Luke 21:16-17).* This world is hostile to God and his ways. Followers of Christ can expect to be persecuted and even martyred for their faith in Christ, but he is worth that cost.

There are severe requirements and serious consequences to following Christ in this life. People have a tendency to gloss quickly over these more difficult demands, rationalizing their meaning and softening their impact—but this is a great danger. Everything in this list was part of Christ's typical message of invitation to follow him, which he gave to crowds as well as to individuals. Jesus did not say merely "believe in me" or "accept me," but "give your all for me and expect hatred, betrayal, and even death in return." The demands of Jesus may be summarized in this way:[5]

❖ *Jesus requires our superior love.* Our love for Christ surpasses our love for everything else in this world, including the people closest to us. This changes our **perspective**.

❖ *Jesus requires our exclusive loyalty.* Through the cross of Christ, we die to our own lives. This changes our **priorities**.

❖ *Jesus requires our total loss.* For the cause of Christ, we give up everything we have. This changes our **possessions**.

Jesus can rightly demand our love, loyalty, and loss because he is the ultimate example of all three—he is supremely loving, supremely loyal, and suffered the supreme loss. To follow Christ demands a sacrificial life of radical compassion and giving, but Jesus is *worth* this because he is the supreme treasure in the universe. The demands of Jesus are indeed radical, but so are the astonishing rewards.

---

[5] David Platt, *Radical: What the Gospel Demands*, sermon delivered September-October 2008, The Church At Brook Hills, Birmingham, Alabama, available at http://www.brookhills.org/media/series/radical/. I highly encourage the reader to watch this challenging eight-part sermon series.

CONCLUSION

How should we live?

Who is wise? He will realize these things. Who is discerning? He will understand them. The ways of the LORD are right; the righteous walk in them, but the rebellious stumble in them.

Hosea (8th century BC)
Jewish prophet
Hosea 14:9

If you call out for insight and cry aloud for understanding, and if you look for it as for silver and search for it as for hidden treasure, then you will understand the fear of the LORD and find the knowledge of God. For the LORD gives wisdom, and from his mouth come knowledge and understanding.

Solomon (c. 1011-931 BC)
King of Israel
Proverbs 2:3-6

Not only do we only know God through Jesus Christ, but we only know ourselves through Jesus Christ; we only know life and death through Jesus Christ. Apart from Jesus Christ we cannot know the meaning of our life or our death, of God, or of ourselves.

Blaise Pascal (1623-1662)
Mathematician, physicist, inventor, philosopher
Pensées, no. 417

How should we live? We should live as if God is there, for surely he is. This is the only reasonable course for the person who wants to live wisely with meaning and purpose and not waste his life. This God who is there has revealed himself in many ways to us because he loves us.

Faith in Jesus

International speaker and author Ravi Zacharias observes, "The message of Christ was not the introduction of a religion, but an introduction to truth about reality as God alone knows it."[1] Jesus claimed he was "the way and the truth and the life" and proved his authority and power by predicting his bodily resurrection and then fulfilling that prophecy. The prophecies, person, and work of Christ, his resurrection from the dead, and numerous other affirmations are verified from history. If you test his claims, you will find him and his teaching thoroughly trustworthy. Jesus provides answers to our five fundamental questions of life in a way that corresponds with reality and satisfies our souls unlike any other world leader or religion.

We have seen that Jesus Christ is the focal point of creation—*everything* pivots around him. The very last book of the Bible is introduced in its first verse as "The revelation of Jesus Christ." Early in the book John describes Jesus as "the faithful witness, the firstborn from the dead, and the ruler of the kings of the earth" (Rev 1:5). This verse answers three important questions about Jesus.

Can we trust him?

Jesus is the faithful witness. His words are absolutely true and authoritative. He came to testify to the truth, so that we could know it and live it. He is totally trustworthy and deserving of our complete faith and obedience.

Does he have the power to help us?

Jesus is the firstborn from the dead. He has the power to defeat death. He was the first person to be raised from the dead who never died again, so this guarantees that we also will be raised and never die again. Jesus has the power to help us.

Will he take care of our future?

Jesus is the ruler of the kings of the Earth. The world is a mess today, so Jesus as ruler and king may not look true from our limited perspective, but it only *seems* that way. God is sovereign. He is always in control. Jesus Christ presently sits at the right hand of God the Father, and has promised to come again to judge the Earth, to vanquish all evil forever, and to set up his eternal kingdom of peace, joy, and harmony with no more suffering or sin. Jesus will take care of our future.

---

[1] Ravi Zacharias, *Jesus Among Other Gods* (Nashville: Word Publishing, 2000), 34-35.

Full commitment

It is a delusion to think that a nominal faith is worth anything to God. Jesus wants fully devoted followers, not half-hearted admirers or part-time pretenders. Jesus chastised the Pharisees for being hypocrites that honored him with their lips when their hearts were far from him (Mark 7:6). A fully devoted follower is committed to steadfast obedience to Jesus' demands. Jesus said, "If you hold to my teaching, you are really my disciples. Then you will know the truth, and the truth will set you free" (John 8:31-32).

When the most glorious person in the universe pays all your debts and then commands that you come to live with him and enter into his joy, there can be no more desirable demand imaginable.[2] The commands that Jesus has given us reveal how a true disciple should live in an obedient relationship with him. Jesus demands are not meant to make us constantly struggle to live up to his expectations. In fact, Jesus demands what we cannot actually do on our own. We can only consistently live out his commands when we trust Christ to give us the desire and power to do so. When we do we experience peace, joy, and fulfillment that begin now and last forever. We will also hear "well done good and faithful servant" from the One we obeyed when he returns to judge mankind (Matt 25:23). However, for those who reject Christ and his demands there is only condemnation: "There is a judge for the one who rejects me and does not accept my words; that very word which I spoke will condemn him at the last day" (John 12:48). The time to decide is now. Which will you choose?

Further reading

The supremacy of God

> *Counterfeit Gods,* Timothy Keller
> *Crazy Love: Overwhelmed by a Relentless God,* Francis Chan
> *Desiring God: Meditations of a Christian Hedonist,* John Piper
> *God is the Gospel,* John Piper
> *One Thing: Developing a Passion for the Beauty of God,* Sam Storms
> *The Dangerous Duty of Delight,* John Piper

Following Christ

> *Don't Waste Your Life,* John Piper
> *Radical: Taking Back Your Faith from the American Dream,* David Platt
> *The Divine Conspiracy: Rediscovering our Hidden Life in God,* Dallas Willard
> *What Jesus Demands from the World,* John Piper

---

[2] Piper, *What Jesus Demands from the World,* 26.

Future Hope

We have this hope as an anchor for the soul, firm and secure.
Hebrews 6:19

All I have seen teaches me to trust the Creator for all I have not seen.
Ralph Waldo Emerson (1803-1882)
Essayist and poet

The mystery that has been kept hidden for ages and generations is now
disclosed to the saints. To them God has chosen to make known among
the Gentiles the glorious riches of this mystery, which is Christ in you,
the hope of glory.

Paul (c. AD 5-67)
Apostle, missionary, teacher, author
Colossians 1:26-27

The secret of the universe and of your life lies behind this door [to
Heaven], according to the wisest and best men who have ever lived;
how should we describe someone who won't bother to lift the key to the
lock and see whether it opens?

Peter Kreeft (1937-)
Scholar, philosopher, author
Christianity for Modern Pagans

We have discovered that God is at the root of every one of our
answers to life's most important questions. God explains where everything
came from. God explains what is wrong with the world. God determines
what happens after we die. God has given us knowledge of these and many
other wonderful things by revealing them to us in creation, in a book, and

in himself in the person of Jesus Christ. And it is God who tells us how we should live.

Peter Kreeft insightfully observes, "The major obstacle to faith for modern man is the secular utopian idea that he can find wisdom and happiness without God."[1] By now we have come to appreciate the foolishness of this approach. This is clearly a theistic universe and more specifically a Christ-centered universe. A major difference between Christianity and other worldviews is that Christianity is entirely grounded in knowledge. We have abundant evidence for its truth, which gives us excellent reasons to believe it. Competing worldviews are vastly inferior in this respect and should be rejected. This is not a matter of personal preference, but a matter of objective truth—the way the world really is. Christianity makes sense philosophically, intellectually, and emotionally.

The Christian faith is not only about having a change of mind and coming to accept a new worldview, however. It is about coming into a new relationship with God and becoming a new person. God is the creator and lover of our souls, and he offers us the possibility of deep, fulfilling communion with him. He desires that every person he created respond to him in love, faith, and obedience so they can enjoy this relationship forever. This is the great hope in our universe.

The greatest hope

With all that is wrong with the world, the only thing we really have to live for is hope—hope for a better present and an even better future without pain, suffering, and death. Man tries in vain to manufacture hope through education, government, business, science, religion, retirement plans, and countless other man-made institutions, programs, and ideas. However, none of these bring any authentic and enduring joy, peace, or human flourishing.

Present and future hope is found only in God, the One who created everything to begin with. He created the universe and human beings with a purpose, and he is working out that purpose to a conclusion of his own timing. We need not fear life *or* death. This is where faith comes in. We need to place our full and complete trust in this sovereign, mighty, wise God. Our hope is not mere wishful thinking on our part, however. It is a firm and sure hope because God has revealed himself to us and shown that he is able and faithful to deliver on his promises.

What we hope for in the future will drive our behavior in the present. When we apprehend the grand vision of God for our lives we *want* to be

---

[1] Kreeft, *Christianity for Modern Pagans*, 49.

part of it. It will change the way we think and act. We will reorient and readjust everything to be involved in God's kingdom.

May this be true of your life and may you experience the fullness of joy offered by this great God who created our universe and fills it with real value, meaning, and purpose.

A word to those who may not be convinced

Thank you for sticking with me to the end! Even though you may not be fully convinced I hope that you have found the journey rewarding nonetheless.

I encourage you to continue seeking. Seventeenth century philosopher Blaise Pascal makes a helpful observation: "Wishing to appear openly to those who seek him with all their heart and hidden from those who shun him with all their heart, [God] has qualified our knowledge of him by giving signs which can be seen by those who seek him and not by those who do not. There is enough light for those who desire only to see and enough darkness for those of a contrary disposition."[2] God's claim is that you will find him when you seek him with all your heart (Jer 29:13). This claim is neither disproven nor even fairly tested if you do not fulfill your part of the experiment, which is to seek. Therefore, someone who is indifferent, no matter how sincere or intelligent he is, is in danger of forfeiting eternal life for not seriously considering Christ. God is there to be found and wants to be found, but he will not force himself on anyone.

Please do not view this merely as an intellectual inquiry about God, though. I am not asking you to become a Christian because of the arguments and evidence pointing to its truth. All the reasons given in this book should simply convince you that Christianity is intellectually sensible and satisfying. This should be a genuine search of your soul—a spiritual quest done in humility and with a contrite heart.[3] You should become a Christian not *just* because it is true, but because you find Jesus Christ completely captivating—certainly as a man, but more importantly, as your Lord and Savior. Peter Kreeft summarizes this thought by saying, "Christianity is not a hypothesis, it is a proposal of marriage."[4] This is the depth of intimacy Christ desires to have with you. He stands at the door and knocks. Will you answer?

---

[2] Pascal, *Pensées no. 149*, Kreeft, 69.

[3] William Lane Craig, "Is God's Existence Evident to Every Sincere Seeker?", http://www.reasonablefaith.org/site/News2?page=NewsArticle&id=8927, accessed Jul 18, 2011.

[4] Kreeft, *Christianity for Modern Pagans*, 31.

APPENDIX A

Evolutionary sleight of hand

It is absolutely safe to say that, if you meet somebody who claims not to believe in evolution, the person is ignorant, stupid or insane (or wicked, but I'd rather not consider that).

Richard Dawkins (1941-)
Atheist, evolutionary biologist
New York Times book review

It seems to me that Richard Dawkins constantly overlooks the fact that Darwin...pointed out that his whole argument began with a being which already possessed reproductive powers. This is the creature...of which a truly comprehensive theory of evolution must give some account. Darwin himself was well aware that he had not produced such an account.

Antony Flew (1923-2010)
Former life-long atheist, philosopher
My Pilgrimage from Atheism to Theism, 2004 interview

We are skeptical of claims for the ability of random mutation and natural selection to account for the complexity of life. Careful examination of the evidence for Darwinian theory should be encouraged.

Statement signed by over 800 scientists
www.dissentfromdarwin.org

There is wide appreciation of the fact that if biologists are wrong about Darwin, they are wrong about life, and if they are wrong about life, they are wrong about everything.

David Berlinski (1942-)
Mathematician, author
The Devil's Delusion

Charles Darwin published his book, *The Origin of Species,*[1] in 1859. It is quite an understatement to say that his theory has had wide-ranging impact in the last hundred and fifty years. The effect has been so great because human origins have a tremendous influence on what we think of human beings. Many people believe that Darwin's ideas prove that God is not necessary to explain the origin and development of life. Indeed, Richard Dawkins once famously claimed, "Darwin made it possible to be an intellectually fulfilled atheist."[2]

Definitions

Before we explore this issue we need to distinguish between three different kinds of evolution. The first definition of evolution is simply change over time. Certainly we observe change in populations of living organisms on planet Earth over a period of years. By this general definition, though, almost everything evolves—like culture, language, automobiles, and computers, for example. This kind of evolution is not disputed because everything is changing in this general sense in one way or another. It is obvious that this observation is not very helpful and is not what Darwin had in mind.

The second definition of evolution is referred to as *microevolution.* In this definition small changes take place in an organism over time, producing modifications of its existing characteristics. These are changes within a species that allow an organism to survive and reproduce. Examples of this kind of evolution include changes in the size of finch beaks due to changing climate, color variations in moths, and bacteria's resistance to antibiotics. This second kind of evolution is also not in doubt. This process is real, but it is an adaptive, not a creative process. Microevolution can alter existing animals, but not produce new ones. It explains how finches get larger beaks, how moths turn darker colors, and how bacteria develop resistance to drugs, but it does not tell us how we get finches, moths, or bacteria in the first place.

The third definition of evolution is referred to as *macroevolution.* This definition extends the processes of microevolution to explain all of life on the planet with all of its great diversity. Macroevolution is the theory that life first arose from non-life and then evolved from a single cell

---

[1] The full title of Darwin's book was *On The Origin of Species by Means of Natural Selection, or The Preservation of Favoured Races in the Struggle for Life.*

[2] Richard Dawkins, *The Blind Watchmaker: Why the Evidence of Evolution Reveals a Universe Without Design* (New York, W.W. Norton & Company, 1996), 6.

up to present-day human beings. This was Darwin's revolutionary idea, which gave atheists their intellectually satisfying answer to the origin of the human species.[3] This is the kind of evolution we are concerned with; it is what we mean when we speak of *Evolution* with a capital "E". Since evolution is an ambiguous term as we have just seen, I will refer to it as Darwinism—meaning macroevolution—in honor of its most popular advocate, Charles Darwin.

It is important to grasp the central premise of Darwinism and hence its appeal to atheists. The idea is that all of life is comprised of only material ingredients, which have developed by random and blind processes that can be described solely in terms of biochemical reactions and physical laws. There is no immaterial or non-physical aspect of life, nor is there a supernatural explanation for any of it. All of life can be explained exclusively by natural and physical processes.

Assessing the evidence for Darwinism

In this book we have examined an abundance of reasons and evidence to believe in a transcendent Creator God, which makes theism the most plausible overarching worldview. If we are correct about this, then it seems Darwinism cannot really make good on the claim to make it possible to be an intellectually fulfilled atheist. There is simply too much *other* very strong and persuasive evidence weighing in against atheism.

In fact, upon closer examination we find that Darwinism is a theory with little to commend it as an explanation for the many complex structures and forms of life. Mathematician David Berlinski writes, "Suspicions about Darwin's theory arise for two reasons. The first: the theory makes little sense. The second: it is supported by little evidence."[4] The evidence against Darwinism comes in three main categories.

1. *It lacks explanatory power.* Darwinism fails to offer adequate explanations in terms of how its processes could actually work in the real world to do what it claims.

2. *It lacks sufficient physical evidence.* Darwinism fails to demonstrate that the physical evidence we presently have can support its claims. In fact, the physical evidence actually opposes Darwinism at several points.

---

[3] Actually, Charles Darwin was not the first proponent of Evolution, but his theory of natural selection earned more scientific credibility than his predecessors' ideas.

[4] David Berlinski, *The Devil's Delusion: Atheism and its Scientific Pretensions* (New York: Basic Books, 2009), 187.

3. *It lacks explanatory scope.* Darwinism fails to explain features of the world that it legitimately needs to explain as a theory of how complex, intelligent life arose and developed on planet Earth.

Lack of explanatory power

Darwin believed that all life forms in existence are descended from a single common ancestor by way of a slow gradual process of billions of cumulative changes. This is often called *descent with modification.* Given enough time, Darwinism holds that nature can produce every kind of animal we see today, all originating from one single celled life form.

Unfortunately for Darwinists, the biological pathways they suggest to do this—natural selection and random genetic mutation—are inadequate to explain how new classes of complex animals can develop. Michael Behe explains, "If there is not a smooth gradually rising, easily found evolutionary pathway leading to a biological system within a reasonable time, Darwinian processes won't work."[5] Darwinism fails because it does not have the explanatory power to accomplish what it needs to do.

Natural selection

Darwin saw the process of natural selection as the primary force behind biological evolution. It is the process by which organisms with genetic traits that make them more fit for their environment pass on their beneficial genes to the next generation, while the less fit organisms, along with their unfavorable genes, diminish within the population. This process continues from generation to generation, producing better adapted organisms, while weeding out the weaker ones. Because these more fit organisms tend to live longer and reproduce more, this process is often referred to as the *survival of the fittest.*

Darwin thought that natural selection had an endless capacity to generate new traits and create brand new animal classes. He writes, "I can see no limit to the amount of change, to the beauty and infinite complexity of the coadaptations between all organic beings, one with another and with their physical conditions of life, which may be effected in the long course of time by nature's power of selection."[6]

Darwin began developing his theory of natural selection during his work in the Galapagos Islands in 1835. He discovered 14 species of finches there and observed that they differed dramatically in the size and shape of their beaks. Darwin thought that the various species had evolved

---

[5] Behe, *The Edge of Evolution*, 7.

[6] Charles Darwin, *The Origin of Species By Means of Natural Selection* (London: Penguin Books, 1985, first published 1859), 153.

from "an original paucity of birds in this archipelago, one species had been taken and modified for different ends."[7]

Darwin thought that natural selection operated over very long periods of time and could not be observed. However, biologists Peter and Rosemary Grant conducted a detailed 30-year study of the Galapagos finches from 1972-2001 and observed that the finches changed body size and

beak traits several times over that period.[8] Differences in their food supply due to weather changes led to natural selection on their beaks in both directions. A severe drought brought deep, strong beaks to get the larger, harder seeds in difficult-to-reach places; but when the rains returned the birds adapted to eat the smaller, softer seeds.

This was hailed as a great triumph for Darwinism, with the Grants winning awards for their work. However, there is a problem when the interpretation of this study is taken too far. The change in the finches is evidence of *micro*evolution, not *macro*evolution. There was *no net change* in the finches over the 30-year period. Beak sizes increased during a severe drought and returned to their normal size when the drought ended. This showed that variations do occur within an animal kind, however the finches remained finches! They did not become some new kind of animal.

Natural selection is a real process that causes adaptive changes within and sometimes across species, and this is a bona fide example of microevolution that is not disputed. However, no new traits or characteristics appeared in the finches. Only the existing traits, shape and size of the beak, became more adapted to the surroundings. It is a big leap—and a completely *unproven* one—to extrapolate a microevolutionary process like natural selection to achieve macroevolutionary results.

Darwin was mistaken to think that natural selection is a creative process that would produce new kinds of creatures. Natural selection cannot create information at the genetic level. Rather, it is only capable of deleting or modifying *existing* genetic information from the less adapted creatures who do not survive to reproduce. It can only select among pre-existing traits for the surviving creatures—it cannot create new ones. New information is required to cross animal classes because the blueprint that directs what a living organism will be is encoded in its DNA. As we saw in

---

[7] Charles Darwin, *Voyage of the Beagle*, as found in Appendix B of Joseph Carroll, editor, *On the Origin of Species* (Ontario, Canada: Broadview Press, 2003), 457.

[8] Peter R. Grant and B. Rosemary Grant, "Unpredictable Evolution in a 30-Year Study of Darwin's Finches", http://www.sciencemag.org/content/296/5568/707.abstract, accessed Feb 14, 2011.

chapters 2 and 3 though, physical processes cannot create information. It has to come from somewhere else. This means there is a conceptual gap between microevolution and macroevolution that cannot be bridged without intelligent action to add new information.

Genetic mutation

Darwinists eventually recognized that natural selection cannot produce the new information required by Darwin's theory. They theorized that genetic mutations would have to provide it since there simply is no other mechanism that can make changes within an organism's DNA. They thought that mutations would supply the new genetic information and then natural selection would guide the evolutionary process from there.[9]

We noted earlier how genes are comprised of long, extremely complicated, molecules of DNA, which form the blueprint of all living  things. In rare instances, errors can occur during the replication of a DNA molecule so that the information is somewhat altered. A "copying" error is referred to as a mutation. Mutations can also occur if the organism is exposed to radiation, chemical agents, or viruses.

Darwinists started experimenting to prove that mutations can produce upwards, positive evolutionary change. They tried breeding the fruit fly for many years and documented thousands of mutations, yet none of them were beneficial. All of the mutations were harmful, producing less fit flies with such things as unusable wings. None of the large number of beneficial mutations needed for Darwinism was found. More importantly, all the flies remained flies all their lives. They never evolved into anything else. Genetic mutations simply cannot produce new classes of animals. There are several problems with the idea that genetic mutation can accomplish the evolutionary change that Darwinists require for their theory.

First, mutations are very rare. Darwinism requires millions of constructive changes, but mutations normally occur once in every hundred million replications of a DNA molecule in a generation of an organism.[10] Mutations are simply too rare to have produced all the necessary traits of even one life form, much less all the creatures that are found on Earth.

Second, mutations are always random. They are totally uncontrollable, chance events. They have no goal or purpose that they

---

[9] Evolutionists who appeal to genetics are often called *neo-Darwinists*.
[10] Behe, *The Edge of Evolution*, 11.

work toward, yet Darwinism requires very many continual, cumulative, and beneficial changes to improve an organism. Behe remarks, "When more than a single tiny step is needed for an evolutionary improvement, blind random mutation is very unlikely to find it."[11]

Third, mutations are almost always harmful. In many cases mutations cause death in a short time or severely limit the fitness of the organism, reducing its ability to reproduce. Some mutations are neutral, but there are few known favorable mutations.[12] We have all seen various deformities that some human beings have had since birth. We call them genetic birth defects. We certainly do not consider them to be evidence of positive evolutionary progress.

Fourth, mutations do not provide the new information needed for the organism to evolve. Darwinism needs new information, but mutations never provide it. Behe explains, "Randomly duplicating a single gene, or even the entire genome, does not yield new complex machinery; it only gives a copy of what was already present...Mutation has to work with the pre-existing cellular machinery, so there is a very limited number of things it can do."[13] Mutations only duplicate, distort, or delete already existing information, so the key ingredient needed to create new complex structures—additional information—cannot be generated by this process.

The limits of Darwinian processes

Darwinian processes have been observed to occur in certain limited cases, but these are always examples of microevolution, not macroevolution.

What Darwinian processes can do

Random mutation and natural selection *can* account for relatively minor changes in life forms. Two common examples are increased resistance to parasites and drugs, and relatively inconsequential changes in the appearance of animals, such as their size, shape, and color. Let's take a closer look at increased resistance.

One change to a single gene can sometimes cause a beneficial effect in an organism. For example, a single amino acid change in the human sickle cell hemoglobin protein confers resistance to malaria. Very rarely, several mutations appear simultaneously to provide a beneficial effect, such as malaria's stubborn resistance to drugs. However, since mutations

---

[11] Ibid., 19.

[12] Francis S. Collins, *The Language of God: A Scientist Presents Evidence for Belief* (New York: Free Press, 2006), 131.

[13] Behe, *The Edge of Evolution*, 74-77.

occur about every 100 million births,[14] these sorts of rare changes require an enormous population size of organisms in order to have sufficient mutational opportunities. Those numbers are present for microorganisms such as malarial parasites and bacteria, but they are not there for larger creatures.[15] For example, bacteria are by far the most numerous type of organisms on Earth, with about a million trillion trillion (10^{30}) bacterial cells formed each year[16] compared to about a 100 million (10^8) annual human births. These kinds of resistance improvements are therefore far *less* likely to occur in anything larger than a microbe.

It is also important to remember that mutations do not provide new information. They always break something that already exists, rather than build something new. Behe likens resistance mutations to biological trench warfare because they "burn a genetic bridge" or "break a genetic lock" to stop an invading parasite.[17] The desperate measure of breaking molecular machinery merely to survive can hardly be described as an overall improvement for the organism.

What Darwinian processes cannot do

The incredibly complex and coherent systems in the cell are not built from only one or two random amino acid changes to proteins that are currently doing other jobs. Instead, they consist of dozens of different proteins dedicated to specific tasks that arose, not by a few broken genes, but by the coordinated construction of many new genes. Behe provides a helpful analogy: "Such coherent, complex, cellular systems did not arise by random mutation and natural selection, any more than the Hoover Dam was built by the random accumulation of twigs, leaves, and mud."[18]

The cell is often compared to a modern human factory because of its great complexity and coordinated elegance, but this really understates the case. The cell is actually a whole level *more* complicated than that, for it also contains all the instructions and components to *create the factory itself*. The cell is full of sophisticated mechanisms that can replicate its entire structure in a very brief period. Michael Denton marvels about this: "It is astonishing to think that this remarkable piece of machinery [the cell], which possesses the ultimate capacity to construct every living thing that ever existed on Earth, from a giant redwood to the human brain, can construct all its own components in a matter of minutes and weigh less than 10^{-16} grams. It is of the order of several thousand million million

---

[14] Ibid., 68.
[15] Ibid., 101.
[16] Ibid., 63.
[17] Ibid., 69.
[18] Ibid., 102.

times smaller than the smallest piece of functional machinery ever constructed by man."[19]

The two main problems for Darwinism at the molecular level are *steps* and *coherence*. Steps represent a sequence of numerous individual changes and coherence represents the interrelatedness and progressive building of those steps one upon another in order to produce an overall improvement. Behe explains, "The more intermediate evolutionary steps that must be climbed to achieve some biological goal without reaping a net benefit, the more unlikely a Darwinian explanation...A telltale signature of planning is the coherent ordering of steps toward a goal. Random mutation, on the other hand, is incoherent; that is, any given evolutionary step taken by a population of organisms is unlikely to be connected to its predecessor."[20] Simply put, the more parts there are to a system, and the more they interact with one another in sophisticated ways, the more opportunities there are for Darwinism to fail in building the system. It does not take much to imagine the enormous complexity of creating an animal, for instance. Behe concludes, "The molecular developmental program to build an animal must consist of many discrete steps and be profoundly coherent."[21]

It simply is not reasonable to believe that Darwinian processes can solve these problems. Many more than one or two steps (mutations) have to occur before there is a net beneficial effect. If an intermediate state is harmful or is less fit than an earlier state, then it will result in an evolutionary dead-end. Imagine the probabilities for thousands of coherent steps to produce even one overall benefit to an organism—like an improved eye or organ—and then consider that this must occur not only once or even a few times—but millions of times to produce a life form like a human being. Denton observes, "Aside from any quantitative considerations, it seems intuitively impossible that such self-evident brilliance in the execution of design could ever have been the result of chance. For, even if we allow that chance might have occasionally hit on a relatively ingenious adaptive end, it seems inconceivable that it could have reached so many ends of such surpassing 'perfection'."[22]

The failure of Darwinian pathways

If mutations could produce new animal classes then we should observe Darwinism at work producing new creatures in radioactive environments. Instead, we have seen precisely the opposite results in the

---

[19] Denton, *Evolution: A Theory in Crisis*, 338.

[20] Behe, *The Edge of Evolution*, 104.

[21] Ibid., 179.

[22] Denton, *Evolution: A Theory in Crisis*, 327.

atomic bombing of Hiroshima and the Chernobyl nuclear disaster.[23] The radiation from these events caused massive disease and death and produced deformed children and animals that did not have improved capabilities.

Furthermore, if these pathways actually did what Darwinism wants them to do, they would likely often work *against* one another. Natural selection maintains the stability of a species by weeding out the weak and vulnerable organisms. Just when a mutation might have a remote chance to begin the macroevolutionary process of changing one creature into another, natural selection would squash it before it went anywhere.

Natural selection and genetic mutation cannot be the pathways that create all the complex life we observe around us. There is no physical proof that these pathways *actually* do what the Darwinists need them to do, but this is not surprising since they cannot even *theoretically* do what the Darwinists need them to do. Information is the major problem for Darwinism. DNA information is the fundamental building block for living organisms and that requires intelligence, not random chance.

Lack of physical evidence

A theory that alleges all the diversity of life we observe today has developed slowly and gradually from a single cell to millions of species over eons of time would surely have a great deal of physical evidence to support it. The physical evidence does not support Darwinism, however. Not only does it fail to confirm the theory, it actually undermines it at several points.

Discontinuity of nature

Living things are classified into groups based on their similarities.[24] Each class of organism possesses a number of unique and fundamental characteristics which are the same in all the species of that class, and are not found in any species outside the class. Take for example, mammals, which have a large cerebral cortex, a four chambered heart, a diaphragm used for respiration, three middle ear bones, mammary glands, body hair, and several other unique traits. Each of the characteristics in the list describes *all* mammals. All identifiable groups of organisms in existence

---

[23] The Chernobyl disaster was a catastrophic nuclear accident that occurred in April 1986 at the Chernobyl Nuclear Power Plant in the Ukraine.

[24] Biology classifies all of life into eight major ranks within the following hierarchy: Domain, Kingdom, Phylum, Class, Order, Family, Genus, and Species.

today can be classified in like manner. The animal groups are well-defined and remarkably isolated from one another.[25]

Accordingly, the primary description of the various animal kinds is one of *discontinuity*, and not of *continuity* or *sequence*. The animals fit nicely into distinct groups that appear to have been formed in an isolated manner, with no particular connection to other groups. Furthermore, any change is limited and contained within the boundaries of the established population types. This is not what we would expect if Darwinism were true, however, since change should be happening all the time and everywhere in the long gradual process of creating new classes and species. These apparently discontinuous groups, so the theory goes, were really formed in a sequential manner from other groups. All life forms are linked together and ultimately lead back to a single primeval cell. Therefore, we should be able to identify the transition sequences between all the groups.

The challenge for Darwinists is to convince us that the distinct types we see in nature are the result of sequential, interconnected changes between groups. There are no intermediate groups by the very definition of the classification system in wide use today, though. Every group is distinct, with its own unique set of traits. Even if biologists were to discover an intermediate specimen that truly shared characteristics across different groups, this would *still* be insufficient to validate their evolutionary model, though. The existing patterns are simply too numerous, too systematic, and too well-established to be deposed by a few apparently contradictory samples, even if they existed.[26] Denton explains, "To refute typology and securely validate evolutionary claims would necessitate hundreds or even thousands of different species, all unambiguously intermediate in terms of their overall biology and in the physiology and anatomy of all their organ systems."[27]

The fossil record

Darwinists claim that each species on Earth came from a single, primitive, common ancestor through minor changes that accumulated over great periods of time. It would require millions of intermediate life forms to arrive at the many complex species we have today, since the changes

---

[25] Denton, *Evolution: A Theory in Crisis*, 105-110.

[26] The lungfish may be such an example and will be discussed shortly.

[27] Denton, *Evolution: A Theory in Crisis*, 117.

would be small and gradual. Therefore, we would expect to find fossil evidence of these gradual transitions from one form to another.[28]

Imagine for a moment what it would take to evolve from a fish to a land animal one very small step at a time. Even to have only the fins evolve into fully formed and fully functional legs and arms would take thousands of incremental changes, not to mention the changes needed in the respiratory, circulatory, digestive, and other body systems. Each "transitional" form would die and be preserved in the fossil record. Many of them must certainly have been fossilized; thus the fossil record would bear witness to many of these gradual changes. In fact, gradual transitions from one form to another should be the rule rather than the exception.[29] We should expect to see *continuity*, and not *discontinuity*, in the fossil record.

Lack of transitions

The problem for Darwin is the lack of convincing evidence for transitional forms in the fossil record. Yet if Darwinism were true, the fossil record should be rich with clear transitional forms of numerous individual organisms, over millions of years, representing thousands of species. Darwin was aware that no intermediate forms had yet been found and regarded this as a major dilemma facing his theory:

> Why, if species have descended from other species by insensibly fine gradations, do we not everywhere see innumerable transitional forms? Why is not all nature in confusion instead of the species being, as we see them, well defined?...But, as by this theory innumerable transitional forms must have existed, why do we not find them embedded in countless numbers in the crust of the earth?...But in the intermediate region, having intermediate conditions of life, why do we not now find closely-linking intermediate varieties? This difficulty for a long time quite confounded me.[30]

Darwin tried to explain this by the supposed fact that transition fossils should be rarer;[31] yet he also admitted that "the number of intermediate

---

[28] Fossils are the preserved remains of animals, plants, and other organisms from the past. These remains are embedded within sedimentary rock formations, and the totality of these remains is referred to as the *fossil record*. Paleontology is the science of the study of fossils.

[29] Greg Koukl, "Why I'm Not an Evolutionist", Ambassador Basic Curriculum, Stand To Reason, 1999.

[30] Darwin, *Origin of Species*, 205-207.

[31] Ibid., 209.

and transitional links, between all living and extinct species, must have been inconceivably great."[32] In the end, he took comfort in the fact that the fossil record of his time was simply insufficient.[33] He thought the fossil record would eventually vindicate his theory through future discoveries, but in the subsequent 150 years, after millions of fossil discoveries, not a single one of them has proven Darwin correct.

Alleged missing links

Darwinists have been searching for their legendary "missing links" since Darwin first published his *Origin of Species*. These so-called missing links are the yet-to-be-discovered fossil remains of all the alleged intermediate forms that must have existed in the Darwinian view. Every so often we hear about some great new discovery that is supposed to fill in one of these gaps. There have been some false alarms, but not a single legitimate missing link has been found. As we just noted though, we would not expect to find only a small number of missing links. Rather, we anticipate many thousands of them, but they simply are not there.

Perhaps the most famous so-called missing link is *Archaeopteryx*, which was thought by some to be an intermediate specimen between reptiles and birds.[34] This primitive bird, roughly the size of a raven, did

indeed possess certain reptilian features like teeth, a long tail, and claws on its wings. Its most interesting feature, however, is that it had flight feathers as fully developed as any modern bird making it capable of powered flight. Although *Archaeopteryx* hints at reptilian ancestry, the fully developed wings make this an unconvincing intermediate.[35] The reptilian traits are curious, although we know of at least one contemporary bird that has claws on its wings— the South American Hoatzin. Indeed, bird origin researchers on both sides of this controversy now agree that modern birds are not descended from *Archaeopteryx*.[36]

Another famous so-called intermediate is the *Rhipidistia*, an ancient lobe-finned fish, once thought to be the ancestor to terrestrial vertebrates. This judgment was based on a number of skeletal features which closely resembled the earliest known amphibians. The key assumption made by

---

[32] Ibid., 293.

[33] Ibid., 298.

[34] Ten of these fossil specimens have been discovered in Germany, the first occurring in 1861.

[35] Denton, *Evolution: A Theory in Crisis*, 175-176.

[36] Jonathan Wells, *Icons of Evolution: Science or Myth? Why much of what we teach about evolution is wrong* (Washington DC: Regnery Publishing, 2002), 134.

paleontologists was that the soft tissue of the fish would also be transitional.[37] However, in 1938, fishermen off Cape Province in South Africa made an astonishing discovery when they caught a close living relative of the *Rhipidistia*—the coelacanth. This fish was thought to have been extinct for a hundred million years. When the anatomy of the coelacanth was examined, it showed no evidence of having internal organs pre-adapted for use  as a land animal. Not surprisingly, its anatomy resembled that of a fish.[38] Despite a few skeletal similarities to amphibians, the coelacanth was far removed from them in anatomy and therefore not a transitional form.

The lungfish is another proposed intermediate between fish and amphibian. It has fins, gills, and an intestine like any fish, but lungs, heart, and a larval stage like an amphibian. Although this is definitely puzzling, the problem is that the organs are clearly fully-developed forms of their respective modern-day counterparts. Denton explains, "Although the lungfish betrays a bewildering mixture of fish and amphibian character traits, the individual characteristics themselves are not in any realistic sense transitional between the two types."[39] If the lungfish were a true intermediate, we would expect to see a set of new and strange half-fish/half-amphibian organs, representative of some transitional stage from fish to amphibian. Macroevolution has to work in small, gradual steps, not huge, sudden leaps.

An extensive fossil record

The fossil record today is extraordinarily rich with the discovery of millions of fossils from all over the world. Yet no conclusive intermediate form has ever been found among these countless fossil specimens. Instead, newly discovered fossils almost always fit into currently known groups. When they do not, they are found to be distinct and isolated from the existing groups and in no sense intermediate or ancestral as required by Darwinism. Even though 99.9% of the fossils known today were discovered *since* Darwin's time, the fossil record remains as discontinuous as it did in Darwin's day.[40]

---

[37] Ninety-nine percent of the biology of any organism resides in its soft anatomy, which is not accessible from a fossil since it all decomposed soon after its death. This is the great danger in judging overall biology solely on skeletal remains (fossils). Denton, *Evolution: A Theory in Crisis*, 177-178.

[38] Denton, *Evolution: A Theory in Crisis*, 178-179.

[39] Ibid., 109.

[40] Ibid., 159-162.

The fossil record is so substantial now that it appears highly improbable that any genuine intermediate fossils will be discovered in the future. This seems like a safe bet considering our expectation of finding tens of thousands of transitions. If we are still looking for the first real transition with millions of fossils already discovered and classified then Darwinism has a major problem.

Evolutionary biologists have admitted this serious impediment to their theory. Paleontologist Stephen J. Gould admits, "The absence of fossil evidence for intermediary stages between major transitions in organic design, indeed our inability, even in our imagination, to construct functional intermediates in many cases, has been a persistent and nagging problem for gradualistic accounts of evolution."[41] George Gaylord Simpson, perhaps the most influential evolutionary paleontologist of the twentieth century, acknowledges, "This regular absence of transitional forms is not confined to mammals, but is an almost universal phenomenon, as has long been noted by paleontologists."[42]

Theoretical difficulties in bridging the gaps

The lack of fossil transitions is probably best explained by the fact that the so-called intermediates between classes and species never existed. Not only does the fossil record bear this out, but even working out a detailed *theory* of transitional organisms that cross a species gap proves to be virtually impossible. If Darwinism were true, then it should be possible to provide general descriptions of the intermediates to show that they could have *actually* existed. This would include the important details of their biology, anatomy, physiology, and behavior. However, even the best schemes invented by evolutionary biologists to create a series of hypothetical and fully functional transition forms have been unconvincing.[43] We will look at the origin of birds as an example.

The bird feather and wing

Evolutionary biologists are virtually unanimous in thinking that birds evolved from reptiles since they are more closely related than other possible ancestors. Before we look at the theoretical possibility of this occurring we need to briefly examine the hallmark feature of birds—the feather. Denton explains:

---

[41] Stephen J. Gould, Paleobiology Journal (1980), vol. 6, 119-130.
[42] George Gaylord Simpson, *Tempo and Mode in Evolution* (New York: Columbia University Press, 1944), 106.
[43] Denton, *Evolution: A Theory in Crisis*, 199-202.

Each feather consists of a central shaft carrying a series of barbs which are positioned at right angles to the shaft to form the vane. The barbs which make up the vane are held together by rows of barbules. From the anterior barbules, hooks project downward and these interlock with ridges on the posterior barbules. Altogether, in the flight feather of a large bird, about a million barbules cooperate to bind the barbs into an impervious vane.

The feather is a magnificent adaptation for flight. Flight feathers are remarkably light and strong and anyone who has played with one will know how easily a ruffled feather can be repaired merely by drawing it between the fingers. In addition to its lightness and strength the feather has also permitted the exploitation of a number of sophisticated aerodynamic principles in the design of the bird's wing.[44]

Denton goes on to describe how feathers reduce turbulence by smoothing out flight and how they provide the bird with an aerofoil of variable geometry so the wing shape can be altered to support take-off, landing, flapping, gliding, and soaring. The positioning of the feathers is maintained by an intricate system of tendons. The bird feather and wing are truly exquisite in their appearance and function, and are engineering marvels.

At issue is how they might have evolved in a gradual, Darwinian fashion. The only real way to get a bird feather in this view is for it to evolve from a reptilian scale. The consensus view is that as the proto-bird[45] reptile began its first flight tests, either by leaping from the ground or jumping from the trees, the outer edges of its scales became frayed by the friction of the air. Over the course of time, the frayed scales gradually changed into a perfect set of feathers and wings. Even on the surface this seems like a highly questionable process, but let's look at it a little closer.

There are several critical difficulties with the gradual scale-to-feather scheme. An aerofoil will only work if its components are strong, can resist deformation, and are able to form a vane that is impervious to the wind. Moreover, the surface area of the wing must be large enough to achieve lift, which in this case requires a sufficient number of feathers. Flight is a very exacting activity that imposes very stringent mechanical criteria. This

---

[44] Ibid., 202.
[45] *Proto* means the first or earliest form of something.

is why every single flying bird has possessed a highly developed wing with a complex arrangement of fully-developed flight feathers.[46]

It is not at all clear how an impervious reptilian scale could be gradually converted into an impervious feather without passing through a number of frayed-scale intermediates which would be weak, easily deformed, and quite permeable to air.[47] Simply put, these creatures would not fly. If a Darwinian process did happen to get started, these intermediates would not survive. It appears that both the avian wing and its individual feathers are more examples of irreducible complexity. They need to be fully formed in order to be functional and intermediate forms would be non-functional.

There are also difficulties with the origin of powered flight. Darwinists believe that gliding was the forerunner of powered flight in proto-birds, but there are serious doubts about the feasibility of the transition from gliding to powered flight because the physical adaptations for powered flight are in *opposition* to those of gliding flight. Denton explains, "The aerofoil of a glider, for example, is usually a membrane attached to the body of the animal which extends out to the fore and hindlimbs. In the case of a powered flyer, lift and thrust are usually generated by surfaces such as the wings and tail, which are some distance from the main mass of the animal."[48]

The bird lung

The origin of the wing is not the only challenge for Darwinists regarding birds. The lung and respiratory system of the bird are dramatically different from their supposed ancestor, the reptile. This poses a major problem that defies Darwinian explanations. Both birds and reptiles are vertebrates, which mean they have a backbone. In all vertebrates, *except* birds, air is drawn into the lungs through a system of branching tubes which terminate in tiny air sacs. During respiration, air is moved in and out through the same passage in a bi-directional manner.

In the case of birds, however, the major branching tubes break down into smaller tubes which permeate the lung tissue. These tubes eventually join together again to form a looping circulatory system. The air flows only in one direction by a complicated system of interconnected air sacs. The existence of this air sac system requires a highly specialized and unique compartmentalization of the bird's body cavity. No lung in any

---

[46] Denton, *Evolution: A Theory in Crisis*, 207-208.
[47] Ibid., 209.
[48] Ibid., 205.

other vertebrate species is even close to the avian system, and this system is nearly identical in all types of birds, from hummingbirds to ostriches.[49]

The structure of the respiratory system in reptiles and birds could hardly be more different, which raises the crucial question of how any of the intermediate life forms could survive the intervening steps to get from one breathing system to the other. Obviously, if an organism cannot breathe, it will not survive very long. Denton thinks this Darwinian problem is even harder to overcome than the feather: "In attempting to explain how such an intricate and highly specialized system of correlated adaptations could have been achieved gradually through perfectly functioning intermediates, one is faced with the problem of the feather magnified a thousand times."[50]

The gaps cannot be bridged

The gradual, step-by-step Darwinian process is at odds with our empirical experience of irreducible complexity. Most life systems we find in nature cannot operate at all to sustain life unless they are fully intact.

A feather cannot support flight until its hooks and barbules are integrated precisely together. A wing will not generate lift until a sufficient number of feathers are present and precisely arranged. A lung cannot support breathing until its complicated components are in place and cooperating with one another. There are many other examples like this of irreducibly complex organs, structures, and systems among the multitude of life forms on our planet.

The Cambrian explosion

We saw earlier how the fossil record fails to support Darwinism. The transitions we would expect to find among the fossils simply are not there. However, it gets much worse for Darwinism because the evidence that *is* in the fossil record substantiates the exact opposite of what Darwinism predicts.

Most major animal groups appear for the first time in the fossil record during a relatively brief geological time known as the Cambrian Period. This was a sudden appearance accompanied by a profound diversification of life. *Phylum* is the highest category within the animal kingdom,[51] and the Cambrian fossil record reveals *every known phylum* originating at nearly the exact same time, including phyla that no longer exist today.

---

[49] Ibid., 210-211.

[50] Ibid., 212.

[51] In biology, a *phylum* is a taxonomic rank below *kingdom* and above *class*. Example animal phyla include mollusks, segmented worms, arthropods, and chordates (the human phylum). Experts do not agree completely, but there are somewhere between 35 and 40 animal phyla.

There are *no* examples of phyla that originate outside of the Cambrian period.

This is a stunning discovery and totally contrary to Darwin's theory. We do not see evidence of life beginning with one or even a few groups that diverged gradually over millions of years. Instead, the Cambrian starts with the abrupt appearance of many diverse and fully formed animal body plans. *The highest levels of the biological hierarchy appeared right at the start.*[52] The fossil evidence is so strong and the event so dramatic that it has become known as the *Cambrian explosion* and also the *Biological Big Bang*. To put the suddenness of this event into perspective, philosopher of science

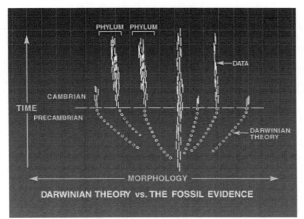

Stephen Meyer explains, "If you were to compress all of Earth's history into twenty-four hours, the Cambrian explosion would consume only about one minute."[53]

Darwin thought that nature could make no big leaps: "Why should not Nature take a sudden leap from structure to structure? On the theory of natural selection, we can clearly understand why she should not; for natural selection can act only by taking advantage of slight successive variations; she can never take a leap, but must advance by the shortest and slowest steps."[54] Darwin was aware of the Cambrian explosion and considered it a major problem for his theory. He writes, "The case at present must remain inexplicable; and may be truly urged as a valid argument against the views here entertained."[55] Contemporary paleontologists have had to admit this problem as well. Gould sums it up: "We do not know why the Cambrian explosion could establish all major anatomical designs so quickly."[56]

---

[52] The accompanying diagram illustrates this discrepancy between Darwin's theory and the Cambrian data. What Darwin would expect to see in the fossil record is below the line—all the phyla branches originating from a single ancestor. However, as the actual data above the line shows, the phyla appear abruptly with no evidence of common ancestry. http://winteryknight.files.wordpress.com/2010/02/cambrianexplosion.gif, accessed Nov 19, 2010.

[53] Stephen C. Meyer, as quoted in Strobel, *Case for a Creator,* 239.

[54] Darwin, *Origin of Species,* 223-224.

[55] Ibid., 314.

[56] Stephen J. Gould, *Scientific American* (October 1994), 97.

The molecular evidence

Despite the clear distinctions among classes, it is also apparent that there are very many anatomical similarities among organisms of different classes. For example, the bone pattern in a bat's wing is similar to that of a porpoise's flipper, though the wing is used for flying and the flipper for swimming.[57] This kind of structural similarity between animals is often referred to as *homology*. Forelimbs of vertebrates (arms, legs, and similar appendages) are the most common examples of homologous structures.

Darwin appealed to homology as evidence that all organisms had descended from a common ancestor and this continues to be a key part of the Darwinian argument even today. However, there is a major problem with Darwinism's appeal to homology.

For common ancestry to be the correct explanation for homology, it must be shown to be true at the genetic level. All the anatomical features of an organism have their origin in its genes, so any homologous structures between organisms must be specified in their own homologous genes. This is, in fact, how Darwinists argue for common ancestry in general—similar genes produce similar traits. However, the attempt to prove a genetic basis for homology has been a massive failure.

Biologists have studied the embryos of organisms whose adults have homologous structures. Since an embryo contains information inherited from its parents' genes, and that information directs its development, biologists can infer similarities in genetic patterns of cell division, cell movement, and tissue differentiation by comparing embryonic characteristics.[58] These comparative studies have found that there are great dissimilarities in the early stages of embryogenesis in the different vertebrate classes that exhibit homologous similarities. Organs and structures considered homologous in adult vertebrates could not be traced back to homologous cells in the earliest stages of embryogenesis.[59] The conclusion is that homologous structures are *not* the product of genetic similarities. The evidence is simply not there.

The evolutionary basis of homology was further damaged by two discoveries that complicate the Darwinian scenario even further. First, homologous structures are specified by different genes in different species, which clouds the alleged ancestral interconnections. Second, almost every gene that has been studied in higher organisms has been found to affect more than one organ system, which means that non-homologous genes are involved to some extent in the specification of homologous structures.[60]

---

[57] Wells, *Icons of Evolution*, 59

[58] Ibid., 71.

[59] Denton, *Evolution: A Theory in Crisis*, 146.

[60] Ibid., 149.

Denton thinks this evidence is the death knell for the whole idea of descent with modification. He concludes, "Without the phenomenon of homology—the modification of similar structures to different ends—there would be little need for a theory of descent with modification."[61] These homologous structures must have arrived by a different route than common descent. A better explanation for structural resemblances between species is common *design* rather than common *descent*. Various life forms have similarities because they were purposely planned and created that way. This fits well within a theistic universe, where we have already discovered countless examples of intelligent design.

Biochemical comparisons

It was impossible in Darwin's day to measure the exact distance between any two organisms in quantitative terms. Classifications into various groupings were done exclusively on anatomical grounds. However, twentieth century comparative biologists discovered that the amino acid sequence of the same proteins vary considerably between species. This discovery enabled biologists to align the sequences between organisms and actually count the number of places where the sequences differ, which provided not merely an anatomical, but also a *quantifiable* difference.[62]

They learned that closely related species—as classified by their anatomies—had closely related molecular sequences. Wherever species varied at the anatomical level, there was a corresponding variance at the molecular level. In fact, when biologists classified all the species using this new molecular comparison method, the resulting classes were identical to those from the anatomical method. This was an astounding discovery. After studying thousands of these protein sequences in hundreds of species, biologists were able to mathematically compare the species to determine *how far* each one was from the others. They discovered that *all* the sequences in each group were *equally* isolated from the members of other groups, which means there are no transitional or intermediate classes whatsoever.[63] Denton writes:

> The almost mathematical perfection of the isolation of the two fundamental classes at a molecular level is astonishing!...There is not a trace at a molecular level of the traditional evolutionary series: cyclostomes → fish → amphibian → reptile → mammal...So amphibia, always traditionally considered intermediate between fish and the other terrestrial vertebrates, are in molecular terms as far from

---

[61] Ibid., 154.
[62] Ibid., 274-276.
[63] Ibid., 277-280.

fish as any group of reptiles or mammals!...No amphibian species is midway between other amphibia and the reptiles and the mammals. Similarly, no reptilian or mammalian species is closer to amphibia than any of the others.[64]

This data is entirely consistent, not only with the fossil record, but also with our understanding that the gaps cannot be bridged due to irreducible complexity. It is now well-established that the pattern of diversity at the anatomical level precisely matches the diversity at the molecular level. Both conform to a highly ordered hierarchical system, with no overlapping between groups. Each group is unique and isolated, exhibiting no trace of transitions between groups. The evidence simply is not there to support Darwinism.

Lack of explanatory scope

So far we have seen that Darwinism fails to deliver on physical evidence and also the necessary biological pathways to evolve life from simple to complex forms. It also fails in another significant way. The theory is not broad enough to explain the full range of life features we observe in nature. We will consider this insufficiency in two parts: Darwinism's inability to explain certain material aspects of life and its inability to explain all immaterial aspects of life.

Material realities

The origin of the universe

Darwinism has no explanation for the origin of the universe. Technically, Darwinism is a theory of the origin and development of *life* (not the whole universe), so we might not expect it to be able to do this. However, we are taking a larger view in our study. We want to answer *all* the big questions. Darwinism is a key tenet of the atheistic worldview which must explain how the universe came to be so that life would have an environment and opportunity to form. The overarching worldview of Darwinism—atheism—still has a gigantic hole to fill. Not only must the origin of the universe be explained, but also its amazing fine-tuning of physics, chemistry, and biology to support life.

The origin of life

Even though Darwinism purports to describe how life evolved on this planet, it has no explanation for how life *originated* from non-life. Its

---

[64] Ibid., 284-285.

assumed starting point is a single living cell swimming in a primeval pond, but as we saw in chapter 2, getting that first solitary cell is a monumentally improbable task through purely natural processes. The best Darwinism has been able to muster is the now discredited Miller-Urey experiment from 1953. This is a severe weakness in the theory. We should wonder why we are asked to give our commitment to a theory about life that cannot explain the single most important fact about life—how it all got started in the first place.

Irreducibly complex systems

Even if we give Darwinism a pass on both the origin of the universe and the origin of life, it still cannot explain the irreducible complexity in life that we observe. Darwin prophetically writes, "If it could be demonstrated that any complex organ existed, which could not possibly have been formed by numerous, successive, slight modifications, my theory would absolutely break down. But I can find out no such case."[65] Darwin could find no such case because science at that time regarded the cell as a radically simple organism, and not the complex molecular factory that we know today. We have already looked at several examples of these irreducibly complex systems at various levels, including the bacteria flagellum, blood clotting, bird feathers and wings, body systems and processes such as circulation, respiration, digestion, and so on. Another example is the reproductive system.

Sexual reproduction is very difficult to explain in Darwinian terms. Most species reproduce only when a male and female come together in sexual intercourse.[66] During fertilization, when a sperm enters an egg, the cell from the mother and the cell from the father each contribute half the chromosomes that make up the new offspring's genome. Darwinism would have us believe that two individual organisms of the same species, at the exact same time within evolutionary history, acquired the needed mutations that led to passing on only half of their chromosomes in a very complex fertilization process known as *meiosis*. Not only this, but it required the independent development of compatible sex organs for physical mating. Moreover, all of this had to occur in thousands and

---

[65] Darwin, *Origin of Species*, 219.

[66] Some species do reproduce without sex, which is called *asexual* reproduction. Only one parent is needed to make an identical copy of itself through a process called *mitosis*, where a cell divides itself in half to make two identical copies. This type of reproduction is common among some single-cell organisms. A small number of invertebrates and some less advanced vertebrates are known to alternate between sexual and asexual reproduction, or be exclusively asexual. The fact that some species propagate through asexual reproduction is not an argument *against* design, but rather *for* it, since it proves that a male/female combination is contingent, and not necessary for reproduction. Moreover, the existence of asexual reproduction does nothing to refute the obvious irreducible complexity in sexual reproduction.

thousands of species. No natural hypothesis can explain the origin of sexual reproduction; it must be the result of design.

Vivid sensations

It is fascinating that human beings do not merely perceive the world in ordinary and dull ways. Instead, we perceive and sense it in extraordinarily vivid ways that deeply enrich our enjoyment of it.[67] Consider our amazing ability to see in color or our ability to taste a wide variety of flavors and textures. There is no law of nature that we should have either ability. We could get along nicely seeing only in black and white and not tasting anything we put into our mouths. Why should we be able to speak or to smell or to hear or to sense our world through touch? Why should the mating ritual, at least for humans, be one of the highest forms of pleasure for both sexes?

Not only do we have all these abilities, but we have them to a remarkable and highly tuned level. This could have easily been a colorless, tasteless, speechless, odorless, soundless, nerveless world, but it is not. It is hard to believe that unguided Darwinian processes would result in, not merely one, but a multitude of sense organs that significantly enhance our experiences of the world. Our abilities to create great art, architecture, music, dance, and literature all flow from our exceptional ability to sense our world. All of this is inexplicable on Darwinian terms, since we do not need any of it to survive. Behe suggests that if we find ourselves in a world lavished with extras—with much more than the minimum—we should bet heavily against it being the result of random chance.[68]

Immaterial realities

We examined several immaterial features of life in chapter 2— information, consciousness, reason, free will, language, value, meaning, purpose, love, joy, and morality. Darwinism has no convincing explanations for how *any* of these came to exist by purely natural processes.

Perhaps you are wondering why we should require Darwinism to explain these kinds of immaterial realities. After all, Darwinism proposes only material explanations for physical life, and these are clearly not physical. This would totally miss the point, however. For Darwinism to be a viable theory for the explanation of life, it needs to have sufficient

---

[67] I have listed these features under material realities, but as we learned in chapter 6, sensations are really mental entities, that is, they are immaterial. Of course, our sense organs are physical, so this is really a combination of material and immaterial features.

[68] Behe, *The Edge of Evolution*, 223.

explanatory scope to cover *all* aspects of life. Darwinists cannot simply excuse themselves from explaining certain intrinsic features of life by arbitrarily limiting its scope to include only the material realm. If life contains immaterial aspects, then the true account of life must explain how these immaterial features came to be.

Inability to explain immaterial things

The reason that Darwinism does not explain these immaterial realities is because it is *incapable* of doing so. It simply does not have the necessary creative resources because you cannot get immaterial things from material things. Think about how a physical-only world would operate. Everything must be ultimately explainable at the most basic level in terms of chemistry and physics according to natural laws that determine effects from prior causes. Yet, *by definition*, immaterial things cannot be described in these terms. They transcend physical description because immaterial stuff is of a higher order than material stuff. What can it possibly mean that a collection of chemicals has intentions, desires, needs, or passions? It is a nonsense question that we intuitively grasp by common sense.[69]

William Provine, atheist professor of biology history, admits these conclusions: "Naturalistic evolution has clear consequences that Charles Darwin understood perfectly. 1) No gods worth having exist; 2) no life after death exists; 3) no ultimate foundation for ethics exists; 4) no ultimate meaning in life exists; and 5) human free will is nonexistent."[70] Provine denies the reality of these features of the universe, and he makes a conclusion that is consistent with his understanding of reality. If only most Darwinists would be so honest!

The problem for Provine and for Darwinism is that these things really *do* exist. Darwinism therefore has a major gap in its ability to explain the information found in DNA, consciousness, and our ability to reason, make free choices, and communicate using advanced language. If Darwinism were true then mankind is the result of a purposeless and natural process. We were not planned, we merely happened accidentally; therefore we can have no real value, meaning, or purpose; nor can we explain how love and joy came to be. Likewise, there is no legitimate basis for the existence of objective morality.

---

[69] "Common sense" is another immaterial reality, by the way.

[70] William Provine, "Evolution: Free will and punishment and meaning in life", speech delivered at the Second Annual Darwin Day Celebration, University of Tennessee, Knoxville, Feb. 12, 1998.

Darwinian explanations for morality

Some Darwinists deny objective morality and accept moral relativism, which we showed to be false in chapter 2. There are other Darwinists, however, who recognize the flaws in moral relativism and affirm moral objectivity. Since they are bound to their evolutionary worldview though, they attempt to ground objective morality in evolutionary processes. They usually try one of three approaches to do this.[71]

First, they sometimes assert that morality simply exists with no reason or basis for its existence. They will agree that there are things that are objectively right and wrong, but leave it at that with no further explanation. However, acting in moral ways and having a way to *justify* that morality are separate issues. Saying that morality simply exists is no explanation at all. I could be quite adept at using a computer, but have no understanding of what makes the computer actually work. If I were to claim there is no reason that my computer works—it just does—I should rightfully be ridiculed for providing no answer for something that clearly requires one. It is the same with morality. This answer must be rejected since it provides no explanation for the foundation of morality.

Second, Darwinists sometimes claim that morality comes from our "selfish genes." By this, they mean we are blindly programmed by natural processes to act in moral ways as a means of promoting our survival. For example, helping our family members to survive helps us to survive and reciprocating the kindness of strangers promotes the survival of each. The problem with this understanding of morality is that it is quite shallow and bears little resemblance to the full range of behaviors that we would normally consider to be right and wrong. A survival of the fittest ethic cannot really explain the absolute and universal rightness of self-sacrifice or humility, nor can it explain the absolute and universal wrongness of injustice, oppression, rape, or murder. On the contrary, a survival-only mentality would foster an ethic of radical selfishness, which would include lying, cheating, killing, and doing whatever it takes to survive and reproduce. No reasonable standard of objective morality accepts these actions as good, though. This approach is simply moral relativism in disguise, so it must also be rejected.

Third, Darwinists sometimes say that morality is nothing more than an evolutionary illusion—it does not really exist. Our genes have simply tricked us into thinking that acting in moral ways will help us reproduce and survive. If this view is correct, however, then morality is not really objective and therefore we have no real duty to obey it. Any attempt to live

---

[71] Chad Meister, "Atheists and the Quest for Objective Morality", *Christian Research Journal* (Volume 33, No. 2, 2010), 33-35.

a virtuous life is misguided and offers no real benefit. Moreover, we could not trust our consciences when they guide us about what is right and wrong. This should also make us doubt our other mental processes, like our abilities to reason and make free choices. This view leads us down a slippery slope where we have very little to rely on and must suspect that virtually everything is an illusion.

All of these explanations for Darwinian morality are mere grasping at straws. Morality is not objective just because our genes have compelled us to believe that certain actions are "morally good" in order to gain some evolutionary advantage. We all know deep down that morality is truly objective, not merely something we do to survive.

There is no sensible way to ground objective morality in a Darwinist worldview. Morality cannot be objective on *any* evolutionary account because it provides nothing that transcends humanity to establish the necessary universal standard. More importantly, there is no duty to behave in any particular way because there is no moral authority in the universe to hold us accountable or dispense ultimate justice in this view.

Peripheral Issues

Theistic evolution

Although Darwinism appeals mainly to atheists, some theists have embraced the theory, referring to their particular version as *Theistic Evolution* (TE). If a supernatural agent is added to the mix, many of Darwinism's shortcomings can be fixed, although what remains is far from Darwin's unguided, natural process. For example, where natural selection and random genetic mutation fail, God can supply the supernatural mechanism to change one animal kind into another. Where the time for Evolution to occur is too short, God can speed up the process as needed. Where Darwinism has no explanation whatsoever, God can explain the origin of the universe and its fine-tuning, the origin of life, information in DNA, irreducible complexity, consciousness, reason, significance, and so on. Thus, TE could remedy all the explanatory scope and power problems of Darwinism.

The physical evidence problems remain, however. If God did use something like Darwinian Evolution as the process to create the wide diversity of life, then we should still expect a great deal of transitional fossil evidence. Moreover, we would *not* expect to see the pervasive and overwhelming physical evidence of the Cambrian explosion. Additionally, we would find evidence of anatomical and molecular continuity in animals between classes.[72]

Theistic evolutionists are seeking compromise where none is necessary. They think the physical evidence for Darwinism is strong, so they attempt to explain it in terms of God. As we have seen, however, the evidence for Darwinism is actually quite weak; so there is no compelling reason to bother explaining it through theistic causes and processes.

The whole point of Darwinism is to show that there is no need for a supernatural Creator, so why feel the need to rescue such a theory if there are very good reasons to believe in the supernatural? In fact, theistic explanations have to be inserted at so many points in the TE view that what is left does not resemble Darwinism at all. It is a more rational course to abandon belief in Darwinism altogether.

The age of the universe

Sometimes people confuse the two separate issues of how old the universe is and how life developed on planet Earth. They mistakenly think that an old universe *requires* Darwinism to explain life, but there is no reason to believe this. The universe can be quite old and life still could have developed by some other method, such as through special creation by a divine Creator/Designer.

Rejection of Darwinism therefore does not require embracing a young universe view. The age of the universe is a separate issue from Darwinism. There are different opinions about the age of the universe and life on Earth. The answers to these particular questions do not change the fundamental truth that a Creator exists who is responsible for origins.

I am not trying to make an argument for any particular age of the universe—young or old. This is an interesting, but secondary, question that is not crucial to forming our worldview. In other words, we can hold to a theistic worldview while believing differently than other theists on these matters. We could also change our mind on the issue without being forced to abandon the central tenets of theism.

Conclusions about Darwinism

Darwinism has failed to make its case. It is flawed in three major ways. First, it is unable to prove that its processes can actually do what it needs them to do. New animals require new information and Darwinian

---

[72] It is possible that God used microevolutionary processes to create the wide diversity of species we see today from some basic animal kinds that he specially created at the level of family or genus. He may very well have done something like this, but this is not Darwinian macroevolution, which states that *all* life forms came from a single cell.

processes cannot produce it. Second, it has a severe evidential problem, including the lack of physical evidence to support it and the existence of strong physical evidence that opposes it. Third, it is unable to explain many known features of life, both material and immaterial.

Virtually every piece of actual evidence for macroevolution advanced by Darwinists is instead evidence for microevolution, which is not in dispute. Obviously, there is a sleight of hand taking place when evidence for microevolution is given as evidence for macroevolution. Any evidence for descent from common ancestry can just as easily be interpreted as evidence for common design, which is consistent with a theistic worldview.

Darwin himself provided three specific ways to disprove his theory and each one of them has come to pass.[73] The first was the fossil record. Darwin said that we should expect to find many transitional forms in the fossil record, but this has not happened. Darwin also said that nature takes no sudden leaps, so we should expect only slow and gradual changes. Yet, the Cambrian explosion provides evidence of exactly the opposite happening. Instead of major life forms evolving from simpler forms over eons, we see all major life forms appearing suddenly and fully intact. Finally, Darwin predicted that if it could be shown that life could not be formed by numerous, successive, slight modifications, then his theory would break down. Many discoveries of irreducible complexity at the molecular and anatomical levels have, in fact, demonstrated that they could not be formed gradually. Instead, they have to be formed all at once in order to function and survive.

Intelligent design and Darwinism are mutually exclusive explanations for life. There is no middle ground or third alternative. Either life came about by an intelligent cause or it came about by accidental and random processes. Darwinism offers nothing to refute all the evidence we have collected and examined in this book. Neither can it offer enough, if any, positive evidence to stand on its own.

Further reading

Darwin's Black Box: The Biochemical Challenge to Evolution, Michael Behe
Darwin's Dilemma, Stephen C. Meyer
Darwin on Trial, Phillip E. Johnson
Evolution: A Theory in Crisis, Michael Denton
Icons of Evolution: Science or Myth?, Jonathan Wells
The Edge of Evolution: The Search for the Limits of Darwinism, Michael Behe

---

[73] This is called *falsifiability*, which is the logical possibility that an assertion could be shown to be false by a particular observation or physical experiment. Many scientists regard this as a necessary attribute of any scientific theory; otherwise there would be no possible way to ever prove it false.

Other books by Tom Gender

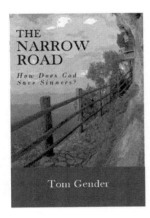

The Narrow Road
How Does God Save Sinners?

Many people assume their salvation is largely completed because the defining episode—a time of conversion—is history, and all that remains is to coast into Heaven. However, salvation is not simply an event in our past, but a lifelong journey that leads to a promised inheritance. All along the way, we make choices that will affect the outcome of that journey. *The Narrow Road* will challenge you to seriously contemplate what the Bible says about how God saves sinners and what that means for your daily life.

10005091R0020

Made in the USA
Charleston, SC
30 October 2011